DEFENCE OF HINDU SOCIETY

Defence of Hindu Society

Sita Ram Goel

VOICE OF INDIA
New Delhi

First published, 1983
Revised reprint, 1987
Third enlarged edition, 1994
Fifth Reprint, 2025

ISBN 978-81-85990-24-8

website: www.voiceofindia.com

Published by Voice of India, 2/18, Ansari Road, New Delhi – 110 002.
Printed at Replika Press Pvt. Ltd.

Contents

1

The Situation at Present

In an earlier series, *Hindu Society under Siege,* I had dealt with the forces which threaten Hindu society, and are striving to throttle it out of existence with aid and abetment from their international allies.

I undertook, at that time, to write another series regarding the steps which Hindu society should take in order to break out of the siege, and snatch the initiative from its sworn enemies.

I have delayed this second series deliberately. Firstly, I wanted to watch and weigh the reactions from the readers of the first series. Secondly, the more I thought over the subject, the more diffident I grew about my own competence to deal with it adequately.

The response from the readers has been positive. I have received many letters of appreciation from Hindus residing in all parts of the country as well as abroad, and belonging to all sections of society and age groups. Most of them have congratulated me for articulating, in clear and concrete terms, what they themselves have felt instinctively and for a long time.

A few scholars and journalists who have never been known for their sympathy for Hinduism or Hindu causes have, however, remarked caustically that I have "failed to frighten them". Some other birds of the same feather have dived deeper and referred to my "mentality" rather than refute my facts or demolish my logic.

It was far from my intention to frighten any one, far less the Hindu society which I aspire to serve. But our hand-to-mouth scholars and journalists have only a number of shibboleths up their sleeves. If one says that some events and trends are pregnant with bright possibilities, they dismiss him as a "dreamer". On the other hand, if one draws attention to dangers that are maturing, they attack him as an "alarmist". What they always refuse to do is to join a serious debate on any subject. And yet they strut around with superior airs as if they know all the answers. Most of the time these superior airs hide only stark ignorance, mental sloth, and moral indifference. I will not, therefore, enter into an argument with this tribe.

MY DIFFIDENCE

My diffidence, however, is an altogether different matter. Defence of a living and complex entity like a society is no easy task. It needs a sure touch which has to be sympathetic at the same time. A defence which does not take into account the spiritual, moral, and cultural aspirations embodied in and expressed by a society, can endanger rather than energize it.

This diffidence is doubly warranted in the case of a vast and variegated society such as the Hindu society, the like of which has been seen only rarely in human history, at least not on this scale. It is perhaps presumptuous on my part to deal with a subject which can be handled adequately and wholesomely only by sages, seers, saints, and visionaries. At the end of this exercise, I may only prove the old adage that fools rush in where angels fear to tread.

Hindu society has grown and shaped itself in the vision of Vyāsa and Vālmīki, Manu and Yājñavalkya, Nārada and Vasistha, and a hundred other exponents of Sanātana Dharma in all its dimensions and dynamics.

Hindu society has been inspired through the ages by such mighty shastras as the Vedas, the Upanishads, the Gita, the Jaināgama, the Tripiṭaka, the various Yogaśāstras, the Vāṇī of Siddhas and Sants, and the devotional outpourings of Alvars and Nayanars.

Hindu society has been defended, during its days of distress, by such high-souled heroes as Chandragupta, Skandagupta,

Vikramaditya, Yasodharman, Bapa Rawal, Jayapala, Bhojadeva, Prithiviraj, Prataparudra, Vir Pandya, Harihara and Rana Sanga.

Hindu society has fought a long-drawn-out struggle for freedom against foreign invaders under the leadership of such veterans as Maharana Pratap, Shivaji, Maharaja Surajmal, Banda Bairagi, Lokmanya Tilak, Veer Savarkar, Mahatma Gandhi, and Sardar Patel.

Hindu society has been reawakened and reformed by such visionaries as Bankim Chandra, Maharshi Dayananda, Swami Vivekananda, Sri Aurobindo, Rabindranath, and Subramanya Bharati.

It is small wonder, therefore, that I feel like an intruder in this august field. No one is more aware than myself of the limitations of head and heart from which I suffer. Adapting a metaphor from Kalidasa, I can state my case in the following śloka:

kva dharma-prabhavaḥ tantraḥ,
kva ca alpa-viṣayā-matiḥ,
titīrṣuḥ dustaram mohād,
uḍupena asmi sāgaram.

(I am a small mind when it comes to understanding the social system which has been shaped by Dharma; It is only in a fit of folly that I am attempting to cross the great ocean by means of a ramshackle raft.)

BUT MY HEART BLEEDS

But my heart bleeds when I see this great society being attacked by sheer barbarians whose only weapon is either a criminal theology masquerading as religion, or a materialist dogma sustained by the lowest in human nature, or a phoney modernism parroting the latest slogans from the West. My mind is deeply disturbed when I witness the leaders of this great society going on the defensive in the face of wanton aggression from inhuman ideologies whose only stock-in-trade is self-righteous spite.

I fail to understand the selective journalism which spotlights *only* the atrocities on Harijans when statistics go to show that caste Hindus provide many more victims to violence in our countryside, which plays up *only* stories of bride-burning without caring to find out what is happening to old parents in many modern homes under the spell of an imported culture which places a premium on what is described as youth, which accuses Hindu organisations of aggression in every communal strife without investigating the hard facts about provocation from the so-called minorities, and which, in short, replaces serious debate on every subject with a few mindless cliches — reactionary and progressive, right and left, capitalist and socialist, revivalist and modern, communal and secular, and so on.

OPENNESS OF HINDU SOCIETY

History stands witness that Hindu society has never refused to listen to those of its critics who have had the good of this society at heart. This society has always accepted every well-intentioned advice, and tried its best to reform and renew itself. This society has always hanged its head in shame before every well-deserved reprimand, and done a penance in good time, provided the reprimand has come from those whose credentials are not in doubt.

Hindu society has never been a closed society which catches cold at the very first whiff of a wind from outside. It has never been a fundamentalist fraternity parroting the pontifications of self-appointed prophets, or burning the entire incense of its reverence at the altar of ridiculous revelations, or ruling out every rational and reflective discussion of its dogmas. It has never been a regimented flock grovelling in an orgy of sinfulness which can be washed only by the blood of God's only begotten son, or waiting helplessly for fiats from God's viceregent on earth.

On the contrary, Hindu society has been the meeting point as well as the melting pot of as many spiritual visions as the human psyche is capable of springing up spontaneously. It has been a willing and welcoming platform for as many seers, sages, saints, and mystics as have responded to the deeper stirrings in the human soul. It has been a repository of as many metaphysical points of view as human reason can render in human language. And it has been a vast laboratory for as many cultural, social, economic, and political experiments as human nature in its widest range can carry out and cope with.

A PAINFUL SIGHT

It is, therefore, a painful sight that the spokesmen of some puny and petrified ideologies should be pointing accusing fingers at Hindu society, and that this society should fail to muster sufficient self-confidence to repel the attack. Hindu society never tries to tick them off in good time with the stern warning they fully deserve. It has never asked them, "Who the hell are you?" It has never told them, "Go and get lost or, better still, do a bit of introspection. You are blind with beams in both your eyes, and yet you have the cheek to raise a hue and cry about a mere mote in one of mine. Here is some sound advice for you. Stop telling lies about me, lest I be forced to tell the truth about you."

What is worse, a brood of professional Hindu-baiters has tried and tested an armoury of cheap gibes — polytheism, pantheism, idolatry, brahmanism, obscurantism, revivalism, fundamentalism, communalism, and the rest — and discovered to its great glee that the gibes hurt. It is a sorry spectacle indeed that this society should take these gibes as well-deserved reproaches for its own good and indulge in an orgy of breast-beating at the behest of every Hindu-baiter. The sworn enemies of Hindu society have made a great game out of some scare-words in order to keep Hindu society on the defensive, and go on drawing apology after apology from the spokesmen of this society, day in and day out.

THE BROOD OF HINDU-BAITERS

Here we have the inheritors of some blood-soaked bigotries holding aloft the flag of monotheism, and denouncing Hindu ways of worship as polytheism and idolatry. Hindu society has yet to scan the scriptures of these criminal creeds, and have a close look at their prophets, saviours, and saints. The day Hindu society does that, these creeds will beat a hasty retreat, and know not how to defend their dark doctrines and horrid heroes.

Here we have the erstwhile traffickers in slave trade trumpeting about "human brotherhood" and "social equality", and brushing aside the whole of Hindu society as a beehive of brahmin domination, caste discrimination, degradation of women, bonded child labour, and what not. Hindu society has yet to review the matrix of their societies, and expose the true character of "human brotherhood" and "social equality" from the annals of their remote as well as recent history. The day Hindu society does that, the "human brotherhood" will give up its bark, and the "social equality" shed its self-righteousness.

Here we have the salesmen of a "proletarian revolution" denouncing Hindu society as primitive, feudal, semi-colonial, capitalist, and full of class oppression in all stages and forms. Hindu society has yet to peep into their "proletarian paradise", and raise the curtain on a vast salve empire sustained by mass slaughter and ceaseless terror. The day Hindu society does that, the socialist swearology will lose its sting, and know not how to hide the horrible scene.*

Here we have the minions of a mercenary culture dishing out lectures on individual freedom, rule of law, parliamentary democracy, secular state, human rights, rate of growth, distribution of prosperity, abolition of poverty, and arrest of population explosion. This imported culture frowns at the "fundamental failures of the Hindu social system" and the "hurdles on the path of progress presented by the Hindu cultural milieu". They advocate "rapid modernisation" of Hindu society in the image of this or that Western model. Hindu society has yet to expose this pompous priestcraft patronized by foreign foundations, multinationals,

* Since I wrote this para in 1983, the "proletarian paradise" has been exposed as the worst hell known to human history.

secret services, and defence departments of the West, and place on public view what is hidden behind its pretentious verbiage.

The day Hindu society does that it will show that their notion of individual freedom does not function beyond a small class of the English-educated fraternity; that their rule of law provides justice only for those who can pay the price; that their parliamentary democracy is a game of multiplying grievances in the minds of people who are then manipulated by self-seeking politicians in a ruthless pursuit of power; that their secular state is a promoter of separatism among the so-called minorities some of which have been artificially carved out of the Hindu society itself; that their human rights mean the right of plain criminals to terrorize innocent citizens; that their rate of growth really refers to the growth of their own bank balances besides what they themselves bemoan as black money; that their distribution of prosperity means distribution of the better and bigger jobs among themselves; that their abolition of poverty means sweeping the mass destitution under the carpet of doctored statistics; and that their arrest of population explosion works out towards reducing the Hindus to a minority in the only Hindu homeland. As regards their Western models, all of them are sick with rising curves of crime, with boredom bred by excess of hedonism, and with pollution at all levels — physical, psychological, psychic, and spiritual — produced by hyper-industrialism and soulless commercialism.

Here we have some two-faced secularists who try to impress Western audiences by talking glibly about Indian yoga and mysticism, Indian schools of philosophy, Indian panorama of sciences, Indian styles of music and dance, Indian languages and literatures, and the Indian genius for unity in diversity; but who go into uncontrollable tantrums if someone tells them that what they are taking pride in is the Hindu cultural heritage, or describes India as the Hindu homeland. The same secularists not only do not object but also approve and applaud when some of this cultural heritage is credited to Islam, or when visiting VIPs from Islamic countries refer to India as the "second largest Muslim country". These are the people who have fashioned India's foreign policy in a manner which makes India look like the leader of an aggressive Islamic bloc rather than a peaceful nation pledged to non-alignment and friendship for all.

Hindu society has yet to affirm that all this spiritual, cultural, philosophical, and scientific heritage is Hindu, and that no one who is ashamed of being named a Hindu has a right to take pride in it. Hindu society has yet to proclaim that India has always been and will always remain a Hindu homeland, and that people who fail to come to terms with Hindu society and culture have no place in this country. Hindu society has yet to point out that the only contribution of Islam has been the ruination of this country in medieval times and Partition with wide-spread bloodshed in the recent period, and that projection of Pan-Islamism in India's foreign policy is neither sanctioned nor supported by the Hindu masses who have no illusions about Islam, or Islamic culture, or Islamic causes, or Islamic countries.

THE FAILURES OF HINDU SOCIETY

Hindu society has so far failed on all these fronts because it has failed to see the closed creeds and criminal ideologies for what they are. It has been suffering from self-forgetfulness, and has been taken in by the self-righteous slogans raised by these creeds and ideologies. It has tried to ransack its own records in search of matching prescriptions. In the process, Hindu society has been yielding ground to wanton aggression all along the line.

Christianity and Islam have only to raise the slogan of monotheism as opposed and supposedly superior to polytheism, and Hindu thinkers go out in search of a similar monotheism in Hindu shastras. At the same time, Hindu scholars line up quotations from the same shastras which are seemingly denunciatory of polytheism and image-worship. The thinkers and the scholars seldom stop to see that the monotheistic creeds are creations of the outer and the lower levels of the human mind, and that nothing which is prescribed by their criminal theologies can have a place in the shastras of Sanātana Dharma which have their source in the highest reaches of the human soul.

So also in the case of the Christian claim of "social service", or the Islamic claim of "human brotherhood", or the Communist claim of "social equality", or the modernist claim of "democracy" and "secularism", etc. Hindu scholars keep busy marshalling quotations from their own shastras in support of similar ideas, or citing examples from Hindu history of those who put such ideas into practice. The wealth of Hindu spirituality, philosophy, culture, history, and society thus goes on getting weighed in a balance which is tilted against it from the very start. It is small wonder that the entire Hindu heritage is found wanting in the final assessment.

THE FIRST PRINCIPLE OF DEFENCE

The first principle which Hindu society has to observe while preparing its defence is that it will stop processing and evaluating its own heritage in terms of ideas and ideals projected by closed creeds and pretentious ideologies. On the contrary, Hindu society will henceforward process and evaluate the heritage of these creeds and ideologies in terms of its own categories of thought, and find out the real worth of Christian, Islamic, Communist, and Modernist claims.

The first need of the hour, therefore, is for Hindus to become aware of the fundamentals of their own faith (Hindu Spirituality), the premises on which their own society has evolved (Hindu Sociology), and the vicissitudes which their own society has experienced in the march of Time (Hindu History). These are the three domains in which the Hindu image has been distorted to the utmost by imperialist thought systems, resulting in a deep sense of inferiority from which Hindus suffer at present.

Hindus have become devoid of self-confidence simply because they have ceased to take legitimate, well-informed, and conscious pride in their spiritual, cultural, and social heritage.

This lack of pride has led to a serious weakening of the Hindu psyche. Hindus are no more prepared to stand up and fight for anything, because they no more believe or feel that anything is worth fighting for, not at least to the bitter end.

The sworn enemies of Hindu society have taken advantage of this enervation of the Hindus. They feel instinctively that threats coupled with some show of violence are sure to frighten the Hindus out of their wits, and make them yield almost anything including precious parts of their homeland.

2

Sanātana Dharma Versus Prophetic Creeds

The one Vedic verse which modern Hindus quote most frequently is the third quarter (*caraṇa)* of Rigveda 1.164.46 — *ekam sad viprāḥ bahudhā vadanti* (it is of One Existence that the wise ones speak in diverse ways).

The full *mantra* reads as follows:

indram mitram varuṇam agnim āhuḥ,
atho divyaḥ sa suparṇo garutmān,
ekam sad viprāḥ bahudhā vadanti,
agnim yamam mātariśvānam āhuḥ.

(They hail Him as Indra, as Mitra, as Varuṇa, as Agni, also as that divine and noble-winged Garutmān. It is of One Existence that the wise ones speak in diverse ways, whether as Agni, or as Yama, or as Mātariśvān.)

Why do modern Hindus quote only one-fourth and not the whole of this *mantra* ? Why do they forget or refuse to cite the rest of it, or at least consider three-fourth of it as irrelevant or superfluous? And why do they assign a disproportionate weight to just one word, *ekam,* out of the five words which comprise what they consider to be the weighty one-fourth?

A careful reading of the full *mantra*, particularly in the context of the *sūkta* of which it is a part, leaves no doubt that the three-fourth which is ignored is not at all a repetition or paraphrase of the one-fourth which is presented. On the contrary, that three-fourth is as significant, if not more, as the one-fourth when we take into account the spirit of the Veda from which the citation has been selected. In fact, the one-fourth which is flourished so forcefully remains meaningless unless it is read with the rest of the *mantra*.

Why do modern Hindus maim in this manner a *mantra* from what they hold as their most sacred shastra? What do they want to prove by this wanton misrepresentation of an entire and ancient ethos in spirituality, philosophy and culture?

The answer becomes obvious as soon as we look into the psychology behind the citation.

HINDU PSYCHOLOGY OF SURRENDER

Firstly, modern Hindus want to stake a claim for admission to the exclusive club of Monotheism maintained by Christianity and Islam. Hindus here are out to convince the monopolists of Monotheism that the earliest Hindu shastra, the Rigveda, also supports and sanctions what is supposed to be the *summum bonum* of religion according to Christian and Muslim theology, or its apotheosis according to the modern Western "Science" of Comparative Religion. At the same time, there is an almost pathetic appeal to the monopolists of Monotheism that they should not be appalled by the multiplicity of gods and goddesses in the post-Vedic Hindu pantheon, and that they should judge Hinduism in terms of the "original aspiration" rather than in terms of the latter-day "aberration".

Secondly, modern Hindus are pleading before the custodians of the "only true" creeds that Hinduism is only a different way of stating the same truths which were revealed to the founders of the former. In effect, Hindus are praying with folded hands, "Please do not denounce Hinduism as polytheism, pantheism, idolatry, paganism, and *kufr*. Please ignore the differences of language and metaphor, and attend to the fundamental spirit which informs your faiths as well as ours."

The Hindu psychology throughout this exercise is one of apology, of shamefacedness, of defence against what is initially conceded as a valid criticism of the idioms and forms in which Hindu spirituality has been spelled out in its shastras. This is a disastrous psychology. It leads to a supine surrender on the one hand, and to a slavish imitation on the other.

The psychology of surrender is best symbolised by the well-intentioned Hindu slogan of *sarva-dharma-samabhāva* when it is extended indiscriminately to Christianity and Islam. Hindus are shouting themselves hoarse in stressing the identity of Brahma with Abraham, of Manu with Noah, of Rama with Rahim, of Krishna with Karim, of Kashi with Ka'ba, and so on. But the monopolists of Monotheism remain far from mollified. The orthodox among the monotheists dismiss with contempt the Hindu claim of sharing the same faith with them fundamentally. The kinder (or craftier) among the monotheists take pity on this plight of poor Hindus, and invite them to renounce their nebulous, if not counterfeit, Monotheism in favour of the fully developed doctrine.

HINDU PSYCHOLOGY OF IMITATION

The psychology of imitation is manifest in modern Sikh scholars who have, over the years, forced the message of the great Gurus into monotheistic moulds. They have almost succeeded in eclipsing, more or less completely, the Upanishadic spirituality of the *nirguṇa* saints among whom Guru Nanak occupies the front rank. They take immense pride in equating the *Ek Oṁkār* with *Allah*, the *Ādigrantha* with *Al-Kitāb*, the succession of Sikh gurus with the succession of prophets in which Guru Gobind Singh is the last like Muhammad, and the injunctions of the last Guru regarding outer symbols with similar injunctions of the Sunnah.

A manifestation of the Islamic spirit could not lag far behind, once Sikhism started Islamicizing itself. It has progressed on the path of a similar exclusiveness, a similar self-righteousness, a similar self-aggrandizement, a similar use of terror in the service of religion, and a similar mob mentality vis-a-vis internal dissent, as have characterised Islam throughout its blood-soaked career. Sikhism is fast moving out of its spiritual moorings, and becoming a politics of power which Islam has always been.

THE WAY OUT

Hindu society will never be able to combat or come to terms with the "only true" creeds like Christianity and Islam, so long as its spokesmen continue to clothe Hindu spirituality in concepts borrowed from Monotheism. The slogan of *sarva-dharma samabhāva* will fail to make any dent in the armour of Christian and Muslim animosity, so long as Hindus fail to recapture the spirit and the context in which this slogan had been evolved.

What, then, is the way out?

Firstly, Hindus have to reawaken to the sublime spirituality of their own Sanātana Dharma, and base their evaluation of other religions and cultures on its pristine premises. That will give them the requisite self-confidence to counter all misinformed or malicious criticism.

Secondly, Hindus have to study and scrutinise the sources from which the "only true" creeds derive their inspiration. That will invest Hindus with an insight into why the monopolists of Monotheism have always been so impervious to appeals for goodwill and understanding among different sections of the human family.

The fundamental difference between the Sanātana Dharma family of faiths on the one hand, and the "only true" creeds like Christianity and Islam on the other, can be drawn out in the form of a dialogue between a Soviet citizen and a citizen from a free society. The story may not be literally true. But it is illustrative of what can happen to human mind when it is deprived of freedom, and is regimented by blind beliefs imposed from outside.

A FREE SOCIETY VERSUS A CLOSED FRATERNITY

A Soviet diplomat arrived in the capital of a democratic country on a commercial mission on behalf of his government.

The mission was to continue for several months, and the hotel in which the diplomat had to stay immediately on his arrival was rather expensive by Soviet standards. Next day, the diplomat approached the enquiry counter of the hotel and asked the lady in attendance, "Where can I find your Housing Committee?"

The lady could not understand his question and asked him to elaborate. The diplomat explained, "You see, I cannot stay for long in this expensive place. I want to apply to the appropriate authority for allotment of adequate but cheaper accommodation."

The lady picked up the telephone directory, opened it at a particular page, and told the diplomat, "Sorry, we have no such committee in this city or anywhere else in this country. You have to go to an estate agent who will show you all kinds of accommodation and negotiate for the one you approve of finally. The leading estate agents are listed on this page. You may phone to any one of them for an appointment."

The diplomat was visibly annoyed. He shoved aside the telephone directory and shot his next question, "And where can I find your Food Committee?"

The lady informed him that there was no such committee either. The diplomat was now furious. He shouted, "How and where, then, do I buy the food which I will need everyday? I must have the necessary permit."

The lady assured him patiently that he needed no permit, and that he could go into any of the hundreds of stores to buy whatever he wanted, whenever he wanted.

By now the diplomat was in tantrums. He taunted, "I suppose you have no Transport Committee either?"

The lady kept her cool and said with a smile, "Why, there are all those taxies standing and cruising all over this city. You can hire any one of them at any time of the day or night and go wherever you please."*

The diplomat gave up in utter disgust. There was sadness

---

* This dialogue was written when the Soviet Union was functioning. Now the Soviet Union is no more. But the point made is still valid.

writ large on his face. He shook his head several times and said to himself, "Very bad! Very bad indeed! There is no system in this country. It is a chaos all around. I feel lost."

SPIRITUAL FREEDOM VERSUS RELIGIOUS REGIMENTATION

A follower of closed creeds like Christianity and Islam finds himself in a similar situation when faced with the spiritual freedom that is Sanātana Dharma. He discovers very soon that Sanātana Dharma does not fit into any of the mental moulds to which he is wedded, and which he seeks in other systems of thought. He is most likely to shake his head in utter disgust and feel lost like our diplomat from a closed social system stationed in the metropolis of a free society. An encounter between a monotheist and an informed follower of Sanātana Dharma is, therefore, sure to develop along similar lines.

The first point in which the followers of closed creeds take great pride is the historicity of the only saviour or the last prophet who was sent by or who received the "full and final revelation" from the "one and only true god." The first question which such a faithful will put to a student of Sanātana Dharma, therefore, is bound to be as follows: "Who is your only saviour or your last prophet? Where was he born and brought up? Where and when and before which apostles or companions did he teach, preach, and reveal?'

A student of Sanātana Dharma cannot but reply as follows: "The very concept of a historical saviour or prophet is foreign to Sanātana Dharma. We do not concede the monopoly of spiritual truth or moral virtue to any historical person, howsoever great or highly honoured. Every one has to be one's own saviour, one's own prophet. One has to discover the spiritual truths for one's own self, if that truth has to have any meaning for one or any validity in one's life. A truth discovered by someone else cannot become my truth unless I rediscover it for myself. Scriptures and spiritual teachers can be my aids and guides, and may help me in my search for truth. But the truth of which the scriptures speak or which the teachers expound cannot become a truth for me unless it comes alive in my own consciousness, and starts transforming my own life. Moreover, the very historicity in which you take pride is for us the hallmark of the ephemeral and the false. We reject a historical religion as *pauruṣeya prasthāna*, idiosyncrasies of a particular person, no matter how you hail him. That which was born in history has also died in history. You are showing devotion to what is dead and gone."

Next, the followers of closed creeds are mighty proud of being as *Ahl-i-Kitāb* or the People of the Book. They are sure that the "only true revelation" from the "one and only true god" is contained in *the* book *(al-kitāb)* which was compiled by the apostles of the only saviour or the companions of the last prophet, after the saviour or the prophet had passed away and could speak no more. They believe that nothing can be taken out from or added to this "book" which is supposed to contain the final truth for all time to come. Therefore, the second question which such a faithful will put to a follower of Sanātana Dharma is as follows: "Which is *the* book in which you believe, or your *al-kitāb*?"

A student of Sanātana Dharma is sure to reply as follows: "What for do we need a book? The whole spiritual truth, every shastra, is secret in the human heart. Any one, anywhere, at any time can have access to the spiritual realm provided one seeks for it sincerely, and prepares oneself for entering it. Many seers and saints have seen it in as many ways, and spoken of it in as many languages and by means of as many metaphors. The Vedas provide one version of it, the Jainägama another, the Tripiṭaka yet another, and so on down to the latest Hindu saint such as Sri Ramakrishna, or the latest Hindu sage such as Raman Maharshi. Different sects of Sanātana Dharma have collected the sayings and songs of different sages and saints in as many books which these sects cherish as their shastras But these shastras are not at all what you describe as *the* book or *al-kitāb*, even by distant definition. Your creed will get lost for good if your *the* book or *al-kitāb* gets lost. *The* book or *al-kitāb* cannot be recovered because the person who preached it or to whom it was revealed is dead and gone. But Sanātana Dharma will lose nothing if all its shastras are lost. All old shastras and many more can be recovered from inside the human heart, where all of them are ultimately enshrined."

By now the follower of a closed creed is most likely to feel flabbergasted by what he has been brainwashed to regard as blasphemy. The third question which such a faithful will put to a student of Sanātana Dharma is as follows: "You have no only saviour, no last prophet. You have no *al-kitāb*. How, then, do you know who is your one and only true god? How do you distinguish this one and only true god from the many false gods which abound all around you?"

At this stage the student of Sanātana Dharma will have to smile and say, "According to our spiritual tradition, testified by a long line of spiritual seekers, the way to God-discovery is through Self-discovery. As one proceeds on that inner voyage one sees spiritual truths in many forms. None of these forms is false. It is only one's seeking which can falter and lead to one's fall from the path of spiritual progress by insisting that this or that form alone is true. Sanātana Dharma stands squarely for a human becoming God in the process of Self-discovery—*Ātman* becoming *Parmātman*, *Puruṣa* becoming *Puruṣottama*. This is the path of world-discovery as well. The deeper one dives into oneself, the faster one's world gets divinised. One starts seeing God in every human being, in every animal, in every plant, in every stone. One feels free to worship God in any from or in all forms at the same time. One also feel's free not to worship God at all, and to dwell within oneself in spiritual self-delight. Sanātana Dharma, therefore, has no use for a God who makes himself known to mankind through the medium of a saviour or a prophet, or through the pages of *al-kitāb* or *the* book. Such a God must always remain external to us, and external to the world in which we live. Such a God does not permit humanhood to grow into Godhood, nor allows this world to get divinised. He has reserved all divinity for himself, and has nothing to spare for his creatures except an abject servitude to his arbitrary commandments conveyed through a saviour or a prophet chosen equally arbitrarily."

The follower of a closed creed now shoots the last arrow in his armoury with what he believes to be deadly effect. He is sure to shout, "You have failed to win the favour of the only saviour or the last prophet by not living a life according to the final commandments of the one and only true God as revealed to his only son or his last prophet in *al-kitab* or *the* book. How will the only saviour or the last prophet intercede for you on the Day of Judgement, and save you from God's wrath and eternal hell-fire? You cannot say in all seriousness that you are not interested in going to an eternal heaven full of fair maidens, flowing with milk and honey, and fanned by ever-fragrant breezes."

A student of Sanātana Dharma will keep his cool and reply as follows: "Sanātana Dharma is not so mean and miserly in deciding human destiny. It gives many lives to every creature. One can start anew from the point where one stopped in one's previous life. And the process does not cease till a creature has attained perfection and achieved Godhood. Every one is a *bodhisattva* destined to become the Buddha in the course of spiritual seeking. The journey is from darkness and bondage to light and freedom, and not from the sensual pleasures of this world to the sensual orgies of a high heaven. On the other hand, the only hell we know is neither situated outside ourselves, nor at the end of time. The hell is within us — in our greed and gluttony, in our hatreds and infatuations, in our self-righteousness and self-seeking, in our dark drives for power and domination, in our self-love and pursuit of pleasure. The only way out of this hell is through an awakening to the divinity within us, and through dispelling the darkness of ignorance in which we live our mundane lives. The favour or disfavour of a saviour or a prophet can neither catapult us into heaven nor drag us down into hell. A saviour or prophet is absolutely irrelevant to the realm of spiritual progress or retrogression."

At this point the follower of a closed creed is bound to give up in utter disgust. He is bound to exclaim, "Very bad! Very bad indeed! There is no system in your bewildered beliefs. It is a free for all. What is worse, it is blasphemy against the one and only true God, against the only saviour or the last prophet sent by Him, and against the only true revelation conveyed by Him through a mighty messenger."

PSYCHOLOGY OF CLOSED CREEDS

A student of Sanātana Dharma can ignore these pronouncements and proceed to examine the "only true" creeds. To start with, he will not judge these creeds for their inner logic or want of it, but instead weigh them on the scales of yogic spirituality systematized by reflective reason. And he will very soon find out that these creeds are not born of a spiritual consciousness at all. On the contrary, they are constructs of the outer mind drawing strength from dark drives of the unregenerate unconscious which Freud and other psychoanalysts have studied and surveyed with some insight.

The one and only true god of these creeds is the embodiment of fear and awe of the dark and the unknown. Their only saviour or last prophet is a father figure in an infantile search for security in a world full of doubts and uncertainties. Their *al-kitāb* is a collection of rationalisations mounted upon human passions like self-love, jealousy, vindictiveness, cunning, covetousness, and aggression. Their heaven represents an explosion of the animal hunger for endless sense-pleasures unmixed with or followed by pain. Their hell symbolizes a deep-seated hatred for follow human beings who refuse to bow down before self-appointed messengers of an imaginary almighty.

Hindu society will acquire self-confidence vis-a-vis the "only true" creeds when it recognizes that Sanātana Dharma stands for self-exploration, self-purification, and self-transcendence, while these creeds stand for self-stupefaction, self-righteousness, and self-aggrandizement. The horrible histories of these creeds are running commentaries on the character of their doctrines. Those histories are full of crusades and *jihāds*, massacres and genocides, inquisitions and witch-huntings, extinction of the freedom of thought and spiritual aspiration, and imperialist aggression against "infidels" in which the latter's religion and culture are destroyed, their properties pillaged, their lands misappropriated, and their men and women and children slaughtered or enslaved. It is a sin to regard them as religion in any sense of the term, and to extend *samabhāva* towards their exclusive and intolerant dogmas. One of the tasks of a resurgent Hindu society will be to rescue those people who have been forced or lured into the folds of these crude and cruel creeds.

3

The Spiritual Centre of Hindu Society

Hindu society has had to go on the defensive against monotheistic creeds masquerading as religion mainly because it has lost consciousness of the spiritual centre round which its religious, cultural and social life has revolved, and which has sustained it through the ages.

Hindu society has failed to fathom the chasm which separates its own sterling spirituality from the "only true" creeds because it has fallen in love with a dead uniformity in place of a living plurality prescribed by its own spiritual centre.

Hindu society will never be able to win the debate with thoughtless theologies unless it rediscovers its own spiritual centre, and holds in its hands the scales of yogic spirituality on which alone all theologies should be weighed for whatever worth they have.

It was an active awareness of its spiritual centre which emboldened Hindu society, at the very dawn of its history, to explore all varieties of religious experience, to evolve endless ways of religious worship, to express its philosophical insights in many metaphysical points of view, and to project its plastic genius in many forms of language, literature and art.

It was an active awareness of its spiritual centre which encouraged Hindu society to experiment with cultural, social, economic, and political pluralism on a scale such as has been unknown to any other human society.

It was an active awareness of this spiritual centre which provided an inner stability to Hindu society in the midst of outer change, and which proved its inexhaustible source of strength in weathering the vicissitudes of worldly fortune.

Hindu awareness of its spiritual centre suffered a steep decline after a long spell of spectacular creativity in all fields of human endeavour. Hindu society also suffered a corresponding decline of its vitality and vigour. Even so the awareness remained sufficiently strong to see Hindu society through a few more storms.

One of these storms was the Islamic invasion which brought death and destruction to large parts of the Hindu homeland. But thanks to the still surviving awareness of its spiritual centre, Hindu society was able to preserve its patrimony in the face of a totalitarian imperialism spreading fire and sword, pillage and rapine for a thousand years.

It was the still surviving awareness of its spiritual centre which enabled Hindu society to stick to its own Gods and Goddesses and to honour its own seers and saints, in the midst of a large-scale desecration and destruction of its temples at the hands of Muslim swordsmen, and harrowing humiliation of its holy men and women by haughty Muslim hoodlums. Some of these swordsmen and hoodlums styled themselves as sultans and sufis, and proclaimed that they had been commissioned by an almighty Allah to spread the latest and the last *ilhām* (revelation). But Hindu society refused to be hoodwinked by the honorifics donned by these disciples of the Devil.

It was the still surviving awareness of its spiritual centre which steeled Hindu society to witness the sacrifice by fire of hundreds of thousands of its daughters who cherished their chastity above every allurement offered by the Islamic marauders. Some of these marauders were known as kings and generals, governors and great dignitaries, qazis and mullahs, living in mansions full of every kind of luxury available in the world at that stage of human history. But few daughters of Hindu society yielded willingly and voluntarily to the amorous advances of these animals masquerading as men.

It was the still surviving awareness of its spiritual centre which inspired Hindu society to send hundreds of thousands of its sons into unequal battles and inevitable martyrdom against a militarily superior monster. Countless Hindu heroes courted death in defence of their heritage and honour rather than seek power and pelf in the courts of Muslims swordsmen masquerading as monarchs.

And it was a resurgence of its spiritual centre which rallied Hindu society round a counter-attack which rolled back the Islamic invasion, and wrested victory from a ferocious and formidable foe. At the same time, a victorious Hindu society was prevented by its spiritual centre from being vindictive towards an erstwhile enemy, and extending to him the same treatment which he had meted out to Hindus during the days of his own domination. Muslims could have easily met the same fate in India as they did in Spain, had not this spiritual centre of Hindu society intervened and saved them from a holocaust which the Quran and the Sunnah of the Prophet have prescribed for defeated adversaries.

Hindu society was humbled once more by another invader who swore by another but a similar closed creed. The Christian missionaries mounted a vicious and well-planned attack on the outer forms as well as the inner core of the Hindu heritage. Hindu awareness of the Hindu spiritual centre revived once more and the Christian attack was not only contained but also reversed. Hindu thought stormed into the strongholds of Christianity in Europe and America. Hindu religion and philosophy lent a helping hand to the revival of humanism and rationalism in the modern West against a fanaticism which had dyed Europe deep with several hundred years of bloodshed.

What is this spiritual centre of Hindu society?

We must first understand quite clearly as to what it is *not*, before we come anywhere near comprehending it in all its dimensions. This negative approach has been rendered necessary because the language of religion has been confused by Christianity and Islam to such an extent that darkness now passes for light, the Devil for the Divine, vice for virtue, and vice versa.

The spiritual centre of Hindu society is not constituted by *the* book or *al-kitāb* revealed by an almighty Jehovah or Allah to a Chosen People through the only saviour or the last prophet, at a particular point in human history. Nor is it a Church or Ummah entrusted with the mission of saving mankind, if need be, by force and fraud. All these formulations of religious doctrine are inspired and sustained by the dark drives of an unregenerate human nature.

THREE SUBLIMITIES OF SANĀTANA DHARMA

Hindu seers and sages as also Hindu shastras, no matter to what Hindu sect they belong, designate this spiritual centre of Hindu society as Sanātana Dharma. This designation can be loosely translated into English as the Perennial Philosophy or the Permanent Principle of Sustenance.

Firstly, Sanātana Dharma says that the aspiration for Truth (*satyam*), Goodness (*śivam*), Beauty (*sundaram*), and Power (*aiśvarya*) is inherent in every soul, everywhere, and at all times, like the physical hunger of the body for food and drink. The satisfaction of this spiritual aspiration is neither dependent upon, nor waits for, a particular prophet or revelation, as the physical hunger has never been dependent upon, or waited for, a particular pioneer in food production or a particular textbook of food technology. The soul of the spiritual seeker in all ages and among all races of mankind has soared upwards till it has found its true status in its own heights.

Secondly, Sanātana Dharma states that spiritual aspiration cannot come to rest till it overcomes all limitations of human nature, lower as well as higher, and emerges as master of oneself. Simultaneously, one emerges as master of the universe also because human nature, in all its dimensions, is a segment of Universal Nature. One arrives at the end of one's spiritual quest *only* when, Buddha-like, one can say to oneself: "I have known whatever is to be known; there is nothing more to be known. I have attained whatever is to be attained; there is nothing more to be attained. I have done whatever is to be done; there is nothing more to be done." This is the boundless bounty which flows from becoming a Buddha. This is the mighty meaning of becoming a Mahavira.

Thirdly, Sanātana Dharma promises this supreme fulfilment, this acme of attainment, to every being born in a world brimming with blind forces of Nature, ignorance, evil, suffering, disease, deprivation, and death. The path is summed up in three spiritual steps—self-exploration, self-purification, and self-transcendence. One has to travel inwards and upwards, and reverse the law of human nature in the raw which is outwards and downwards. This reversal is not brought about by an outer baptism but by an inner opening. The very first perception of the earliest Hindu seers has been — *yathā piṇḍe tathā brahmāṇḍe* (as in the microcosm, so in the macrocosm), that is, the way to world-discovery is through self-discovery.

The Upanishadic prescription, *ātmānam viddhi* (know thyself) is a variation on the same theme. It leads to the same attainment — *aham brahmo'smi* (I am Brahma), *tat tvam asi* (thou art That), and *sah tadasti* (he is That). It is a steep spiritual ascent at the end of which the *Ātman* (Self) becomes *Paramātman* (Supreme Self), and the *Puruṣa* (Person) becomes *Puruṣottama* (Superperson). In the language of Theism, man becomes God.

Here there is no place for an almighty Jehovah or Allah, sitting outside and above the Cosmos, communicating with his creatures through the medium of a privileged historical person, and coercing them through a Holy Roman Emperor or an *Amir-ul-mu'minin* to conform to a closed code of moral and social conduct. Here there is no place for a world-wide warfare between a True One God who has to be wooed and worshipped, and the False Many Gods who have to be disowned and destroyed. Here there is no command for Crusade or *Jihād* by a Church or an Ummah for spreading the "only true creed" at the point of the sword.

Nor is a metaphysical speculation of any sort relevant to this spiritual seeking which has an entirely and intensely practical purpose. The Buddha was so indifferent to metaphysical questions that most of the time he fell silent when he was faced with them. He always repudiated all metaphysical curiosities with the stern rebuke: "How will it avail you if you accept or reject this theoretical postulate or that ? The problem is practical. There is all this suffering. The suffering has a cause. And whatever has a cause can be cured. I tell you of the cause, and also of the cure." Patañjali systematised this curative prescription into a scientific discipline, the system of Yoga, locating all landmarks and signposts along the path in purely psychological terms, without reference to any metaphysical proposition.

One is, therefore, free not to give any name to the Self which seeks the Truth. One is free not to accept the ontological language of *Ātman* and *Paramātman*, *Puruṣa* and *Puruṣottama*. One is free to describe the spiritual experience in cryptic aphorisms or sonorous songs, or to say that it is indescribable and fall silent. It is the discovery and not the description which is significant. All sects of Sanātana Dharma share this discovery in common, and have their starting point in it.

It is this spiritual centre of Hindu society which has been the watershed of many ways of worship, each with its own outer forms; many religious sects, each with its own private and public rituals; many shastras, each with its own language and metaphor; and many metaphysical points of view, each with its own ontology, epistemology, axiology, and ethics. They are like the streams of crystal clear water which spring from the same snow-clad Himalayan heights, which become many rivers as they meander through the plains with many villages, towns and ferries on their banks, and which merge in the same Great Ocean to become one wide spread of water once more.

TRUE AND FALSE UNIVERSALISM

This is the basis of true universalism envisaged by Sanātana

Dharma. One is free to take a start according to one's own individual stage of spiritual evolution and preparation (*ādhāra*), and also free to follow along the curve of one's own cultural moorings, one's own individual inclination and aptitude (*adhikāra*). The pace of spiritual progress can be slow or fast, evolutional or revolutional, depending upon the drive towards divinity which one feels within oneself. One is free to choose this form of worship or that, this round of ritual or another, this religious sect or a different one, this philosophy or some other speculation.

Here there is no place for that counterfeit universalism which has only one closed concept of God, one dogmatic designation of the deity, one fixed form of faith, one regimented mode of worship, one rigid code of moral conduct, and one strait-jacket of social culture. Here there is no place for hysterical harangues to conform to the One True God's commandments in the only life one has, and no forced pace by fear of an eternal hell or promise of an eternal heaven. On the contrary, here one can start again after every false step, wander away and wait till the inner call comes again, and resume the journey in as many rebirths as are required to arrive at the ultimate goal of final freedom from bondage.

It is this sterling universalism of its spiritual centre which has sustained Hindu society as a spacious platform for the free play of a large number of spiritual traditions, and for the fullest functioning of a still larger number of religious denominations. Hindu society has never known the religious strife which has characterised the closed creeds throughout their history.

There have been prolonged and many a time heated debates among different Hindu religious sects and Hindu schools of philosophy. Some sects and schools have also used sometime a vituperative language about the precepts or practices or both of some other sects and schools. But there has never been breaking of heads, nor killing of heretics, nor a desecration or destruction of rival shrines or shastras, nor a marshalling of military forces in a war against another religious community, such as has blackened the annals of Christianity and Islam.

Hindu history has known many monarchs who subscribed to this or that particular religious prescription in their private lives. But Hindu history has seldom known a prince who patronized his own sect to the exclusion of others, or persecuted sects other than his own, as has been the standard practice of potentates most highly honoured in Christian and Muslim history.

Hindu society has sent out many saints and sages to distant lands down the ages. But Hindu society has never equipped an armed force to impose its own Gods on other people by fire and sword, as has been done by Christian and Muslim societies whenever they got an opportunity.

There is no sociological explanation for the votaries of the Vedas, the Jains, the Buddhists, the Vaishnavas, the Shaivas, the Shaktas, the Alvars, the Nayanars, the Sikhs, and many other Hindu sects never exchanging blows in pursuit of power, or privilege, or prestige for people of their own persuasion. There is no sociological explanation for several members of the same family subscribing to as many religious doctrines and yet living amicably under the same roof.

There is no political explanation for princes engaged in warfare but never quoting a shastra in support of their defensive or aggressive designs. There is no political explanation for no conqueror casting a covetous eye on any religious place, howsoever rich its coffers may have been in gold and silver and precious stones.

There is no economic explanation for rajas and rich men contributing with even-handed munificence towards the building of rival religious shrines or towards maintaining the monasteries of rival religious orders. There is no economic explanation for every householder extending equal hospitality to monks and mendicants who come to their doors in multifarious attire, and who invoke for their hosts the blessings of different deities.

It is very often stated by students of Hindu culture that Hindus have a genius for unity in diversity. But Hindus have never claimed to be the Chosen People who are radically different from other members of the human family, either in terms of native propensities or in terms of creative capacity. In fact, Hindus are never tired of repeating that all human beings, in all places and at all times, are similarly constituted, have the same appetites and aspirations, can descend to the same depths and rise to the same heights. In fact, Hindus have always failed to understand why people do not practise religious tolerance, and continue to quarrel over questions of no relevance to spiritual seeking.

The only explanation for this Hindu broad-mindedness, this Hindu spirit of religious tolerance, and this open psyche of the Hindus towards all currents and cross-currents of thought and culture, is to be found in the spiritual centre of Hindu society. It is this spiritual centre which has given to Hindu society a calm and quiet dignity of its own, and a compassion which reaches out equally not only to all members of the human family but also to all elements in the human environment—the insects, the animals, the birds, the creepers, the plants, the trees, the rivers, the oceans, the mountains, and the minerals deposited in the womb of Mother Earth.

4

Hindu Spirituality Versus Monotheism

It is an intuition ingrained in the Hindu psyche to inhabit our entire environment — celestial, physical, vegetable, animal, and human — with innumerable Gods and Goddesses. Some of these divinities are installed in temples as icons, and worshipped with well-defined rituals. Some others are worshipped as and where they are invoked. Hindu shastras, saints and sages have paid homage to many Gods and Goddesses in many sublime hymns.

The Sky which forms the firmament, and permeates the whole universe as space including the interstices in human and animal and vegetable anatomies, is a great God. It is the abode of all sounds. And it harbours in its vastnesses many other Gods such as the Sun and the Moon and the Stars, and Goddesses such as the Dawn and the Dusk. These celestial Gods and Goddesses are worshipped in their own right, particularly the Sun and the Moon and the Dawn.

The Air which fills the hollow between the sky and the earth, which rages as storm and blows as breeze, and which sustains the respiratory system in all that is alive, is also a great God. It is not visible to the eye but it manifests itself by its power to touch and turn.

The Earth which bears all burdens, which bestows boundless bounties from beneath and above its surface, and which is the symbol of forgiveness and forbearance, is also a great Goddess. The mountains which soar up till they become snow-capped are the abodes of Gods and Goddesses. So are the forests which are full of flowers and fruits and varied wealth. Some creepers and plants and trees are veritable Gods and Goddesses, harkening us to pay our homage to them.

The Water which is clustered in the clouds, which pours down as rain, which flows in rivers and springs, which gets stored up in tanks and lakes and seas and oceans, which showers itself as snow and gets settled as ice on mountain tops, is also a great God. It washes all dirt and slakes all thirst. It nourishes our field crops and our forests. It becomes the sap in all vegetables and fruits, and circulates as blood in all animals and humans. Lakes like the Mānasarovara are specially sacred because Gods and Goddesses play their games in and around them. Rivers like the Ganga and the Godavari are themselves Goddesses.

The Fire which blazes in the sun, which heats up every hearth, and which is stored as energy in all fuels, is also a great God. It manifests itself not only as heat but also as light which shines in the stars, which reveals itself in a riot of colours, which endows everything with form, and which lends vision to every eye. It maintains every metabolism as vital heat without which nothing can remain alive. The Fire God is worshipped daily in the family hearth, is regarded as the ambassador of Gods in every sacrifice, and is a witness to the sanctity of all sacraments.

The birds, the fishes, and the animals are the venerable vehicles of Gods and Goddesses, and are revered as much as their riders. The Garuḍa is the vehicle of Vishṇu, the bull that of Śiva, the lion that of Durgā, the mouse that of Gaṇapati, the swan that of Sarasvatī, and the owl that of Lakshmī. The horse is yoked in the chariot of Indra as well as that of the Sun. The snake is *nāga-devatā*. And the cow is sacred above all, a Goddess par excellence.

Nearer home, the mother is a Goddess and the father a God, to be obeyed while they are in their prime and served when they grow old. They are to be remembered with reverence, and their protection is to be sought after they pass away and become *pitris*. The wife who looks after the family welfare, who brings up the children, and who participates in all sacraments, is a Goddess. The Guru who is the repository of wisdom and learning, is also a God to be propitiated with gifts as profuse as one can afford. The Guest who comes to our home by chance is a God deserving of our warmest hospitality. The King who protects us from evil-doers and presides over the welfare of his *prajā* is also a God.

And so on, the roster is endless. Every family has a *kula-devatā*, every community a *jāti-devatā*, every village a *grāma-devatā*, every city a *nagara-devatā*, and every region a *janapada-devatā*. The Bhāratamātā who came to be worshipped as *rāshtra-devatā* in more recent times, and who inspired the national song, *Vande Mātaram*, is a projection of the same Hindu psyche which sees a God or a Goddess in everything, everywhere. It is a belief common among Hindus that the Gods and Goddesses worshipped by them add up to thirty-three crores.

The Hindu psyche has always harboured a deep sense of sanctity towards all elements and forces of Mother Nature, in all their forms and transforms. It worships these elements and forces not only outside the human body but also within it. In fact, it sees the human body as a magnificent mansion in building which all these elements and forces of Mother Nature have participated, and feels grateful towards what it greets as great Gods and Goddesses.

What is more significant, this Hindu psyche intimates that as all that is without is also within, all that is within must also be without (*yathā pinde tathā brahmānde*). It, therefore, invests everything outside with life, with consciousness, with thought and feeling, and also with will. The inanimate thus becomes animate, the unconscious becomes conscious, the thoughtless becomes thoughtful, the insensitive becomes sensitive, and the inert becomes active.

This power of the Hindu psyche persists till long after a Hindu gets converted to Christianity or Islam, and invites frowns and fierce lectures from the missionary and the mullah. This power of the Hindu psyche is illustrated by the story of a Hindu lady in Kerala who got converted to Christianity for some reason. The missionary who had presided over the conversion paid a visit to her home one day, and found her worshipping the old Hindu Gods and Goddesses of the family. The missionary was red in the face and rebuked her in the name of the only True God. The lady smiled and said, "So what? My becoming a Christian does not mean that I have renounced my *Dharma* !"

It would not do for Hindu society to fight shy of this pervasive Hindu psyche which is as old as the oldest Hindu shastras, the Vedas, and perhaps much older. It would not do for Hindu society to disown this deep-seated Hindu psyche which sustains practically the whole of Hindu religion and culture. In fact, Hindu society has to go back to the source of this psyche, reawaken to the spiritual centre which gave birth to this psyche, and reaffirm an abiding faith in its reaches and ramifications.

HOSTILITY TO HINDU PSYCHE

Western sociology is trying to explain this psyche as a hangover from a primitive past when human reason was not so developed and could not discriminate between fact and fancy, or, worse still, when a "puerile priestcraft" succeeded in deceiving people for its own private profit. The Western "Science" of Comparative Religion, which is only another name for Christian theology, is trying to pooh-pooh this psyche as a vestige of primitive animism which was at best only a crude form of religious awakening.

A more serious attack on this Hindu psyche is mounted by the Christian missionary. He pronounces that Hindu psyche has been heavily "polluted" by pantheism which sees a God or Goddess "in every bug that bites, and every cockroach that crawls". He believes that Hindus can be "cured" of this "perverse" psyche only by being baptised in the Christian Church, and by accepting Jesus Christ as the one and only saviour.

Similarly, the Muslim mullah frowns on this Hindu psyche as *shirk*, that is, a mixing up of the divine with the mundane. He sees no future for Hindus, either here or hereafter, unless they accept Allah as the only true god, and Muhammad as the last prophet of Allah.

And the missionary and the mullah are not mere preachers of some distinct doctrines. They are also crusaders and *mujāhids* who believe that Hindus should either be converted to the "true faith", or killed and consigned to eternal hell-fire. Destruction and defilement of the images of Hindu Gods and Goddesses, demolition of Hindu temples and monasteries, desecration of Hindu places of pilgrimage, and burning of Hindu shastras are the fundamental tenets of their faiths.

What is this other psyche which is suffused with such smug self-righteousness, and which finds such satanic satisfaction in hurting the deepest sentiments of people belonging to another faith? Hindu society will have to understand this other psyche if it wants to save itself from the inroads of Christianity and Islam, both of which are eating into its vitals with the aid of international allies and resources.

THEOLOGY OF MONOTHEISM

Let us for the time being forget the Freudian analysis of Christianity and Islam, though that analysis provides an intimate peep into the psyche of these primitive creeds. Let us have a look at the philosophy underlying their doctrines, and find out if they have any share in the spiritual seeking which is intrinsic to human beings and which stands systematized in Sanātana Dharma.

Christianity and Islam differ on many points of detail. But they share a common view of what they invoke as the creator and controller of the cosmos, as well as of the cosmic process. In the language of theology, they describe their basic dogma as Monotheism as opposed to what they denounce as Polytheism and Pantheism. It is this basic dogma which needs a philosophical probe deeper than that to which it has been subjected so far.

The term Monotheism casts such a magic spell on certain minds that they stop at its literal meaning — the concept of one God as opposed to many gods. But the literal meaning tells us little, almost nothing, about its theological inspiration or its practical implications.

In the theology of Monotheism, God is extra-cosmic. He created the cosmos out of *Nothing* in order to demonstrate his almightiness and, consequently, kept himself outside and above the cosmos. There is nothing in God's creation which can partake of God's divinity. The elements and forces of Nature are devoid of any divinity whatsoever. The sky is empty space, and the Sun and the Moon and the Stars are only bright spots in that sky. Matter is absolutely material, and animals and birds are mere brutes unless they are domesticated when they show some improvement. Trees are timber, and the flowers embody no more than colour and fragrance. Air and water and fire and earth are what they are, and point to nothing beyond.

It is only man who is placed on a higher pedestal because the Almighty God blew His own breath into the handful of dust which He used in order to manufacture Adam, the male ancestor of the human race. Woman cannot share man's status because Eve, the female ancestor of the human race, was carved out of Adam's rib without the benefit of God's breath being blown into it. Man is thus the best of God's creation, the *ashraf-ul-makhlūqāt*.

But it is an unpardonable folly and a cardinal sin for man to fancy that he shares even an iota of God's divinity. The only privilege which man enjoys as God's best creation is to lord it over the lower creation which God has made for man's use and benefit. Man can exploit the material resources of the earth in whatever way he pleases. Man can eat every bird and fish and animal for God has created them specifically for man's consumption. And man can marry and divorce and keep as his concubines any number of women, at any stage of his three score and ten years. (The monogamy we find in Christianity is not prescribed by the Christian scripture. It was an institution which it borrowed from the pre-Christian Romans.)

As man is likely to be carried away by the freedom of will

which has been bestowed on him, and forget his creator, God has been sending prophets from time to time to restrain him from worship of false gods and philosophical speculation, and to turn his thoughts towards a higher purpose — obedience to God's will as revealed through the prophets. The complete code of such do's and dont's has been conveyed by God in his final revelation — the New Testament according to Christianity and the Quran according to Islam — through his only son who is Jesus for Christianity or the last prophet who is Muhammad for Islam.

The supreme purpose of man's life is to worship this extra-cosmic God with whom man cannot communicate directly, lead a life of piety according to rules laid down in the final revelation which man cannot question, and seek the intercession of the only son or the last prophet whose claims man cannot scrutinize in terms of his natural reason or normal moral sense. If man can thus bid good-bye to his critical faculty and conscience, "the seats of the Satan", he can hope for an eternal heaven at the end of the only life God has granted to him. But if man wavers, or questions, or criticizes, or tries to understand, or judge these mysteries by using his own mind or moral sense, he becomes bound for an eternal hell from which there is no escape, and where the torment turns worse and worse with the ticking of every moment.

Whether all this applies to woman as well has been a point of dispute among Christian and Muslim theologians. Nevertheless, this much is clear that Islam at least assigns the same role to woman in heaven as she is expected to play on this earth — to serve man in servile obedience and to provide sexual pleasure to her male master. The only concession extended to woman after she enters heaven is to be spared the pains of maternity and old age. She becomes a houri endowed with eternal youth and unfading beauty. In Christianity, woman is essentially a temptress who leads man to hell. Her role in the hereafter has not been clearly defined.

An added duty of all true believers is to band together in a

Church or an Ummah for propagating the only true religion, and to prop up the only son or the last prophet by all means including force and fraud. The fraternity thus formed is expected to invite all unbelievers to get converted to the only true creed, and to declare a crusade or *jihād* against all those who refuse to be persuaded peacefully for saving themselves from eternal perdition and for securing an eternal heaven. The Church is expected to secure the aid of its secular arm, and the Ummah is expected to convert itself into a theocratic state in order to carry forward the struggle.

There is no limit to what these holy wars can legitimately do to the unbelievers except the limit imposed by power equations at any time. The least that the wars should do at the first available opportunity is to destroy the false gods of the unbelievers, and the unholy temples where those gods are worshipped. The holy warriors are under no obligation at all to prove that they are better human beings as compared to those they are expected to convert, or kill, or enslave, or subjugate. Their only qualification is that they believe in the only son or the last prophet, and follow the only true religion.

MONOTHEISM IS DISGUISED MATERIALISM

One may spend a lifetime searching this theology of Monotheism for a factual or rational proof of what it proclaims so pompously. But the search will be in vain. For, all the time it assumes what it wants to prove, and proves what it has already assumed. At its best, it is a syllogism of which the major as well as the minor premise are arbitrary assertions.

Is there a proof that a being called Almighty God exists, and controls the cosmos? The answer is that the only son or the last prophet has said so. Who has sent this son or appointed this prophet to tell us about God and his doings? The answer is that it is God who has proclaimed the son or the prophet. What is the proof that what the son or the prophet pronounces as a divine revelation comes from God? The answer is that the revelation says so. And so on, it is an endless exercise in casuistry with no reference to human experience or human reason at any point.

In the last analysis, God is really a superfluity in this system of thought. A time comes when God imparts his final revelation to the only son or the last prophet, and retires to a well-deserved rest after entrusting the fate of his world as well as of his creatures to the keeping of the son or the prophet. In due course, the son or the prophet also is dead and gone after bequeathing his monopoly over truth and virtue to the Church or the Ummah. The Church or the Ummah, in turn, is dominated by a single man or a clique that can control and use a mighty military machine which has been built in the meanwhile. In the final round, it all ends up as imperialist aggression against other people in which a veneer of religious verbiage is retained in order to sustain the self-righteousness of the aggressor. The idols of the conquered people are destroyed and their temples pillaged, not because their Gods have been found to be false but because an imperialist always aims at destroying the self-respect of a people upon whom he wants to secure a stranglehold. It is in the nature of imperialism to indulge in cultural genocide on the slightest pretext, or at the first favourable opportunity.

The plight of the Allah of Islam is portrayed by Shykh Muhammad Iqbal when he puts the following question to Allah in his *Shikwā* "*Tujhko ma'lūm hai letā thā kuī nām tirā / Quwwat-i-bāzū-i-muslim nē kiyā kām tirā* (Do you know of anyone who bothered about you before we came forward? It was the muscle-power of the Muslim which came to your rescue)." The God of the Bible is in no better position. He has been held aloft all along by Christian bayonets or Christian bags of money.

History is witness that Christianity as well as Islam have always expanded by the power of the sword, and seldom by power of any truth contained in their scriptures. In the words of Iqbal again, "*Par tire nām pē talwār uṭhāī kisnē* ? *Kāt kar rakh diyē kuffār kē lashkar kisnē* (But who did draw their swords in defence of your name and fame? Who was it that slaughtered the armies of the infidels for your sake ?)." It is obvious that the Allah of Islam had to be thrust down people's throats at the point of the sword. Otherwise poor Allah was a non-existent entity which no one was prepared to affirm. The same can be said of the Jehovah of Christianity, though no Christian poet has had the honesty of Iqbal to come out with the naked truth in a frank and forthright manner.

It is small wonder, therefore, that this politics of power masquerading as religion, cannot understand the language of spirituality which speaks in terms of a Divinity secret in everything, everywhere, and which enables human beings to dwell constantly in the company of Gods and Goddesses. This politics is too busy amassing wealth and power and pleasures of a material world to care for things which belong to the realm of Spirit.

Pained by the poverty of Muslims and the decay of the power of Islam, Iqbal has lamented: "*Qahar tō yēh hai ke kāfir ko milē hūr-o-qusūr/ Aur bechārē musalmāṅ kō faqat wa'da-i hūr* (The terrible tragedy is that the infidels live in palaces and make love to houris in this life while the poor Muslim has to remain content only with the promise of houris hereafter)." This is the highest aspiration to which this venerable Allāma of Islam could ever attain. It speaks volumes about Islam as a religion. Christianity too aspires towards no goal higher than this. Only its spokesmen are not so crude (or honest) in putting forward its case.

Hindu society has not only to recover the source of its own psyche which speaks in the language of Gods and Goddesses, it has also to realize that the psyche of Christianity and Islam hides vulgar materialism and imperialist ambition under a welter of high-sounding verbiage.

5

The Basis of Universal Spirituality

Sri Ramakrishna was one day taunted by a sceptic that the Kali he worshipped at Dakshineshwar was only a slab of black stone carved into a bizarre female figure and decked with glittering trinkets. The saint was taken aback. So far he had not cared to see the sacred icon in its supreme spiritual splendour. He had been content to witness the Divine Mother in all Her majesty in the cave of his heart whenever he was in a state of *samādhi*. Now he had been challenged to find out if what he worshipped was a figment of his fevered imagination.

He entered the *sanctum sanctorum*, and stood before the sacred icon. He fixed his gaze on the holy figure, and prayed with all his concentrated psychic power: *Mā* ! *dyākhā dē* (Mother! Reveal Thyself). And lo and behold! The Divine Mother dazzled his physical eyes with the same indescribable infinities as he had witnessed with his inner eye while meditating on Her form. He looked back at the sceptic who had accompanied him, and smiled with compassion. The sceptic had seen nothing which he had not seen before. To his physical eyes, the Goddess was still a slab of black stone. And it had not been given to him to train the inner eye.

The point which was made that day at Dakshineshwar was that to the physical consciousness a slab of stone in any shape or form will always remain a slab of stone, while to another consciousness which has awakened to some sublime dimension the same slab will reveal its innermost mysteries. To a consciousness such as that of Sri Ramakrishna who had already scaled the highest spiritual heights, the slab of stone became an incarnation of

Sat (Truth), *Cit* (Consciousness), and *Ānanda* (Bliss). It was not the icon which was inert and inconscient; it was the witness within the sceptic which had not yet awakened to its own spiritual power. It is not the Gods who are unwilling to reveal themselves; it is the worship which has not yet known how to woo them.

This is the spiritual secret discovered by the Vedic seers. This is the mystery and miracle witnessed and vouchsafed by Hindu saints and sages throughout the ages. And this is the vast vision which forms the spiritual centre of Hindu society.

There is a consciousness, inherent in all beings, everywhere and at all times, which, when reached and brought forward, witnesses the world-play as a drama of divine forms and forces. There is not a thing, nor a thought which does not get transfigured from the terrestrial into the celestial, whenever and wherever this consciousness comes into play. Everything then returns to and resumes its supreme spiritual status, or becomes the outer symbol of an inner sublimity. It is these sublimities which invite the seer's worship as Gods and Goddesses. It is these sublimities which spur the *bhakta* to burst out in song and *stuti*, the paens of praise pouring out of a grateful heart for being permitted to witness what has been witnessed.

The Vedic seers were not primitive animists who invested the phenomena of physical Nature with anthropomorphic attributes, as the "Science" of Comparative Religion will have us believe. They were spiritual explorers who discovered and employed well-defined yogic disciplines to raise up human consciousness from its terrestrial turmoil to its transcendent tranquility. Nor were the Vedic Gods and Goddesses born in the poetic hyperboles of some barbaric bards, as the "higher criticism" of modern Indologists will have us imagine. The poetry did not *precede* the birth of the Vedic pantheon. On the contrary, it *succeeded* that birth when the Vedic seers saw the inner secrets of outer forms.

SECRET OF IMAGE-WORSHIP

Sages such as Sri Aurobindo who have meditated on Hindu iconography, and savants such as Ananda Coomaraswamy, Stella Kramrisch, and Alice Boner who have studied the subject, assure us that the forms and features of Hindu icons have a source higher than the normal reaches of the human mind. The icons are no photocopies of any human or animal forms as we find them in their physical frames. They are in fact crystallizations of the abstract into the concrete, of the infinite into the finite. They always point beyond themselves, and a contemplation of them always draws us from the outer to the inner.

Hindu *Śilpaśāstras* lay down not only technical formulas for carving holy icons in stone, and metal, and other materials. They also lay down elaborate rules about how the artist is to fast, and pray, and otherwise purify himself for long periods before he is permitted, if at all, to have a psychic image of the God or Goddess whom he wants to incarnate in a physical form. It is this sublime source of the *Śilpaśāstras* which alone can explain a Sarnath Buddha, or a Chidambram Naṭarāja, or a Vidisha Varāha, to name only a few of the large assembly of divine images inhabiting the earth. It is because this sublime source is not accessible to modern sculptors that we have to be content with poor copies which look like parodies of the original marvels.

The same sages and savants inform us that the Hindu temple architecture and the rituals that are performed at the time of *pūjā*, also have a sublime source. This is a deep and difficult subject, largely beyond the reach of the present writer. I shall, therefore, not proceed with it. What needs to be emphasized is that the plurality of Hindu Gods, the icons in which they are embodied, the temples in which they are installed, and the rituals with which they are worshipped, are not mere accessories and aids towards some deeper spiritual vision; instead, they incarnate the vision itself.

Ram Swarup has presented the proper perspective on the plurality of Hindu Gods as well as their incarnation in concrete images, in his recently published book, *The World As Revelation: Names of Gods*. His discussion leaves no doubt that the plurality of the Hindu pantheon, and the large use of concrete images is not only quite in keeping with but also necessary corollaries of (1) the spontaneous processes of human psychology, (2) the normal growth of human knowledge culminating in spiritual vision, and (3) the natural development of human language for incorporating and communicating that knowledge and vision. I will quote at length from Ram Swarup's book because I find it difficult to clothe his insights in my own language.

PLURALITY OF GODS

He introduces the subject as follows:

"If we look at the word 'God', we find that though today it has acquired a forced, intellectualized outward meaning appropriate to the mentality of the present age, yet it still retains the memory of the idea of a deity of a more intuitive people and of more spontaneous times.

"Etymologists connect this word with Gothic *guth*, which is Skt. *huta*, which means 'one to whom oblations are made' and, therefore, one who is worshipped. It connects us with the period when fire was a great living symbol of the deity within and around. In later times, the symbol was denounced as nature-worship by some sects but there was a time when it claimed, along with the Sun and the Sky, universal acceptance. Even Moses who belonged to an iconoclastic tradition had a glimpse of his God through the medium of fire. And in the *Old Testament* itself, certain hymns are considered 'nature hymns' by its scholars.

"Etymologists also connect the word with the German word *gotse* whose original meaning was an image or a figure. In the Norse language also, the word meant 'image of a deity' So the word perhaps referred to the practice of worshipping God through various images and figures a practice quite common amongst different peoples all over the world, ancient as well as modern.

"There is another feature worth noticing. Spengler tells us

that the Old German word for 'God' was a neutral plural and was turned into a masculine singular by Christian propaganda. The same is true of the word in the Norse and Teutonic languages. But after the heathens were converted, God changed his gender and number. This can hardly be regarded as the deepening of its meaning and conception.

"The Hebrew word *Elohim* too is plural in origin, form and sense. The same is true of the Semitic word *El.* It is not the name of the deity common to all but is a common name for different deities in the Semitic world.

"Thus we see that the untutored and the more spontaneous intuition of the human race excludes neither the plurality of Gods nor the use of images and nature symbols from its religious sensibility. The denial comes when the mind becomes too conceptual; or when dogmatic faith develops faster than understanding.

"If we study the ancient religious literature of the Hindus, particularly the Vedas, the Upanishads and the Mahabharata, certain things stand out prominently. The very first thing is a very large use of concrete image. There are Gods like Indra, Pūṣana, Varuṇa, Aśvins for whom there are no physical correspondences, but many important Gods like Sūrya, Agni, Marut take their names after natural objects.

"There is also another important feature that we notice. The spiritual consciousness of the race is expressed in terms of the plurality of Gods. In these two respects, at least, the Hindu approach agreed with the spiritual intuition of other ancient peoples.

THE PHYSICAL AND THE SPIRITUAL

"The physical and intellectual are not opposed to one another. The names of physical objects become names of ideas, names of psychic truths, names of Gods; sensuous truths become intellectual truths, become spiritual truths. As the knowledge of the senses becomes the knowledge of the *Manas* and the *Buddhi*, the knowledge originating in the higher organs of the mind also tends to filter down to the levels of the *Manas* and the senses. So in this way even the highest knowledge has its form, colour and sound. This need not lower down its quality in any way. In fact, this is the only way in which the sense-bound mind understands something of the higher knowledge.

"This reverberating, echoing and imaging takes place up and down the whole corridor of the mind, at all levels of abstraction. Here, as we traverse the path, we meet physical forms, sound-forms, vision-forms, thought-forms, universal forms, all echoes of each other. We meet *mantras* and *yantras* and icons of various efficacies and psychic qualities. In one sense, they are not the light above but they are its important formations. They invoke the celestial and raise up the terrestrial.

"There is another reason why images in the Vedas and the Upanishads are concrete. When the fever of the soul subsides, when the mind becomes calm, when the spiritual consciousness opens, things are no longer lifeless. In this state, things which have hitherto been regarded as ordinary are full of life, light and consciousness. In this state, 'the earth meditates as it were; water meditates as it were; mountains meditate as it were.'[1] In this state, no need is felt to separate the abstract from the concrete because both are eloquent with the same message, because both image one another. In this state, everything expresses the divine; everything is the seat of the divine; everything is That; mountains, rivers and the great earth are but the Tathāgata, as a Chinese teacher, Hsu Yun, proclaimed after his spiritual awakening.

"According to Hindu thought, the names of Gods are not names of external beings. They are names of truths of man's own highest Self. So the knowledge of the epithets of Gods is a form of Self-knowledge. Gods and their names embody truths of the deeper Spirit and meditation on them in turn invokes those truths. But those truths are many and, therefore, Gods and their

---

[1] Chāndogya Upanishad, 7.6.1

names too are many, though they are all held together in the unity of a spiritual consciousness."

THE ONE GOD OF THEOLOGY

Next, he provides a peep into how the Western-Christian mind views the Vedic pantheon. He proceeds:

"This way of looking at the Godhead is disconcerting to the Western schematic mind. In the Vedic approach, there is no single God. This is bad enough. But the Hindus do not have even a supreme God, a *führer*-God who presides over a multiplicity of Gods. If there has to be a plurality of Gods as is the case in all polytheistic religions, there could at least be a tabulated statement of Gods arranged in some order of superiority and inferiority, each God having some distinctive characteristics of his or her own. But here we have no such thing, no ranking, no order of seniority and precedence, no hierarchy, no recognizable magistracy; it is all anarchy. This melee could not even be called a pantheon — a body of Gods, however disordered (Gk. *pan+theos*); it is a body of demons and evil spirits, pandemonium (*pan+diamon*).

"It seems that the Hindus were either confused about their Gods or that these Gods were not jealous enough to be like the God of the Bible. The Hindus worshipped their Gods in turn with the same supreme epithets. It seems to be like a philanderer wooing several women at the same time with the same vows, promises, and protestations and telling each in turn that she is the only beautiful and true one for him. If they only knew what the man was doing there would be trouble enough for him. In like manner, if a Hindu God knew what his worshipper was telling his rival God, it would either expose the devotee's insincerity or the powerlessness of his God."

NO OPPOSITION BETWEEN ONE AND MANY

Finally, he presents the Vedic point of view in the following words:

"But there is another approach, quite a different one, which was adopted by the people of the Vedas. According to this approach, 'Reality is one but the wise call it by different names; they call him Indra, Mitra, Varuṇa, Agni, Yama, Mātariśvān.'[2] Reality is like the Ganges: different villages along its banks are differently named but they are all on the same river; the people drink the same water and their soil is watered and fertilized by the same source. The Reality is like an ocean rolling against different continents; you taste it anywhere, it is the same. The Reality is like a nugget of gold; it is the same at the corners, at the top, or at the bottom, or in the middle. Like a lump of sugar, it is sweet at all points. Similarly, whether you go East or West, South or North, you move in the same pervading space and you meet the same truth and principle of things.

"The Hindus do not call their Gods either 'One' or 'Many'. According to them what they worship is One Reality, *ekam sat*, which is differently named. This Reality is everywhere, in everything, in every being. It is One and Many at the same time and it also transcends them both. Everything is an expression, a play, an image, an echo of this Reality.

"In Vedic literature, the question of the number of Gods was no point of dispute and agitated no mind. The number could be increased or decreased at will. It all depended on the principle of classification, on the context, and on the viewpoint.

"There are two ways of regarding the Godhead. In one approach, God is a jealous one. He brooks no other. He is Ismael-like, his hand against everyone and everyone's hand against him. But in the Vedic concept, all Gods are friends, one and equal. Brahmaṇaspati is associated with Indra, Soma and Dakṣiṇa; they are invoked jointly. The Maruts are requested to come along accompanied, *saṁjagmāno*, by Indra, and both are called of 'equal splendour', *samāna varcasa*.[3] Indra and Varuṇa are offered con-

---

[2] Rigveda, 1.164.46

[3] Ibid., 1.6.7.

joint praise, *sachastut*.[4] They are invoked together. 'I invoke you both,' says the worshipper;[5] or, 'come Agni with the Maruts,' is the repeated prayer of the devotee in another hymn.[6]

"Spiritual life is one but it is vast and rich in expression. The human mind also conceives it differently. If the human mind was uniform without different depths, heights and levels of subtlety; or if all men had the same mind, the same psyche, the same imagination, the same needs; in short, if all men were the same then perhaps One God would do. But a man's mind is not a fixed quantity and men and their powers and needs are different. So, only some form of polytheism alone can do justice to this variety and richness.

"Besides this variety of human needs and human minds, the spiritual reality itself is so vast, immense, and inscrutable that man's reason fails and his imagination and fancy stagger in its presence. Therefore, this reality cannot be indicated by one name or formula or description. It has to be expressed in glimpses from many angles. No single idea or system of ideas could convey it adequately. This too points to the need for some form of polytheism.

OPPOSITIONS BETWEEN TRUE AND FALSE WORSHIP

"In this deeper approach, the distinction is not between a true One God and the false Many Gods; it is between a true way of worship and a false way of worship. Wherever there is sincerity, truth, and self-giving in worship, that worship goes to the true altar by whatever name we may designate it and in whatever way we may conceive it. But if it is not desireless, if it has ego, falsehood, conceit, and deceit in it, then it is unavailing though it may be offered to the most True God, theologically speaking. 'He who offers to me with devotion a leaf, a flower, a fruit, or water,

---

[4] Ibid., 1.17. 9.
[5] Ibid., 1.17.7.
[6] Ibid., 1.17.10.

that I accept from that striving devotee,' says Lord Krishna in the Gita.[7]

"He also assures us that 'those who worship other Gods with faith worship me,' for 'I am the enjoyer of all sacrifices.'[8] Devotion, faith, austerity, striving in the soul — they all belong to Him; they are His food: they can never go to a false God though so declared by a rival theology.

"The fact is that the problem of One or Many Gods is born of a theological mind, not of a mystic consciousness. In the Atharvaveda, the sage Vena says that he 'sees That in that secret station of the heart in which the manifoldness of the world becomes one-form', *yatra viśvam bhavatyekarūpam*[9] or, as in the Yajurveda where the world is rested in one truth, *eka nīḍam.*[10] But in another station of man, where not his soul but his mind rules, there is opposition between the One and the Many, between God and Matter, between God and Gods. On the other hand, when the soul awakens, Gods are born in its depths which proclaim and glorify one another.

"Worship is in man's soul and the divine glory is reflected in every symbol. Therefore, the Vedic seers worshipped Him in many forms and under many Names. 'Veneration to the great Gods, veneration to the lesser, veneration to the young, veneration to the old, we worship all the Gods as well as we are able,'[11] that is their attitude. A true heart's homage cannot go waste; it cannot go to false Gods; in a divine economy it is taken up by That which is the secret meaning and the principle of truth in everything."

It was this all-pervading sense of divinity which inspired Hindu seers and sages to sense the same *Sat-Cit-Ānanda* sleeping in the stone, stirring up in the sapling, smiling in the flower,

---

[7] Gita, 9.26.
[8] Ibid., 9.23-24.
[9] Atharvaveda, 2.1.1.
[10] Yajurveda, 32.8.
[11] Rigveda, 1.27.13.

singing in the bird, shining in the sun and the stars, and resuming its own supreme status at the summit of spiritual experience. It was in this crucible of concrete spirituality that they saw the one Divine Substance manifesting itself in a multiplicity of forms, and many Divine Diversities dissolving themselves in one ubiquitous Unity.

It was these intimations from infinity which invited Hindu saints and mystics to invoke the same Reality in many Names and Forms, and make it accessible to each aspirant according to his or her aptitude (*adhikāra*) and in keeping with the stage of his or her spiritual development (*ādhāra*). They devised many ways of worship and sang their devotion unto the same Divinity in many languages. It was this vision of the One-in-Many and the Many-in-One which is the source of the Vedic verse, *ekam sad viprāh bahudhā vadanti*, which has now been torn out of context and turned from a trenchant truth of Sanātana Dharma into a tawdry slogan of Monotheism.

This Vedic verse is neither a defence mechanism to be put into operation whenever the monopolists of Monotheism mouth their war-cry of the 'true One God', nor a secularist slogan to be shouted whenever a Muslim mob stages a riot over music before a mosque or over a pig wandering away into a Muslim *mohalla*. On the contrary, it is the statement of a profound principle which informs sincere spiritual seeking everywhere, at all times. It is the basis of a universal spirituality.

6

Revival of Universal Spirituality

The Hindu and Buddhist Gods and Goddesses in India, Nepal, Bali, Burma, Japan, Korea, Sri Lanka, Thailand and elsewhere are only local expressions of a universal spirituality. In this respect, spirituality is akin to science. Astronomy, Biology, Chemistry, Geology and Physics reveal the same secrets of Nature to all men everywhere and at all times, no matter in what language those secrets are couched or communicated. In like manner, the spontaneous expressions of spirituality have been the same everywhere and at all times, though the language and metaphor of those expressions have been different according to culture and clime. In the final analysis, they are variations on the same sublime theme.

ALL ANCIENT NATIONS WORSHIPPED MANY GODS

There was a time when the ancient Assyrians, Babylonians, Chaldeans, and Egyptians worshipped a multiplicity of Gods in the form of icons installed in innumerable temples. The ancient Iranians paid homage to the Fire God in their sacred shrines. The Gods of the Greeks and the Romans are well known in spite of a large-scale destruction of their physical manifestations by the vandals of Christianity. The Britons, the Celts, the Franks, the Germans, the Scandinavians, and the Slavs also sensed their Gods as residing in many a mountain, river and forest. The pre-Islamic Arabs had many Gods and worshipped them in many sacred shrines besides the principle one at Ka'ba before the prophet of Islam presided over their destruction.

Nearer home, the pre-Islamic Turks in Central Asia and the

pre-Islamic Indonesians and Malaysians to our south were Hindus and Buddhists with similar ways of worship as we have in this country. The Cambodians, the Chinese, the Laotians, the Mongolians, the Tibetans and the Vietnamese had their own Hindu-Buddhist Gods till the other day before they fell into the clutches of the Communist monolith.

The Red Indians in North, Central, and South America practised what their Christian invaders from Europe denounced as 'idolatry'. The so-called aborigines of Africa, Australia, New Zealand and the far-flung islands of Oceania did the same, and met the same punishment at the hands of Christian invaders and missionaries.

The physical destruction of the icons and temples does not mean that the Gods have been destroyed. Nor have the Gods become outdated. They do not belong to a distant past. On the contrary, they are always there, waiting to be witnessed and worshipped by any one who prepares oneself to be admitted to their presence. For they dwell in a dimension which defies time and space. They dwell in the depths of the human heart, in the innermost sanctuary of the human soul. Their disappearance from the physical scene only means that human spirituality has become shallow, and suffered a steep decline.

HINDU GODS PROVIDE A LINK WITH ALL ANCIENT GODS

Ram Swarup has drawn our attention to this eclipse of the ancient Gods of many people after those people were forcibly converted to Christianity or Islam, and their temples were destroyed or converted into churches or mosques. I shall, therefore, quote again at some length from his book, *The Word As Revelation: Names of Gods:*

"There was a time when these Gods satisfied the religious urges of their devotees. But in the course of time they came under attack from new Gods that were appearing on the horizon. They are by now completely replaced but the old persecution still continues though in a modified form. The new persecutors are not theologians and religious zealots but staid academicians. To them these Gods are not false but primitive. They hold that these Gods represented the attempt of the primitive mind to express, however imperfectly, through Nature's symbols and objects, its groping for a unitary principle. At this stage of human evolution, it was difficult for man's mind to rise above the sensuous to the intellectual and the spiritual, and from the many to the one. That was left for a later generation to achieve, reaching its high water-mark in Christianity and modern Europe.

"If Gods are born of religious urges and spiritual intuitions, it is difficult to see how modern European Christians are superior in this respect and, therefore, how their 'one God' could be truer than the 'many Gods' of their ancestors.

"A look at the Hindu Gods may throw light on this aspect of the subject. The Hindu pantheon has changed to some extent but the old Gods are still active and are still understood though under modified names. Hindu India has a sense of continuity with its past which other nations, that changed their religions at some later stage, lack. It is also known that the Hindu religion preserves many old layers and forms. Therefore, its study may link us not only with its own past forms but also with the religious consciousness, intuitions and forms that prevailed in the past in Europe, in Greece, in Rome, in many Scandinavian and Baltic countries, amongst Germanic and Slavic peoples and also in several countries of the Middle East. In short, the study may reveal a fundamental form of spiritual consciousness which is wider than its Hindu expression.

"This discussion should help to promote our understanding not only of Vedic religion and Vedic Gods but also of a whole archetypal spiritual consciousness which expresses itself in the language of Many Gods; and as a result should also help us to understand better the old religions of Europe and Asia which are no more; it should also help us to see in a new light the old Gods of Egypt, Persia, Greece, Rome, the Gods of the Scandinavian and Baltic countries, the Gods of the Germanic, Celtic, and

Slavic peoples.

RETURN OF ANCIENT GODS

Ram Swarup pleads that a revival of universal spirituality should lead to a return of ancient Gods eclipsed by Christianity and Islam:

"In the cultural history of the world, the replacement of Many Gods by One God was accompanied by a good deal of conflict, vandalism, bigotry, persecution and crusading. These conflicts were very much like 'wars of liberation' of today, hot and cold, openly aggressive or cunningly subversive. Success in such wars played no mean role in making a local deity, say Allah of certain Arab tribes, win a wider status and assume a larger, monarchical role.

"Looking at the whole thing from the perspective of today, it is difficult to say whether the replacement was enriching or impoverishing in the spiritual and cultural sense. In most cases like these, outer symbols change without making any significant changes in their psychic meanings. It would, therefore, be difficult to hold that the present Gods of Semitic origin are superior to the now defunct pagan Gods. There was a time when the old pagan Gods were pretty fulfilling and they inspired the best of men and women to acts of greatness, love, nobility, sacrifice, and heroism. It is, therefore, a good thing to turn to them in thought and pay them our homage. We know pilgrimage, as ordinarily understood, as wayfaring to visit a shrine or a holy place. But there can also be a pilgrimage in time and we can journey back and make our offerings of the heart to those Names and Forms and Forces which once incarnated and expressed man's higher life. They are holy Names and Symbols.

"The present generations of many countries tend to regard their past as a benighted period of their history. A more understanding approach towards their Gods of old will work for a less severe judgement about their past and their ancestors. It will also fill the generation gap, not the one we talk about the most these days but a still wider one, the general rootlessness of a whole nation. Gods provide an invisible link between the past and the present of a nation; when they go, the link also snaps. The peoples of Egypt, Persia, Greece, Germany and the Scandinavian countries are no less ancient than the people of India; but they lost their Gods, and therefore they lost their sense of historical continuity and identity.

"Today, there is a spirit of revolt amongst Western youths against their parents' religion. Some are seeking light in new symbols. One of the most fruitful channels for them could be to explore the symbols of their more remote forefathers. This could help to broaden and deepen the religion of their parents with the religion of their ancestors.

"What is true of Europe is also true of Africa and South America. The countries of these continents have recently gained political freedom of a sort. But it has done little to help them and to give them a spiritual identity. If they wish to rise in a deeper sense, they must recover their soul, their Gods, their roots in their own psyche; there has to be a spiritual reassertion, a resurrection of their Gods. If they need any change, and there is no doubt they do, it must come from within themselves as a part of their own experience. If they do enough self-churning, then their own Gods will put forth new meanings in response to their new needs. They have to make the best of their own psychic and spiritual gifts and discover their own Gods within themselves. No people can import their Gods ready-made and rise spiritually under the aegis of imported deities, saviours and prophets.

"But one cannot retain old Gods or revive their memory artificially. One should develop a spiritual way of looking at things. One should live with these Gods and spend much time with them. In a sense, all Gods are jealous Gods. They want a person wholly with themselves before they become wholly his. One has to dwell with them and meditate on them before they become vivifying forces. If there is sufficient aspiration, invoking, and soliciting, there is no doubt that even Gods apparently lost could come back again. They are there all the time. For nothing that has any truth in it can be destroyed. It merely goes out of manifestation; but it could reappear under propitious circumstances. So could the old Gods come to life again in response to new summons."

Hindu society has to help the peoples of Asia, Africa, America, Europe, and Oceania to go back to their own Gods, their own ancient shastras which their Gods will reveal again. Hindu society can perform this onerous task only if it reawakens to its own Gods, repels the attack which monotheistic creeds are mounting again on its own spiritual traditions, and turn the tables on mullahs and missionaries who are stinkingly sick with self-righteousness.

MONOTHEISM IS THEOLOGY, NOT SPIRITUALITY

The very fact that Christianity and Islam fall outside the commonwealth of this universal spirituality, goes to show that there is something seriously wrong with the consciousness which has constructed these coercive creeds. The very fact that Christianity and Islam are intensely hostile to universal spirituality expressing itself through diverse deities, goes to prove that there is something particularly perverse in the psychology of these thoughtless theologies. A special effort has to be made to psychoanalyse the pathological behaviour of Christianity and Islam, and spot the source of their spiritual sickness.

Ram Swarup has something significant to say about Monotheism which also I shall quote:

"Ancient Rome, Greece and Egypt, all polytheistic cultures, were relatively free from religious wars though they had their full quota of wars otherwise.

"In polytheistic Rome too, men of different religious persuasions and sects met and built their temples and worshipped in their own way. But this freedom disappeared when Christianity, the religion of One True God, took over.

"Monotheism was not always a spiritual idea. In many cases,

it was an ideology. It was consolidated in wars and in turn it led to further wars. There were wars between different tribes, each tribe claiming its own God to be supreme. Eventually, the Gods of the tribe that lost in battle were supplanted by Gods of the winning side. Or, sometimes, a tribe exchanged its Gods for power. It accepted the Gods of the conquered people in order to consolidate its power over them. Or, perhaps there was a larger association to create, an empire to consolidate, or other nations and tribes to conquer, and the idea of a 'One True God' was handy in the pursuit of this object. Thus, diplomacy, the sword, systematic vandalism, all played their part in making a particular god supreme. From very early days, the One God of Christianity was bound up with the imperial needs of Rome In more recent times, the Biblical God has tried to consolidate what the European arms and trade have conquered.

"When the urge for unity is spiritual, the theology of One God is no bar and the seeker reaches a position no different from *Advaita*, from *ekam sat*. He realizes that God alone is, and not that there is only one God.

"But if the motive for unity is merely intellectual, it helps little, spiritually speaking. God remains an outward being and does not become the truth of the Spirit. It does not even help to reduce the number of Gods; instead it multiplies the number of Devils if Christianity is any guide in the matter. We know how Medieval Christianity was chock-full of them. In fact, they occupied the centre of attention of the Church for many centuries to the exclusion of everything else. During these centuries, it was difficult to say whether the Church worshipped God or those devils. One authority calculated that the number of demons was six and a half million. According to another authority, there were 7,905,926 lesser demons presided over by 72 Princes of Hell. All of them were intriguing against the Church and were undermining its work and authority. Each of the Princes had his allotted work. Lucifer promoted pride, Asmodeus lechery, Belphegor sloth, and so on."

Christian and Islamic imperialism gave wide currency to monotheistic theologies during periods of Christian and Muslim domination over large parts of the world. These theologies, in turn, supported totalitarian tyrannies practised by Christian and Muslim theocracies, and mobilised mobs against subject populations belonging to other faiths. The worst thing that happened was that these theologies confused the language of religion and philosophy. Their impact on imbecile minds can be judged by the thesis of Dr. Tarachand and his tribe that *Advaita* was a concept coined by the Adi Shankaracharya in imitation of Islamic Monotheism brought to Kerala by Muslim merchants (mind you, merchants!) in the early years of the 8th century AD.

MONSTROSITIES OF MONOTHEISM

Monotheism, polytheism, in fact, the whole brood of concepts born of the basic concept called theism, are products of a petrified mind and an inert intellect. These are theological concepts and not spiritual perceptions. That is why they move so mechanically, back and forth, without illumining any corner of the human mind or improving any part of human behavior. They create a lot of casuistry and cantankerous cant. They are not only irrelevant to any practical spiritual purpose, but also positive impediments on the path of spiritual progress. Anyone who is interested in the upliftment of human life as lived should shun these concepts like a plague.

What is worse, Monotheism has manufactured a number of hate-filled words — infidel, *kāfir*, unbeliever, *munkir, mushrik*, heathen, heretic, hypocrite, polytheist, pantheist, pagan — which raise unbreakable barriers between brother and brother, and which divide the one human family into a number of warring camps. These swear-words are hurled at unoffending people belonging to other faiths like stones thrown by street hooligans at peaceful citizens. These malicious words have motivated many crusades, *jihāds*, inquisitions, genocides, imperialist aggressions, and campaigns for pillage and rapine. Rivers of innocent human blood have been made to flow in the service of these spiteful words, and for causes that are of no consequence at all, either for the moral upliftment or the spiritual illumination of mankind. The only way a monotheist can conceive of human brotherhood is that everyone accepts his exclusive creed.

What is still worse, Monotheism and the monstrosities that logically follow from it such as *the* saviour, *the* prophet, *the* revelation, *the ilhām*, *the* church, *the* ummah, have been selling the most degenerate type of idolatry known to human history. Being dead to the intimations of immortality conveyed by icons of Gods, the monotheistic mind manufactures any number of myths about its all-too-human saviours, prophets, saints, and sufis, and attributes any number of miracles to them. Being bereft of any true sense of divinity, this materialistic mind starts seeing the supernatural in the dirt and dross of its prophets and saints such as the saliva, the hair, the shoe, the shirt, and the shroud. And this mind ends up by kissing and kowtowing before these dead objects in a surfeit of sickening superstition. There is a brisk trade in 'holy relics' till the total number or weight of each relic reaches fantastic proportions, far in excess of what had really survived the prophet or the saint. Stinking tombs and sepulchers take the place of sublime temples. Less said about the slaughter of innocent animals in a round of so-called sacrifices, the better.

The monotheist reaches the limit of the ludicrous when he struts around as an iconoclast or a *butshikan*, saying that the false Gods of the infidels could not save themselves from his sword and fire. He secretly expects the idols to perform the same sort of miracles as he attributes to the saliva, the hair, the shoe, the shirt, and the shroud of his own prophets and saints. But if he is requested that his own relics be subjected to the same physical test, he loses his balance, shouts that his religion is being insulted, and takes to violence at very short notice.

No one who knows anything about the sanctity of icons has ever attributed any powers or miracles to them, except the power to point to a still greater sanctity beyond themselves and the miracles they work in human hearts. No one who knows the mystery of icons manifesting themselves has ever expected them to rise in self-defence, sword in hand, against gangsters styling themselves as *ghāzīs*. Yet the monotheistic mind has spread many yarns about Hindus and Buddhists believing that their icons were repositories of magical powers, and could raise deadly storms and armies of demons!

PIETY WITHOUT UNIVERSALITY IS POISONOUS

Some people are impressed by the piety displayed by some merchants of Monotheism such as poverty, penance, patience, chastity, obedience, etc. No doubt these are great virtues, and can add a lot to the loftiness of human character. But a piety which is not preceded by self-purification and which is not permeated by universality (*samatā*) born of wisdom (*prajñā*), can easily turn into poison in the human soul. This sort of self-flattering piety lacks charity and compassion, and feeds self-righteousness as is evident in the case of Muslim mullahs and sufis, and Christian monks and missionaries. They have been not only advocates of inhuman persecution of those they describe as infidels, but also privileged members of imperialist establishments. They have always been out to save others without ever having a look at their own hardened hearts and closed minds. Quite a few of them have been sanctimonious humbugs selling salvation to others without first trying to salvage themselves from hatred towards fellow human beings. St. Francis Xavier is an excellent example of spiritual lepers deluding themselves that they are spiritual healers.

The Buddha is very emphatic that mere piety leads nowhere, and saves no soul. He says: "It is the blockheads who believe about me that I preach piety (*śīla*). I say that I teach meditation (*samādhi*) and wisdom (*prajñā*)." The self-transcendence and the opening of a universal vision in which Hindu spirituality specializes have been predicated not on piety but on purification. According to the Bṛhadāraṇyaka Upanishad, the journey is from darkness to light (*tamaso mā jyotirgamaya*). Piety alone cannot be of much help on this inner pilgrimage, not at all when it consists of only an outer code of conduct such as laid down in the Ten Commandments, or the Sunnah of the Prophet. It needs be added that the *śīla* which the Buddha finds inadequate is much larger and loftier than the pretentious piety which is prescribed by Christianity or Islam, and which degenerates into exhibitionism more often than not. Sufis have been the exhibitionists par excellence. Read the lives of Shykh Farid Ganj Shakar and Nizamuddin Awliya, for instance.

7

Starting Point of Universal Spirituality

Hindu seers and sages could tap the sources of universal spirituality because they did not start with an *a priori* assumption of an Almighty God whom man had to fear and obey in awe and abjection. Nor did they fortify this *a priori* assumption with a framework of deductive inferences drawn from an observed order in the workings of the outer world. They never asserted that an Almighty God had to be accepted as a matter of faith as the creator and controller of the cosmos. Nor did they dogmatise that faith in an Almighty God could not and should not be subjected to the test of human experience and reflective reason.

The starting point of Hindu sages and seers was not God but man. Their testing ground for what they divined was not fanatical faith but direct perception (*pratyakṣa pramāṇa*). Whether it is the Mahabharata of a very distant date, or the songs of Chandidas who came quite late, the refrain has always been, *sabār ūpar mānuṣa satya*, that is, the highest truth is man, the ultimate mystery (*paramam guhyam*) above all other mysteries.

Man is neither an *a priori* assumption nor an abstract concept like God. On the contrary, man is a concrete reality accessible to direct (*pratyakṣa*) perception which is the only valid evidence (*pramāṇa*) recognised by Hindu spirituality. The first question which a Hindu seeker puts to himself, therefore, is: "Who am I (*ko'ham*)?" This is the question asked again and again in the Upanishads. This is the question which Raman Maharshi asked himself in the twentieth century, only to reaffirm the ancient answer: "I am That (*aham brahmo'smi*)."

Lest this starting point of Hindu spirituality be mistaken for modern humanism, it may be made clear that the former does not stop short at the first few faculties of knowledge possessed by man. It searches for and finds some other and more powerful human faculties of higher and wider knowledge. Modern humanism views man mostly as a rational, or a social, or a tool-making (*homo fabricus*) animal, or, at best, as a scientist, or an artist, or a seeker of ethical and aesthetic values. Hindu spirituality does not deny or discount these definitions of man. Man can indeed be placed in all these categories. What Hindu spirituality has discovered specifically is that man is very much more than his body, his mind, and his intellect. His reach is far beyond his inventive, his imaginative, and his intuitive genius. Hindu spirituality proclaims that man in his innermost being is God—*Shivo'ham*, as the Adi Shankaracharya sang.

The concept of an Almighty God *can* yield an experience of the Divine if it is employed as a subject of meditation in order to purify and raise a person's concentrated (*ekāgra*) consciousness, as Patañjali has prescribed (*īśvara-praṇidhānāt vā*), or as an object of selfless devotion described in the Gita and other compendiums on Bhakti. But in the mind of the unmeditative, the self-centred, and the self-righteous, it can become a source of serious mischief. A passionate (*rājasika*) preoccupation with God can lead to delusions of sonship and prophethood. The best that can be said about such self-appointed sons and prophets is that the road to hell is paved with good intentions. In the case of the prophet of Islam, even the intentions are highly doubtful. The cunning, the covetousness, the carnal craving, and the calculated cruelty come through quite clearly even though covered with a liberal coat of Allah and his ninety-nine names. The Almighty Allah of Islam is no more than a tape-recorder which relays back obediently what has been fed into it.

THEOLOGY VERSUS SPIRITUALITY

As one reads the scriptures of Christianity and Islam with a morally alert mind, one starts getting sick of the very sound of the word 'god' which word is littered all over this literature like dead leaves in autumn. The deeds which are ascribed to or approved of by this God are quite often so cruel and obnoxious as to leave one wondering that if these are the doings of the Divine, what else is there which is left for the Devil to do.

On the other hand, the literature of Hindu spirituality employs a vocabulary which breathes an altogether different atmosphere. It deals with the soaring up of a purified human consciousness, and comes up with words and phrases and figures of speech which embody intimations from the infinite (*ananta*) and the immortal (*amrita*). It speaks of *ātman*, *brahma*, *rita*, *sat*, *cit*, and *ānanda*; of *rūpa*, *vedanā*, *saṁjñā*, *saṁskāra*, and *vijñāna*; of *śīla*, *samādhi*, *prajñā*, and *nirvāṇa*; of *yama*, *niyama*, *āsana*, *prāṇāyāma*, *pratyāhāra*, *dhyāna*, *dhārṇā*, and *mokṣa*; of *cittabhūmi*, *manas*, *buddhi*, *bodhi*, *sattvaśuddhi*, *kṣetra* and *kṣetrajna*. The list can be extended and many more terms of a similar import can be cited.

These psychological and psychic terms inspire no self-righteousness which Hindu spirituality stigmatizes as the fundamental frailty of unregenerate human nature. There is no malice in these words, nor spite, nor proclivity to put the other person in the wrong. They only invite one to improve oneself, and to start on a journey towards a fuller and larger life — from the unreal to the Real (*asato mā sadgamaya*), from darkness to Light (*tamaso mā jyotirgamaya*), from death to Immortality (*mrityormā amritam gamaya*).

It is an altogether different matter that Hindu seeking for the deepest and the vastest and the highest and the holiest in man has led to visions of Gods and Goddesses, and that the *Ātman* has ascended into the *Paramātman* and the *Puruṣa* has been perceived as *Puruṣottama*. The significant point is that at no stage of its search, Hindu spirituality has got separated from its starting point, namely, that man and not God is the only proper subject of exploration.

There are strains of Hindu spirituality which have no use for

God. Jainism and Buddhism have plenty of Gods but no God as the creator and controller of the cosmos. Buddhism discards even the concept of a Soul or Self (*ātman*). In fact, the entire range of technical terms used by the Buddha are of psychological and psychic intent; none of them suggests philosophical speculations. The several schools of the Shaktas have a Goddess instead of a God to denote the supreme power they worship. The six systems of Hindu philosophy — Nyāya, Vaiśeṣika, Sāṁkhya, Yoga, and the two schools of Mīmāṁsā — also have no notion of God. It is only in Shaivism, Vaishnavism, and the other sects of Bhakti that we come across God besides Gods. But this God again is nothing like the God of Christianity or the Allah of Islam. Shiva and Vishṇu grow directly out of the Vedic and the Upanishadic pantheon; they are Gods invested with the attributes of all other Gods; they represent and are represented by all other Gods.

This is a very significant feature of Hindu spirituality. A spirituality which does not have its base in humanism can soon become a sham and a self-deception. It can emerge as a closed creed leading to a closed culture, a closed society, and a closed polity. Similarly, no true universalism can be built or sustained except on the basis of humanism — the validity of human experience and the objectivity of human reason raised to its highest power.

It is not an accident that the modern West made a worthwhile progress in science, technology, and a culture of general human welfare *only* when it rejected the dogmas of Christianity derived from an *a priori* concept of God, and returned to the humanism of ancient Greece and Rome. It is not an accident that the Western humanists alone appreciated the Hindu heritage at a time when it was under an unprecedented attack from the crusading Christian missionaries and the bearers of the white man's burden. And it is not an accident that Communism ended by becoming a closed ideology, a closed culture, a closed society, and a closed polity when the Bolsheviks led by Lenin abandoned the humanism of Marx and Engels, adopted the Almighty God of the

Bible as Almighty History, and came up with the doctrine of a permanent war between two sections of mankind *a la* Christianity and Islam. The brutalities committed in the name of Almighty History are now known. On the other hand, the Western democracies retained the humanism of Marx and Engels, and revised only such of their formulations as had gone off the rails of rationalism or were proved to be defective by subsequent social developments. How they created welfare societies, how they came to have a bad conscience about their empires, and how they retired from the colonies, is recorded history.

HINDU CONCEPT OF MAN

Humanism by its very definition must be rooted in some concept of man. What is man? — that must remain the quintessential quest for humanism. Different cultures have given different definitions of man. Here we are concerned with the definition evolved by Hindu spirituality from an endless exploration of the human personality, uncontrolled by any preconceived ideology and led only by an unbounded curiosity to get to the bottom of it all. The results of this exploration are the core of Hindu culture, and the spiritual centre of Hindu society.

The earliest definition of man that we come across in Hindu tradition is to be found in the Upanishads. The rishis who started their search with the eminently empirical formula of 'know thyself' (*ātmānaṁ viddhi*), and employed yogic methods to reach the farthest frontiers of the inner in man, arrived at the conclusion that man was constituted of five faculties or sheaths (*kośas*), one within the other. These they enumerated as follows: (1) human body or the physical sheath (*annamaya kośa*), (2) human desires and drives, or the vital sheath (*prāṇamaya kośa*), (3) human sense perceptions or the mental sheath (*manomaya kośa*), (4) human intellection and intuition at their highest and most universal or the spiritual sheath (*vijñānamaya kośa*), and, (5) human self-delight or the blissful sheath (*ānandamaya kośa*).

The spiritual science of Sāṁkhya spelled out the same structure of human personality in a different language. So did the various Yogas and Tantras. But the purpose of all these statements always remained practical — the human personality was to be explored, purified, uplifted, and made to reach and rest on its highest perch. Many mystic methods were devised, experimented with, and perfected in order to achieve this ultimate aim. But the central theme always revolved round human consciousness and what can be done with it as it rose from one level to another. The metaphysicians engaged themselves in their round of abstract discussions. But the yogin and the bhakta and the mystic pursued their path towards perfection without bothering about mere metaphysics and without anchoring their boat at this scholastic shore or that.

That explains why it is the seer and not the scholar who has all along dominated the scene in Sanātana Dharma. That explains why it is the saint and not the pandit who has always sat at the centre of Hindu society. That explains why it is the mystic and not the man of letters who has ruled the roost in Hindu culture. The most honoured names in Hindu history, above even those of the heroes, are the names of seers, sages, saints, and mystics — Vyasa, Valmiki, Yajnavalkya, the Buddha, Bhagvan Mahavira, Shankara, Ramanuja, Gorakhnath, Kabir, Nanak, Tulsidas, Mira, Ramakrishna, Raman — to mention only the most notable in a galaxy of great names. It is said that there is not a village in India which has not known an authentic saint within a radius of three miles around it. The *vāṇī* and the *vacanāmṛta* of these great souls has sustained Hindu masses in their allegiance to Sanātana Dharma even when subjected to the most harrowing hooliganism as during the medieval Muslim rule, or under the Portuguese pirates in Malabar, Tamil Nadu, and Kerala.

THE MYSTIC QUEST IS UNIVERSAL

Mysticism is not a monopoly of Hindus who have never claimed to be the Chosen People, or organized themselves into the Church or the Ummah. It is the universal religion of the human race wherever and wherever it has not been forced or harangued into shutting itself against the higher message by pontifical prophets and ridiculous revelations. The record has not survived but the sculptures and hymns of ancient Egypt leave no doubt that this was a land of lofty mysticism to which the Greeks acknowledged a great debt. The mysticism in the ancient cultures of Mesopotamia can be gleaned from the points of odium attached to their religions in the Old Testament. The pre-Islamic Iranians had their full quota of mystics, the same as in the medieval period under Islam before the sufis were made subservient to the Shariat. So also the pagan Arabs. The Jews have had giant mystics. The Greeks had their Thales, Heraclitus, Pythagoras, Socrates, Plato, and Plotinus. The annals of Rome reveal the same mystic spirit. China scaled the same spiritual heights in Lao-tse and Confucius.

It is only when we come to countries and ages dominated by Christianity and Islam that we find systematic theological tirades against mysticism. The ancient traditions of mysticism derived from Egypt, Iran, India, and Greece had survived for some time in many Christian and Muslim countries. They were particularly prominent in Iran and Iraq which gave us such great sufis as Rabia, al-Hallaj, Junaid, Abu Yazid, Attar, and Rumi. Europe under Christianity also gave us great mystics such as Eckhart, St. Teresa, and St. John of the Cross. But the theologians of Christianity and Islam were vigilant. So were the tyrants propped up by the Church and the Ummah. They could not tolerate for long such erosions of their exclusiveness by what they denounced as an unsanctioned universalism.

SUBJUGATION OF MYSTICISM TO THEOLOGY

The theocratic hand that came down on the Christian mystics and Muslim sufis was quite heavy to start with. The mystic and the sufi spirit was irrepressible like all other sterling expressions of the human spirit. But theology and theocracy were equally uncompromising. After a lot of terror inspired by theologians and theocrats, a compromise was made between the two. The Christian mystics could continue their 'mumblings' provided they swore by the primacy of the Catholic Church, and paid homage to the Pope. The sufis could sing and dance and indulge in other 'frivolities' provided they swore by the Muhammad, conformed to the Sunnah in their outer conduct, and served the sultans in the extension of Islamic imperialism.

This victory of theology over theosophy is very much manifest in the functioning of sufis and their *silsilās* in India. One never meets a sufi in the large number of this tribe in India who even whispered a word of protest against what the mullahs were saying about Hindu religion and culture, and what the sultans were doing to Hindu temples, places of pilgrimage, and holy men. But one meets many sufis who were furious with the sultans for stopping short of converting or killing all Hindu *kāfirs,* and destroying all Hindu places of worship. Some of them never got reconciled to the recognition of Hindus as *zimmīs* and the imposition of *jizyah* on them because in their theology it was tantamount to bartering away the mission of Islam for mammon. The only choice which Hindus had, according to them, was between Islam and death.

A typical example of such sufism was Shykh Nuruddin Mubarak Ghaznavi (died 1234-35 AD), a disciple of Shykh Shihabuddin Suhrawardi (1144-1234 AD), and one of the founders of the Suhrawardia sufi *silsilā* in India. He propounded the doctrine of *Dīn Panāhī,* and presented it to Sultan Iltutmish (1210-36 AD). This doctrine declared its very first principle as follows: "The kings should protect the religion of Islam with sincere faith. And kings will not be able to perform the duty of protecting the Faith unless for the sake of Allah and the Prophet's creed, they overthrow and uproot *kufr* and *kāfirī*, *shirk* and the worship of idols. But if the total uprooting of idolatry is not possible owing to the firm roots of *kufr* and the large number of *kāfirs* and *mushriks*, the kings should at least strive to insult, disgrace, dishonour and defame the *mushrik* and idol-worshipping

Hindus, who are the worst enemies of Allah and the Prophet. The symptom of the kings being the protectors of religion is this: When they see a Hindu, their eyes grow red and they wish to bury him alive; they also desire to completely uproot the Brahmans, who are the leaders of *kufr* and *shirk* and owing to whom *kufr* and *shirk* are spread and the commandments of *kufr* are enforced. Owing to the fear and terror of the kings of Islam, not a single enemy of Allah and the Prophet can drink water that is sweet or stretch his legs on his bed and go to sleep in peace." Such statements from sufis can be multiplied. Amir Khusru, the dearest disciple of Nizamuddin Awliya (Chishtiyya luminary of Delhi), mourned loudly that if the Hanafi law (which accommodated Hindus as *zimmīs*) had not come in the way, the very name Hindu would not have survived.

Similar examples can be cited from the annals of Christian mysticism as well. In the process, Christian mystics and Muslim sufis not only drifted away from their spiritual search, but also prolonged the life of such falsehoods as Christianity and Islam by making the dogmas of these creeds sound deeper than they were intended to do. Their personal tragedy turned, in due course, into a tragedy for universal spirituality which had initially inspired them to deepen and widen the dogmas propounded by the Founding Fathers of the Church and prophet Muhammad. This double tragedy was inevitable because Christian mystics and Muslim sufis failed from the beginning to see that what they were being made to serve was not religion but a politics of power and imperialist aggression.

MISINFORMATION ABOUT MONOTHEISTIC CREEDS

Hindu society has never had an organised hierarchy like the Christian Church. Nor has Hindu society ever been a fanatical fraternity like the Muslim Ummah. Hindu spirituality, therefore, never became an instrument of predatory imperialism. Hindu princes in pre-Islamic India fought many wars. But none of them was a religious war. The scene changed to a certain extent when

Hindu society was attacked by an imperialist ideology named Islam which pretended to be a superior religion, and which swore that Allah and his last prophet had mandated the whole earth to the Muslim Ummah. Hindu sword had to be drawn in defence of Hindu society and culture, and some Hindu saints blessed the enterprise. Even so, Hindu saints of the stature of Kabir and Nanak kept on pleading with the mullahs and the sufis to give up their exclusiveness, and accept the Hindu spiritual insight that all paths lead to the same goal. Hinduism thus retained its spiritual character and universality all along.

Kabir and Nanak and numerous other *nirguṇa* saints failed to carry any conviction with the mullahs and the sufis and the sultans. The latter were either too self-righteous or too enamoured of the power and pelf which the exclusiveness of Islam had earned for them. Kabir had to suffer persecution from Sikandar Lodi for questioning this exclusiveness. Guru Arjun Deva and Guru Tegh Bahadur had to lay down their lives in defence of Sanātana Dharma.

In the final round, however, the *nirguṇa* saints succeeded only in confusing Hindu society into believing that Islam was just another religion and not an ideology of imperialism. Fortunately, the impact of *nirguṇa* saints on Hindu society was marginal. The *saguṇa* saints and the *āchāryas* did not even so much as mention Islam even in the heyday of its power and sway. They found it beneath contempt.

The *nirguṇa* saints have been revived in more recent times, and presented as social reformers who stood for a casteless and classless society and as the precursors of what passes for Secularism in present-day India. This monstrous misrepresentation has been mostly the work of Hindi scholars working for doctoral degrees. They have succeeded to a large extent in misleading the Hindu intelligentsia. Now it is the turn of the Buddha and Bhagvan Mahavira who are also being dressed up in the same secular plumes.

The confusion has by now become very widespread, and is

symbolized by the sanctimonious slogan of *sarva-dharma-samabhāva*. This slogan was coined by Mahatma Gandhi and included in his *Maṅgala Prabhāta* as one of the sixteen *mahāvratas*. The result was an unprecedented appeasement of Islam starting with the Mahatma's support of the Khilafat movement. The Mahatma had believed sincerely that he could touch the heart of Islam and win over the Muslims to nationalism by paying handsome tributes to the Quran and the Prophet. But he also ended as a colossal failure like Kabir and Nanak. In the final upshot, he had to pay the price with his own life, and the nation had to suffer partition of the motherland.

For, Islam has no heart which can be touched. The heart has been drained of all human feelings and hardened into a calculating machine which manufactures only imperialist ambitions. Hindu society will never be able to soften that heart, or make that machine produce anything except contrived grievances and repeated rounds of violence. Let Hindu society make no mistake. The same is true of Christianity, though it has been forced to soften it face and language due to its collapse in the modern West. The heart of Christianity, too, has been hardened into a calculating machine.

A RESCUE OPERATION NEEDED

The only hope lies in the mystical elements which still survive in Christian as well as Muslim communities in India due to the Hindu converts carrying with them a lot of Hindu culture and also due to the intrinsic urges of universal human nature. These urges have nothing to do with theological Christianity or prophetic Islam. It is not an accident that Aldous Huxley could not find a single mystical passage in Christian theology or the Quran which he could cite in his *Perennial Philosophy*. He quotes only from Christian and Muslim mystics.

One of the enterprises which a reawakened Hindu society will have to undertake is to rescue Christian mysticism from the clutches of Christian theology, and salvage sufism from the stranglehold of prophetic Islam. This can be the only basis on which Hindu society can come to terms with Christian and Muslim communities in India. One can be sure that there are many Christians for whom the message of Christian mysticism is more important than Christian theology, as there are many Muslims in whom Attar and Rumi touch a deeper chord than is touched by the pronouncements of prophetic Islam and its stultified sufi accomplices.

Hindu society has to make it clear, once and for all, that there can be no compromise with a Christian theology which preaches that Jesus Christ is the only saviour and that it is the mission of Christianity to save all mankind. At the same time, Hindu society has to tell the Muslims, in an unmistakable voice, that it will not permit the permeation of prophetic Islam according to which Muhammad is the last prophet and the Ummah has inherited the lands of the *kāfirs* as a mandate from Allah.

8

Christianity and Islam: Ideologies Of Imperialism

The story which I am now going to tell is true. I remember it word by word, although it happened twenty-five years ago.[1]

A young Muslim sufi from Kashmir was telling us about the teachings of his *guru* (this was the word he used for his teacher) who had died some years earlier. *Pranayam* was a prominent part of these teachings. This again was the term he used, though he did not know even the Hindi language properly, not to speak of Sanskrit.

The sufi was a very simple and unassuming person. He had had no schooling and he made his living by the humble occupation of a tailor. But we were fascinated by what he told us about the techniques used by his *guru* for his spiritual training. His language was straightforward without the slightest touch of pedantry.

As the conversation drew to a close someone from among us started to play a record of *padāvali kīrtan* by one of the few famous female specialists from Bengal. The sufi was visibly moved by the pathos in Radha's pining for Sri Krishna who had left Vrindavana for Mathura. Soon after the music stopped, he exclaimed, "*Aisā gānā hamnē ēk hazār baras bād sunā* (I have heard this sort of music after a thousand years)." His eyes were brimming with tears which he was trying to hide.

We were amazed. He was in his thirties. He could not have been in this world a thousand years ago. What did he mean by

---

[1] In 1958.

that statement? We requested him to explain. He said in a voice full of innocence: "*Pahle janam mēṅ sunā hogā* (I must have heard it in an earlier life)."

I became agog with curiosity. He was talking of transmigration. So I asked him, "*Āp kyā is zindgī sē pahlē janam kī bāt mānatē hain* (Do you believe in a birth before this present life)?"

The sufi seemed to be somewhat annoyed. He asked a counter-question in a tone which had a touch of temper: "*Āp mazhab kā sawāl kyoṅ uthātē hain* (Why are you raising a theological controversy)?"

I was puzzled by his reply, as was everybody else. I had not the slightest intention to annoy him. He was our guest. I had asked the question out of sheer curiosity. So I came forward with a clarification, and said, "*Sufijī, āp musalmān hain. Islām ēk hī janam mānatā hai. Āpnē pahle janam kī bāt kahī, isliyē sawāl uṭhāyā thā* (You are a Muslim. Islam recognises only one life. You talk about an earlier life. That is why I had asked the question)."

He relaxed and explained: "*Mazhab tō wahī bāt kahtā hai. Lekin maiṅ tō rāz kī bāt kah rahā thā* (It is true that theology says that. But I was talking of the esoteric way)."

We were surprised by this distinction. This was a new revelation to us — this separation of esoterism from theology. The sufi continued: "*Rāz kī bāt ham sab kē sāmanē nahīṅ kahtē. Yeh tō maiṅ āp logoṅ se kah rahē thā* (We do not talk of the esoteric way before everybody. It is only to you people that I was talking about it)."

All of us asked simultaneously: "*Kyoṅ* (Why)?"

The sufi said, "*Woh log* (those people)"... and without completing the sentence he put the edge of his outstretched palm on his throat and moved it across. He was trying to convey that "those people" would cut his throat.

We asked him about "those people". Who were they? He did not name any. But he became gloomy. It was obvious that he did not like to continue the dialogue, which we dropped immediately.

I was sure in my mind that nobody was going to cut his throat these days even if he proclaimed publicly what he believed privately. Times had changed. Moreover, he was a citizen of India, not of an Islamic theocracy. Yet the alarm in his voice was unmistakable.

I knew how Mansur al-Hallaj had been tortured to death by an Islamic state prompted by Islamic theologians for saying that he himself was the *Haqq* (Truth). But that was all. I had not yet read any detailed history of Sufism, nor compared or contrasted the doctrines of Sufism with the dogmas of prophetic Islam. It was years later when I made such a study and came to know of the *rishi* tradition in Kashmir Sufism, that I was suddenly reminded of that talk with the young sufi that day. He was obviously referring to the tradition of terror which had silenced the sufis of the *rishi* tradition, and forced them to keep in their breasts the best of their knowledge. The memory of that terror, it seemed, was still intact in the mind of this sufi.

THE SUFI AS A FANATIC

My studies in Sufism also brought back to my mind another encounter with another sufi at about the same time. He was an elderly man. He was quite learned in his own way, and could discuss various religious and philosophical doctrines with some knowledge. He could also manage some English in which language he also wrote an occasional pamphlet. The incident which I shall now relate took place when I met him for the first time, though I had heard a lot about him from a close friend.

I was staying by myself in the house of this friend when this sufi dropped in one day. I requested him to stay with me for a few days and give me the benefit of his company. He agreed and we had quite a few fruitful sessions during which we talked about mysticism and the rest, without touching the subject of Islam or Hinduism. I was impressed. His language was quite forceful, particularly when he made fun of atheists, materialists, and mere philosophers.

One day I was reading an Urdu translation of Sarmad's Persian poems when the sufi came into my room and sat down by my side. I put away the book and had another long talk with him. Then I left the room because I had a few other things to do. When I returned after about half an hour, I found the sufi reading the same book by Sarmad. A few days earlier I had heard him talking about Sarmad with reverence and in a language of fulsome praise. So I sat down quietly in a corner and waited for him to read out and explain some significant lines from that book.

But I was taken aback when he suddenly threw the book against the opposite wall with some violence and shouted, "*Harāmzādā kāfir hī thā* (The bastard was an infidel indeed)!" I picked up the book, brought it back to the sufi and asked him to show me the lines that had enraged him so uncontrollably. He leafed through the book and finally put his finger on two lines almost towards the end. I cannot recall the exact words of the couplet but I remember very well the message that was conveyed. Sarmad had addressed himself as follows: "O Sarmad! What is it that goes on happening to you? You started as a follower of Moses. Next you put your faith in Muhammad. And now at last you have become a devotee of Rām and Lachhman."

I could see nothing wrong or improper in this couplet. Sarmad was only telling the story of his seeking which had led him from Moses to Muhammad to Rāma and Lakshmaṇa. I had not read the book as fast and as far as the sufi had done. Nor did I know the real reason for which Sarmad had been beheaded in Delhi by the order of Aurangzeb. All I had heard was that Sarmad used to roam about naked on the roads of this imperial city. I had supposed that he had been punished for his impudence in the midst of a polished society which placed immense importance on being properly dressed. It was years later that I learnt the real nature of Sarmad's "crime". It was apostasy which is punishable with death according to the law of Islam laid down by the Prophet himself during the days of his tussle with the polytheists of Mecca.

I have never lost my respect for this second sufi. He is a man of character endowed with a keen mind and a good knowledge of what passes for mysticism in Islam. But he becomes absolutely impregnable, indeed an insufferable fanatic, when it comes to the dogmas of prophetic Islam. His contempt for everything Hindu comes through clearly whenever he publishes a pamphlet. Hindus, he says, are worshippers of *kankhajūrās* (scorpions), *khaṭmals* (bugs), *gāy kā gobar* (cowdung), and *Kālī*. How he has worked out this combination of four "filthy" things has always defied my imagination. But one thing becomes obvious whenever he opens his mouth, namely, that he derives immense satisfaction by portraying Hinduism in this picturesque manner. Sometimes I feel that the very vehemence of his language against Hinduism helps him keep the fire of his fanaticism burning. Whenever he is in this mood, it is impossible to have a word edgewise with him, or make him realize that he is being downright ridiculous.[2]

THE CHRISTIAN MISSIONARY AND THE MYSTIC

I had the same experience an year earlier with a Catholic missionary who was trying to convert me to his own creed. He had taken me to a monastery in a mountainous region, and put me into what the Christians call a retreat. The very first sentence he uttered in his very first lecture was that I should not expect him to give "some funny feeling inside you". I did not get the point at that time. Later on I learnt that he was referring to the mystic experience for which we Hindus are supposed to have a special weakness. The Father failed to give me any feeling, funny or otherwise, and the retreat was a total failure. I had started as an ordinary Hindu and came out of it in the same condition. The dogmas of Christianity he had dished out sounded to

---

[2] This sufi remained a friend till he saw my writings, particularly *Hindu Society under Siege*. In my last meeting with him he said that I had "stabbed him in the back". He died a few years ago.

me, to say that least, rather infantile. But what pained me the most in my meetings with this otherwise lovable man was his contempt for Hinduism which he always equated with the "worship of every bug that bites and every cockroach that crawls around".

In later years I met another Christian missionary who made it a point to call on me whenever he visited Delhi. His first fascination in India (he was a foreigner) was for Raman Maharshi. That led him to Vedanta and the Upanishads which fascinated him still more. Finally, he gave up his missionary station in the south and moved to the Himalayas for a quiet life of study and meditation. He was a prolific writer. He died a few years ago.

In my first encounter with him I made him feel somewhat uncomfortable by asking him some unconventional questions about Christian theology, particularly about Jesus being the only saviour. Next time we met, he asked me to avoid doctrinal disputation and join him in a deeper communion of minds in meditation. I agreed with him very gladly, and we never discussed theology again. Most of the time I listened to him as he as spoke about the Upanishads, particularly about the experience of *Advaita*. He had made a very deep study of the subject, and I was nowhere near him in my own knowledge of it.

But I was puzzled when I read some of his writings. Here he was trying very heard to reconcile the experience of *Advaita* with what he called the Christian experience. I referred the matter to Ram Swarup. He told me that Christian experience was the new name which they were now giving to Christian theology.

I knew nothing about any experience, advaitic or Christian. Nor do I know it now. But one thing I know for certain is that human experience, whatever its level, is human experience. There is nothing Hindu, or Muslim, or Christian about it as such. The fact that *Advaita* is a Sanskrit word — a language which flourished in India and is now honoured by Hindus — as also the fact that it has been discussed most exhaustively in the Upanishads, which are now known as Hindu shastras, does not make it a national or sectarian word. For the word only refers to a state of human consciousness which Kabir has described so aptly as *bāhar bhītar ekai jānō, yēh guru gyān batāī* (it is the same everywhere, whether without or within; this is the secret taught by the teacher).

Here was a man who was moved so sincerely and so deeply by his seeking for *Advaita*. Why could he not concentrate on the experience itself, and forget Christianity for the time being? Why could he not throw his theological luggage out of the window and travel straight to the station towards which the train of his own experience was heading? Why should he look out every now and then to find out if the stations on the way had their nameplates inscribed in a language which he had inherited by the accident of his birth? I could not find at that time any satisfactory answers to these questions.

The young sufi was afraid of being slaughtered for saying what he believed to be true. The sincere Christian seeker was trying to stick a label where it failed to stick. Their plight was pathetic.

On the other hand, the old sufi was so sure about himself, about his Islam, and about the abomination that was Hinduism in his eyes. So was the Catholic missionary who had tried to save me from perdition. They seemed to know what was wrong, and where. They seemed to know what was right, and how. What was it that made them feel so secure in their beliefs, and so self-righteous in their swearing against Hinduism?

POLITICS MASQUERADING AS RELIGION

The questions remained unanswered till I had a chance to read the life of prophet Muhammad and the history of the rise of Christianity. I knew a lot of Muslim history in this country, and also abroad. I knew how blood-soaked it was in all its chapters. I also knew a lot of Christian history in Europe, and America, and elsewhere. I knew what a horrible story it was in terms of death and destruction it brought to many lands. What I did not know for a long time was the genesis of these creeds which had inflicted so much sufferings on mankind.

It was only when I looked into the source books of these 'religions', and examined the character of their founders that I discovered the *āsurika* roots from which they had sprung. It was only then that I realized the grave error in recognizing these creeds as religions in any sense of the term. I could see quite clearly that what we were faced with were purely political ideologies inspired by imperialist ambitions. It was only then that all pieces of the puzzle fell into a pattern — the theologies, the histories, the swearologies, and the rest.

Before I take up the genesis of these creeds I should like to make one point very clear. There are no non-Christian records available about the birth, rise, and spread of Christianity till it captured state power in the Roman empire. Whatever I write below about the genesis of Christianity is based entirely on early Christian records. Similarly, no non-Muslim records have survived about the rise and spread of Islam in Arabia. What I write below about the genesis of Islam is based entirely on Islamic records.

GENESIS AND CHARACTER OF CHRISTIANITY

Some historians in the West have serious doubts about the very existence of a man called Jesus Christ.[3] And almost all historians agree that if he existed at all, nothing can be known about his person or teaching because all contemporary sources, Christian and non-Christian, are either silent or unreliable regarding the subject. Thus all we have is the Jesus of the Gospels which are now regarded as theological statements rather than a record of historical events. And Jesus of the Gospels is a questionable character. He makes tall claims about himself, and curses all those who do not accept those claims. He denounces his own people as sons of the Devil and killers of prophets.

---

[3] See Sita Ram Goel, *Jesus Christ: Artifice for Aggression*, Voice of India, New Delhi, 1994.

In due course, Christian theology came to proclaim that Jesus was the only-begotten son of the only true god; that he had been sent down in order to wash with his own blood the sins of mankind by mounting the cross; that he had risen from the dead on the third day and appeared to his apostles in flesh and bones; that he was the same as his father whose divinity he shared in full; that those who accepted him as the only saviour had all their sins washed by his blood; that he had entered his apostles as the holy ghost and entrusted them with the mission of saving all mankind from eternal hell-fire; that the Church founded by the apostles and joined by the converts was his body and bride; and that the whole world had been mandated to the Church by the father and the son and the holy ghost.

What one finds striking about these ridiculous statements is that none of them can stand the test of human reason or experience. The Church declares them to be mysteries beyond the reach of human understanding. The apostles had tried to sell these 'mysteries' to the Jews in Jerusalem. The only response they met was dismissal with contempt. Next, they tried these 'mysteries' on Jewish communities settled in Syria, Asia Minor and Greece. They had some small success but most of the time met with considerable resistance. Finally, they took this merchandise to the metropolitan mart at Rome where their business found some firm footing for the first time. It was in Rome that the methods of missionary salesmanship were matured over a period of time. The structure of the Roman empire provided a model for the structure of the Church. The missionaries got busy building a state within the state.

In the next two centuries, the Church became a rich and powerful organisation with members in many leading families of Rome. It found many adherents among politicians who wielded power, among military commanders who were superstitious or in need of political support, and among merchants who had money but no brains for philosophical questions. The mother of emperor Severus (222-235 AD) became a Christian. So did emperor Philip the Arabian (244-249 AD). Helena, the mother of Constantine, was also a Christian convert. Now the Church extended the Divine Right to rule as a despot to anyone who was prepared to declare Christianity as the sole state religion and suppress all pagan religions. Constantine who wanted to secure a dynastic succession for his family — a practice unknown to Roman politics so far — saw his opportunity in this new doctrine, and proclaimed in favour of the Church. The common people in Rome resisted this royal renegade. So he removed his capital from Rome to Byzantium which was renamed Constantinople.

The precedent set by Constantine in consolidating a dynastic despotism with the help of the Church was copied by many crowned heads all over Europe in subsequent centuries. The king in pagan societies was only the first among equals. The Church enabled him to become an unbridled autocrat who derived his authority not from the community over which he ruled but from God Almighty. The conflicts which developed between these autocrats and the powerful Church with a Pope at its head, came much later, after the common people all over Europe had been enslaved and deprived of their traditional institutions which safeguarded their fundamental freedoms. For quite some time, the Church cooperated with the kings to convert the common people everywhere into hewers of wood and drawers of water.

This was one part of the story. Another was a large-scale destruction of ancient religions all over Europe, Asia Minor, and North Africa where the Church spread its tentacles with the help of despotic rulers. All pagan schools were closed, all pagan temples were demolished or converted into churches, and all pagan images were publicly defiled and destroyed. Pagan books were burnt and pagan priests were killed, mostly by Christian monks who led Christian mobs after lecturing them into fevered frenzy. That is how Christianity triumphed over pagan religions and societies — not by the power of its moral or spiritual superiority or the logic of its doctrines, but by the power of the sword wielded by despicable despots.

GENESIS AND CHARACTER OF ISLAM

Muhammad followed in the footsteps of Jesus in making the same sort of claims for himself, cursing his own people in the choicest language of monotheism, and threatening them with slaughter. He, however, did not have to struggle against a centralized state when he found that his prophethood had no attraction for the people of Mecca. He migrated to Medina which was more receptive to monotheism because of a large presence of Jews in that town, and emerged as a powerful potentate. He ended by exiling or killing en masse the Jewish population which resisted him as soon as he came out in his true colours. Meanwhile, he had amassed much wealth by plundering merchant caravans and scattered Arab settlements. He created the nucleus of a standing army out of the toughs and desperados who flocked to him in increasing numbers for committing crimes and sharing the loot. In short, he built the apparatus of a military state in Medina and used it for imposing his closed creed on the tribal settlements of Arabia by means of armed force. The doctrines of Islam were tailored to the needs of this galloping tyranny, and sold with the help of the sword. And the sword was stamped with the name of an almighty Allah in whose service the ancient religion and culture of Arabia were destroyed root and branch.

THE MISTAKE MADE BY HINDU SOCIETY

Hindu society has to understand very clearly that what it is faced with in the form of Christianity and Islam are not religions but imperialist ideologies whose appetite has been whetted by running roughshod over a large part of the world. Hindu society is making a serious, almost a fatal mistake, in appealing to these ideologies in the name of reason and morality which are supposed to accompany religion. This sort of appeal is bound to fail because it falls on deaf ears. The menace has to be met by methods and means which are suited to the nature and magnitude of the menace. Hitler had said that "if the chicken and geese pass a resolution about peace, the wolf is not convinced". There is little chance that Hindu society will ever be able to contain Christianity or Islam if it continues to regard these aggressive and imperialist ideologies as religions, and extend tolerance to them.

9

Character Of Nehruvian Secularism

Twenty years ago I had been invited to a seminar on Hurdles To Secularism.[1] It was presided over by the late Shri Jayaprakash Narayan (JP). The Working Paper had been prepared by the late Professor A.B. Shah. It was a surprising departure from the usual norm of such papers. While he had repeated the current cliches about 'Hindu communalism', Professor Shah had been equally unsparing about what he had nailed down as 'Muslim communalism'.

In the event, however, the paper remained irrelevant to the discussion that took place. The several speakers that rose, one after another, became red in the face and foamed at the mouth as they fulminated against Hindu society for denying employment to Muslims in the public as well as the private sector, for reducing the Muslim minority to the status of second class citizens, for committing untold atrocities on the poor and helpless Muslims in a repeated round of riots, and so on so forth. All these speakers wore Hindu names. The most vociferous of them was Balraj Puri who has managed to masquerade for many years as a martyr in the service of what he proclaims to be humanist causes.

There were four or five Muslim participants present in that seminar. One of them was a professor of Arabic from a leading university. Another was a lawyer well-known for his championing of all communist and Islamic causes at all times. They were invited to speak next. But they all smiled and said that they had nothing to add to what their 'Hindu brethren' had already said so

[1] It was in 1963.

'loudly and so lucidly'.

And then all of a sudden I saw some fireworks from the same silent and satisfied Islamic fraternity. They had all stood up, shaking with uncontrollable rage, and were shouting at the same time, "He is lying!" They were pointing their fingers at the gentleman who had been invited to speak by the president, and who had said only a few sentences. Balraj Puri kept sitting. But he looked as if he would burst out of his skin

This was the late Hamid Dalwai. I had heard of him. But this was the first time I saw him. He was a tall man with a slight stoop, a smiling face, and a rather relaxed self-possession. He was saying, "All that has been said about Hindu communalism today is nothing new. We have heard it for the nth time. The intention of the working paper of this seminar, however, was to highlight for the first time what has so far been ignored by all progressive people who swear by secularism. What I want to expose today is Muslim communalism which has already divided the motherland, and which is still strong enough to poison our body-politic..."

It was at this point that the Muslim gentlemen had stood up and started shouting. I had been asked by JP not to speak at all. He was of the view that I being a well-known 'Hindu communalist' was quite likely to say something wild and thus mar the proceedings. It was Professor Shah who had extended the invitation to me, and then conveyed to me the condition laid down by JP if I wanted to be present. So I had kept quiet in spite of the insufferable Balraj Puri staring at me provokingly, off and on. But I could restrain myself no more. I stood up and addressed JP as follows: "For almost an hour and a half we have been listening patiently to what so many Hindus have said about Hindu society. Now a Muslim gentleman wants to say something about Muslim society. Why should we not listen to him with the same patience? Why should this gentleman, who is attending this seminar not as a gate-crasher but as an invited participant, be shouted down in this shameless manner?"

JP had also come to feel very strongly the iniquity of it all. He looked at the Islamic fraternity with annoyance on his face, and said with a touch of temper in his voice, "I insist that Hamid should be allowed to say whatever he wants to say." The Islamic fraternity collapsed in their seats with pained and perplexed expression on their faces. They felt betrayed. It was the most unkindest cut of all, coming as it did from a man of such eminent standing in the world of India's Secularism.

Hamid continued:

"Hindu society has produced many communalists. Admitted. But it has also produced men like Mahatma Gandhi who went on a fast unto death to save the Muslims of Bihar from large-scale butchery. It has produced men like Pandit Jawaharlal Nehru who had the Bihari Hindus bombed from the air when they did not respond to the Mahatma's call. These have not been isolated men in Hindu society, as Rafi Ahmad Kidwai and M.C. Chagla have been in Muslim society. The Mahatma was a leader whom the whole Hindu society honoured. Pandit Nehru has been kept as Prime Minister over all these years by a majority vote of the same Hindu society.

"Now let me give you a sample of the leadership which Muslim society has produced so far, and in an ample measure. The foremost that comes to my mind is Liaqat Ali Khan, the first Prime Minister of Pakistan. Immediately after partition, there was a shooting in Sheikhupura in which many Hindus who were waiting for repatriation in a camp, were shot down. There was a great commotion in India, and Pandit Nehru had to take up the matter in his next weekly meeting with Liaqat Ali in Lahore. The Prime Minister of Pakistan had brought the Deputy Commissioner of Sheikhupura with him. The officer explained that the Hindus had broken out of the camp at night in the midst of a curfew, and the police had to open fire. Pandit Nehru asked as to why the Hindus had broken out of the camp. The officer told him that some miscreants had set the camp on fire. Pandit Nehru protested to Liaqat Ali that this was an amazing explanation. Liaqat

Ali replied without batting an eye that they had to maintain law and order. This exemplifies the quality of leadership which Muslim society has produced so far. This...."

All hell now broke loose as the Islamic fraternity stood up again, and started shouting that they had not come to the seminar to be insulted by "a hired hoodlum of the RSS fascists". JP could restrain them no more, and declared the proceedings closed with a note of anguish in his voice. As we walked out, I saw that the Hindu champions of Secularism avoided Hamid as if he was a snake. He was trying to take leave of them by approaching each one of them with a smile still lingering on his face. I was the only Hindu who shook hands with him, and patted him on the back for the brave stand he had taken in the face of a rowdy opposition

GENESIS OF SECULARISM IN EUROPE

Ever since then I have pondered over the subject of Secularism which has become a political cult next only to Socialism,[2] and to which all political parties subscribe without so much as a why. What has Secularism come to mean in the Indian context? How did the concept arise? Who were those that gave to it its current shape and content? I have absolutely no doubt in my mind that Secularism in its present Indian form is no more than an embodiment of anti-Hindu animus, and is supported by all those who want to destroy Hindu society and culture.

Secularism is essentially a political concept which originated and took shape in nineteenth century Europe. Till about the middle of the 18th century, the State in all European countries was allied with one denomination or another of the splintered Christian Church. In fact, the State was described by the Church as its secular arm. It was not unoften that the State carried out pogroms against 'heretics' and 'dissidents' at the behest of the dominant Christian denomination. The King of England is still

[2] Thank God, the cult of Socialism is now dead except for some orphans of the Soviet Union and Dr. Ram Manohar Lohia.

described as Defender of the Faith whenever the full array of his titles is trotted out. This is a relic and a reminder of that dark period in European history when the king in every country was used by the Church to maintain its stranglehold, and when he used the Church in turn to sustain his unbridled despotism.

Then came the Enlightenment when the exclusive claims of Christianity were questioned, and a wave of anti-clericalism attracted the intellectual elite in all European countries. This was followed by the rising tide of rationalism and humanism, fostered and fed by the empiricism of modern science. The churches defended their dogmas very doggedly. But there was very little in those dogmas which could survive a rational or moral scrutiny. That was why the Church had needed a secular arm to maintain its monopoly of truth for more than fourteen hundred years.

It was in this atmosphere of revolt against Christianity and its closed culture that the concept of Secularism was evolved and employed in country after country in Europe. The secular power of the State was no longer to be the secular arm of the Church. It was to become secular on its own, that is, a power which secured equal rights to all its citizens without bothering about their beliefs. The Church was separated from the State which was no longer supposed to interfere with the religious life of the citizens, or to discriminate against any citizen on the basis of his on her religion or absence of it. Religion was now to be treated as a purely private matter in which the state was not supposed to pry, and which was not to be projected in public affairs.

HINDU SOCIETY HAS ALWAYS BEEN SECULAR

India had never known a theocratic state till the advent of Islam in this country in the first quarter of the eighth century AD. Hindu Dharma has always been a pluralistic religion. Hindu culture and society too have been pluralistic throughout their hoary history. It was, therefore, impossible for the Hindus to erect an established church or to proclaim a state religion and call upon the State to impose it by force. The Hindu state extended its patronage to all religious sects equally, even when a king and his courtiers adhered to a particular sect in their private lives. Religious strife followed by bloodshed had never blackened the fair face of Hindu society.

Things changed radically when Islamic imperialism invaded India, and brought with it a fully developed theory as well as the apparatus of a theocratic state. The Islamic state had already destroyed by fire and sword the ancient religions of the Arabs, the Persians, and the Turks. It started to do the same in India, and succeeded to a large extent in several parts of the North-West. But the resistance offered by Hindu nation in the rest of the country was too strong. The Mughals under Akbar had to abandon the experiment in order to save and extend their empire. And the Islamic state met the fate it deserved when Aurangzeb tried to reverse the trend.

The Hindu experience of a theocratic state was a very painful experience, spread as it was over several centuries. Even so, the Hindus did not learn any lessons in theocracy. The Hindu states which re-emerged under the Rajputs, the Marathas, the Sikhs, and the Jats were secular states which did not molest the Muslim population in spite of Hindu memories of what Islam had done to Hindu religion and culture during the days of its domination. The same Secularism characterised the national movement for freedom from British imperialism which was manned overwhelmingly by the Hindu masses. Hindu leaders tried their best to take along the Muslim masses in the fight for freedom.

THE RISING TIDE OF MUSLIM REVIVALISM

On the other hand, the Muslim society in India which consisted almost entirely of those whose forefathers had been converted by force, started throwing up one revivalist movement after another throughout the period of British rule. All these movements reminded Muslim society that it had lost political power in India due to its own fall from the faith, that it had to purify itself in the image of the first four Khalifas who had founded the world-wide Islamic empire, and that it could not and should not rest till it recaptured political power and restored its theocratic state. It is debatable whether any of these movements achieved any purification of Muslim society except a spasmodic outburst of beards on many Muslim faces. But it is on record that every one of these movements turned into a *jihād* against the Hindus wherever the latter were found in a minority and unable to defend themselves. The British power had to intervene against the mullahs and the *mujāhids* not to protect the Hindus so much as to restore law and order. Some of the Muslim fanatics got killed in these encounters and were hailed by Muslim society as martyrs (*shahīds*) for the greater glory of Islam. Recently the Communist Party of India has been resurrecting these riots staged by Islamic lust for Hindu blood as illustrious instances of the Muslim fight for freedom against the hated British imperialism!

Muslim society in India, therefore, looked at the freedom movement with suspicion, and frequently denounced it as a Hindu conspiracy to capture power to the detriment of Islam. The British had started feeling the impact of the freedom movement in the opening years of the twentieth century. They saw an ally in Islamic revivalism, and made up their mind to pit it against a nation in revolt. The foundation of the Muslim League in 1906 was a command performance at the instance of a British Viceroy as is now very well known. It followed immediately after the partition of Bengal (1905) in order to carve out a Muslim majority province in the east of India. The partition had to be undone due to fear of Hindu revolutionaries. But the alliance that was thus forged between British imperialism and Islamic revivalism continued and got consolidated in the years to come. Muslim society now started staking its claims for a lion's share whenever the British were forced to make any concessions to the freedom fighters.

By the time Mahatma Gandhi appeared on the scene, the Muslim League had acquired a position which the British could play up on every bargaining counter between Indian nationalism on the one hand and British imperialism on the other. The mischievous message conveyed by the British rulers was that it was not they who were blocking India's progress towards freedom but the Hindus themselves by their refusal to come to terms with the "Muslim minority". At the same time, the British made it clear that they were not going to quit under "Hindu pressure" and leave the "Muslim minority" to the "tender mercies of a brute Hindu majority". It was this stalemate that the Mahatma tried to break by his sudden decision to support the Khilafat agitation.

The agitation ended as a farce when Mustafa Kamal forced the Turkish Sultan (who was also the Khalifa of Islam) to abdicate and sink into oblivion. But it had created an illusion of Hindu-Muslim unity in India for as long as it lasted. The streets in most Indian cities resounded with the emotionally surcharged slogan of *Hindū-Muslim-Bhāī-Bhāī* which frightened the British authority, at least for the time being. Not many Hindu nationalists were able to notice that the Khilafat agitation was just another recrudescence of Islamic revivalism which was now making a bid to use the national movement for its own imperialist purposes. The few doubting Thomases who raised their voice of warning, were silenced by the prevailing euphoria for communal amity.

The curtain was raised on the reality behind the rhetoric when the Moplah Muslims of Malabar started another *jihād* against their Hindu neighbours who were caught uncautioned and unprepared. The British had to send some armed forces before the Muslim butchery of innocent Hindus could be brought under control. The Moplah violence was the opening scene of unprecedented riots staged by Muslims all over India. The Muslim leaders were once more taking it out on the Hindus for their frustration over Khilafat. It was the same story all over again — music before a mosque, or a pig in a Muslim *mohalla*, or a private fracas between two toughs belonging to the two communities. The Muslims have never needed a more substantial excuse whenever they are in a nasty mood. Nor has the nasty mood been able to mend itself for long because of the continued Muslim failure to recapture power all over India and re-establish their 'lost empire'. In case the Hindus failed to provide the necessary provocation, the Muslims could always slaughter a cow in the presence of Hindus or abduct and molest a Hindu girl in keeping with the best behests of Islam, or take out a rowdy *tājiā* procession through a thoroughfare thickly populated by Hindus.

The need of the situation was to remind Hindu society that Muslim objection to music before the mosque was a legacy of Islamic imperialism under which the *kāfirs* were not allowed to celebrate their religious and social festivals loudly, and that cow-slaughter and *tājiā* processions through Hindu *mohallas* were discriminatory privileges enjoyed by Muslims during the days of their dominance. Muslim society had to be told in no uncertain terms that Islamic rule in India was no more, and that the privileges enjoyed by the Muslim and the disabilities imposed on the Hindus were not going to be tolerated. At the same time, Hindu society had to prepare itself to meet effectively the violence to which Muslim society had become addicted under inspiration from the Quran and the Sunnah of the Prophet.

GENESIS OF SECULARISM IN INDIA

But Hindu society did not take any of these steps, though there were several voices which warned this society to mend its fences while there was still some time. The Indian National Congress came to be increasingly dominated by constitutionalists who wanted to settle with the Muslim League on terms of the latter's choosing in order to be in a better position to bargain with the British. And failing to persuade Muslim society to shed its separatism, these constitutionalists started training all their guns against those who objected to Islamic revivalism, or criticized it as an obstacle in the path of national progress towards freedom. The Congress started undergoing a transformation which was fraught with fatal consequences. In the process, the phrase 'Hindu communalism' gained currency as a pejorative phrase.

The constitutionalists were soon reinforced and then replaced by a brood of Leftists most of whom were educated in the West where they had caught the contagion of Communist thought-categories. Their animus against Hindu society to which they belonged by accident of birth was incurable because they had pawned their brains to what they glorified as progressivism. It was these Leftists who branded Indian nationalism as Hindu communalism, and then placed this swearology at the service of Islamic separatism in India. It was these Leftists who converted the Hindu-Muslim conflict into a class conflict in which Hindus were presented as the parasitic landlords and capitalists and the Muslims as the poor peasants and the proletariat whom Hindus were out to exploit and oppress. It was these Leftists who started the game of parading Islam as the champion of social equality and human brotherhood while pooh-poohing Sanātana Dharma as the bulwark of brahmin domination and caste discrimination. And it was these Leftists who divided the Indian National Congress into "progressives who stood for eradication of poverty" and "reactionaries who were out to safeguard and extend the Birla empire". Most Congressman who had any feeling for Hindu society and who saw the menace of Islamic imperialism were in this "reactionary" camp of the Congress. The Leftists started lampooning them as "Hindu communalists" as soon as the "reactionaries" opened their mouths.

The Leftists were small in number to start with. But they were ideologically equipped and spoke in a language which was prestigious in the eyes of the fast multiplying English-educated Hindu elite. They were supported by university professors and student leaders who had become fascinated by Marxist phraseology with which the country was being flooded by both Soviet Russia and Western democracies, and which the British authorities patronised to wean away the nationalist revolutionaries from what was described as terrorism. But what was most significant, the Aligarh school of Islamic imperialism in particular and the

Muslim League leadership in general picked up the refrain in no time, and converted Islamic separatism into a peasant and proletarian protest against "Hindu exploitation and oppression". The wolf was now going about in sheep's clothing, and the poor sheep was being portrayed as a man-eater.

Hindu society was not ideologically equipped to meet this new challenge. The language of nationalism was the only language it knew and could speak with conviction. But the double-speak devised by the Leftists had already made this language of nationalism sound like the language of "reaction" and "sectarian self-interest". Nor did Hindu society suspect that the Leftists were, by and large being financed and made to function in the service of Soviet imperialism. Hindu society was taken in by the loudness of their language against British imperialism. Traitors were stealing a march on the patriots, and those who failed to jump on the bandwagon were left by the roadside.

What followed was inevitable. The Indian National Congress surrendered to Islamic separatism in stages, and finally sold millions of people to slaughter and slavery on both sides of the border. And the Leftists who had worked untiringly to bring about this disaster and bloodshed blamed it on "Hindu communalism", while they themselves slipped into positions of power for which they had bargained with the British in the meanwhile. The leader of this perfidious operation was Pandit Jawaharlal Nehru, who became the Prime Minister of truncated India. The erstwhile Muslim Leaguers who failed to find a berth in Pakistan flocked to the Indian National Congress to strengthen "secularism" which was now proclaimed as the new religion of India that is Bharat.

SAPPERS AND MINERS OF SEVERAL IMPERIALISMS

This is the genesis of the Nehruvian Secularism. A concept which was evolved in Europe in order to free societies from religious fanaticism has been converted by the Nehruvian ruling class into a cover for furthering the cause of religious fanaticism.

The verbal shell is the same. But it has been surreptitiously stuffed with the potent poison of Islamic imperialism. Secularism in India today is the single most powerful shield for protecting the further progress of Islamic imperialism in the truncated Hindu homeland.

It is small wonder that the Muslim leaders in independent India have revived in stages all the old strategies of Islamic imperialism — contrived grievances, the posture of being a persecuted minority, street riots, and so on. The Leftists who now style themselves as secularists are again shouting themselves hoarse against "Hindu communalism". Only the whipping boy has changed. It was the Arya Samaj, Purushottam Das Tandon, the Hindu Mahasabha, and Sardar Patel in pre-independence India. It is the RSS and other patriotic organisations in the post-independence period.

What is worse, the success of Islamic imperialism in dividing India and in continuing to steal another march on the Hindu homeland, has encouraged another Indian community, the Sikhs, to copy the Islamic model as well as the Islamic methods. The *Ek Oṁkār* has been converted into Allah. The *vāṇī* of the Gurus has been converted into *wahī* which is supposed to be the latest and the best. The Gurus themselves are being paraded as prophets who proclaimed exclusive power for the *Panth*. And the *Panth* itself has been made into an Ummah which claims a monopoly of virtue for its members simply because they swear by a book and wear a distinctive hairdo.

The *Panth* now proclaims that its scriptures do not permit it to separate religion from politics. It accuses Hindus of a conspiracy to destroy its religious and cultural identity. It is uncontrollably angry with the "brute Hindu majority" for denying to it what it "more than amply deserves by virtue of its achievements in the past". It has passed a resolution which demands an exclusive domination over a well-defined area without reference to the wishes of other inhabitants of that area. And it is increasingly taking to violence to frighten the "*kālās*"[3] into surrender. It will not be long before the *Panth* opts for a separate homeland "after having exhausted all peaceful methods of an honourable accommodation with the Hindus". The slogan has already been raised by a section of the *Panth*. Meanwhile, the *Panth* has grabbed and is enjoying more than its fair share in the economy, polity, and administration of the country. Here is another wolf prowling around in sheep's clothing.

The response from the secularist ruling class is bound to be the same old stereotype which was evolved in the face of the Muslim wolf. The secularists have started by being concerned over the "communal situation" in the Punjab, and have thus already placed the aggressor and the victim of aggression on the same pedestal. In the next round, the "legitimate" demands of the *Panth* will be conceded. And "illegitimate" demands will go on becoming "legitimate" as the tempo of violence increases. In the final round, the demand for separation is bound to become fully "legitimate". The dreadful deed will then be blamed on "Hindu communalism" which "refused to see reason at the right time".[4]

HINDUS SHOULD REJECT THIS SHAM SECULARISM

Hindu society will fail to defend itself unless it sees through this Secularism and rejects it not only as a counterfeit coin but also as high treason to the Indian nation. Hindu society will never be able to defeat this gangster game unless it stops going on the defensive every time a secularist shouts his subversive slogans. Hindu society will have to tell the secularist that a Hindu cannot be a communalist in his own homeland. Anyone who accuses a Hindu of being a communalist is like the *thug* who accused the brahmin of buying a dog while, in fact, the brahmin had bought a calf. The *thug* is out to hoodwink and steal.

---

[3] A term of contempt coined by the Muslim League for Hindus in general. Now the Sikhs had made it a part of their swearology.

[4] This section was written in 1982, before the rise of Bhindranwale and the demand for Khalistan.

An honest Secularism had a lot to learn from Hindu history and culture. It would have held up Hindu society as the model of a secular society. It would have informed Muslim society, in very firm language, that the seeds of its trouble lay not in "Hindu communalism" but in the exclusiveness of Islam. It would have tried to re-educate Muslim society so that this society shed its self-righteous aggressiveness, and learnt to live peacefully with non-Muslim societies. And it would have carried the same meaningful message to the Christian and Sikh communities. In short, an honest Secularism would have been a defender of Hindu society instead of raising a brood of the sappers and miners of Islamic imperialism in particular and of other imperialisms in general.

10

The Trap and the Way Out

It was my intention to include in this series a few essays on Hindu Sociology and Hindu History as I see them after many years of study and reflection. But these themes would have to wait for some time. I will return to them later and discuss them with reference to Hindu Spirituality as I have presented it so far.

I have received many letters from the readers of this series as I did when I wrote some earlier ones. Most of the readers have appreciated what I have said. A few friends have reacted against my repudiation of Monotheism. It has not been possible for me to reply to these readers individually in spite of a strong desire to do so. But I have felt immensely encouraged. The appreciation as well criticism confirms that there is a large number of my countrymen who are conscious of their spiritual and cultural heritage, and who are moved by more than mundane matters.

Before I conclude, I should like to summarise what I have said so far in the context of Hindu Spirituality.

1. Hindu society has been sustained by its spiritual centre throughout the ages, particularly in the face of Islamic and Christian barbarism. Countless Hindu heroes and heroines have defied death rather than renounce their ancestral religion. Hindu society will be revived and revitalised only by recovering its spiritual centre which is Sanātana Dharma.
2. Hindu society has been thrown on the defensive by blood-soaked bigotries, clay-footed creeds, and a mercenary modernist culture because Hindu society is suffering from self-forgetfulness. A re-awakened Hindu society will not evaluate its own heritage in terms of ideas and ideals pro-

jected by imperialist ideologies. On the contrary, Hindu society will process these ideologies in terms of its own vision and world-view. That will restore the self-confidence of Hindu society as also Hindu pride in the ancient Hindu heritage.

3. The self-forgetfulness of Hindu society is symbolized by a wide-spread misinterpretation of the Vedic verse *ekam sad viprāḥ bahudhā vadanti* to mean that the Vedas also advocate Monotheism. This misinterpretation is motivated by a psychology of surrender as signified by the Hindu slogan of *sarva-dharma-samabhāva* vis-a-vis Christianity and Islam. A psychology of imitation is also at work. It has led some Sikh theologians to cast into monotheistic moulds the Vaishnava spirituality of the *Ādigrantha*.
4. Monotheistic creeds like Christianity and Islam view Sanātana Dharma as chaos and anarchy because Sanātana Dharma does not (1) swear by a historical prophet or saviour, (2) grant a monopoly of truth to a book (*al-kitāb*), (3) prop up a True One God against False Many Gods, and (4) seek the intercession of a prophet or saviour for escape from an eternal hell and get admitted into an eternal heaven. But that is not the fault of Sanātana Dharma. That indicates only the limitations from which the monotheistic mind suffers. A monotheist feels lost in the spiritual freedom of Sanātana Dharma like a Soviet citizen who fails to understand the functioning of a democratic society.
5. Evaluated by Sanātana Dharma, Christianity and Islam turn out to be constructs of the outer human mind, drawing upon dark drives of the unregenerate unconscious. Sanātana Dharma stands for self-exploration, self-purification, and self-transcendence, while Islam and Christianity stand for self-stupefaction, self-righteousness, and self-aggrandizement.
6. The central message of Sanātana Dharma is that (1) the spiritual aspiration for absolute Truth, Goodness, Beauty

and Power is inherent in every human being, everywhere, and at all times, (2) the spiritual striving cannot come to rest till a seeker overcomes all limitations of human and universal nature, and emerges as master of himself as well as of the universe, and (3) the way to world-discovery and God-discovery is through self-discovery. At the same time, Sanātana Dharma proclaims that there are as many ways of spiritual seeking as there are seekers, and that spiritual seeking does not express itself in any single and set doctrine or dogma. This is the basis of true universalism enshrined in Sanātana Dharma, as opposed to the counterfeit universalism of Christianity and Islam which prescribes one fixed, fossilized, and uniform system of belief and behaviour for everyone.

7. Sanātana Dharma is ingrained in the Hindu psyche which sees the same divinity in everything and everywhere, and which invests our entire environment with innumerable Gods and Goddesses. The mullah and the missionary denounce this Hindu psyche as poisoned by Pantheism and Polytheism. But that is the language of Monotheism which is incapable of understanding any type of spirituality whatsoever. Monotheism is disguised materialism which makes God extra-cosmic and denies divinity to God's creation. The God of Monotheism is soon replaced by the only son or the last prophet who, in turn, is replaced by a monolithic Church or Ummah out to conquer the world by force and fraud.

8. Hindu spiritual consciousness is expressed in terms of a plurality of Gods. These Gods are many a time symbolized by concrete images such as Sūrya, Agni, Marut, etc. This is because Sanātana Dharma allows many variations on the same spiritual theme, and does not put Matter in an irreconcilable opposition to Spirit. The forms and features of Hindu icons have a source higher than the normal reaches of the human mind. Idol-worship is the only way by which

the sense-bound human mind reaches something of the higher spiritual knowledge.

9. History is a witness that the spiritual consciousness of mankind everywhere had expressed itself in a plurality of Gods and in widespread idol-worship, before Christianity and Islam destroyed many ancient religions by fire and sword and imposed monotheistic materialism on large sections of mankind. Hindu spirituality which still retains its ancient intuition and genius, has to help many societies in Asia, Africa, America, Europe and Oceania to reject these impositions and revive their old Gods. That is the only path towards their spiritual and cultural emancipation from the imperialist and inhuman yoke of Christianity and Islam.
10. Monotheism of Christianity and Islam is not only an impediment on the path of spiritual progress, it also divides mankind into warring camps by giving currency to a number of hate-filled words such as infidel, *kāfir*, heretic, idolater, polytheist, etc. What is worse, Monotheism promotes the most degenerate type of idolatry by manufacturing myths and miracles about its all-too-human apostles and prophets, saints and sufis, and by seeing the supernatural in dirt and dross such as the hair, the saliva, the shoe, the shirt, and the shroud. It expects the idols of the infidels to perform the same supernatural miracles, and breaks them when the miracles are not forthcoming. Monotheism thus turns out to be the most abominable superstition.
11. Hindu sages and seers could tap the sources of universal spirituality because they did not start with an *a priori* assumption of an Almighty God as the creator and controller of the cosmos. Their starting point was the human person. That is why Hindu spiritual literature abounds in psychological and psychic terms. Hindu sages and seers explored human consciousness till they discovered the highest dimension of humanhood. It is seldom that Hindu spirituality speaks in the language of Theism. God as the creator and

controller of the cosmos is unknown to the Vedas, to the Upanishads, to Jainism, to Buddhism, and to the six systems of Hindu philosophy. Hindu spirituality never renounces its base in humanism; it only raises humanism to its highest meaning and significance.

12. Christian mystics and Muslim sufis continued to travel on the same path of universal spirituality because the new creeds sat lightly on them, and discovered the true fount of freedom from bondage. But Christianity and Islam used the power of theocratic states to suppress this natural and spontaneous mysticism and sufism. In due course, the mystics and sufis were made to serve the imperial establishments of the Church and the Ummah, and they became degenerate accomplices of predatory imperialism. Hindu spirituality has to rescue Christian mysticism from the clutches of Christian theology, and salvage sufism from servitude to prophetic Islam. That is the only basis on which Hindu society can come to terms with Christian and Muslim communities in India.

13. The true character of Christian theology and prophetic Islam is revealed when one studies the genesis of Christianity and Islam in the Gospels and biographies of the Prophet. Such a study leaves no doubt that Christianity and Islam are not religions but political ideologies pregnant with imperialist ambitions. Their appetite has been whetted by their conquest of a large part of the world by the power of the sword. Hindu society is making a serious mistake in treating Christianity and Islam as religions, and by extending to them the same *samabhāva* as has always prevailed among the various sects of Sanātana Dharma.

14. Hindu society has never had an established church, nor ever known a theocratic state. This society has always been a secular society. This society, therefore, does not need lectures on Secularism such as are delivered to it daily by the Nehruvian ruling class. An honest Secularism would have

addressed itself to Christianity and Islam which are the strongholds of exclusiveness and the advocates of a theocratic state. This has not happened because the Nehruvian brand of Secularism arose out of surrender to Islamic separatism. Having failed to overcome Islamic separatism, a section of the national movement, particularly the Leftists under the leadership of Pandit Jawaharlal Nehru, blamed their own frustration on what they called Hindu communalism. As a consequence, Nehruvian Secularism is no more than the embodiment of an anti-Hindu animus. The secularists serve as the sappers and miners of Islamic and Christian imperialism. They are also encouraging the imperialism of an Islamicized Akali clique which has been allowed to control *gurudwara* revenues and thereby dominate Sikh society which is only a section of the larger Hindu society.

15. Hindu society should see through this perverted Secularism, and reject it not only as a counterfeit coin but also as high treason to the Indian nation. That is the only way to defeat the gangster game which goes on all around Hindu society, and which threatens to reduce it to a minority in its own ancestral homeland. The secularist who accuses Hindu society of communalism is no more than a *thug* who wants to hoodwink this society into believing that its nationalism is communalism. He has to be unmasked and isolated.

HINDU SOCIETY STANDS TRAPPED BY ITS OWN SLOGAN

What is the situation at present?

The Hindu elite continues to shout its slogan of *sarva-dharma-samabhāva* vis-a-vis Christianity and Islam. It is rare to meet a member of the Hindu elite who does not shout from the housetops that Christianity and Islam are as good religions as his own Sanātana Dharma. There is no dearth of dim-witted but sanctimonious scholars who line up quotations from the Bible and the Quran alongside quotations from Hindu shastras in order to prove the "essential unity of all religions". Matters have come to such a pass that a Hindu who does not subscribe to this slogan suffers ostracism from the elite circles of Hindu society. Hindu politicians are the worst culprits. They are mortally afraid of being branded as 'Hindu communalists'. And they have neither the knowledge nor the courage to change the universe of public discourse. The secularists have only to invent a new slogan, the Hindu politicians are the first to fall in line. The only purpose they serve is to keep Hindu society always on the defensive.

Neither the missionary nor the mullah subscribes to the slogan of *sarva-dharma-sambhāva*. Each one of them is convinced and proclaims publicly that his own creed is the only true one, and that to equate it with Sanātana Dharma is the height of blasphemy. Each of them claims that Hindu society cannot stop him from converting as many Hindus as he can, by all means including force and fraud, without repudiating its own slogan and thus knocking the very bottom out of Secularism. Every Hindu objection to conversions, they say, exposes the Hindus as hypocrites who do not mean what they say. But if you ask the Hindu leaders to renounce this mischievous slogan, they denounce you as one who is trying to upturn an established Hindu tradition. They do not know that this slogan was coined by Mahatma Gandhi, and that it stood totally defeated in his own life-time. The future of Hinduism and Hindu society is dark if this is not debunked, and Islam and Christianity are allowed to march as they are doing at present.

What is the treatment prescribed for Hindus in case Christianity or Islam acquires state power in India? The prescription provided by the missionary as well as the mullah is again unequivocal.

The mullah says: "Allah has mandated the lands of the infidels to his last prophet who, in turn, has bequeathed them to the Ummah. India continues to be a *Dar-ul-harb*. It is our Allah-ordained duty to convert it into a *Dar-ul-Islām*. Our scriptures prescribe a total destruction of *kufr* (infidelism) and *shirk* (idolatry). Allah is very jealous of his own position as the only one worthy of worship. He cannot stand the sight of these Hindu idols imitating his majesty and trying to share his divinity. These idols have to be destroyed and trodden under the feet of the *mu'mins* in order to propitiate Allah. The temples which house these idols have to be demolished and converted into places worthy of our own way of worship. We will, of course, invite all idolaters in India to embrace Islam, willingly and voluntarily. But if they do not come round of their own accord, we are afraid we shall have to use force in furtherance of the only true faith. Allah had sent his last prophet to save all mankind from perdition. The divine duty has devolved on the Ummah after the departure of the Prophet. We cannot turn traitors to his mission."

If a Hindu protests at this revelation of the 'divine duty', he invites an angry howl from the Ummah. And the whole of it thunders: "So you do not want us to be true to our religion as revealed by Allah to his last prophet, as enshrined in our sacred scripture, the Quran, and as enjoined by our sacred tradition, the Sunnah? What sort of a Hindu are you? Have you not read the books written by your own scholars and sages such as Dr. Bhagwan Das, Pandit Sunderlal, Rahul Sankrityayan, and Vinoba Bhave about the sublimity of Islam? Have you not heard the lectures on *sarva-dharma-samabhāva* delivered by your own leaders, day in and day out, and over all these so many years? It seems that you are not secular. It looks as if you are a Hindu chauvinist out to deny to us the fundamental right of religious freedom guaranteed by the Constitution of the country. We appeal to you to shed your narrow Hindu communalism, and be true to your Hindu Dharma. We assure you that we shall not fail to be true to our Islam. This is the only basis on which our two communities can coexist peacefully till, in due course, the true faith triumphs."

The Christian missionary also talks in the same vein, though his language is less crude than that of the mullah, and his manners are more sophisticated. His methods of salesmanship are more mature. Also, the mullah is aggressive because he knows that a whole Islamic world supports his onslaught against Hindu society and culture, and because he finds that the Indian ruling class gets really frightened by his threats to mobilize frenzied Muslim mobs for committing gangster acts. He has demonstrated any number of times that his threats are not empty. The Christian missionary, on the other hand, knows that he does not enjoy such solid support in the West, and cannot mobilize Christian mobs on the requite scale.

Hindu society is thus trapped by a slogan which it has itself coined and made current countrywide. It is the same sort of trap in which a democratic society finds itself the moment it grants that the Communist fifth-column or a fascist phalanx is a legitimate political party entitled to enjoy freedom to function and expand.

THE WAY OUT

What is the way out?

Hindu society has to realize that Christianity and Islam are not religions but political ideologies inspired by imperialist ambitions. These ideologies came to India as accomplices of Islamic and Western armies. Those armies have been defeated and driven away. The ideologies which came with those armies should now find no place in India. They, too, have to be defeated and dispersed. Hindu society has to recover the ground that was lost to these ideologies during periods of Islamic and Christian expansion and domination. Those sections of Hindu society which were forced or lured into the folds of these ideologies, have to be brought back into their ancestral fold. This is the minimum task which Hindu society has to set before itself. The maximum task is to carry the campaign against these ideologies into their own homelands, and to free large sections of mankind from the abominable superstitions which breed intolerance and aggression.

The cultural climate in the modern West is favourable for the spread of Sanātana Dharma. The West has repudiated Christianity and returned to rationalism, humanism and universalism, all of which are values cherished and promoted by the Hindu view of life. But the West does not realize that the massive finances which the Christian missions collect over there in the name of doing social service in "a poor, starved, diseased and illiterate India" is used by the missions for the nefarious work of subverting the only sane society which has survived the depredations of genocidal creeds. Hindu society, particularly the Hindus settled or working in the West, have to provide this information to the West so that the menace of Christian missions is challenged in their own homelands.

It is true that Christian missions are involved in the foreign policy manoeuvres and intelligence networks of the various Western nations. The systematic building up of a Christian missionary like Mother Teresa by the U.S. State Department provides an obvious pointer. But Western foreign policy establishments are using Christian missions because Hindu society has made them respectable in India. The day that respectability is destroyed and Christianity and its missions are exposed for what they are, the Western nations will have no use for them.

Islam is a harder nut to crack. The Islamic countries everywhere are closed societies presided over by theocratic states which do not permit any scrutiny of Islam or the propagation of a rational and humanist view of life. The rise of Islamic fundamentalism in many Muslim lands has let loose a reign of terror against all those enlightened sections which have tried to free their people from the stranglehold of a fanatic falsehood. The Western democracies, particularly the United States of America, are encouraging this fanaticism in the fond hope that it will stand as a bulwark against Soviet imperialism.* A dark night envelops

* The Soviet Union is dead and gone, but the US support for Pakistan, one of the front rank promoters of Islamic fundamentalism and terrorism, continues. The aim of US foreign policy now is no less than the disintegration of the truncated Hindu homeland. Nehruvian secularists are now waiting to be hired by the US establishment, as they were by the Soviet estabishemnt in the past.

the Islamic countries at present due to a combination of historical circumstances, and there seems to be little hope that the Muslim masses will be able to emancipate themselves in the near future.

But it is also a fact that the rise of fundamentalism in a closed creed is a sign of panic, and sounds its death-knell. Christian fundamentalism which surfaced in Europe in the form of Protestantism proved to be the death-gasp of Christianity. For, fundamentalism brings to the fore, in one fell sweep, all the crudities of a closed creed — crudities which normally remain hidden under borrowed cultural trappings.

There is a large number of Muslim students, scholars, scientists technicians, and other sections of Muslim intelligentsia who find no place in their closed societies, and who have fled to other countries including India. Here is a fertile field in which Hindu society can sow some seeds which will bear fruit in due course. These refugees from Islamic terrorism have to be convinced that it is not the politics of their motherlands that has become perverse, it is the culture cultivated by Islam which has poisoned their societies.

But before Hindu society can perform these minimum and maximum tasks, it has to revive its own spiritual centre and reawaken to its own ancient heritage. The rest will follow.

Index

When the Kurinji Blooms

RAJAM KRISHNAN (1925–2014) was born in Musiri, Tamil Nadu, and got married before she completed high school. She wrote her first novel *Swatantra Jothi* in 1943. A prolific and versatile writer, her work spans several genres, including fiction, plays, essays, biographies, short stories and travelogue. Her writing is bold but lyrical and her feminist perspective and socialist ideology are tempered by her deep humanism. Her extensively researched stories are peopled by those who rarely find a place in modern Tamil literature: adivasis, destitute landless farmers, women labourers, salt-pan workers, petty criminals and under-trial prisoners. She has won national and global recognition for her writings, including the Sahitya Akademi Award (1973) for her novel *Verukku Neer* (Water for the Roots) and the Soviet Land Nehru Award (1975) for *Valaikkaram* (Wrist with Bangles). Her works have been extensively translated into other Indian languages and also nationalised by the Government of Tamil Nadu.

UMA NARAYANAN (1940) was born in Bangalore and holds degrees in Home Science, French and German. Her works in translation from Tamil include *Tyagu* by Sivasankari, Rajam Krishnan's novel *Lamps in the Whirlpool*, Ambai's (C. S. Lakshmi) novellas and short stories by other writers, in collaboration with Prema Seetharam. The librarian at the Alliance Française in Chennai for years, she is the founder of SOS Children's Villages India, Chennai, and balances her passion for translation with her dedication to child welfare.

PREMA SEETHARAM (1940) was born in Chennai and holds degrees in Chemistry, History, Library Science and French. She has translated from French *Le Temps d'un Royaume: Jeanne Dupleix, 1706–1756* by Rose Vincent, with Uma Narayanan. Her translations from Tamil, with Uma Narayanan, include Rajam Krishnan's *Lamps in the Whirlpool* and *When the Kurinji Blooms*, and *Two Novellas and a Story* by Ambai. She has also worked extensively with the blind and established Braille and audio libraries for them.

When the Kurinji Blooms

RAJAM KRISHNAN

Translated from the original Tamil by

UMA NARAYANAN
PREMA SEETHARAM

Orient BlackSwan

WHEN THE KURINJI BLOOMS

ORIENT BLACKSWAN PRIVATE LIMITED

Registered Office
3-6-752 Himayatnagar, Hyderabad 500 029, Telangana, India
e-mail: centraloffice@orientblackswan.com

Other Offices
Bengaluru, Chennai, Guwahati, Hyderabad, Kolkata,
Mumbai, New Delhi, Noida, Patna

Originally published in Tamil as *Kurinjithen* (Madras, 1963)

When the Kurinji Blooms first published by
Orient Blackswan Private Limited 2002
Second edition 2023

ISBN 978-93-5442-515-8

Typeset in
Adobe Caslon Pro 11.5/13
by Le Studio Graphique, Gurgaon 122 007

Printed in India at
Kensington Press, Noida

Published by
Orient Blackswan Private Limited
3-6-752 Himayatnagar, Hyderabad 500 029, Telangana, India
e-mail: info@orientblackswan.com

Contents

Author's Preface

Kurinjithen was first serialised in the magazine *Kalaimagal* forty years ago. I wrote it after thoroughly researching the life of the people of the Nilgiris. Though I have written many other novels, equally well-researched, this is the most highly acclaimed of them all. All my readers, academics or otherwise, have identified me with *Kurinjithen*.

Once in twelve years, in the season when the blue kurinji flower blooms in these hills, the bees store honey in combs in the crevices of rocks and on the branches of trees. Nowadays, no one is aware of when the kurinji blooms. Living close to nature is a thing of the past. Today people are primarily concerned with making money. The tea and coffee which are the means to achieve this goal cover the hills as far as the eye can see. While enjoying the aroma of fresh tea leaves and imagining the sweetness of the honey from the kurinji, I have tried to portray the changes in the lives of the people in these hills and the struggles they face. I summoned the courage to write this novel specifically to bring to light this change. Much to my sorrow, this has made people lose the feeling for fellow men that had been deeply ingrained in them. However, let us have faith that love is a natural human feeling. As our elders have said, we can wait for a generation for this feeling to return.

When *Kalaimagal* brought out this novel in book form, Dr Mu. Varatharasan honoured me by kindly writing the preface. That gesture was an opening for a novice like me, who had just then stepped into the literary world, to be introduced to learned men of letters. Though I have written novels before and since, this work made me known as a literary writer to historians, research scholars and students. I will always be indebted to Dr Na. Sanjeevi, who eagerly and enthusiastically made a study of this book from the viewpoint of a literary critic even before I had received recognition.

I encountered innumerable difficulties while gathering the facts for this book. Holding the book in my hand has made me forget them. But I really wonder whether the reader will ever know how painstakingly I have collected the facts, verified each one of them and woven the details into the story.

Four or five years after the book was published, much to my delight, something that I had never dreamt of happened: Dr Na. Sanjeevi who had read and admired the book, presented a paper on its anthropological value. He had studied the book with the same thoroughness with which I had checked facts about the hill people before writing about them. What greater accolade could a creative writer get?

This was the first Tamil novel of its kind. It was published in 1963. It has subsequently run into four editions. I am grateful to Orient BlackSwan for bringing out this English translation. I hope it will be well received by readers.

September 2000 RAJAM KRISHNAN

Translators' Note

When the Kurinji Blooms is a saga of three generations of Badagas spanning fifty years. It begins with the Badagas leading a tranquil and contented life at a time when the Nilgiri hillsides were covered with kurinji flowers every twelve years, and ends with the advent of hydro-electric power in the Nilgiris.

Jogi, a nine-year-old Badaga boy, lives in a *hatti* surrounded by mountains which keep 'at bay the hustle and bustle of the outside world, its colours, scents and artificial glitter.' As he grows up, the environment in the Nilgiris undergoes a remarkable change. All that the mountains had kept at bay creep in despite their protective presence. It destroys the peace and contentment of the inhabitants, and creates dissension and enmity between hitherto united families. Families, which had so far cultivated samai, ragi and potatoes for food, and to whom the taste of money was unknown, take to toiling on the land and growing tea with the sole objective of making money. Once money becomes the primary goal, culture and tradition begin to fade. The family of Jogi, who stubbornly cling to the old ways, remains backward, while that of Kariamalla, who move with the times, progresses. The rift between their two families widens. When Nanjan from one family and Vijaya from the other fall in love, this enmity stands in their way.

The path of enmity is strewn with tragedy: Lingayya's illness; Rangan's wild ways and violent death; Madhi's patience and endurance in the face of difficulties; and the modern man Krishnan, whose repeated efforts to help always end in failure. In the midst of these varied hues of life, the portrait of Paru stands out. We first see her glowing with beauty, then radiant in the first flush of love, after which we see her crushed by marriage to a man who destroys her hopes and dreams; she loses her children and finds solace only in the land. Happiness burgeons when Paru receives Jogi's son as her own. Yet conflicts persist.

In this novel, Rajam Krishnan welcomes progress while her admiration for the old ways remains undimmed.

The Tamil name *Kurinjithen*, honey from the kurinji, is appropriate for this poem in prose. The kurinji grows wild on the Nilgiri ranges. The bushy shrubs are covered with a profusion of bright blue bell-like flowers once every twelve years. One interesting result of the flowering is that there is an amazing increase in bees in the vicinity and immense quantities of honey become available. Due to the destruction of the environment, the kurinji in bloom is a rare sight now. The Badagas use the term kurinji (referred to as a kurinji-span in this book) to denote a twelve-year period.

According to Edgar Thurston in his *Castes and Tribes of Southern India* (Madras: Government Press, 1909): 'The name Badaga or Vadugan means northerner, and the Badagas are believed to be descended from Canarese colonists from the Mysore country, who migrated to the Nilgiris three centuries ago owing to famine, political turmoil, or local oppression in their own country.'

According to a popular legend among the Badagas, seven brothers and their sister lived in a village called Badagahalli near Mysore. During the reign of Tipu Sultan, either the Sultan himself or a Muslim Nawab fancied the sister. To escape from them, the brothers and sister disguised themselves and fled at night to the Nilgiris and settled down there. However, Thurston cites the *Gazetteer of the Nilgiris*, which says, 'When this flitting took place there is little to show,' and that going by their language, it is probable that 'the movement took place nearer the twelfth than the sixteenth century.'

The Badagas live in extensive villages or *hattis* composed of rows of thatched or tiled houses. Each house is partitioned into an outer room (*edumane*) and an inner one (*ogamane*). If the family owns cattle, a portion of the ogamane is converted into a milk-house (*hagotti*). The one who milks the cow wears freshly washed (*madi*) clothes. The milk is collected in a long cylindrical vessel made of bamboo (*honai*).

'Nobody,' it has been said, 'can beat the Badaga at making mother earth produce to her utmost capacity.' They store the fruits of their labour in a wooden box (*palapetti*).

The traditional Badaga man wears a *dhoti* and a *dupatti*, which is a long piece of thick, special weave of cotton, and a turban. The Badaga woman's attire consists of the *thundu*, *mundu* and *pattu*. The thundu is a piece of white rectangular cloth wrapped around the body and reaching the knee. The mundu is a piece of finer cotton cloth worn like a shawl over the shoulders. The pattu is a scarf-like piece of white cotton cloth, worn square across the forehead, and tucked in at the back of the head.

The photographic eye of Rajam Krishnan has missed nothing of the characteristic spirit of the Badaga culture as manifested in its attitudes, aspirations and customs. She spent many years in Kundah. When she went into the hattis, she familiarised herself with the language and became an observer of their way of life and of all their rites and rituals, which she so feelingly and vividly describes. Though *When the Kurinji Blooms* has been acclaimed as an anthropological novel, it is by no means a dry narrative. The emotional turmoil of a people in a state of transition is brought out in all its powerful intensity and pathos.

Rajam Krishnan's use of anthropomorphism renders her descriptions of nature extremely complex and has been a challenge to the translators. She has invested the mountains, the sky, the earth and the sun with moods ranging from gentleness to passion, generosity to cruelty. These passages often appear as a prelude to events in which the characters experience the same emotions.

The grandeur of the Nilgiris and the sweeping changes she witnessed in the lives of the Badagas has had an overwhelming impact on Rajam Krishnan. Her intellectual and emotional involvement with the theme is evident in the delineation of the story and its characters. In her conversations with the translators, she often said that writing this book had been a fulfilling experience.

We are extremely fortunate that we could consult Rajam Krishnan at every step. She has been of invaluable help.

We also owe a debt of gratitude to Indu K. Mallah, our Badaga friend who took us to a hatti, where we saw a typical Badaga home, spoke to people who still followed some of the old ways, and partook of a Badaga meal in the traditional manner. She also helped us by giving us an article written by her on the Badagas that had invaluable information on Badaga customs, tradition and attire.

UMA NARAYANAN
PREMA SEETHARAM

Part I

One

The verdant hillside, mellow in the afternoon sun, was like a mother who had just experienced the miracle of birth: wildly ecstatic, serenely aglow, fulfilled. It was the year of the kurinji flower, which spreads its blue mantle over the hillside once every twelve years, investing it with an exquisite beauty. The hillside, the epitome of youthful beauty in spring and the recipient of the sky's bounteous love, attains the lush maturity of motherhood in the last days of the month of *Kartigai*.

Can mere words capture the glory and enchantment of the Nilgiris or convey the wealth of her treasures? She has the power to dispel heat and spread coolness. She is fertile, repaying tenfold what is entrusted to her, whether grain, fruit or vegetable. She is endowed with *sholas* redolent with the fragrance of sandal, incense and camphor. She has plenty of honey. She has no dearth of healthy cattle heavy with milk. She embraces those who seek refuge in her, irrespective of caste or creed. She showers prosperity on them by providing fertile soil for tea and coffee to grow in abundance.

Is it any wonder then that the beauty, simplicity and caring nature of this mother are deeply ingrained in those who have found a haven in her lap?

That afternoon, on the last day of Kartigai, Jogi reclined on the emerald green carpeted hillside. The *hatti*, a settlement perched on the hill, was his very own, his birthplace. The hatti was protected on three sides by hills—except on the south, where a maze of forests surrounded by sholas stretched endlessly, keeping at bay the noise and clamour of the outside world, its colours, scents and artificial glitter. This hatti in the midst of emerald peaks was called Maragathamalaihatti or 'emerald mountain settlement'.

As one climbed the heights and paused near the houses to gaze into the distance, the eyes met a breathtaking vista of fold upon fold of azure hill ranges resembling herds of elephants, crowned by the peak of Devarbetta. Down below, the forest curved beyond the emerald hillocks; and scattered in the heights and hollows, like red and white dots, were the hattis. Reflected here were the two faces of Mother Nature—the awe-inspiring and the compassionate.

From the time the sun appeared on the horizon beyond the mountain, till it set behind Devarbetta, Jogi was loath to tarry even a moment indoors. The entire world of this nine-year-old boy was encompassed within the wide green slopes and the banks of the rivulet that meandered down the hillock and the hatti. As far as he could recall, he had not known sorrow. Where was the question of sorrow where there was no dissatisfaction? Jogi had a loving mother, a father who was the personification of honour, bosom companions and a *hethai*, a grandmother, to tell him stories; also the pleasant task of grazing buffaloes and cows to while away the time. What could tempt him to look beyond that?

Playing catch, his friends Raman, Belli, Rangan and Krishnan had gone beyond the rivulet. Tired of the game, Jogi lay on the hillside. He had his ear tuned to the crunching sound of cattle chomping on the lush grass. As they grazed, he played a guessing game.

He thought that the 'pdk-pdk' was Sheeli, the cow. The slow 'tup-tup' was surely Nili, the buffalo?

To check whether his guess was correct, Jogi sat up and glanced in the direction of the sounds.

Sheeli the cow sat chewing the cud while Nili the buffalo was nowhere in sight. Raman's buffalo calf was running down the slope with its bells jingling.

Since his guess had proved wrong, Jogi once again laid down, ear to the ground. However, the 'pdk-pdk' noise still persisted. Bored with the game, he turned and gazed at the blue sky. Narrowing his eyes, he imagined that the sky looked back at him intently.

'One cannot look straight at the sun,' thought Jogi, 'and the earth cannot exist without the sun.' The sun was the manifestation of *Isan,* the Supreme Being, to whom they prayed first thing in the morning.

Jogi's father, Lingayya, would worship the red orb emerging from the east. 'Hail God who gives light! O, Great Bestower, who gives rain to make the earth fertile! May you bless us with your love and grace.' With this prayer he would untie the buffaloes and cows and leave for the fields. By the time he returned home, the sun would have set behind Devarbetta. To dispel the darkness, Jogi's mother, Madhi, would place an earthenware lamp, wick dipped in castor oil, in its niche and light it. At night, in the absence of the sun, this lamp was considered the symbol of God. Without this lamp, the harvest would be poor and the yield of milk low; so Jogi believed.

He had a fear of the dark. The forest dwellers, the *Kurumbas,* practised their black magic in secret, in the dead of night. His grandmother had fed him stories of how these folk assumed the form of a dog, a jackal or a cat and cast evil spells. That was not all. It was during the dark nights that nocturnal creatures like panthers, bears and boars roamed. The boars ate the crops and destroyed them. Would they care to come when the sun shone?

He had a sudden flash of inspiration!

Just as they placed a lighted lamp in the house, why not place a myriad lamps all over the fields, the sholas and the cowsheds? Why not cover the hills with them? If there were lamps all over the hills and all around to dispel the darkness, would night be like day? Would the blue skies still be visible?

Jogi shut his eyes. The light of those lamps dazzled his imagination. Would the sky be bright? Would the light reach it?

The picture was mind-boggling. Lamps could be poised atop tall poles. They could be placed on the soaring eucalyptus trees. Enormous wicks dipped in ghee or castor oil could be lit in huge earthenware pots dotted all over the hills.

Could entire hillsides be planted with castor bushes and innumerable herds of buffaloes be raised? Who would have the strength to milk them?

Jogi's father had powerful arms.[1] He only had to place his hands on the udders and foaming milk would gush forth into the *honai*. Jogi's grandmother was given to reminiscing that in the olden days a man's right shoulder was branded with a red-hot iron to strengthen it. It was believed that bearing the pain stoically made one strong. If one man had to milk thousands of buffaloes, he would have to be strong. All the men would have to be really strong.

Even as Jogi's fantasy soared, his mind was beset with doubts. Where would all these buffaloes graze? If all the forests became pastures and fields of castor, where would they cultivate millets like *samai* and *tinai*? Where would they grow wheat? How would they cook without foodgrains? What about potatoes? Could one survive on buttermilk all day long?

Jogi's fertile imagination faltered at this juncture. He felt dejected. Before his train of thought came to a dead stop, his friends were already racing towards him.

'I'm first,' Raman said, touching Jogi with the grazing stick. The others followed, puffing and panting up the hill.

The minute he saw his friends, Jogi asked, 'Krishna, what'll happen if there's no sun?'

Krishnan did not have to graze cattle. His maternal grandfather was the influential *maniakkarar* of Maragathamalaihatti. Krishnan was slightly older than Jogi. Unlike the others, he went to the Mission School in Keezhmalai.

Krishnan laughed. 'Without the sun the day will be as dark as the night. Don't you know even this?'

'Suppose, just for one whole day, there's no sun?'

'We'll snuggle into our blankets and keep sleeping,' said Belli.

---

[1]Badaga men have cicatrices on the shoulder and forearm as a result of branding with a fire-stick when they are lads, to give strength and prevent pain while milking or churning (Thurston).

Belli, who was the same age as Jogi, was their neighbour Kakai's son.

'How can we milk the buffaloes if we don't get up? What about the "night-watch" in the fields, how will he come home? Everything will come to a stop without the sun. Isn't the sun like the eye of *Hiriya Udayar*? If he closes his eyes it will always be dark,' said Jogi.

'A ghee lamp always burns in Hiriya Udayar's temple which means that he will never close his eyes,' said Krishnan.

Rangan guffawed. He was the son of Jogi's father's elder brother, Madhan. The oldest in the gang, he was radical and forthright in his statements.

'Fools! There is no Hiriya Udayar Isar in the temple,' he said.

'*Aiyaiyo*! Shut up! Don't say such things!'

A scandalised Belli slapped his own cheeks with his palms in atonement.

Jogi was aghast at Rangan's audacity.

'Then why is there a temple for *Iswaranar*?' asked Krishnan.

'It only has a stone and a picture,' retorted Rangan.

'Your buffaloes will not give milk; you'll have no grain to harvest,' was Belli's solemn prophecy.

'Who says that Hiriya Udaya Isar is in the temple and the sun is his eye? Does the sun rise from within the temple?' asked Rangan.

It seemed to make sense, yet it puzzled them. Since no one dared contradict him, Rangan continued triumphantly, 'The sun will always rise. The hills will still be there when we wake up every day. As also the rivulet.'

'Do the hills rise and set each day? Do they move around? But the sun is not like that. It rises between the hill tops and after moving the whole day, sets at Devarbetta,' said Krishnan.

'What's so great about the sun? If it doesn't rise, we can always light big lamps,' Rangan said smugly.

'We'll need an enormous quantity of ghee,' said Jogi returning to his old dilemma.

'We'll turn the water of the rivulet into oil,' was Krishnan's solution.

Jogi's eyes widened saucer-like with admiration. How come this had never struck him?

'How stupid can you be! You can't make oil out of water,' said Rangan scornfully.

'You are the stupid one. The sun will always rise,' said Krishnan. Rangan did not relish being contradicted. 'You skinny fellow! You dare to call me stupid?' He tightened the cloth at his waist and got ready for a fight.

'Stupid fool!' Krishnan's patience was exhausted.

Rangan instantly leapt at Krishnan. A scuffle ensued and they rolled together on the ground.

At that moment a child's voice was heard from above. 'Re, Jogianna! Jogianna!' Straightening his shirt and adjusting his head cloth, Krishnan raced up the incline. Jogi was already ahead of him.

A five-year-old girl came running towards them. Round rosy face, dark eyes, curly shoulder-length hair, a few strands brushing her forehead. She wore a *thundu* and a *mundu* like a grown up. Shiny silver bangles that were too big for her, jingled on her wrists. They were large enough to be worn as armlets and could not have been hers.

'Jogianna, my baby sister has come. Mother and all the aunts have come bringing *poriurundai*, groundnuts and oranges. Come quickly.' Standing beside a thicket, she beckoned them to see this wonder. When she waved her hand, one of the silver bangles slipped and rolled among the shrubs. Rangan, who stood transfixed glaring at Krishnan, noticed it at once.

Belli, Raman and the other children raced homeward. Only Rangan remained, seething with indescribable anger and disappointment, and watched them till they vanished from view.

'Uncle is always having guests. Jogi is always feasting on delicious *porimavu* and jaggery, but in our house there's nothing,' he fumed inwardly. Rangan was motherless. His stepmother and father quarrelled constantly. She never served food without an argument. Their only buffalo was a weakling and its calf had died. Why? Why did it have to be like this?

'Paru has come to fetch only Jogi. That chap Krishnan thinks too much of himself because he wears a shirt and cap and goes to school. That cat-eyed fool Belli taunts me for calling a stone a stone. Why should God curse me for that?' As he turned around, his young heart bursting with rage, the skinny buffalo tugging at the grass caught his eye. He found a target for his fury in the ageing animal and unleashed his frustration by striking it repeatedly with his grazing stick. Losing its balance, the buffalo hurtled down the slope with a heart-rending cry that echoed in the hills.

Rangan's anger still smouldered. He uprooted some thorn shrubs and scattered the broken twigs as he climbed upwards. He spotted the bangle lying among the bushes and furtively glancing around him, snatched it up and tucked it in at his waist. Then he ran down the slope.

The buffalo, its forelegs broken by a jutting rock, lay sprawled pathetically, bellowing in agony.

Two

As one walks up the green slopes set aside for grazing, the first structure that looms ahead is the cattle shed. Beyond this is Maragathamalaihatti which comprises twenty houses in two rows. The four houses, which stood apart on the western slope, belonged to the *Toreyas.*

Legend has it that the *Badagas* had migrated from Mysore to the Nilgiris seven hundred years earlier through the dense jungles at Bandipur. There were divisions among them according to occupation. It is said that the leaders, administrators and account keepers were known by specific names such as *Haruva, Udaya, Adhikari, Kanaka* and Toreya. In every hatti the Toreyas are the servant class. However, it is well known that the so-called higher castes regard them as their own children.

Below the hatti there is a small hut-like dwelling, the temple for the divine ancestor *Hethappa*; in front of the temple is a stretch of level ground, where the *panchayat* would meet. From the western side a bridle path winds around the hill towards the south, joining the path that climbs up from behind the temple. At this junction stands a four-feet-high platform from which there is a clear view of anyone approaching the village. Rangan's father Madhan was wont to pass most of the day sprawled on it.

Paru, Jogi, Raman, Belli and Krishnan took the short cut, sped past the Toreya huts, and arrived panting. Jogi's was the last house in the row and it faced the temple. The hatti women were gathered at the entrance.

Paru was the daughter of Jogi's maternal uncle. One had to walk eastwards through the forest along the rivulet to reach Manikkalhatti, the village of Jogi's uncle. Paru's mother had gone to her parental home in Keezhmalai for her confinement and was returning to her husband's home with the baby. On the way, she had halted at her husband's sister's house to receive the grandmother's blessings. She would leave on the morrow for Manikkalhatti.

Jogi's house had a thatched roof and its white walls sparkled with fresh limewash. Krishnan's mother, the maniakkarar's daughter, stood outside the house, cradling the baby in the evening sunlight. The baby smacked her lips, relishing the taste of jaggery and milk, and gave a toothless smile.

As she kissed the baby, she said fondly, 'Just look at her smacking her lips,' Jogi eagerly burst in upon the gaggle of women.

'Ah, so you know him! She is giving him a smile! Look Jogi, she is smiling at you!' Everyone laughed.

Their laughter and teasing made no sense to Jogi. All his attention was focused on the baby. He was wide-eyed with amazement.

What a lovely creature she was! Rosy pink cheeks, coal black hair curling over her forehead, button nose, rosebud mouth, soft hands and tiny feet.

When he stretched out his arms, asking to hold her, there was much laughter.

'She's all yours. Don't you have first claim on your mama's daughter? Look at her smiling at you!' Krishnan's mother showed Jogi the baby.

'She is for Rangan. Jogi gets Paru,' interrupted Jogi's aunt.

Jogi was too young to feel bashful.

'Mm, I don't want Paru. I want only this baby,' he grumbled. More laughter.

'Just hear your son! He flatly refuses Paru. Hey Jogi, what's wrong with Paru? Didn't she come running to see you the minute she arrived? She's a good worker and will bear you fine sons,' said his aunt fondly, stroking his head.

Not understanding what she meant, Jogi said with his usual impetuosity, 'Hm, I like only this baby.'

'You have to pay a thousand sovereigns; you won't get her for nothing!' His aunt teased him affectionately.

'I'll pay,' Jogi nodded vigorously. Again a burst of laughter.

'Where will you get the thousand sovereigns? What a hope!' said Belli's grandmother.

'I'll manage somehow,' Jogi insisted.

'I also want a thousand milch buffaloes,' his aunt demanded with a sly grin.

'Taking advantage of my innocent son! A thousand milch buffaloes as bride price! Is my son a fool?' retorted Madhi.

'Why are you getting so worked up? If your son is that interested, he should respectfully place the gold at his mama's feet and ask for his daughter's hand,' replied Mami in mock anger.

All the women trilled in unison, 'Yes, that's right, that's right!' Krishnan's mother made Jogi sit down and placed the baby on his lap. Holding the infant who was soft as a flower, Jogi was totally enraptured. Two children born to Madhi after him had not survived. As far as he could remember, Jogi had never experienced such happiness.

Worried that Jogi might become fidgety, his aunt lifted the baby from his lap.

'Mami, Mami,' pleaded Jogi.

'Look here, get ten rupees from your father, give it to Mami and ask for her daughter,' his grandmother advised smilingly.

'Mami, if I give you ten rupees, will you give me the baby?'

'Don't be silly!' said his mother.

'Why, Amma?'

'The baby can't stay with us now. When she grows up and you become like your father, we'll give the bride price and bring her home. Then she'll cook for you, fetch water, sow samai and harvest the grain. What can the baby do now?' explained his mother.

His aunt handed the baby to the grandmother, went into the kitchen, and came out bringing a *vattathattu* heaped with sweet poriurundai.

When she placed the poriurundai in Paru's hand, she was startled to find the silver bangle missing.

'Where is the bangle, Paru?'

Paru looked around blankly.

'Where is it?'

'It was too big for you. I told you that you could wear it when you were older! Did you listen to me? Where did it fall?'

'Were you wearing it when you arrived here?' asked grandmother.

'I saw the bangle when she came to call us,' said Krishnan.

'Where else has she roamed?' Paru's mother shook out the child's mundu.

Madhi led the way out saying, 'Come, show us where you've been.'

Jogi's face brightened. 'Will Mami give me the baby if I find the bangle?' he asked his mother eagerly.

'Silly boy, going crazy over the baby,' his mother chided him.

The sun had begun to set and a cold breeze was blowing when they went out to look for the bangle. Paru ran ahead. Madhi, followed by Jogi, searched among the bushes and shrubs. There was no sign of the shining silver bangle.

It was growing dark and the children had begun to lead the cattle home.

Suddenly Madhi asked, 'Where's Rangan?'

'Look there!' A buffalo lay still, its legs splayed.

'Gno… oi.' Its heart-rending bellow reached their ears.

Jogi climbed down swiftly. How had his uncle Madhan's skinny buffalo fallen down? When he saw the blood-encrusted welts on its back, his tender heart melted.

Looking around him, he called out, 'Ranga! Re, Ranga! The buffalo has broken its leg. Ranga?'

There was no answering shout. The boy gently stroked the animal with hands still sticky with poriurundai.

Her bangle forgotten, Paru stared at the crimson pool near the buffalo's leg and shrieked, 'Aiyo, blood!'

Madhi came running towards her. The commotion attracted all the men and women working in the nearby fields.

Rangan's stepmother Nanjammai, who had been skulking at home all this while, resentful of the festivities at her brother-in-law's house, now came towards the field as if to gather twigs. When she reached the spot where the crowd had gathered and discovered the buffalo with its legs broken, her fury erupted.

Needless to say, her anger was directed at Rangan.

'Oh, Iswara! The buffalo's leg is broken! Where has that lazy lout gone?'

'Don't know,' said Jogi.

Nanjammai always compared their lot with that of Lingayya's family. Now she wailed, 'Wealth accumulates in the house of those who are well-off. Poverty seems to beget only further poverty. We've lost the one buffalo we had! The head of the house doesn't do a stroke of work and that boy is also a good-for-nothing! Can one woman slog single-handedly to feed the family? The whole world prospers, only Nanjammai suffers.'

'Tch, tch. How did this happen? Who has done this? How could you beat up the buffalo like this?' demanded Jogi's father Lingayya, who was also trying to lift up the animal.

'Loss upon loss for this family,' muttered Krishnan's grandfather Kariamalla.

'Take this pot and fetch some water from the stream,' Lingayya ordered the boys around him and then sat down to give first-aid to the buffalo.

'Can't take it to the cattle shed. We have to apply a leaf poultice right here. Where is Ranga?'

Lingayya looked up at Nanjammai. His question fanned the flame that was already blazing within her.

'I wonder whose evil eye has brought bad luck upon us! One disaster after another!' And Nanjammai proceeded to berate the good-for-nothing Rangan, cursing his disobedience, wilfulness, laziness and his propensity to steal and lie.

'Don't worry, Anni. It's my turn for the night watch. I'll call out from the watch-platform. Toreyamallan is also with me. If we keep the fire going, no harm will come to the buffalo. In a couple of days, it can be led home slowly,' Lingayya consoled her. Turning to Jogi, he said, 'Go and cut some grass for it!'

When Nanjammai reached home, bemoaning her fate, she found her eight-year-old daughter Rangi hitting her baby brother because he would not stop crying. The dried *mochai* beans that she had left on the fire were scorched. There was no water in the house.

'Our buffalo has been beaten up. And you lazy girl, haven't you fetched water?'

'No.'

'Why not?'

'Because . . .'

'Because what? Why are you adding to my miseries? The father is lazy, the boy is good-for-nothing and you're a useless creature!'

'Mami has come to Jogi's house.'

'How does that concern you, you donkey? Has she brought a groom for you? Gaping open-mouthed at them! Shameless creature! Now that the buffalo has fallen down, there's no milk for the baby.' Mumbling and muttering, she went out, waterpot in hand.

Shortly afterwards, her husband Machan staggered in with blood-shot eyes and fell down in a heap on the *edumane*.

Rangan who had set off towards the stream, the bangle tucked in at his waist, did not return home.

Three

From the time he is born till he stands on his feet, the child draws strength from his mother's love and father's all-embracing support. Infused with self-confidence, he aspires to be independent. Where there is no parental love there is a void and the disappointment dims the spark in him. It was Rangan's lot in life to endure constant barbs instead of loving words. The good fortune of his companions made him seethe with anger. Bitter disappointment and envy gnawed at him and he was seized by a sudden violent desire to show that he could become greater than all the others.

This rush of feeling impelled him to cross the stream and descend eastward into the forest, heedless of the buffalo's pathetic cry.

'Why not run away from Maragathamalai for good?' he thought. His aunt lived in Mookkumalai, so did his uncle.

Or why should he not go off to Othai? In tune with his heartbeat, the bangle tucked in his waist seemed to say, 'I'm here, I'm here!' He could get a whole silver coin if he sold it to the *labbai*. One whole silver coin!

Rangan knew that there was a pawnbroker's shop near the Englishman's estate beyond Keezhmalai.

Surely there would be one in Othai? Third house Dharman had told him how young boys carried baskets for English people when they bought vegetables at the *shanay*, the weekly market, and were paid in silver coins. Dharman worked in a road gang at Othai, earning as much as six *annas* a day that he saved and brought home. What was there for him in the hatti? In his fantasy world, that one silver bangle was transformed into stacks of silver coins and then into countless gold mohurs.

He meandered into an unknown forest path. He breathed the eucalyptus-scented air. He had heard that there was a path leading to Othai, but he had never seen it. His destination lay beyond Mookkumalai, Mottamalai and Pulikunru which could be seen to the north-east of Maragathamalai.

Once he reached Othai, he would earn silver coins. When he had saved enough, he would return to Maragathamalai in triumph. The whole hatti would be wide-eyed with wonder when he arrived on horseback, resplendent in a serge coat and turban.

Suddenly aware of the isolation of his surroundings, he checked his princely stride. The rustling of leaves; the frightened chirping of fledglings as he approached the bushes; the descending darkness; the paths suddenly petering out—all these combined to sap his courage, urging him to turn back.

But Mookkumalai had seemed so near when viewed from Maragathamalai! How could he possibly cross all these forests?

'Re, Ranga, what brings you here?' It was the voice of Belli's elder sister. She was tying together the twigs she had gathered.

Five or six girls from the hatti gave him curious glances. Could they have guessed his secret intentions? He was inwardly nervous.

'Have you come to gather twigs? Have you come looking for wild guavas and berries?'

'Where are the wild guavas? There are hardly any blooms on the bushes.'

'Has your *chinnamma* come for twigs? Have you come with her?'

They bombarded the silent Rangan with questions.

Dusk had fallen; there was no point in attempting the hazardous trek to Othai now.

'We were playing and I lost my way, Akka.' Rangan turned back.

As they walked home with their load of firewood, Rangan followed them at a distance.

As they crossed the stream and went past the pasture to the hatti, Rangan walked along the riverbank to the fields where Mother Earth was clad in wondrous colours. Darkness descended.

Here and there, bare fields proclaimed their owner's laziness. Plots which were a tangle of shrubs and weeds revealed the discord between the husband and wife who owned them. Rangan was well aware of this. He identified the owners of the various rectangular, square and triangular plots. The samai, heavy with grain, bent low like a shy maiden. The healthy knee-high potato plants in the triangular patch belonged to Krishnan's grandfather Karamalla. Nearby, plump radishes pushed their way out of the earth as if rebelling against their confinement underground. Lingayya had recently acquired the little square near Kariamalla's land. It belonged to Jogi. The cauliflower plant, like a protective mother, shielded with its leafy arms the flower inside from the harsh sun. So did the cabbage. Jogi's father Lingayya was a true son of the soil; Jogi's mother believed that tilling the earth with her own hands was a reward in itself; what Jogi's grandmother sowed, she reaped ninefold.

The sight of Lingayya's land and the thought of their house was like a thorn piercing Rangan's heart. Madhan's one and only buffalo was sickly. His land appeared parched and barren. The soil in that area was red and infertile. However, Jogi's father had worked on his barren land till it gave forth in abundance. He also had two cows and three buffaloes, so hunger was unknown in his household. And, to the south, where the stream curved, the land belonging to Krishnan's grandfather was dark and fertile.

Rangan's father Madhan was too lazy to work on the land; nor did his stepmother put in much effort. If she worked for two days at a stretch, she would disappear for a week with her baby and take refuge with her brother in Kothai. Rangan's father would occasionally work as a coolie in Othai, squandering the six annas he earned on drink.

Seeing the contrast between the two patches of land, the resentment and anguish simmering in Rangan flamed anew. In his fury, he pulled four or five plump radishes out of the soil. He washed them, crunched them with relish and walked on.

He halted at the watch-platform. In the light of the burning torch, the injured buffalo was visible. Someone was standing beside it. Who was it? Could it be Chithappa?

He was afraid that Chithappa would spot him and he furtively looked up at the platform.

Two short poles and two longer ones supported the platform on the slope. Steps led up to the top.

Armed with flaming torches and horns, two men accompanied by their dogs normally kept vigil over the fields at night, from on top of the platform. Blowing the horn kept away the porcupines that dug up the tubers and the deer that nibbled at the young leaves.

Whose turn was it to keep watch today, he wondered.

Rangan shrank from the thought of going home. He finished eating the radishes and took refuge from the cold and the dark in a corner of the platform.

Four

That day, as was his custom, Lingayya returned home, had a bath in hot water, went into the *hagottu*, the milk-house, and put on his *madi* clothes. The hatti dwellings, each one a replica of the other with their low narrow doorways, consisted of two main parts. Adjacent to the small verandah-like portion in front was the *edu nane* or outer house. In the *ogamane* or inner house, a doorway in line with the front door led to the kitchen. At the right-hand corner of the ogamane, the hagottu abuts an arched doorway set in the wall. In the centre of the ogamane, at the kitchen doorway, a lamp placed in a niche in the wall illuminates the whole house. Overhead are the bamboo lofts used for storage.

Lingayya went to milk the buffaloes after paying obeisance to the lamp, which at night was the visible emblem of the deity. Jogi's mother, bursting with the news of the lost bangle, stood aside when she saw him set forth with the honai. Her brother's wife, who sat rocking the baby in her lap, got up abruptly, moved out of his way and went into the kitchen.

The milking hour was sacrosanct. The rules prescribed for the worship of the *Devaru* also governed the ritual of milking. When Lingayya returned from the cattle shed with the enormous pot into which he had transferred the milk from the honai, women would not cross his path, nor would they speak to him. They could not enter the hagottu as it was sacred, nor could they boil the sacred milk. Girls who had attained puberty could not drink milk when they had their period.

Bringing the milk into the hagottu, Lingayya first poured some milk for the household into a *kalam* placed outside by Madhi. He kept some milk for his brother's household in another kalam. After setting aside the remaining milk for curd, he changed out of his madi clothes.

When he set out with milk for his brother's house, Madhi stopped him, 'Milk for your brother's house?'

'Yes, why do you ask?'

'It is because you show such consideration that your brother's family doesn't come up in life, everyone says so. You shower them with grain and milk. They don't do a stroke of work.'

It was the first time she had stood in his way. She could no longer suppress the bitterness that had been rankling within her for a long time.

'Why pick today to start preaching?'

'It is Anni who drinks this milk!' Madhi burst out furiously.

'So you don't want me to give them milk, Madhamma? Their only buffalo is injured. My brother and I are branches of the same tree. For one branch to stand aloof and watch the other one wither is despicable. Each one has his share of misfortunes because of his sins in his previous life. Don't stop me.' Controlling his emotions, Lingayya went to the opposite house.

His brother lay inebriated in the edumane. The whole house was plunged in darkness. Only eight-year-old Rangammai's sobs could be heard.

'Rangi, isn't Ammai at home?'

At her uncle's voice, the sobs subsided. 'Ammai has gone to the stream,' she replied.

'So late? Why haven't you lit the lamp, child? Have you no castor oil?'

Actually, she had dropped the castor oil container in the dark and had broken it. She would have to face her mother's wrath when she returned! At the very thought of that, Rangi burst into fresh sobs.

'What is it, Rangamma? Why are you crying, child?' When her uncle tenderly raised her chin up, the sobs increased. At that moment, Nanjammai returned with the waterpot.

'Why is the lamp not lit? Hey, Rangi, who is there?' she demanded. Then she noticed her brother-in-law.

'Be careful, Anni, it's dark.' Even as Lingayya was warning her, she slipped on the spilled castor oil and landed on the floor. The water pot tumbled to the ground and shattered, flooding the place.

'Iswara!' she shrieked.

Lingayya quickly ran home and fetched a lamp. Madhi, Paru and Jogi were behind him.

'So you've all come to gloat! Wretched girl. You've broken the castor oil container and now you're keening! Our buffalo has gone, our son is missing and now we've lost the water pot.' The lament went on and on.

'Put the milk away inside. It was just a mishap in the dark. Madhi, mop up the mess. Don't get so upset, Anni.'

Lingayya went out after consoling her and Rangi picked up the crying baby and made good her escape with Paru and Jogi.

While Madhi, obedient to her husband's command, cleaned up the house, Nanjammai continued to sit cross-legged on the floor, weeping and wailing. Madhi was used to such scenes. But today a new baby had come to her house and she was angry at the events that conspired to rob the celebration of all joy.

Reaching home, Lingayya heaved a sigh of relief. He sat down surrounded by all the children including Rangi. When they sat together like this, it was a signal for his wife to place the big brass vattathattu in front of him and serve the food that had first been offered to God.

Madhi brought her little niece and placed her on his lap.

'Oh, *Thangachi*, when did you come? Is everyone well?' he enquired.

The child's mother peeped out of the kitchen and replied, 'I came this evening, but Anna seems to have been very busy.'

'Oh, has the Toreyan come?'

'Yes.'

Even before he had finished saying, 'Bring some milk, Madhi,' she was there, with a *kinnam* of sweet milk.

He moistened the baby's tongue with the milk and uttered a blessing, 'May you be married into a good house. May you reap a thousand-fold whatever you sow. May you be blessed with a house full of children.' Then he asked 'What is the child's name?'

'Girijai.'

'It's a lovely name.' He handed the baby to her mother.

'We haven't found Paru's bangle. The minute she arrived, she rushed off in search of Jogi. Who knows where it fell? Only Rangan remained behind after all the children returned. There's no sign of him yet.'

Lingayya understood Madhi's subtle insinuation.

Rangan sometimes stole jaggery, *pori*, flour or honey from the *palapetti* when Lingayya was asleep. His behaviour was the result of having grown up in a house where prosperity was unknown. Lingayya turned a deaf ear whenever Madhi complained about his habit.

'Who knows where the bangle fell? Don't accuse him without proof,' he chided his wife.

Madhi placed the *vattil* in front of him and first served cooked samai and ghee, the aroma of which filled their nostrils. Then she served mochai *kuzhambu* cooked without tamarind.

Lingayya mixed the food and served the children. But he himself could not eat. The thought of Rangan huddled somewhere, cold and hungry, made the food taste bitter.

He forced himself to gulp down the milk that Madhi brought him and then set out for the night-watch.

Five

Swathed in a black blanket that covered his head, Lingayya made his way to the watch-platform, carrying a horn and a matchbox. His feet, clad in *chappals*, crunched the cold earth. Ten to twenty days of night-watch preceded the harvest.

The crescent moon had appeared in the sky and was now over Devarbetta. The clear sky was like a vast expanse of water where myriad tiny stars frolicked. At the sight of the crescent moon over Devarbetta, Lingayya's lips involuntarily murmured, '*Harahara Sivasiva Basavesa.*' His legs mechanically negotiated the rocky spur and descended the path leading to the Toreyar settlement. Mallan was waiting for him, equipped with a sack, a blanket and a flaming torch.

'Mallan?'

'Yes, Ayya,' came the reply.

Lingayya walked ahead, with Mallan close on his heels. From the forest opposite rose the continuous howl of a jackal. Mallan's dog ran ahead, howling in reply. 'Yesterday a jackal took away my hen,' complained Mallan. Lingayya's thoughts were elsewhere. The distinct nip in the air heralded the advent of frost. This was a cause for worry because the crop would have to be harvested before the frost intensified.

The frost would begin to intensify at the end of the month of *Margazhi* and the harvest would normally be over before the festival of *Thai Pongal.* After the fire-walking on live coals, in front of the temple on an auspicious day in the month of *Masi*, the sowing festival would be celebrated. But there was something that worried Lingayya now to the exclusion of all else, even the crop and the frost. Why should one branch of the same tree wither while the other flourished?

Unless his elder brother's land yielded well, how could he give the forest Kurumbas their due? 'Who is casting evil spells? Who is setting the demons on us?' was his sister-in-law's constant refrain. She feared the evil spells cast by the Kurumbas.

For some days now, his worry about Nanjammai had taken a new turn.

When a new bride enters the family, she considers her husband and his land as her wealth and toils for both; she also holds the family together, ensuring its well-being. No praise is too high for the Badaga woman who slogs tirelessly, giving her best to her husband and children, content to eat just the coarse remains of the *korali* flour after it has been sifted. Is it not the man's duty to appreciate and cherish this priceless gem?

The indifference of his elder brother, the first-born of the family, filled Lingayya's tender heart with boundless pain and sorrow. It was not just his elder brother; there were several men who did not appreciate the worth of their womenfolk. They treated gold as though it were brass and exploited the hard work of the womenfolk for their selfish needs; they had forgotten how to nurture the bonds of love, the life force behind the well-being of the family. Without this life force, the bonds had weakened and families were no longer close-knit. How pernicious were the miseries and evils spawned by these elders! Lingayya felt that the marriage bond was eternal, a unique privilege given to man. Also, that the option of breaking a marriage should be exercised only in extreme circumstances; for when the bonds of marriage were treated casually, it would greatly affect the lives of the children!

Madhan and Lingayya were stepbrothers. Madhan was the son by the first wife. After her death, the father married again and Lingayya was born. Did Madhan sense the lack of love in his step-mother's treatment of him? Lingayya was not sure but he suspected it. Madhan did not care for family ties. However, he was certain that his younger brother would not let him go hungry. He never did a day's work, had no care in the world and had earned the reputation of being a pleasure-loving wastrel. Typical of a motherless child, it was said.

Lingayya's father had divided the land between his two sons during his lifetime. He had also toiled on his elder son's land till his dying day.

Madhan himself was married twice. Rangan was his son by his first wife. Lingayya could picture Rangan's mother in his mind's eye. Her complexion had glowed like sandalwood paste. In their community, she had been a rare beauty with her round face and guileless childlike smile.

Impressed as much by her beauty and figure as by her capacity for hard work, Lingayya's father had paid a bride price of a hundred rupees for her. It was a pity she had died within a year of marriage.

Madhan had the most mellifluous voice and as a dancer he had no peer. Wherever there was a festival for the *Devar* or a funeral, he was the first in the community to be invited to dance to the Kothar's music. When he sang in praise of the Devar, his sonorous voice enthralled one and all.

On the day his wife had wilted like a white blossom and crumpled, Madhan had not been at home. He had gone to Kothai for some festivities.

When she went into labour, she was shifted to an enclosure outside the house. It was as if she had lived until that day only to fulfil her duty of delivering the child in her womb. Once it was born, she had slipped away, as though she had handed over her responsibility.

That child, Rangan, had never done anyone any harm. Did he have to suffer the same fate as his father?

It was not Lingayya's mother who had reared her step-son's child; it was Lingayya who had been a mother to him. A mere six months after the death of Rangan's mother, Madhan brought home Nanjammai, having paid fifty silver coins for her.

As Lingayya wandered around aimlessly, lost in the past, a puzzled Mallan reminded him, 'You said you wanted to see the buffalo?'

'Oh …' Brought back to the present, Lingayya said, 'You go.'

As Mallan departed with the torch, Lingayya climbed up the watch-platform. He stumbled against someone's leg. Startled, he struck a match and peered down. Rangan lay curled up there. Had he beaten up the buffalo and hidden from his step-mother's wrath?

Lingayya removed the blanket from his shoulders and spread it out on one side of the platform. As he was tenderly lifting up Rangan, his fingers brushed against Rangan's waist. He felt something hard.

As Lingayya tried to extract the object, Rangan woke up in alarm, grabbing the hand at his waist. Even in the dark, his uncle's concerned face was visible.

Lingayya realised that the object he had felt was the bangle. Tears welled up in his eyes.

'Rangan!' his voice was unsteady. 'How could you do a thing like this, Thambi? You are the eldest in the family; I carried you in my arms and brought you up. I never thought that you, who were so much part of me, could do this.'

In the dark, Lingayya could not see Rangan glaring angrily at him.

'Is it right to steal at this young age, Ranga?'

'Who stole? If I pick up something from the ground, is it stealing?' Rangan retorted furiously.

Lingayya bit his tongue. The boy might have been telling the truth.

'So it was lying on the ground?'

'Do you think I came to your house to steal it?'

'If you didn't, I'm happy. As happy as I would be if the injured buffalo were to walk home. All right, Ranga, you found the bangle, picked it up and tucked it in at your waist. As soon as Mallan returns, we'll go home and you can eat and sleep.'

'I'm not coming home.'

'Why, Thambi?'

'What is there for me at home? Who is there? I have no father, mother or brother. No athai, no mama. No one wants me.'

As he uttered the last words, his pent-up anguish found release in tears.

Lingayya stroked his back reassuringly.

'Don't talk like that, Ranga. Why do you say you have nobody? Am I not there for you? Why do you think no one cares for you? There's Paru, your cousin. Listen to me and come and stay in my house. Here's Mallan, let's go home.'

Turning to Mallan who looked on in amazement, he asked, 'Did you check on the buffalo?'

'Yes. Is that Rangan on the platform?' asked Mallan.

'Yes. You stay here. I'm going home now, but I'll be back.' Stepping down from the platform, Lingayya took the torch from Mallan.

As Lingayya led him by the hand down the platform and then up the slope, Rangan seethed with resentment. Why did it have to be his uncle's turn to do the night-watch? Now he had been caught red-handed. His rebellious nature had urged him to run away, but Chithappa had cut off his escape route.

As though applying cool sandalwood paste on an angry sore to soothe it, Lingayya was trying to assuage Rangan's feelings. But Rangan couldn't take it. How long could he hide himself in his uncle's house? Even if he stayed there, his step-mother would continue to taunt him. He had never been under any delusion that his relatives and the hatti folk would support him. Naturally, the thought of escape had given him great joy and comfort.

Though angry, he lacked the courage to shake off the hand that led him up the slope. To make matters worse, he was hungry and cold. At that moment, his need for the warmth of that hand outweighed his anger.

Unaware of the boy's state of mind, Lingayya prayed, 'Madalingeswara, keep this child from harm. With the light of this torch and reaching out to him with this hand, I lead him out of the dark abyss. Let this torch and my hand always be there to keep him on the right path.'

The lamp in the Hethappa temple was the beacon that guided them to the village. The village was silent, like a huge house when all the children in it have gone to sleep. In that silence rose a mellifluous voice singing in praise of God.

'Aha! What a wonder! Is it Anna's voice? Is it that of a mere mortal? Or is it that of a *yaksha kumara*, a celestial singer? Does this voice in the stillness of the night emerge from the throat of Anna? Anna, who has the reputation of being a lazy irresponsible wastrel! Is he aware he is singing or is he possessed by the spirit of God?'

Lingayya was spellbound by the music. Utterly moved, he stood at his door, forgetting even to knock.

The music was all-pervasive. Was it perhaps soaring higher and higher, to the limits of the sky, calling out to Siva, the Three-Eyed One?

How fortunate Madhan was! House, cows and land, were they the only enduring things in life? He, Lingayya, had all those, but did not possess the divine gift of being able to call out to God!

The rising strains of this exquisite music, just when he was praying for a good life for Rangan, seemed a good omen. Did the music augur that Rangan would shine like the light from the lamp and not tarnish the reputation of his forebears? Rangan also stood still, spellbound by it.

Inside Lingayya's house, Girijai, the baby, had begun to cry. Recollecting himself, Lingayya knocked at the door. 'Madhi, Madhi.'

Picking up the lamp from its niche, Madhi hurried anxiously to the door. Lingayya had not eaten properly that night. Was he suffering from a chill or fever?

'What is it? Are you not feeling well?' she asked in alarm, raising the lamp higher.

'There's nothing wrong. Ranga, come in…'

It was only then that Madhi noticed Rangan. Haru's mother, who was sleeping in the passage, folded her mat and stood aside.

A surprised Madhi followed Lingayya to the kitchen, lamp in hand.

'Where did you find him?

'Don't say anything,' signalled Lingayya. 'Is there anything to eat?' he asked aloud.

'There is *kali* and kuzhambu.'

Lingayya did not wait for Madhi to serve the food. He took the lamp from Madhi and replaced it in its niche. He washed the bell metal vattil. Balls of ragi had been kept in cold water in a vessel. He took one ball, placed it on the vattil and poured kuzhambu over it from the covered pot on the stove. Mixing the two, he took a handful of it and put it in Rangan's palm. Jogi, awakened by his father's voice, joined them.

'Why did you get up? Go and lie down,' ordered his mother.

'Why are you shooing him off? Let him be. Sit here, Jogi,' said his father.

It was a novel experience for Jogi to see the runaway being fed by his father at midnight. Involuntarily, he stretched out his hand. Lingayya put some kali in it and also ate some himself.

'Just as you are eating from the same vattil, you must always live together and share everything. If you go your separate ways, there will be trouble and misery. Do you understand, Jogi? Ranga?'

Both nodded.

He poured water for them to wash their hands, washed the vattil and came out of the kitchen.

'When I served you food, you refused to eat. Now you are eating kali,' said Madhi.

'I couldn't swallow a morsel then. Ranga, Jogi, go and lie down in the same cot. Think of Iswara and go to sleep.'

After they lay down together, he covered them with a blanket.

Feeling content, he decided to return to the watch platform and stepped out. Madhi, lamp in hand, came to bolt the door behind him.

He beckoned her outside. Wondering why, she joined him. Lingayya said nothing. He loosened his waist cloth and held out the bangle to her. 'When I went to see the buffalo, I saw it glittering on the ground and picked it up. It had slipped off Paru's wrist and you accused an innocent child.'

Madhi took the bangle without comment. 'Where did you find Rangan at this hour?' she asked.

'He had taken refuge from his step-mother on the watch platform. He was huddled there, cold and hungry. I brought him home. Don't talk about it. Children are innocent. Adults should not speak harshly and hurt them.'

Madhi kept silent.

'I am going now. Bolt the door!'

He shook out his blanket and covered himself. Madhan's music had died away. It was not a clear night. The mountain had shrouded herself in a gauzy robe of mist. As he descended swiftly, his mind was not entirely at peace. He was a little uneasy. Would Madhi wholeheartedly and impartially look upon Rangan as a son? To be left motherless was indeed a great tragedy.

As he walked on, he felt as though wave upon wave of his brother's music was still wafting over him. His body tingled to the sweet strains that seemed to linger in the air.

Madhan was cast in a different mould; he had always shrugged off the cares of this world but grabbed its pleasures. Let his land lie fallow, let his wife be aloof and go her way, it was all the same to him. How could such a man take care of his son?

Yet, in the balance, Madhan's plate was lifted up by the music, while Lingayya felt that his plate, weighed down with responsibilities and possessions, was in the nether world. Would an extra son be a burden to his family? If he turned out well, would he not be an asset?

Why should Lingayya give an impression to the world that he and his brother were two disparate entities? What was the point in having partitioned the land? Didn't everyone in the hatti share all duties including the night-watch? If a Toreya fell sick, did not everyone send him food? When he and his brother felt that they were one family, why had his father divided the land? Why had Lingayya let Madhan's portion lie fallow?

He had to toil on Madhan's land for his brother, for Rangan, for the other children, so that it would give forth untold wealth.

After the festival of Thai Pongal, Lingayya would make sure that Rangan was initiated into the ritual that would accord him the privilege of milking the cattle. After the purification by walking on live coals in front of the Madalinga temple, he would till Madhan's land and sow grain on an auspicious day in Masi.

Having arrived at this decision, Jogi's father approached the watch-platform with firm steps.

'Boom…boom…boom…' Mallan was there with his horn and torch.

Jogi's father felt that that the sound signified approval of his decision. He experienced a feeling of fulfilment like that of a joyous mother at the birth of a son.

Six

That night, during the watch, Jogi's father slept as he had never before. Nidra Devi, the goddess of slumber, who did not spare a glance for those tormented by debts, worries, bribes and poverty, lulled him into tranquil repose. Later in the night, he had a dream; not a dream born out of worry, not an illusion conjured up by an unquiet mind seeking to fulfil unfulfilled desires. It seemed to him that God in his kindness was bringing him a message of hope.

In his dream he saw an enormous fire in the east: a crimson blaze, a dazzling column of light, a mountain of flame that can dispel even the impenetrable darkness. In this circle of light, the face of an old man is visible. Noble lofty brow, eyes of a warrior, sharp nose, serenely smiling lips; gem-studded eardrops glisten in his ears, red sandalwood paste glows on his forehead. Lingayya feels he could gaze unblinkingly at that face forever. That face, a repository of knowledge and wisdom, seems to beckon him again and again. Who is he? The god of fire? Or is it God in human form bearing fire? Or Dharmadeva? Yama? Or the god of light…?

Drawn by the radiance on that face, he begins to walk towards east. It is only after a while that he realises that he is not alone; there is a young boy with him. His mind knows that the boy is Rangan. The boy is not clad in his usual garments, but wears a *dhoti* and a *dupatti*. His hair is in a topknot and he has a sandalwood spot on his forehead. Every time his dupatti slips off his shoulder, he drapes it back.

'Come fast, Ranga,' says Lingayya, turning around.

Ah! It is not Rangan! Surely this innocent face with its sandalwood spot belongs to Jogi?

'Is it you, Jogi? The fire will scorch you. You are too small. Go back,' he orders.

'It won't scorch me. I also want to come and worship Hethaiswami,' says Jogi skipping along.

'I don't want you, Jogi, I want Rangan. Where is Rangan? Ranga!' Shaking off Jogi's hand, he turns around.

In the east, the sun had crept through the dense forest sholas and set off on his journey around the world.

Waking up with a start, Lingayya, still bleary-eyed, raised his hands in salutation to the bright orb in the east. When his mind cleared and he looked around, the sun was smiling. There was no old man's face, no boy skipping by his side. He sat on the watch-platform, which was drenched with dew. Mother Earth laughed joyously as her flowers unfurled their petals at the sight of the sun.

'Aha! What a marvellous dream! Did my Ayyan who lives in the temple appear before me? Yes, that is what he has in mind for Rangan. My Ayyan has shown the way for the boy born in this soil to become pure of heart and feel like he belongs to the land. Ayyan himself will protect Rangan till he becomes a young man and give him strength to face life. That will silence people's tongues. This is the only way to redeem my elder brother from poverty. My Ayyan has come to me with these auspicious tidings. I will see the maniakkarar today. I will summon a panchayat of the village elders to the maidan in front of the temple and convince them to decide in favour of

Rangan.' His head full of lofty plans, Lingayya got down from the platform.

As he returned with a spring in his step, the hatti was welcoming the day with animated activity. Young girls and grandmothers with babies in their arms looked eastwards towards the sun and greeted the day. People were sweeping their houses, pounding millet, gathering twigs for the stove or cleaning out the cattle sheds and throwing the muck in the manure pit behind the village. Madhan sat smoking a cheroot in the sunshine.

Remembering the music of the previous night, Lingayya smiled at him.

'Come, Thambi, are you returning from the night-watch? I hear the buffalo has broken a leg? *Appappa*! What a woman, Thambi, she kills me with her constant nagging.' Madhan spoke with bitterness.

These words brought Nanjammai out of the house as swift as an arrow.

'Who is killing whom? Which woman will live in this house? You are a good-for-nothing and everyone makes fun of you. That useless boy hasn't shown his face since yesterday. The baby has fever. There's not a grain in the house and not even oil for the lamp…'

This tirade only amused Madhan.

'The waterfalls may dry up but she won't stop talking. Where is Rangan? Did you see him?' He asked.

'He was asleep on the platform last night. I took him home and fed him. He is sleeping there. He is still wayward, but a little responsibility will sober him up. We must choose an auspicious day and initiate him into the rite of milking,' said Lingayya.

Nanjammai pounced on him, 'Just listen to what he's saying; your younger brother is ridiculing you. He may not say it in so many words, but he's mocking us indirectly. Yet you do nothing. I am so ashamed, I wish I could die. I wish I had not come to live in this house. Your son has pushed our only buffalo down the slope. When we have nothing at all, your brother wants us to perform a ceremony!'

'Why do you misunderstand me, Anni? We may live in separate houses, but we are one family. Accept it, at least now. Don't say, "you have" say rather, "we have". There is no difference between Rangan and Jogi. Aren't we cattle from the same cowshed?' said Lingayya trying to placate her.

Madhan was moved by his brother's words. He was aware of his own weakness, but had become a slave to it and had no hope of conquering it.

'Thambi…!' Filled with emotion, he gripped his brother's hands. His own hands trembled. Tears poured down his rough-hewn face, like the music that poured forth from his throat.

Nanjammai could not believe her ears.

'We can till your land with hired labour, Anni. Don't worry any more about your household. Take whatever you need from our house or send for it,' said Lingayya. He went home and hurried through his daily chores.

As he was leaving the house again, Madhi approached him to discuss Rangan.

'It's one thing to keep their son here. But Nanjakka's talk is unpleasant. She says we have kidnapped their son. She created a scene when I went to fetch water. It is absurd to think that water from one pool can be transferred to another pool which has dried up.'

Jogi's father glowered at her but she refused to be cowed down by him.

'That old man, your father, divided the land. Why should you change that? There's no need to toil on their land, no need to treat their son as ours.'

'Madhi!' thundered Lingayya, 'What has come over you today? Why pay heed to Anni's words? Do you think she'll remain for long in that house?'

Lingayya's voice was heavy with sorrow.

'I have a strong feeling she will summon the panchayat one day and get her freedom, Madhi.

'What else can we do? It is the crow that builds a nest, not the cuckoo. Yet the crow does not refuse to rear a single baby cuckoo. Madhi, look at the *Todas*. They dont work on the land. Just because we live on their hill, we give them grain every harvest. We also give grain to the *Kothars* who make our pots and implements and provide music at our funerals. Fearing the spells of the forest Kurumbas we give them whatever they ask for. When we live in brotherhood with all the hill folk, what harm has Anna done that we should let his family starve? In this house, the first-born is equal to Ayyan. Can I starve him? Tell me, Madhi!'

His words silenced Madhi.

'Well then, keep the hot water ready, I'll pay the maniakkarar a visit,' said Lingayya as he left.

The last house in the row belonged to the maniakkarar, Krishnan's grandfather, Kariamalla. He was the village elder. He had been married twice but had no son and heir, only three daughters. All of them were married and had gone away. The youngest lived in neighbouring Manikkalhatti. Her son Krishnan was grandfather's favourite. He attended the Keezhmalai Mission School clad in serge coat and cap. Kariamalla was an official who was like a protective bund, preventing petty differences from escalating into big disputes. His word was law and he was respected in Maragathamalai, Manikkalhatti and the surrounding hattis of Chinna Kombai, Keezhmalai and others that were under his control. Those who lived in those four or five hattis worshipped at the same temples and celebrated their festivals together. They assembled regularly to discuss the sowing and reaping of crops and to decide the dates of the various festivals.

When Lingayya visited Kariamalla, he was supervising a Toreyan plaiting rope for a cot.

The minute he saw Lingayya, he invited him into the edumane, enquiring, 'Are you well? How is the injured buffalo?'

'There's no change. I came to consult you about something important,' said Lingayya.

'Is that so? I was also planning to send for you to discuss something important; sit down.'

While they engaged in impersonal conversation about the crops and the harvest, Krishnan's mother came out to welcome Lingayya. She brought him some buttermilk.

'Anna never comes to Manikkalhatti,' she complained.

'I'll come and stay with you for months on end and expect a feast every day,' joked Jogi's father.

'Your sister won't get fed up even if you stay for years,' she laughed in return.

Lingayya looked at Malla and cleared his throat. Before he could open his mouth, Kariamalla spoke again.

'It's something important, Thambi. It's five years since that Keezhmalai boy came to tend the fire in our temple. His uncle feels that it's time he got married and raised a family. Now we need another boy to tend the holy fire. We have to select a boy of good character, who doesn't cheat or lie, who will not covet the offering made to Ayyan or be a glutton. Has your son completed one kurunji-span?'

Lingayya was overjoyed to hear Malla broach the topic even before he could speak of his dream. What a good omen it was! However, Malla mentioning Jogi specifically instead of Rangan struck a discordant note. 'No, Rangan is the right age…I had a dream last night,' he began and proceeded to narrate the dream. Totally absorbed, Mallan nodded from time to time. Eyes moist, he saluted in the direction of the east.

Describing Ayyan and the light, Lingayya deliberately changed the identity of the boy in the dream, substituting Rangan for Jogi.

Kariamallar sat still with his eyes closed.

The temple was dedicated to Hethappa, their first ancestor who had settled down in the hills. It was a common belief that all the hill folk of the region were his descendants. Only a boy innocent of the carnal desires of youth was fit for the sacred task of tending the fire in that temple. That fire was the deity of the temple. Even though the villagers' offerings of buffaloes and grain belonged to the boy tending the fire, he was to exercise moderation and not attract attention. His only task, to the exclusion of all else, was to tend the holy fire. He could eat only once a day and the food had to be cooked by him. His body was not permitted the comfort of a cot or mattress. He could not go outside the temple and the sacred *maidan* without informing the elders. Young girls would never enter the temple precincts. Even if they did, the guardian of the fire of Ayyan could not talk to them. It was not easy to find such a paragon.

Kariamallar broke the silence. 'Let the panchayat meet in front of the temple this evening. I'll send word to everybody,' he said.

'I feel the divine voice of Ayyan has spoken,' said Lingayya.

'Let us mull over it together. When you narrate the dream, no one will refuse you.'

'The boy has not yet been initiated into the rite of milking. We plan to do it next Monday. As an elder, you must grace the occasion and bless him.'

'I surely will. It is all the Hiriya Udayar's doing. Is your brother at home, Linga?'

'I have yet to tell him my dream. Isn't it the boy's good fortune to serve Ayyan? Why should my brother refuse? We may live in two separate houses but he and I are one.'

'You think I'm not aware of it? You are a brother in a million.'

'Shall I take your leave? We'll meet in the evening.'

'All right. Ask the boy and consult your brother. Then we can make all the arrangements,' said Kariamallar seeing him off at the door.

Lingayya did not go straight home; he went to the slope to have a look at the buffalo.

By the time he reached home, the news had spread like wildfire through the mouths of the village women and men. To Madhi, this news was unexpected. In a way she was happy. Four, five years of strict regimen and the boy would shape well. A part of the offerings would belong to him. What a stroke of luck for a family who wanted to live well without doing any work!

Rangan was playing with his catapult amidst the bushes on the riverbank when Jogi and Belli went running to him. Bursting with excitement, they poured out the news of what was in store for him. Rangan stood rooted to the spot, his hands still, and stared at them without blinking.

'I? For Hethappa's temple?'

'Yes; I believe my father had a dream in which Ayyan appeared and told him. On Monday they'll give you the honai for milking the buffalo,' said Jogi.

Rangan was stunned 'I won't milk the buffalo,' he retorted.

'How can you refuse? They say Ayyan wants only you,' replied Jogi.

'All lies. I won't serve in the temple,' said Rangan.

'Yesterday you said there was no Hiriyan in the temple and the buffalo broke its leg. Now when Ayyan has come in a dream and asked for you, how can you refuse to go?' asked Belli.

'What will they do if I refuse?'

'What sacrilege! Evil will befall you.' Belli frightened him.

Rangan was flabbergasted. He was furious, but didn't know whom to blame; he was not unaware of the restrictions placed on the guardian of the fire. He could cook only once a day. He had to empty the rice from the cooking pot by turning it over only once and eat what fell on the leaf. He was not free to leave the temple precincts.

He was terrified at the prospect of all that it entailed. Was his uncle plotting against him? Was his affection mere play-acting? It was not fair to choose him, disregarding all the boys in the neighbouring hattis.

How many years would he have to spend in the temple? It would be like living in prison. Why couldn't he refuse?

Even though he had defiantly denied the existence of Hiriyan out of bravado, fear pulsated at the bottom of his heart. The buffalo was unimportant. But this? Was it because of his denial that Hiriya Udayar was punishing him by asking for him in his uncle's dream?

Angry, disappointed and miserable, he felt like crying. In a fury, he uprooted a few bushes. He plucked the beautiful yellow *vaadamalli* flowers and flung them in the stream. Why hadn't he made good his escape in the dark, the night before? He had also had the bangle with him. What bad luck had taken him to the watch-platform! Couldn't someone else have been on night-watch? Now his uncle had taken away the bangle. How could he run away to Othai without a single coin in his hand? How would he go?

Jogi was staring at him. As if he had worked it all out, he announced, 'Hiriya Udayar has chosen you because he likes you. If you tend his fire, you'll get grain. The land will produce without being tilled and Iswaran himself will speak to you in your dreams.'

Rangan came to a decision after weighing the pros and cons for a whole day. If he refused to do as he was told, there would be a hue and cry. Everyone would get together and shout him down, making escape impossible. It would be better to go through the milking ritual. A big crowd would be there. He knew his uncle hid silver coins in the hagottu. After the ritual, he would somehow take some of the coins and run away.

The following evening, the village elders and the headman representing the various hattis assembled in the flat area in front of the temple, the maidan. Kariamallar, as the eldest, sat on the platform beneath the tree. Rangan, bathed and dressed in a dhoti and dupatti, was wedged between his father and uncle.

Kariamallar rose and introduced the subject, 'Elders representing five villages, I bow to Hiriya Udayar and explain why we have all gathered here today. The boy, Devan, appointed to tend the temple fire will be twenty years old next month. He should now leave the service of Ayyan and do his duty as a householder for the growth of his family and his clan. Do you agree?'

'Yes, yes,' came a chorus of voices.

'The task of tending the temple fire is no ordinary one. One has to be pure in mind and speech and respect the rules governing it. Devan has performed this task to perfection, gladdening the hearts of our ancestors and villagers. We were worried about finding a replacement. But Ayyan has spared us, his children, this worry. He has shown us the way last night. He himself has chosen a boy. Is there anyone in Maragathamalai who does not know Dharmalingan?'

'No.'

'He was a true devotee of Siva. He reached the holy feet of God without committing any of the three hundred sins even in thought. This boy is of his lineage, his eldest son's eldest son. Ayyan has chosen this boy for us, so who are we to disobey him?'

'The boy has all the qualities essential for this sacred task. Last year he completed one kurinji-span, so he is now thirteen. Is there anyone in these hills who has not been enthralled by Madhanna's music? The boy's uncle, Lingan, has a golden touch. Do I need to say anything about this gem found in such fine soil? Hiriyar's choice only confirms the greatness of this family.'

'Without doubt, without doubt!'

'Ranga, come and bow to the elders.'

When Rangan bowed, all the elders blessed him with the words, 'May the holy fire always burn. May the boy be dedicated to his task and bring prosperity to all the villages.'

'As usual, a handful of grain from each house and the milk from the temple buffaloes will be given as a token of gratitude for his service. If the boy's father agrees to these terms let him come forward and convey his acceptance.'

When Kariamallar finished his solemn speech, Rangan's father got up.

For a while, he stood dazed, eyes glistening.

'*Hara Hara Siva Siva Basavesa,*

Hara Hara Sankara Paramesa!'

The melody, which rose from his throat mingled with the mountain breezes, hallowing the atmosphere and uniting all those present as they invoked the God adorned with the crescent moon and mother Ganga.

Music was his brother's life. The glory of it brought tears to Lingayya's eyes.

Seven

It was Monday. The day of the ceremony that would confer on Rangan the right to enter the hagottu. Before dawn the house had been swept and mopped. Hot water was ready so that everyone could have a bath. The families of the two brothers gathered together. The tiny kitchen was piled high with enough potatoes, greens, mochai beans, samai, tinai, rice and jaggery to feed a hundred people. Rangan's father scrubbed the plump buffalo, which stood with her first-born calf, and adorned her with bells. Jogi and Rangamma enjoyed themselves hugely, running around with the hatti children, laughing, playing and munching jaggery and poriurundai.

Only Rangan stood like a decorated doll, clad in his new dhoti and dupatti. He did not want to be involved in this activity. His thoughts were far away, beyond the hill ranges that looked like herds of elephants, beyond the dense forests, beyond the peak of Doddabetta. He thought longingly of the town of Othai, hidden behind Doddabetta.

A meeting place for different kinds of people. A town where the streets were crowded with swift horses and carriages. What wares would the shops hold? It was said that there was no dearth of silver coins in Othai. Hadn't he once seen the tea and coffee bushes in the Johnson estate to the west? Hadn't he heard of the Labbai's pawnshop and the old woman's shop nearby where she sold savouries like *murukku* and *sundal*?. One Englishman could employ so many men to work on his estate! When so many Englishmen and women lived in Othai, what marvels it would hold! He vowed he would escape from the hatti and reach that fabulous town.

As time went on, he became more and more nervous. The following week the sacred fire of the Hethappa temple would be extinguished. The week after, a new fire would be lit by striking twigs against each other after which they would imprison him to guard the temple boundaries.

His uncles and aunts from Mookkumalai and Manikkalhatti had come for the occasion. The house came to life, resounding with cries of welcome and joyful greetings.

It was neither scorching hot nor bitterly cold that day. A cool breeze wafted slowly by and caressed the body.

At the crack of dawn, Lingayya had a bath, put on madi clothes and cleaned the hagottu. He scrubbed the milk vessels and washed them with hot water while the women stood aside. He then washed the honai, which had been handed down from generation to generation and brought it outside. Then he led Ranga by the hand to the buffalo, which was adorned with *manjal* and *kumkumam* like a freshly-bathed woman. Offering the honai to his elder brother, he said, 'Anna, you milk the buffalo first, then hand over the honai to Ranga.'

Madhan returned it to Linga saying, 'Thambi, your hands are blessed. I've never seen buffaloes yield milk as they do at your touch. You are the one who tends them. So you should be the first one to milk them; then bless the boy and give him the honai.'

The younger brother, Lingayya, looked around at the assembled faces. No one spoke. He turned once more to his elder brother, Madhan.

'You are older. Tradition demands that you hand over the honai,' he said gruffly, in a voice choked with emotion.

'So what? Mama, as an elder, advise us. Mallanna, what do you think? I am the eldest in the family only in name. Don't burden me with responsibility. I don't want to be tied down. The one who toils to fill the family palapetti, who makes the younger generation aware of the value of tradition and instils in them a love of labour by setting an example, has the right to be called the elder. My cattle did not flourish in my care. You should hand over the honai, Linga; do not refuse,' pleaded Madhan.

Both the uncle from Mookkumalai and Kariamalla supported him. 'Yes, that is right. You do it, Linga, take the honai,' they urged. Unable to refuse them, Linga stretched out both his hands to receive the honai. Facing east, he began the sacred ritual.

Whenever Jogi watched his father milking the buffaloes, his fingers itched to do the same. At his father's magic touch, foaming milk would gush forth into the honai. He would then transfer the brimming milk into the milk vessels without spilling a drop.

Even on that day, Jogi watched with an eager light in his eye. The milk spurted for the suckling calf and then, Lingayya held the honai tightly between his knees and showed Rangan how to milk the buffalo. When the honai was three-quarters full, he handed it over to Rangan.

With a thudding heart and trembling fingers, Rangan tried to imitate his uncle's action. He could draw out only two jets of milk.

As he entered the house with the milk, everyone made way for him. Madhi stood aside after placing the vessels and the big bell metal vattil, which was reserved for the head of the house, on the floor.

'First, pour the milk into the vattil. From today you will share in the responsibilities of the household. Ranga, pray to our God, the Hiriya Udayar, to give sufficient milk for the family and make you prosper,' prompted his uncle. Feeling neither excitement nor enthusiasm, Rangan could not bring himself to utter these words.

Was he destined to languish in this hatti, milking cattle, digging earth and sowing seeds?

No, he was not!

As every heartbeat thundered 'No No! No!' his hand trembled while pouring the milk in the vattil; before Lingayya could put out a steadying hand, the honai shook, spilling some of the milk.

This untoward accident jolted Lingayya. People who had gathered there started whispering. Lingayya quickly guided Rangan's hand. The whispers of the womenfolk grew louder.

How dare they chatter during a sacred ceremony? The uncle from Mookkumalai glared in their direction.

There was a reason for the whispers. Nanjammai did not like the idea of the ritual being performed at her brother-in-law's house. Wasn't there a hagottu or an *unkalam* in their house? The 'first milk' should have been poured in their unkalam. Didn't Rangan have any responsibility towards his own house? When the elder brother had honoured his younger brother, couldn't the younger brother's wife have returned the honour? At least for the sake of politeness? Were they scheming against her? Snatching away the son from his family?

She expressed her displeasure.

The aunt from Mookkumalai placated her, 'Let him go to his house and pour milk there too.'

Signalling his assent, Lingayya went to his own kitchen and made Rangan sprinkle milk on all the vessels there. Then they went to the house opposite. It was not Nanjammai who put out the unkalam, but an aunt. On his uncle's instructions, Rangan sprinkled milk on it, then on his parents and finally on the elders in the gathering.

'May you always have milk in abundance; may the cows and buffaloes thrive.' The elders gave their blessings. Rangan followed his uncle into the hagottu and left the remaining milk there.

The ceremony was over. 'Ranga, you have to milk this buffalo from tomorrow,' said his father.

Rangan's face was like a thundercloud.

'The boy is hungry. Feed him first,' advised Kariamalla.

Lingayya's mother, who was the oldest woman present, served Rangan fragrant pongal, made with milk, jaggery and ghee, on *minigey* leaves. Rangan toyed with his food. It was distasteful to him and he choked on it.

'Thambi, aren't you hungry? Eat,' said Grandmother.

'He doesn't like to eat all by himself. Isn't it so, Ranga?' enquired Lingayya.

By this time Madhi had brought out the big unkalams and started serving food to everyone on platters made of minigey leaves. It was customary for the immediate members of the family to sit around one kalam and eat out of it. As the women served sweet kali, rice, kuzhambu and buttermilk, the men ate, extolling the bond between the two brothers.

'Do you think the buffalo will recover?' someone asked suddenly.

Lingayya, disconcerted by the reference to the accident at such a happy moment, made haste to reply, 'If the leg sets, it will walk. In four or five days we can carry it gently to the cattle shed.'

Raman, who had been on night watch the previous night, butted in, 'Yesterday a dog howled continuously. I could see eyes like glowing coals across the river. I have my suspicions. Some creature from the forest has smelled the buffalo. I hadn't taken my spear. I was frightened.'

As Lingayya was reeling from the shock, Bojan from the fourth house demanded, 'Is it a wild animal? Or have you mistaken a jackal or goat for a tiger?'

'Am I that blind? Ask the Toreyan who was with me,' came the indignant retort.

Lingayya was extremely perturbed.

'Then shouldn't we alert the surrounding villages and send for the hunters? If it has come up to the riverbank, doesn't it spell danger for our cattle?' he asked.

'Let us send word,' said Karamala, getting up to wash his hands. After the repast, everyone came out to smoke or to chew betel leaves. The younger lot went towards the Hethappa temple, animatedly discussing whether or not any of them could lift up the heavy round stone at the corner of the maidan.

Something impelled Lingayya towards the injured buffalo. He had last seen it the previous evening. Jogi would normally have taken it grass in the morning. Had he remembered to do so in the excitement of the morning?

As Lingayya crossed the rocky outcrop, two boys who grazed cattle came running towards him. They were not from Maragathamalaihatti.

'Tiger. Tiger!' they shouted, 'It has attacked the buffalo and dragged it off!' Lingayya was shaken. With a churning stomach and deep foreboding, he ran towards the shelter.

A terrible sight met his eyes from the makeshift shelter on the slope.

The buffalo's head had been severed and it lay savaged and bloody. Half the body was missing. There was a trail of blood along the riverbank and beyond.

Lingayya's eyes filled with tears—his life had always been bound up with his land and cattle.

What did this presage? What an evil portent on the day of the sacred ceremony! Ayyane!

He had been born on that soil and had grown up there, but he could not remember having seen such a gory sight. People spoke of tigers. In fear, they would take protective measures. Only once before had third house Mallan's grandfather speared a leopard. He had heard that the Englishmen at the Johnson estate only shot partridge, quail and rabbit, averring that no tigers existed in those parts. And yet, a tiger had perpetrated such an outrage in broad daylight! Was it a tiger? Or had someone cast an evil spell or resorted to black magic?

A thought struck him, making him tremble from head to foot.

Rangan—was Rangan not worthy of the Hiriya Udayar? Was it Ayyan questioning him, 'Son, it was Jogi I chose. You have cheated me…' Was this Iswara's way of testing him? Eyes streaming with tears, he could only stand and stare. In a short while, every man, woman and child from the hatti had rushed to the spot.

There was one person who did not join them, one person who was relieved, happy and excited at that moment. That was Rangan.

Eight

Dark clouds had gathered, threatening a downpour. Just as the hillside glowed when the sun rose suddenly to disperse the clouds, that unexpected occurrence melted the desperate anxiety weighing heavily on Rangan's heart and infused vigour into his mind and body. Barely ten minutes after the decapitated buffalo had been discovered, he had left behind Maragathamalai, his home since birth, and was running along a lonely bridle path towards Othai, his dream town. The two silver and three copper coins at his waist gave him confidence. When the panic-stricken household had rushed out in frantic haste, he had removed the coins from his uncle's savings, which were kept in a silk bag in a vessel in the hagottu. Like a calf let loose from its restraining rope, he ran, not turning back nor looking ahead. The sun was warm on his body. By the time it began to set in the afternoon, he had passed the Englishman's tea estate. Pausing a moment for a last look at the Englishman's bungalow and the white horse tethered in front of it, he ran on. Beyond the tea estate stretched hills and forests.

But which hills were these? Which forests?

Rangan had not the faintest idea how to find his way through the unknown forests and hills. He followed the bridle path in the forest. Thorns and sharp stones pierced his tender feet. Whenever he caught sight of any Kurumba or Kothar, he fearfully hid himself. When he climbed to a hilltop and looked around, though he could spot Maragathamalai and Devarbetta by the position of the sun, the fabulous city of Othai, spread out like the peacock's varicoloured plumage, was not visible.

Rangan climbed down the hill and kept on running, his heart beating fast.

With the kali, jaggery and poriurundai bouncing in the pouch at his waist, he reached the next slope. Below him lay a hatti. His courage ebbed away. His legs wobbled. Would anybody recognise him? Which hatti was that? What if he ran into a relative or someone who knew his uncle?

He went down the forest path avoiding the hatti. Strange sounds reached him, striking terror in his young heart.

'Hiriya Udayar Isare, keep me safe today. Take me safely to Othai.' At that tense moment, the heart that had denied the existence of God pleaded that his sins be forgiven.

He was terrified that tigers might be lurking among the bushes and rocks. After he had run a long distance over the forested hills, he lost all sense of direction. He could not spot Maragathamalai or Devarbetta. Only a hill, surmounted by a rock shaped like an eagle's beak, loomed ahead. Footsore and lost in that vast forest, he broke down.

'Ayyane! I will come with gold and donate four buffaloes to your temple. Protect me!' he cried aloud. Calming down, yet wondering if he would survive the night, he walked on, munching pori.

At dusk, when he looked down from the summit of the hill he had climbed, his spirits rose. In the midst of the curving hills stood a patch of green huts woven from *kanak* grass with curved, narrow, low doorways; there was a stone spire on one side; on the other, a herd of buffaloes.

It was a *Todamund.* Buoyant at finding human habitation after the desolation of the forest, he walked boldly towards the *mund.* He met a freshly-bathed priest on his way back from the stream who looked at him intently and walked beside him.

The Toda asked Rangan something in his own language. Rangan's heart beat violently. Without answering, he walked on and sat down at the entrance to a hut. A young man and an old woman swathed in a blanket were sitting there, and the priest said something to them. A beautiful girl, her twisted coils of hair gleaming with butter, emerged from the hut. In a while, a crowd collected around Rangan. They asked him all sorts of questions in their own tongue which disconcerted him.

He said nothing. Worn out after his trek, he took some kali and jaggery out of his pouch and started eating.

An old man came up to him, tilted his face up and asked affectionately in Rangan's language, 'Are you coming from the hatti? What brings you here?'

'I belong to Othai. I came with my brother to Manikkalhatti. He returned earlier. I was going to Othai, but lost my way.' He lied so convincingly that it brought tears to his own eyes.

'Is that all? Don't worry. You can go to Othai in the morning,' the old man said reassuringly.

Accepting their hospitality, Rangan ate samai and ghee, slept in their hut and prepared to set out at dawn for Othai.

Accompanied by a Toda youth, he reached the city limits before the sun climbed to its zenith.

Rangan drank in the beauty of the roads that snaked around the mountains and criss-crossed them. Many buildings stood on the heights and hollows. Rangan marvelled at the cross-tipped spire of the church. Was it a Toda temple?

There were throngs of Englishmen on the streets; gaily-painted *tongas*, drawn by horses with their majestic gait; turbanned men; elegant Englishwomen walking their dogs. Were they divine creatures with their berry-red lips and milk-white skin?

Rangan turned to his Toda companion and said, 'I can manage now.'

The Toda looked at him as if to say, 'Don't venture out alone in the future,' and stopped at a wayside shop.

Rangan was open-mouthed with wonder. He roamed the streets and went into raptures over the roses in the Botanical Garden. From a distance, he gaped awestruck at the horses and bodyguards in front of the Governor's mansion. He walked on and on. He bought a *pice* worth of sweets from the *lala* in the bazaar and savoured it to his heart's content. He wandered around the market place till nightfall.

It was a cold, frosty night and he wondered where he could find shelter. That night, he curled up in a shop doorway, wrapped in his dupatti. The next day he bought a basket from the bazaar.

'Coolie, coolie sir, coolie.' By evening, he had become adept at hailing the Englishmen and women who came to buy vegetables, eggs and fish.

The very first day he earned two annas. He was elated. Money! Had he ever set eyes on money in the hatti? He had known only the taste of samai and kali.

He grimaced with distaste at the recollection. In Othai there was an old woman, who had migrated from Coimbatore to the hills, and cooked *aappams* for a livelihood. They were one for a pice. Every morning he would polish off six of them. From his earnings, he could feast on varied fare, unheard of in the hatti.

Since it was winter, the stalls in the shandy were heaped high with fresh potatoes, cabbages, cauliflowers, brussels sprouts and radishes. As the English folk approached, the shopkeepers would call out to them, extolling the quality and cheapness of their vegetables. Most of the customers were the white people. Carrying a basket on his head, Rangan worked as a coolie in the bazaar. There he struck up a friendship with Subbu Pillai, who sold eggs, cauliflowers and cabbages. He would often short-change his customers and then disappear quickly. One day Subbu Pillai gave Rangan ten of his cauliflowers and twenty of his eggs to sell. Rangan did so and handed over the money to him.

The lure of silver was stronger than the call of the land. Rangan possessed shrewd business acumen and the ability to make money multiply. Subbu Pillai soon realised this.

Subbu, who had joined an army major's household as a skinny odd job boy a few years earlier, was now Subbu Pillai, the capable steward in charge of the army of servants who worked in that palatial bungalow: stable hands, cooks, kennel hands, butlers and ayahs. The money he sent to his family in Dindigul and the house he had bought in Othai bore eloquent testimony to his shrewdness. There was a vegetable garden and a poultry run attached to the bungalow. He needed a boy like Rangan to sell the surplus produce on the sly and keep track of the money. If the boy earned Subbu Pillai a rupee a day, surely he could be spared one anna? Subbu Pillai found a way to save even those one or two annas.

'My house is in Vandushola. Why don't you come over in the evening? I will give you a meal,' he offered.

Rangan did not need a second invitation.

Could anything be better? Rangan's share of food also came from the bungalow. Rangan who had enjoyed aappams, sweets, pulikuzhambu and white rice, now learned to relish the meat dishes prepared in the Englishman's kitchen.

He enjoyed life. Copper and nickel coins jingled in his purse. He looked forward to the day when they would turn to silver.

For fear of being recognised by any of his kinsfolk, he stopped winding a cloth around his head. He wore full-sleeved shirts and learnt a smattering of Tamil and pidgin English. His progress in Othai was phenomenal. Not once did he spare a thought for his native village.

Nine

Two winters had passed since Rangan had left the hatti and now the second spring had arrived. The ritual of walking on live coals had been performed in the Madalingeswara temple of Keezhmalai, the soil tilled and the sowing festival celebrated. The crop had started growing. Like a fevered body rejuvenated by fresh blood, the bare branches sprouted new leaves. Nascent green shoots burst forth exuberantly from the parched grassland like gleeful children leaping up to welcome home a sea-faring father. Tiny blooms in a riot of colours peeped through the grass and smiled guilelessly at the rising sun like demure girl children. Where had these blooms been hiding all this time? As teeth-chattering cold gave way to gentle warmth, the joy of Mother Nature caressing her precious children was reflected in beauteous scenes everywhere. The forests were alive with groups of hunters in search of prey, while Devarbetta peak and the Kumari falls basked in the admiration of English tourists. It was the season when visitors came to Othai.

Spring, the harbinger of joy, had brought no happiness to Jogi's house for the past two years. There had been many changes in that household.

One spring day, Jogi awoke even before he heard the sweet twittering of the birds at dawn and the crowing of the cock. He lay gazing up at the roof. Up above was the bamboo loft, where grain and potatoes for the household were stored. Thanks to his father's labour and mother's unstinting support, there had always been plenty of grain in the house. Jogi's young mind had never known the meaning of worry.

From early childhood he had been proudly confident that his house was not like Rangan's; that there was enough grain to feed any number of guests. That confidence was now shaken. Worries and household responsibilities weighed on the mind of this child, barely a kurunji-span old.

He turned his gaze from the loft to his father sleeping beside him, blanket drawn up to his chin.

Why was his father sleeping though it was so late? Normally, by now he would have been off to untie the cattle after his morning prayers. Jogi was worried that the grain in the loft would last them only till the harvest. What would they do after that?

Did Jogi's uncle, Madhan, work at least now? Not at all. It was Madhan's household that had suffered change and losses; it was their buffalo that had been carried off by the tiger; it was his son, Rangan, who had run away.

Yet, his uncle ate and drank as before and staggered home in the evenings. His aunt hollered and cursed as usual. She took milk and grain from Jogi's house. Her daughter, Rangi, continued to run around with her playmates, dragging the crying baby with her. Nothing had changed in his uncle's house.

But many changes had taken place in Jogi's house.

Jogi's father was heartbroken by Rangan's desertion. 'Hiriya Udayar, I did wrong. I tried to cheat you. You've cheated me. I'm a sinner, a sinner,' he had wept, beating his forehead. How was his father responsible for Rangan's disappearance, Jogi wondered.

The whole hatti had come forward to console him.

Kariamallar had sent men to search the four neighbouring villages. Rangan's uncle and aunt lived in Kothai, but nowhere was there any sign of Rangan.

Where could Rangan have gone? How did he have the guts to run away? Paru's father had come from Manikkalhatti one day to tell them that his enquiries in Othai had drawn a blank. Had the tiger, which had carried off the buffalo, taken Rangan as well?

Was the tiger real or had it been conjured up through one of the Kurumba's evil spells? For the past two years, Madhan had not paid the Kurumbas their dues. Had they taken revenge on him?

The very thought made Jogi tremble. His father had fallen ill and was not able to work in the fields; was it also the Kurumbas' doing?

His father was racked by a strange fever accompanied by violent shivers and chattering of teeth. His mother would hold him down, covering him with all the blankets at hand. Then he would burn with such high fever that it was impossible to sit near him. His eyes would be closed and he would become delirious. He would cry out, 'Ayyane, I thought of cheating you. I'm a sinner, a sinner.' Or 'Hey, Ranga, where have you hidden the bangle? Didn't you also steal money from the silk bag?' Sometimes he would get up and start running, eyes bulging. One day the fever would rage; the next night it would come down, leaving him drenched in sweat. In the morning, after drinking *kanji* and hot water, he would listlessly attend to the milking, after which he would be exhausted. He would push himself to work in the fields by sheer willpower. The next morning, the chill and fever would reappear as if by appointment.

One day, next-door Belli had told Jogi that his cousin had also suffered from fever induced by an evil spell. The fever had disappeared on making offerings to the Kurumba leader. If some such thing were not done to save Jogi's father, how would the family survive the following year?

Lingayya had had high fever the previous day and had been unable to get up. And his poor mother! It was she who laboured on the small portion of land sown by Lingayya. No wonder she slept on, weary and exhausted.

As Jogi lay awake worrying, his grandmother, who could not see very well, got up and felt her way around. Feeling as though her responsibilities had increased because her son was ill, she had taken over the task of cleaning the dung from the shed and filling the manure pit.

'Ammai, Amma…' The feeble voice drew Jogi to his father's side. 'Appa,' he murmured, sympathy and worry mirrored in his eyes.

'Has Hethai got up? Hot water, I'm thirsty.' Lingayya could barely speak.

Jogi did not call his grandmother or mother. He leapt up and hastened to light a fire with twigs and dry leaves. Taking water from the pot, he heated it in a wide-mouthed vessel.

The smoke and the crackling of twigs woke Madhi. Arranging her mundu and *pattu*, she quickly headed to the kitchen.

'Jogi, is that you?'

'Appa asked for hot water; he says he is thirsty.'

'*Kanne*!' she cried putting her face against his. What a comfort he was! What a solace and a joy!

Jogi's eyes reflected his worry.

'How long will Appa have fever? If like Periappan, Appa also doesn't work, what will we do?'

'Who knows what Isan has in his mind for us?' Madhi wondered tearfully.

'Amma, Belli says the Kurumbas have cast an evil spell. Could it be true?'

'Spell or no spell, this flourishing branch of the family has fallen on evil days. Jogi, will you go with a Toreyan and fetch Thatha from Manikkalhatti?'

'How will Thatha get rid of the fever?'

'He'll give medicine, child.'

At that point, the water boiled. Madhi added fresh tea leaves, cooled the brew and took it to her husband.

Her husband's complexion that had been the colour of red-black earth enriched with manure had turned sallow; his face had grown gaunt. When Madhi looked at him, she was assailed by fears that she could not suppress.

'What were you saying, Madhi?'

'Nothing,' she murmured, eyes downcast, 'How long can we go on like this?'

Noticing the tears coursing down her face, Lingayya wiped them tenderly. 'Why are you crying? There's nothing wrong with me,' he said.

'I'll send word to my father in Manikkalhatti. Don't be obstinate. We'll go and live there, taking our buffaloes with us. I'm too scared to stay here.'

She had worked out everything in her mind. A hand skilled with hoe and hook could always find work. How could they possibly be relieved of the burden of Madhan's household unless they left Maragathamalai? Rangan had run away and extinguished even the faint hope they had had that he would grow up and support his family. Madhan's family was as helpless as a toddler barely able to walk. Would they ever grow up and stand on their own feet?

She felt that they could be free only if they shook the dust of Maragathamalai off their feet.

Sensing what she had in mind Jogi's father said firmly, 'There's no need to call anyone. I cannot leave this place.'

'Then ask your brother's family to go somewhere else and fend for themselves.'

'How could you say this to me, Madhi? It is our duty to share and share alike. Isn't it cowardly to run away?'

'Should one die to keep the other in comfort?'

'What would you have done if I had married a second time and had another family?'

'Another wife would have borne sons. She would have worked on the land. She would not have provoked a fight and driven her son away,' retorted Machi sharply, alluding to Rangammai.

'She did not drive the son away, I did. Madhi, I drove him away. I did not obey Hiriya Udayar's command.'

'It's all your imagination. Why do you keep harping on it?'

'Madhi, last night I dreamt I was fighting a tiger. It pounces on me to savage my arms. I push it down. It does not die but keeps attacking me. I fight back, alive and undaunted.'

'Then?'

'The fight did not end … Jogi turned in his sleep and his cold arm brushed against me. I woke up. Jogi's hand is cool like Anna's, so is his body.'

'Why do you compare the child with your brother? This morning he got up and boiled water without bothering his grandmother or me. After untying the cattle and calves, he is now helping his grandmother sweep the house. It moved me to tears. He is your son through and through.'

'The dream ended with the fight unfinished. Do you understand what it signifies?'

'Does it signify anything?'

'My life is going to be a constant struggle. I'll have to face the odds as I had faced the tiger. I'll struggle with illness, but I'll survive.'

'Don't talk like this!' With an expression of alarm, she quickly covered his mouth with her hand.

'Impressed by her beauty and figure, my father brought a bride for Anna paying a hundred rupees. The beauty and figure did not last. She died young. Mama gave me his thin, plain daughter. He gave me priceless gold for a mere fifty rupees. If I continue to struggle, you won't hate me, Madhi?'

'Will I ever leave my Jogi? What kind of talk is this? Will I leave our child to be brought up by another mother? Wherever you are—that is my temple. My children are the glowing lamps within.' Her toil-worn hands were wet with his tears.

When the sun grew hot, Jogi's father dragged himself out of bed. He went to the hagottu and changed into madi clothes. Holding the honai in his emaciated hands, he went to the backyard where the buffaloes were tied. While Jogi untied the calf, the buffalo licked the hand of its beloved master.

In his enfeebled condition, Lingayya could hardly hold the honai that day. Though the milk gushed forth at his touch, his strength gave out. Before he could milk one buffalo, he felt his body tensing. Pouring the milk into the vessel, he slumped down, totally exhausted.

Madhi was alarmed. Custom dictated that she move out of his way when, clad in madi, he went to milk the cattle, but now she ran to support him against the wall.

'Aiyo! What is this! I would have sent for Kakaianna. Your body is clammy and cold.' Panic-stricken, she called out to her mother-in-law.

Jogi, standing by with a grazing stick in his hand, broke into loud sobs. Hearing him, his father slowly opened his eyes and gestured to him to sit down.

'Madhi,' he murmured.

'What is it?'

'Today is a Monday, an auspicious day.'

'Yes.'

'Give Jogi a hot bath and dress him in good clothes; is there jaggery in the house? Have a bath and make sweet pongal.'

Madhi flicked the tears from her eyes. It did not take her long to divine his intention. The ceremony, which had occasioned a grand celebration for the other boy, would now be performed without fanfare for his own son. Would Jogi, the child, have to shoulder responsibility so soon?

'Jogi is too young,' she said.

'Don't argue. Jogi can't wait to milk the buffalo! Isn't that so, Jogi?'

'Yes, Appa. Didn't I ask if I could milk it at Rangan's ceremony?'

'Today it's your turn to enter the hagottu. Go and bathe the buffalo while your mother heats up water.'

Jogi ran off, exultant.

In the forenoon, the father made his unsteady way to the buffalo which had been freshly bathed by Jogi and drew a little milk into the honai. Giving it to his son, he silently exhorted the gods above, 'Basavesa, let this boy take on this responsibility today. I promise to allow him to tend Ayyan's fire. Forgive me. Let our families prosper.'

Jogi reached out with both hands and gripped the honai. His tender fingers performed the task of milking as though long accustomed to it. Foamy milk gushed into the honai.

Part II

One

Once every twelve years in spring, this wondrous hill region, bewitchingly beautiful like a nubile maiden, stands resplendent in blue, shyly averting her eyes from her beloved, the sky. As far as the eye can see, everything is blue. The buzzing of bees eager to suck the honey from the kurinji flower can be heard from every side. The gurgling waterfalls create their own music. The sky seems to descend every twelve years to embrace this beloved mountain damsel, who has been waiting for him since the beginning of time. The blue of the sky is reflected in the new buds that cover the joyous maiden. Mother Nature, too, awaits the bridegroom, having spent twelve years weaving a garment of blue flowers for her dear daughter. The rising sun smiles warmly at the maiden with the tantalising smile, who stands half veiled by clouds, as if to say, 'You foolish creature, I am your lover, not the sky. I give life to the sky. Look at me!'

As Krishnan sat in the middle of the forest at the edge of his village, watching the cascading waters of the Kumari River, these thoughts flowed from the wellspring of his imagination.

He had just returned to his father's home at Manikkalhatti after completing his studies. After finishing his schooling at Keezhmalai and at Othai, he had obtained his degree from Madras. He had returned to the hills that year, bringing honour to his family, clan and soil. His entire childhood had been spent at his grandfather's house in Maragathamalai, and thoughts, which had never entered his mind back then, rose in him for the first time during this visit. He had had no time to enjoy nature all these years as he had been totally occupied, climbing the ladder of fame even as he was crossing the threshold into the world of adulthood.

In his visits home during the holidays, he had been pained to see the simple hatti folk, who were untouched by so-called education and culture, being labelled 'backward' by the world outside. His dream of getting a university degree had come true. He had returned to be feted by his loving parents, brother and sister. He was flooded with the pleasurable feelings and dreams unique to youth.

As he sat alone, watching the Kumari River as it cascaded down the hillside, nature in its early spring splendour was all around him. It was not surprising that such riotous thoughts overwhelmed him. For the last couple of days, he had given full rein to his imagination.

The people who lived beyond the hills and their varied lifestyles fascinated Krishnan. At first, he had been amazed by the women in multi-coloured saris, their long black tresses adorned with *mullai* and *malli* flowers, who seemed to enjoy a lot of freedom. His eyes, unused to the sights of the city, marvelled at the straight roads, multi-storeyed buildings, colleges, shops and the sweeping sands of the Marina beach which embraced the vast blue waters of the Bay of Bengal.

However, his eyes had never grown tired of the sight of his native hills, which remained beautiful throughout the changing seasons.

Was it because his people were one with nature that they were untouched by progress, Krishnan wondered. He felt that their society was a reasonably contented one.

Certain that there was nothing more to life than tilling the soil and cultivating it, praying, eating and living with women and having children with them, they craved nothing more.

Earlier, Krishnan had not believed that this contentment was a barrier to progress. The word progress had meant nothing to him then. He felt differently now. Not thirsting for anything else in life had prevented his people from reaching great heights and enjoying so many pleasures. What joy he had found in learning and acquiring knowledge! A man who learnt to think because of his education used his time productively.

Lost in his fantasy about the hills being the beloved of the sky, Krishnan was in an ecstatic mood. The word love lingered in his thoughts and he closed his eyes as a thrill ran through his body. He imagined the beautiful girl who belonged to him as the *nayaki*, the heroine, and himself as the *nayakan*, the hero, of the poems he had read.

He did not have an uncle whose daughter he could have claimed as his wife as a matter of course. The only girl he could have claimed as a bride was the daughter of a distant aunt in Thenmalai. He had last seen her many years ago at the fire-walking festival, when she was four or five. She would now be of marriageable age. He could not recollect her face. What would she be like now? As was their custom, a white thundu would cover her chest, above which shoulder blades like bamboo shoots would be visible. She would be wearing chunky silver bangles on her rounded wrists and rings on her slender fingers. The swirling black hair peeping out of the white pattu tied around her head would enhance the beauty of her moon-like face. And when she glanced at him sideways and smiled, her coral-red lips would part to reveal beautiful pearly teeth… He was startled when he heard voices and tinkling laughter above the roar of the Kumari River.

It was a mild day. The Kumari River plunged down between two hills, then swirled and formed a whirlpool. He saw a group of young girls walking through the undergrowth. They were going down to bathe in the river. All of them were of the same age and they were laughing and enjoying themselves.

The thought that a young man would be perched on a rock watching their frolic would never have occurred to them. The noise they made almost drowned the rushing sound of the river. The sun's rays, enthused by the sight of the young girls, pushed aside the veil of mist, pierced through the foliage, crept into every crevice in the forest and hills and embraced the river maiden and the girls, who looked as beautiful as flowers.

The river, jostling the boulders and swirling in the hollows, fell over the rock face, creating an illusion of iridescent crystal. Some of the girls sat on rocks, dipping their feet in water, some were busy making a paste of the *vekki* plant to cleanse themselves, while others tried to light a fire. One, more daring than the rest, had smeared her head with vekki paste and then plunged into the river, splashing water. Was it not cold? Or was she tough enough to endure it? She was the only one who was enjoying herself in the water. She was dripping wet and she teased everybody by splashing water on them. This ruined the efforts of the girl who was trying to get a fire going with twigs. The girl grew angry and chased her. Trying to evade her pursuer, the daring girl slipped and fell into what appeared to be a deep pool. Her hair floated like a dark cloud over the expanse of water.

The river, at this point, was only knee-deep in places. But the depth of the water in the pool, which was dammed by encircling rocks, could not be gauged. The fast-flowing water had formed eddies around the slippery rocks. The girl was caught in a whirlpool and was in grave danger. The joyous laughter of the others stilled in a second when they saw her struggle.

'Aiyo!' they cried aloud. As they were wringing their hands in despair, the unexpected happened.

Krishnan, who had been watching from above, ran swiftly as though hurtling down along the stream and jumped into the pool. The girl kept sinking and surfacing. He lifted her up as though she were as light as a handful of flowers and set her down beyond the slippery rocks. Gripping the branches of a tree, he reached the other bank and stood there, soaking wet.

Realising that it was a man who had saved her, she looked up at him. Did he also recognise her in that instant? A smile played on his lips. Looking as if every trace of mischief in her eyes had been suppressed, she wrung out her wet clothes.

'Krishnanan!' with a teasing smile, one of the girls called out.

The girl he had rescued pointed to the girl who had chased her and said in mock anger. 'She's the one who pushed me.'

'She fell purposely and now she is blaming us,' laughed the one who had been accused, gathering dry leaves to light the fire again.

'Isn't that so, Paru? You saw Krishnan and jumped into the water.'

'That's true! That's true,' laughed the girls, as they fed the fire with dry leaves and twigs

Paru's cheeks actually turned red. Her lips, which had become blue due to the cold, did not need the warmth of the fire to make them rosy again.

Krishnan left before they changed their clothes.

'Why are you dripping wet?' his mother asked him, wide-eyed with curiosity, when he reached home.

He felt bashful to confess to her that he had rescued a girl from drowning. 'I went to the stream. I thought it was shallow and stepped in and got wet.' Brushing her aside, he hurried in to change his clothes.

His mother did not take her eyes off her highly-educated son. He had grown so tall!

He was tall like his grandfather. He was not very fair. His face, which had never been exposed to sunlight and cold, was delicate and had a tinge of femininity to it.

Her heart brimmed with pride. How many books had he read! How many years had he spent studying, this son of hers! Where could she find a girl fit for him? The girl who married him need not till the soil. She should suit Krishnan's modern ways. She should wean her husband from his preoccupation with the land and cultivation. She, the grandmother, would enjoy the sight of her son's children filling the courtyard and playing in it.

While his mother plotted and planned, Krishnan changed into dry clothes.

He was deep in thought. The girl with the complexion like a *champak* flower had seemed a stranger, but in reality, that was not the case. The Paru he had known in his childhood had become a beauty. She was the only girl in that group with a face like a full moon and the air of a princess. What a coincidence, just when his thoughts had begun to dwell on love!

The excitement within him spread over his entire body. That mischievous girl pretended not to know him. Why? Was it her lack of education that lent her a special charm?

'When I am here, unattached and beautiful, how dare you think of that girl in Thenmalai?'

In his mind he could see her, pretending to be angry. She tells him, 'I possess all the qualities that you attributed to the Thenmalai girl in your imagination. Even if you search hard, you won't find anyone like me.' She disappears like a flash of lightning.

Krishnan's mind was filled with joy. He was lost to the world, savouring the thought of the girl who had almost drowned in the whirlpool and had now entered his heart.

Two

Since dawn, there had been hectic activity at the Snowdon dairy farm. It was the twentieth of the month of *Panguni*. It was the season when the Governor and his entourage shifted to Othai.

The special train, which normally preceded him, had arrived the day before. The responsibility of supplying milk to the Governor's household was that of the Snowdon Dairy. There were fifty Jersey cattle and ten to twelve buffaloes which provided fifteen bottles of fresh milk three times a day. The short-horned, black and white shaggy cows, udders sagging with milk, grazed all day on the green slopes of the Snowdon pasture. Durai, who owned the dairy farm, was the son of the first wife of the steward at the Government House. The steward supervised the running of the kitchen in the Government House and earned five to six hundred rupees a month. As the official supplier of milk, the farm received a government grant. Even after the Governor left for the plains, his wife normally remained at Othai until the week before Christmas in the month of Margazhi. Till then, a whole world functioned for her in the mansion. There was no let-up in the demand for milk. During the remaining three months, the milk was converted to cream and butter, which was then despatched to Madras.

Durai kept a strict watch over the milking of the cows, which stood in rows in the cowshed.

The milk was ready for distribution after it was filtered through cotton wool into large vats and poured into cans with a holding capacity of ten to twelve bottles.

That morning, Rangan was standing in for his master who was away hunting for two days. He was ordering the men about.

'Hm! Get on with it! Hurry up! Dey, Betta, keep this bottle aside. See that it is sent to Smith *durai's* bungalow when you have finished delivering milk to the Government House,' he said, rapidly filling the bottles himself.

Rangan did not have to restrict himself to diluting ten bottles of milk with just one of water that day as he was in charge. He was generous with the water. By ten, the distribution was over.

He took out a notebook and wrote the accounts. In his unlettered scrawl he made the entries: 40 bottles to the Government House, 25 to the hospital, 8 to the garden durai, 10 to the doctor durai. If he diluted such a large quantity of milk by adding a mere ten to fifteen bottles of water, it would not be detected. Ten bottles cost a rupee, a whole silver coin. Without his superior's knowledge, he supplemented his monthly salary of twelve rupees by another forty to fifty by selling milk on the sly.

In the span of twelve years, there was little trace left of the young Rangan who had run away from the hatti. He was unrecognisable with his budding moustache, thick lips and crafty eyes. Even his mentor Subbiah Pillai, who had initiated him into the art of shady deals involving stolen potatoes and poultry, had severed connections with Rangan, who had become thoroughly worldly-wise by this time. When Rangan realised that Subbiah had seen him hiding a bag of silver coins in a crevice in a rock, he too had decided to part company with Subbiah.

Rangan had looked after the poultry for a few years in the house of the garden durai of the Government House. Then he had worked in some of the big gardens and sold the flowers grown there. He had also learnt to arrange flowers in vases and to make wreaths. His silk bag went everywhere with him.

He started testing his luck on the racecourse. Whether he won or lost, he would not risk more than five rupees each time. In the previous week's sweepstake he had been especially lucky and had won four hundred rupees.

He had four hens of superior strain, six goats and two Jersey calves in his Vandu Shola hut, and he had also saved up a sum of six hundred rupees. When he had moved to his hut eight years ago, all he had brought with him was a single pear tree. Even that had blossomed and was heavy with fruit. In the past twelve years he had become wise and had mastered the art of survival.

He closed the doors of the milk-shed and took the path leading out of the Government House, cradling ten bottles of milk in his arms.

His heart swelled with happiness. The beauty of the green earth in early summer had been heightened by a shower which had settled the dust and cooled the place. In the distance he could see the trees in front of the Governor's garden covered with blue flowers. It reminded him of the kurinji in bloom.

One whole kurunji-span had gone by since he had left his hatti! The beauty of his hatti would be greatly enhanced by the riot of kurinji flowers in bloom this year.

A desire to go home arose in him. Till then he had had no inclination to see or meet anyone from the hatti. He had saved enough to eat well, live well and dress smartly in a coat and cap. Was it not natural to turn homewards, to fulfil the physical desires of youth?

He was not the only one to have grown in the last twelve years. So had Othai.

Its roads were teeming with activity. Handcarts, horses and horse-drawn carriages bearing Englishmen and their wives had been replaced by swift horse-less carriages. The road was lined with cloth shops owned by people from the North, and other stores that sold a variety of wonderful things. Exclusive clubs for princes and Englishmen had sprung up, as had cafes, lodges, streetlights, double-storeyed buildings, schools, churches and assembly rooms.

That was not all. His people, who for centuries had huddled in hattis, ignorant of town life, now grew potatoes and had learnt to sell them in the Othai market. They even came in droves to the races.

Perhaps, even his uncle, Lingayya, might have taken to potato cultivation in a big way at Maragathamalaihatti. He might be selling the potatoes in the town. Perhaps he had made money. Jogi would be a young man now! Rangammai could well be married and living in her husband's house! What about that fellow Krishnan who had gone to Mission School? Perhaps he had been converted and had joined the Christian priests!

And Paru? She would have blossomed like a newly-opened bud. He had first claim on her. With his wealth, he could ask for her hand in marriage.

So far he had achieved everything he had wanted, without a hitch. Surely it would be possible to go and bring Paru back with him? The thought did occur to him that she might be married to Jogi. Jogi was near at hand and in contact with her. If so, would there be other girls in the hatti who would suit him?

The minute such thoughts arose in his mind, the urge to proceed straight to Manikkalhatti became stronger. It quickened his footsteps as he went to the houses of his customers. He quickly distributed the milk. The sun gently warmed him as he came to the market. The streets were lively as the races were scheduled for the morning; many of his kinsmen were around, wrapped in blue and red blankets.

He entered the market, milk bottles in hand. The old woman from Coimbatore who had sold aappams was no longer there. There was a shop selling snacks like *puttu* and *masal vadai* instead. After buying six vadais for an anna, he entered the Sait's cloth store. He bought mulmul dhotis, shirting, blouse pieces and woollen mufflers. As he was leaving the shop bearing his purchases, a man who had been watching him for a long time from outside, seized his arm and exclaimed, 'Aren't you Rangan?'

Rangan looked up, startled. When their eyes met, the surprise was mutual. It was Paru's elder brother, Bheeman. As he took in Rangan's appearance from head to foot, Bheeman was overawed. Rangan was wearing a blue serge coat! He was dressed like a *maistry* in charge of the dairy farm! What youthful vigour! In his eyes was the proud gleam of a man who had arrived in life by his own efforts.

'How many years it's been! We thought you had disappeared somewhere! Where do you live now, Rangan?'

Elated at finding Paru's elder brother just as he was thinking of her, Rangan replied, 'In Vandu Shola.'

Bheeman noted with surprise that his voice had broken and become manly, his tone firm and authoritative. 'I've been a frequent visitor to Othai the last two, three years. Ayyan also comes there, so do many others from the hatti. No one has spotted you, Rangan! Have you bought land?'

Rangan's appearance proclaimed to Bheeman that he lived a prosperous life. Bheeman himself had always had a blind belief that he could make a fortune in Othai. Though he had tried, he had not been successful. He could only save two to three annas of the six he earned as a coolie. His family appropriated even that. He had tried his hand at betting in the races. It gobbled up his money and impoverished him further.

Attracted as he was by money, he was dazzled by Rangan's apparent prosperity.

'I plan to buy land. Is everyone well at home?' asked Rangan.

'Yes. But Paru…'

'What!' Rangan exclaimed.

'Nothing. We are looking for a good husband for her. There did not seem to be anyone who has a rightful claim to her. How happy I am to meet you! Come, let's go.'

'Where? To Manikkalhatti?' asked Rangan.

'Where else? I'm not going to lose sight of you. I'm going to take you home straightaway,' Bheeman said gleefully.

Rangan interrupted him, 'How are the others? Jogi? Chithappan? And Appan, is he well?'

'Jogi has been a priest at the Hiriyar temple the last eight years. The Kurumba's evil spells have made Chithappan very ill with fever. They are not as well-off as they used to be. Your father and stepmother have not been getting along and the panchayat has permitted them to part.'

All this in a single kurinji-span! Adeyappa!

'Is Rangi married?'

'Don't you know? A short fellow from Osahatti in the west married her. Your father had to borrow around two hundred rupees. They are now staying with your father and cultivating the land. I believe he has planted potatoes and is repaying the debt.'

'Is grandmother alive?'

'She passed away a year before the last festival.'

Rangan felt that there was nothing to be gained by going to Maragathamalai. A kaleidoscope of memories whirled in his brain.

'I ran away because Chithappan planned to push me into the temple. Could I have earned even one silver coin there? Chithappan is devious. He tried to cultivate our lands so that he could take them over. In the end, he is the one who suffers! So Jogi is in the temple?'

'Yes, Chithappa had no option. He fell ill Their family continued to struggle for three or four years. The villagers, taking pity on them, gave them one to two harvests of samai and korali. Of the four buffaloes they owned, they gave one to the temple. It is then that Jogi entered the temple. It is eight years to date. The boy who replaced you ran away all of a sudden.'

Rangan took a deep breath. He had six hundred rupees with him. Why couldn't he lease land and start cultivating potatoes?

He took Bheeman home. The woman who cooked for him was asked to prepare a whole chicken. They ate and drank well. They spent the night pleasurably.

The next day Bheeman left for Manikkalhatti, bearing news of Rangan.

Three

Welcome light showers fell on the earth like rose water from heaven. The sun rose with a benign smile. A soft breeze blew gently, heralding the month of *Chittrai*. The lush green shoots glistened in the fields. Jogi was loosening the earth and pulling out the weeds that were sucking the nourishment from the soil. The small plot was proof of his green fingers.

Before Jogi's time, the boys tending the temple had not bothered about cultivating the plot. They had whiled away their time grazing buffaloes in the nearby jungle, roaming, playing on their own and engaging anyone passing by in gossip.

Jogi was straightforward and God-fearing by nature and had had a disciplined upbringing. A high moral character and good conduct were riches that had come to him from his father. However, the greatest wealth he had inherited from his father was a passion for the soil and this was deeply ingrained in him.

At the crack of dawn, he would have a bath, milk the cows and attend to the morning chores. After cooking a handful of grain, he would gather wood to feed the eternal fire. After serving Hiriyan, he would loosen the soil in the plot behind the temple, enjoying the task. He sowed seeds and watered them from the rivulet. He took immense pleasure in seeing tiny shoots emerge from the soil, become sturdy and green, and grow heavy with grain. When he reverentially placed the harvest in front of the deity, he experienced an indescribable thrill and joy. He was unafraid of solitude. Never tired or bored, he did not fret, nor did he complain that his parents and others had enforced this incarceration on him.

Mother Earth, considering him her beloved son, gave proof of her vitality and delighted him. The task of constantly keeping the fire alive and concern for the seeds he had planted, kept his thoughts unsullied.

He did not harbour any resentment at being confined to this narrow existence that excluded him from the vast array of experiences offered by the world outside. As a matter of fact, he rejoiced at the blessings showered on him.

Jogi accepted this severe existence, which sometimes irked even ascetics and wise men, thanks to his virtuous nature and unshakeable belief in God. As he continued to dwell on a spiritual plane, his appetite shrank and he thought little about sensual pleasures. This lent a special serenity to his countenance. He had a certain aura of dignity. Though lean in appearance, he was a man of great strength.

As he wielded the hook that day in Chittirai, his dupatti kept slipping off his shoulders and his knotted hair came undone. Laying the hook down, he retied the dupatti tightly and retied his hair in a knot firmly. Entering the temple from the front, he chopped dry twigs and fed the fire with them. When he came out, the stone pillar was already in the shade.

Why hadn't his uncle, Madhan, come?

Madhan came daily to fetch buttermilk. The vessel of buttermilk, which Jogi had set aside for him, was still there. Jogi could use the milk from the six buffaloes belonging to the temple. Ghee from this milk was used to keep the lamp alight at all times. Why was there no sign of his uncle? He normally came every day carrying Rangammai's chubby one-year-old son, who was short like his father.

His uncle was his only link with the world outside. He was the only person who came every day to chat with Jogi. While Jogi was chopping wood, breaking twigs, cleaning the milk vessels or watering the plants, his uncle would sit on the *thinnai*. He talked of bygone days or sometimes gazed at the sky as though deep in the thoughts of an unknown world. At other times, haunting melodies would emerge from his throat, and his soft voice would thrill every fibre of Jogi's being.

His uncle's voice had made his father completely oblivious to the world.

Where was uncle? Why had he not come today?

Leaving his patch of land, Jogi went behind the temple and gazed in the direction from which his uncle would come.

He had no idea how long he stood there. He took in the panorama of the scintillating blues and greens of the curving silhouettes of the hills against the horizon. As he stood, forgetting himself in that vastness, feeling free, an excitement was unleashed from deep within him. Those feelings were not new to him. He had experienced them as a child, even before he could analyse them. When he used to lie on his back on the grass while grazing buffaloes, subconsciously he would feel something from within him leaping towards the sky. Eyes closed, he would drown in the pleasurable sensation.

Now, as he basked all alone in the gentle rays of the sun in a similar mood, the loud insistent chirping of two little sparrows distracted him. Two tiny sparrows were screeching and fighting, pecking at each other with their tiny beaks. Both were male and had black patches below the neck on the breast, their down as soft as silk-cotton. He did not have to look far for the reason for the fight. To the right of him a small bird was flapping its wings and chirping excitedly. It was a female; her youth and softness were evident in her beak and her body.

Captivated by the scene, a thrill ran through his body. He had seen mynahs and sparrows before. Yet, until then, he had never been held spellbound like this.

Two male sparrows fighting over one female! The female bird chirped agitatedly. Where did her preference lie? She was anxious for her lover to win and take her soaring to the heights of ecstasy. Jogi was unusually keyed up about the outcome. Which of the two male birds would emerge the victor?

Pecking viciously at each other, wings fluttering, they chased one another, flew across the maidan and disappeared into the forest. The twittering female perched herself on the stone pillar. Dipping her neck from side to side, she admired herself with a sideways glance and combed her feathers with her beak in an unconcerned manner. Was she confident that her beloved would win?

As Jogi, quivering with anticipation, waited for the result of the battle for love, one of the birds returned swiftly, looking triumphant. He perched beside his ladylove. Jogi's body trembled as he watched them.

That female was a crafty one! She tilted her head, giving the male a shy glance. He came closer and closer. She flew off and sat on the other side. The male again sidled up to her. She darted off towards the temple roof. He followed.

Jogi's eyes remained riveted on the pair till they flew out of sight. The upsurge of feeling was unabated. He sat on the small thinnai. For the very first time, he felt a sense of dissatisfaction that his life was incomplete.

Yes, the kurinji flowers were in bloom again. He had entered the temple before he had completed one kurinji-span. Wasn't he now eligible to leave the temple precincts?

Those two birds would live together in the bushes or in the hollows of trees and have offspring. While picking twigs or going to fetch water, Jogi would hear the frightened fledglings chirping, 'Our parents have left us to fetch food. We don't have wings to fly.' But beneath those piteous cries lay an assurance about their future. Their goal in life was to grow feathers and have their own young ones. In the last eight to ten years, the Rangammai who used to play 'seven stones' with him had become the mother of a chubby baby.

He suddenly recollected the day Mami had brought home Girijai as a baby and Paru had fetched him from the grassy slopes. He also remembered the teasing voices of Krishnan's mother and the other women when he refused to let go of the baby in his lap.

'When she becomes a big girl, she will come to our house to cook for you and till your land.' His mother's words flashed in his mind, taking on a new meaning. He shivered.

Paru was yet to be married. Once his father had said that Paru would be Rangan's wife. But no one knew where Rangan had gone or what had become of him.

Paru had an unusual face as beautiful as the full moon. How lovely she would be now!

When released from the temple, he would return home to take on the responsibilities as head of the household.

Fever had emaciated his father. Jogi would take over his father's tasks and ensure that his father had complete rest. Like his father, he would rise early and say his prayers, and Paru, like his mother, would heat the water while he untied the cattle. She would wash the vessels. She would pour water over him for his bath and then lovingly offer him kanji or buttermilk. When he returned for his midday meal, she would serve him cooked gram and kuzhambu in a shining vattil. The food cooked by her would have a special aroma. Before he came home in the evening, she would light the lamp in the niche and wait near the door, smiling, and there would be a glow in those big black eyes.

Appappa! Just thinking about it made him ecstatic.

By next year, like Rangi, she would become the mother of a chubby baby boy.

He had spent many years in the service of Hiriyar. Surely, He would bless him with a baby boy to continue the lineage.

His uncle, who had never been attached to the family, now carried Rangi's baby all the time. What boundless joy a baby would bring! Nothing could compare with it.

His father, mother and uncle would carry Paru's child in turns. His uncle would delight in teaching the baby to clap his hands, sing and dance. Jogi would sow enough for the entire family. He would watch over the crop night and day and bring home a plentiful harvest. He would tend to the cows and milk would flow. As the head of the house, he would welcome his friends, aunts and others warmly when they came on visits and ply them with hospitality. Paru would help him to look after them. The families would feast together at least once a month and the house would resound with joyous laughter…

He was shaken from his sweet reverie by the sound of hurrying footsteps. His uncle did not bring the baby or the vessel for buttermilk; he came with betel-stained lips, evidence of his having partaken in a feast.

'Periappa, where is the vessel for the buttermilk? Has anything special happened at home? Where's the baby?'

'Today we had a grand meal, Jogi. Do you know Krishnan has returned?'

'Krishnan from the manakkarar's house?'

'Yes, he has learnt so much in the city. The way he talks! It was feared that all of you would get converted in the Mission School, otherwise Thambi would also have sent you. Many went there, but none of them studied as well as Krishnan. He speaks about so many things.

'Hm.'

'I believe even girls go for higher education there. He has studied for so many years and read so many books. He is able to reel off the heights of hills and lengths of rivers. I believe that only by studying more and more can we get better yields from our crops. We'll be able to afford fine clothes. Then…'

Uncle's attempts to remember all that he had heard seemed novel and amusing to Jogi.

'I believe there are lights as bright as sunshine in the Governor's bungalow at Othai, which don't need oil or wicks. They need something called power, Krishnan tells us. We couldn't understand anything. The carriages and 'pleasure cars' used by white folk will soon be seen here. Roads have to be built; also, schools. He says all of us should work hard.'

Jogi listened with interest to this news from the world beyond.

Had Krishnan studied so much? Who could say? Perhaps one of these days these marvels would come to Maragathamalai.

Jogi had not seen carriages without horses or cows, nor had he set eyes on wickless lamps

As he was trying to digest this information, his uncle continued, 'Isn't it the white man who brought us trains? Isn't he the one who planted coffee and tea? Don't we pay taxes and think that the Collector and Governor are great men?'

'Hm.'

'The white man is just another human being like us. To be frank, he is like the lower castes, eating goat and cattle.' Lowering his voice he continued, 'He took over our country and is ruling us. He makes money by cultivating our lands. Krishnan says we should all go and demand that our country be returned to us. Adeyappa, how he speaks! I can't understand all that he says. Wait and see, he is going to bring honour to our hatti.'

Jogi continued to look at his uncle. 'Is that where you were all this time, Periappa?'

'Yes, Kariamallan is rightly proud of his grandson. He held a feast for us. Oh Jogi! I forgot something! I believe all their food contains tamarind, Jogi. Here we believe that tamarind is bad for our blood. Adede! There is something else I forgot! Something important!'

Jogi felt like laughing.

'I believe they want Paru as a bride for Krishnan. Krishnan wants to marry her. He has already said so this morning. Isn't Paru a lovely girl? Doesn't he deserve a good wife?' Jogi felt as though a weight had come up from the bottom of his heart and lodged in his throat.

Paru for Krishnan! For Krishnan, who had gone places, studied and earned degrees.

The little sparrows came to his mind.

Like a drowning man who manages to surface, Jogi shook himself and tried to look squarely back at his uncle.

Four

The stone grinder went round and round, grinding ragi into flour. Four tender hands were on the job. Girijai sat rotating the handle while Paru scooped and fed the ragi into the hollow of the grinder. The two of them were alone at home. Their grandfather was away at Thenmalai and their parents were in the potato field.

While Paru's hands were doing the job like a machine, her thoughts were elsewhere. A shadow had fallen on the flawless crystal of her mind. That shadow was causing ripples in her mind, which had till then been like a pristine pool. She had never felt that way before.

Her mind had been in a turmoil ever since she had heard that Krishnan had gone to Maragathamalai. People in that area looked up to him as though he were a king. Men of wealth and standing with daughters must be vying for his hand. She wondered who would be the lucky girl to enter that household.

'What is the matter, Akka, you've stopped feeding the ragi into the grinder. It's getting late.'

Paru was abashed at her sister's words and at once threw in a handful of ragi.

What if Krishnan's parents failed to come in the next few days to ask for her hand in marriage?

Madhi and Lingayya would be coming shortly from Maragathamalai. Rangan had vanished without a trace. The understanding was that she would be Jogi's wife. On one hand, there was the handsome man who had gone into the modern world, had lived through varied experiences and had returned to capture her heart; on the other, there was Jogi, who had not stepped out of the precincts of the Hiriya Udayar temple these last ten years. Where was the comparison between them?

It was evening; Paru lit the lamp and placed it in its niche. As she waited for her parents' return, she saw her elder brother Bheeman and her mother coming home, deep in conversation.

Her mother entered by the rear entrance and set down a bundle of twigs. When Paru saw the brand-new tiffin carrier dangling from Bheeman's hands, she reached out for it eagerly.

She opened it and then turned to him with a smile, 'Haven't you brought anything for me, Anna?'

Bheeman winked slyly at her. 'Oh! Haven't I brought anything! Ask Ammai and she'll tell you what I've got for you.'

She had told her brother about the new silk material available in Othai for making women's blouses, and had asked him to buy a few yards of it. Was her mother hiding it in her mundu?

She ran to her mother and demanded, 'Show it to me! Amma, please let me see it!'

Her mother laughed. Paru was too impatient to sense the subtle undercurrent in her laughter. She first pretended to be angry, then wheedled her, 'Where is it, Amma?'

'Look! I don't have it. It's Annan who has it... Giri, fetch some hot water.' She shook out her pattu and got ready to wash her feet and hands.

Paru was nettled by her mother's evasive reply and her brother's laughter. She sat angrily at the woodstove and pushed a glowing piece of firewood viciously into it.

Her mother, who was vigorously washing her hands, smiled inwardly at the beauty of her daughter's angry face in the light of the blazing fire.

When she had finished, she came to her daughter and said, 'Have you asked Anna what he has got you from Othai?'

'How many times must I ask? Let him give it to me if he wants to. Otherwise, he needn't.'

Bheeman went near her. 'Ade! Ade! Ade! Turn your face this way. Look at me and say that you don't want the present I've brought you.'

Paru was still sitting angrily with her chin buried in her knees. Bheeman whispered in her ear 'I've brought a handsome bridegroom for you from Othai. Now tell me you don't want him.' He lifted her chin and guffawed.

Red in the face, she masked the shyness in her eyes with mock anger. For a moment she was puzzled.

A bridegroom from Othai? Who could it be? Could Krishnan have gone to Othai?

Her heart leapt with joy. Her black eyes were aglow. She was tongue-tied. Clapping his hands, Bheeman broke out into fresh laughter.

'Now tell me you don't want him!'

'I did not ask you for that. I wanted only some silk from Othai,' she said, still pretending to be angry.

'Silk! Is that all, Thangachi? How much silk do you want? Shiny silk, gold and silver; it's all coming your way. A wonderful groom who can make ten rupees out of five, hundred out of ten, a thousand out of a hundred. Tall, well-built, fair, a beautiful moustache…'

At this point, Paru really lost her temper. Pushing him aside, she marched off to sit in the edumane. She was livid with rage.

The handsome young man to whom she had lost her heart had neither beard nor moustache. Who was this wonderful groom who could turn a hundred into a thousand?

Much later, her mother came and sat beside her in the dark and asked her lovingly, 'Paru, why are you angry?'

'I'm not angry,' she replied, averting her eyes.

'Does that mean you don't like Rangan?' Paru's heart missed a beat. Rangan?

'Peria Maman's son?'

'Yes. I believe Bheeman met him at Othai. He serves the white man and earns many silver coins. He owns goats and cows. He gave Bheeman a feast. He wears a coat and cap and is very smart.'

'Was Athan in Othai all these years?'

'Yes.'

'Are you in favour of this, Amma?' Paru gazed at her mother with sorrowful eyes.

Her mother understood what those eyes conveyed. News of the episode of her daughter caught in a whirlpool, her rescue by a young man and the brief love scene that had taken place, had reached her ears through Paru's friend in the opposite house. In spite of this, she said with a teasing smile, 'When one who can claim you as his wife comes with silver coins and falls at his mama's feet, demanding his daughter's hand in marriage, how can your father refuse?'

Paru pouted. 'No Amma… I… I…' she mumbled, burying her face on her mother's shoulder.

Her mother laughed aloud.

'Will Krishnan give two hundred? Will he give you a gold chain, bracelet and bangles? Have you asked him?'

'I'm certain he'll give me everything.'

'You silly girl. Let his grandfather Kariamallar approach us. It's not proper for us to make the first move,' her mother explained.

Every time Paru heard footsteps or saw a shadow fall, she watched from behind the door, her heart beating anxiously for the arrival of Kariamallar, carrying his ferruled walking stick.

Five

In spite of his promise to Bheeman, Rangan could not leave Othai immediately. He leased a small patch of land near the Todamund and got the soil prepared so that it was ready for sowing potatoes. There were showers within fifteen days of sowing. He then stayed on for the Governor's Cup, after which he shopped for gifts like multi-coloured silks and cakes.

The following day, he finished the morning chores, asked his boss for two days leave, had a look at the potato field and returned to his hut. Samuel, his boss's butler, was waiting for him. Samuel took out the expensive liquor bottles which he had tucked in the folds of his clothes.

Rangan put them away carefully with his other purchases. Opening his silk bag, he took out two and a quarter rupees and placed them in Samuel's palm.

'Look, Maistry, this stuff is good. Each bottle costs eight to ten rupees. Can't you give me at least one extra rupee?' grumbled Samuel.

'Don't tell me you spent eight rupees from your pocket,' Rangan said mockingly.

'I had to do it without rousing the durai's suspicions. It was not easy.'

'Are you trying to fool me? When the durai is inebriated, don't you fill up the half-empty bottle with water? You probably add the water used for cleaning the table! Be grateful for what you've got and push off.'

Samuel knew he could not try his tricks on Maistry.

Rangan tied up his bundle. He put on his newly-tailored coat and turban and left.

He had no intention of going to Maragathamalai. He had never wanted to share his wealth with anybody. Would it be wise to go there when his uncle, Lingayya, had fallen on bad times? Wouldn't his visit be like timely rain for the withering crops? He had even thought of going directly to Manikkalhatti, offering the silver coins and gifts to Paru's father and concluding the ceremony of making her his wife.

Two miles from the city limits, there was a strong chilly wind portending a heavy thundershower. He had never in all these twelve years gone beyond the city limits with the intention of visiting his hatti. He could not recognise the mountains and forests that he had crossed twelve years earlier on his way to Othai. Appappa! Though he had run away convinced that he would make a fortune, how many longings, difficulties and fears had he experienced on that journey!

With his brisk stride, he had covered quite a distance when it started pouring. His dhoti billowed in the strong breeze. Fearing that his bundle would get wet, he took shelter under a tree. A flash of lightning split the sky, followed by a clap of thunder. In front of his eyes, a conifer fell with a loud crash.

He remained beneath the tree, trembling with fear, nagged by doubt as to whether he had set out at an inauspicious hour. The path was deserted as it was raining. He had not even come across any of the rich men riding on ponies. He wished he had thought of hiring a horse and arriving at the hatti on horseback like a prince.

The rain, which had lashed furiously and filled the air with a fresh smell, stopped suddenly. He resumed walking. He crossed the valleys and climbed the hills till he reached some parched earth that had not seen rain. Branches of trees with dry leaves brushed against him. All of a sudden, waves of melodious music flowed, spread in ripples and flooded his ears, sending a thrill through him.

He stood still, as if shocked by the sensation. Who was creating such moving music, so much in tune with the pent-up yearning that had been smouldering in his heart for a long, long time?

Like a snake mesmerised by the snake charmer's *magudi*, his feet were irresistibly drawn to that voice.

There he sat, eyes half-closed, soaked to the skin, leaning on a rock. As Rangan drew near, it was evident that the singer had been drinking. Submerged in drink and music, he took no notice of Rangan.

In twelve years, his body had shrunk and withered. He had lost so much weight that his cheekbones jutted out. He was so emaciated that he could not possibly become any thinner. His appearance revealed the condition of his younger brother's household.

Even though Rangan was blinded by greed, could the love for his father that throbbed in every pore of his being be extinguished? That love now surged forth.

His eyes wet, Rangan threw his bundle down, sat by his father and touched his hand.

'Appa!... Appa!'

There was wonder in the half-open eyes. The music died in his throat.

'Is that you... you...'

Disbelief made him stutter.

'Yes Appa... I... am... Rangan... Rangan.'

The eyes shone brightly in their sunken sockets. 'Rangan... Rangan... are you really Rangan... Ranga...'

He gathered his son in his arms. Their faces touched. His son Rangan, on the threshold of adulthood! Yes, it was Rangan. Yes, the face was his. He could even see the resemblance to his own face. Yes, it was his son Rangan. His eyes gazed and gazed at his son with joy and an insatiable hunger. The next minute, he lifted his hands towards the sky in homage.

'Isa... What compassion! Ranga, I swear I was on my way to Othai. I couldn't walk more than half the distance. Look at my feet.'

Rangan's eyes filled with tears when his father showed him the soles of his feet. There were deep cracks in them. Had the fat drained out of his body, leaving his feet bone dry?

'I couldn't walk any more. What could I do? I sat here calling out to Isan for help. My voice reached His ears. He has brought you here! He has brought you here!'

Heedless of the pain in his feet, he got up and danced with joy. With tears streaming from his eyes, he hugged his son repeatedly, his happiness unbounded.

'Where were you all these years, Ranga? Your Chithappan kept assuring me that you were alive. I did not believe him!' Again, he looked skyward with folded palms.

'Why don't you wear these slippers? Let's go home.'

'No, Thambi, you wear them. Devar heard my plea and took pity on me. That's enough for me. Now I can walk for hours and hours.'

Though Rangan would have given anything to avoid this unexpected encounter, he feared that an unseen power had ordained it.

He had purposely set out on this little-used path and met the one person he did not want to meet.

In a moment, Rangan changed his plans. His father gave him news of the family and hatti as they walked together. Rangan told him about his job as maistry in the dairy. They neared the hatti.

The evening sun had bid farewell and Mother Nature was spreading her mantle of darkness. Grateful for the rains that had cooled the earth, Lingayya, wrapped in a blanket, was sitting in front of the house. He had borrowed a little money from the labbai to sow potato seeds. The principal and interest on the sum he had borrowed for his mother's funeral rites already burdened him. For every step that he took upwards, he seemed to slide two steps down. Life was a constant struggle for him.

After lighting the lamp and placing it in its niche, Madhi stood by his side.

'Will the date of this year's Deiva Habba[1] be fixed for the end of the month?' she asked.

'Why do you ask?'

'Our stock of grain will not last till then! How can we harvest the new crop before the festival? The Kurumban asked for money, we could give him only korali.'

Lingayya had no answer. Ever since his health had started failing, they had gone through troubled times and the lack of grain was nothing new to him. Why was Devar trying him all the time? Would a self-respecting man like him have to stoop to beg?

Darkness had descended. Only the forms of the passers-by were visible. 'Why are you sitting in the cold? The buffaloes have to be milked,' his wife prodded him gently.

Before he could get up, Madhan came in, swift as an arrow, and hugged him.

'By the grace of Devar, Ranga has returned. See, he is here. It's Rangan. I'm not lying.'

In the all-pervading darkness, all that could be seen of Rangan was a tall form in a coat and turban with a bundle tucked under his arm.

Lingayya looked up. His lips quivered as he tried to suppress a strong surge of emotion.

'Bring a light… a light,' shouted Madhan.

Lingayya remained still. When Rangan had been a child, he had carried him on his shoulders, cuddled him, bathed him, fed him milk and pampered him. And now after a gap of twelve years, here was the boy he had looked upon as a son, standing before him, tall as a mountain.

The courage that Rangan had displayed when he had met his father failed him when he was face-to-face with his uncle.

When he saw the figure in the light of the lamp held by Madhi, his false veneer of respectability was shaken. His heart,

[1]Deiva Habba is celebrated on a Monday in the month of '*Vaikasi*' or '*Ani*'. A single sheaf of tinai is cut first and offered to God and only after that could the crops be harvested.

which was filled with deceit and selfishness, was wracked with uneasiness when he met his uncle's piercing glance.

The hands that should have embraced him shot out and slapped him on his cheeks.

Madhi and Madhan shouted, 'Aiyo!' while Lingayya, his eyes bloodshot, screamed in rage, 'Why have you come? You thief. Get out. Don't stand before me. You don't belong to this house. Go… go away…'

For a moment, Madhan believed that his brother's senses had come unhinged by the shock and he tried to pacify him.

'Leave me alone.' Turning to Rangan, Lingayya continued his tirade, 'What did you take me for, you blackguard! I looked after you and fed you milk with these hands. You repaid me with treachery. So now you are wiping the white man's table. You Holaya, you low-caste fellow, eating meat and beef! Get out… go…'

Alternating between tears and passionate anger, he got up to pounce on Rangan. Madhi led him inside with great difficulty, while the crowd that had gathered at the doorstep stood in stunned silence.

Six

Rangan had never imagined that his uncle's welcome would be like this. Did he harbour the memory of the small misdeed committed by him years ago? Or was he perhaps jealous of Rangan's new-found wealth?

However, Rangammai's joy could not be contained. The minute Rangan brought his bundle into the house, she opened it and displayed its contents. Shiny glass bangles, silks, things they had never set eyes on before.

Rangammai immediately draped her child in silk and admired him. 'Are all these made in Othai?' she asked. Her husband was busy eating pieces of cake and shoving them into the child's mouth as well.

When the villagers had witnessed the uncle's wrath, they had all melted away! What kind of welcome was that? Rangan seethed and boiled inwardly.

'Rangi, should we not cook a feast to welcome Anna? Make rice and kuzhambu,' said Madhan.

Where was the rice to cook? She ran out of the house. Her feet automatically took her to Kariamallar's house.

'Our Rangannan has returned from Othai. He has brought silks and cakes for all of us. He has bought land and planted potatoes in it. Please let me have some rice, Annan is used to eating rice,' she burbled excitedly.

'I believe Chithappan shouted at him?' Kariamallar's eldest daughter asked her.

Merely saying, 'Oh! That's because he's not well,' she took a measure of rice and ran back. She started a fire and made rice and kuzhambu.

Rangan was infuriated that no one from Krishnan's house had bothered to come and see him and listen to his boastful tales. 'Is Krishnan not at home?' he asked. His father had told him that Krishnan had returned home after getting a degree, but had failed to mention that he wanted to marry Paru.

As though the thought had just struck him, Madhan said, 'You know, Krishnan is going to marry Paru. He was here till yesterday. He just left for Manikkalhatti,' thus pouring oil on fire.

'What?! Marry Paru?'

Alarmed at Rangan's boiling anger and bulging eyes, Madhan hastily added, 'I believe Paru herself is for it. It is said that the marriage will be celebrated as soon as the Devar festival is over.'

'How can that be possible? After all, there is someone who has a claim on her. How much money will Krishnan offer? I'll give more.'

The father opened the bottle of superior liquor brought by his son and took a swig.

'What are you saying, Thambi?' he asked with a foolish smile.

'What am I saying? How can Paru marry an outsider? Even if Jogi is languishing in the temple, am I not here? How can Krishnan marry a girl who is mine by right?' The spark of jealousy that Rangan had carried with him since childhood towards Kariamallar's family now found an occasion to flare up.

Madhan gaped. Was sheer youthful bravado making this youngster challenge the all-powerful Kariamallar's family or had he accumulated that much wealth?

'Appa, listen. I'll go in person to Manikkalhatti maman either today or tomorrow to ask his consent to bring Paru home,' said Rangan.

'Thambi, is Paru the only girl around? Aren't there other girls in the world for you?' asked his father, his voice slurred with alcohol.

Rangan's pride was piqued.

'You talk about Krishnan's degree! What has he achieved? I ran away twelve years ago with nothing. I have learnt to stand on my own feet and earn a living. Can he earn his living? What if it is Kariamallar or any other big shot? Why should this Rangan give up his claim?' he demanded.

In his anger he slapped the child who was crushing the silk, grabbed it from him and carefully folded it. Rangammai's face fell.

The only one who relished the feast prepared by Rangammai was her husband. Madhan, who was in a drunken stupor, hardly tasted it. Rangan felt envy and rage burning within him; it was as though he were facing defeat.

How could Paru marry Krishnan? In what way was Krishnan superior to him? Would Paru forget the man to whom she rightfully belonged?

All night long, he tossed and turned, his questions unanswered. Wealth could not buy a warm welcome or fulsome praise. Wouldn't he even get the girl of his choice? He had already sent word through Bheeman. Bheeman had also spoken as though he supported him.

Could there have been a connection between Krishnan and Paru for a long time? What then?

Haunted by these questions, he could not spend the day peacefully at Maragathamalai. After the morning meal, he left for Manikkalhatti.

Afternoon had given way to evening when he reached the hatti. The sky was cloudy. The people in the hatti did not recognise adult Rangan dressed in a coat and turban till he was almost upon them. Wide-eyed with curiosity, women and children came close to have a good look at him.

'Oh! Madhanna's son. Aren't you Rangan? How you have grown! Are you well?' A chorus of voices greeted him, while the elders and the women encircled him.

Among them was Krishnan's mother. Hearing the excited babble, Krishnan came out of his house; an open book in one hand, gold rings on his fingers, full-sleeved shirt.

Disengaging himself from the group, Rangan stared at Krishnan. Krishnan's eyes were calm.

'What, Krishna? Don't you recognise me? Are you well?' he enquired, swallowing his jealousy. A smile played on Krishnan's lips. He said, 'So, at last you have remembered your folks.' At that moment, Paru appeared, followed by Girijai. Rangan was bowled over.

Adeyappa! She dazzled the eyes like lightning! What a rounded, youthful body!

Her thundu was slightly disarrayed. Quickly covering her shoulder blades which were like bamboo shoots, she laughed gaily.

'The runaway anna. Come, Ranganna. Are you well? You ran away without a word and you have come back without warning.'

Her tone was mocking. Rangan was stung.

'One doesn't need to inform Maman's daughter before returning. Isn't that so, Krishnan?' he said, swallowing his anger.

Krishnan did not like the tone of his voice one bit. Culture could be imbibed only by mingling with people of learning. Rangan might have learnt to speak English by mixing with butlers and servants, but could that have taught him to be polite to people?

'Am I not right, Krishnan?' insisted Rangan.

'What am I supposed to say?' Krishnan's tone was indifferent.

'Don't tell me you've nothing to say. Everyone is talking admiringly of Krishnan and his B.A. degree.'

Krishnan did not reply.

'Are you coming from Othai, Thambi?' an old woman enquired.

'Yes, I've planted potatoes. They have sprouted with the first showers,' said Rangan looking directly at Krishnan.

'Paru, don't just stand there. Even if your ammai and appan have gone to the fields, is this the way you look after guests?' prompted a young girl.

'She is perhaps stunned to see the man who has a claim over her,' another girl remarked mischievously.

'Look at that, Krishnan! They imply that I have come as a rival!' said Rangan.

To a man of refinement like Krishnan, the conversation was distasteful. Meanwhile, Paru's grandfather and parents had hurried back. They stood around Rangan and rained questions on him.

Krishnan tried to slip away. Paru's grandfather would not let him go. With one arm around him and the other around Rangan, he led them both into the house. Paru had already gone inside.

'Thatha, I'm asking you openly. I met Bheeman, didn't he inform you? When Paru is already mine by right, is it fair for someone else to claim her as a wife?' asked Rangan bluntly.

'Who said that, Thambi? It was decided long ago that Girijai was for Jogi and Paru ..'

'Amma,' a red-faced Paru interrupted sharply.

Rangan's face fell. Krishnan's brightened. The grandfather looked at both of them. He smiled.

Girijai came in with tumblers and a vessel of buttermilk.

'Have some buttermilk,' Paru's father said

Krishnan could not bear to be put on par with Rangan. When fixing a girl's marriage, should the decision be based solely on a man's claim on her? To his evolved mind, the marriage bond was an eternal one, never to be loosened or severed.

There was no doubt, that in their community, the expectations from a marriage were very high. The Badagas believed that the marriage bond was like a loosely strung garland of flowers. If the string was tightened to hold the flowers in place, the flowers withered. So the flowers had to be loosely tied so that they remained fresh. That was the reason why the rules governing marriage were not very strict. But when two hearts were naturally bound by love, there was no necessity for rules. In an ideal marriage, the bride brought prosperity to the house she had entered and kept its flag flying.

Krishnan felt that people should not be unmindful of these lofty ideals and should not take advantage of the leniency in the marriage rules to break their bonds for selfish reasons. He firmly believed that the conventions that governed marriage were necessary if one wished to take a wife and live in harmony with her. He wanted to put his ideals into practice.

He sensed Paru's love for him and reciprocated it in full measure. Why was Rangan behaving in this obstructive manner?

While Krishnan was preoccupied with these thoughts, Rangan was bragging about himself. He even hinted that he could offer as much as five hundred silver coins as bride price.

Paru's grandfather, deep in thought, kept nodding his head. When Rangan paused momentarily, he said authoritatively, 'Now... the question is not one of money. You'll give enough and Krishan will not offer less. Let there not be competition about money. Why don't we have a trial of strength?'

'That's a good idea. There is no better entertainment than two men locked in a trial of strength for a girl,' Paru's father agreed.

'That's right,' seconded his wife.

Just then, the voice of Madhi, who had come in through the kitchen and ogamane, rang out. 'There are not just two, but three men. Doesn't Jogi also have a right to Paru's hand, Anna?'

Krishnan looked up, startled. Rangan stared at Madhi, who was standing on the threshold.

'Ade, when did you come, Thangachi?' Her brother asked her.

'Just at the right moment. Jogi will leave the temple in ten days. He is also in the contest,' she said firmly.

'Tell us what this trial of strength is all about, Thatha?' Rangan demanded impatiently.

'Fifteen days from today, on Monday, the one who lifts the round stone in front of the Maragathamalai Hethappa temple and takes two steps forward, wins the contest.'

The old man spoke calmly.

Krishnan grew red in the face.

Rangan crowed inwardly, 'Hm, Paru is mine. That fellow Jogi on a single meal a day will be as thin as a stick. Krishnan is a puny fellow. He blushes like a woman.' Following this train of thought, he turned to Paru who stood there, her dark eyes fixed pleadingly on her grandfather.

The next moment, her eyes, still wearing the very same expression, shifted to Krishnan. It was then that Rangan swore to himself with determination, 'If I don't make you mine, I am not Rangan.'

Seven

For a long time, Jogi could not believe what he had heard. Nothing ever happened according to plan. In his life, at every step, unforeseen events had proved that all was God's will! He was given the right to milk and also the right to serve in the temple in a most unexpected manner. In the same way…

Long after Periappan had left after conveying the news to him, he felt like a man awakened from a long dream; a dream in which the sudden appearance of the blazing sun had opened his eyes to the unreal nature of his visions. The belief that Paru belonged to him had been somehow deeply rooted in him. Whenever he had thought of a life with her, he had felt as happy as a plant in bloom. It was as if his uncle had cruelly axed the plant when he had told him that Krishnan was to marry Paru.

Jogi, however, was by upbringing magnanimous and honest. When the plant was axed, he stood stupefied, but not for long. He tried to console himself in many ways. When Paru herself had set her heart on Krishnan, what was the use of mourning? Krishnan was, after all, superior to him. He was a wealthy young man. He was the first in his community to go to college and earn a degree. How could Jogi put himself on the same plane as Krishnan? If Paru was dear to him, his happiness lay in seeing her and her children prosper.

Just as he would have trained an animal with effort, he had calmed his mind and had been at peace with himself when his uncle, Madhan, brought the news of Rangan's visit to Manikkalhatti. Madhan kept back the bit about Lingayya's reaction to Rangan.

The next day, when Lingayya's fever became worse, the panchayat met hurriedly and took the decision to release Jogi from the temple precincts. The fire was put out. Jogi became a free man and returned home. The panchayat did not stop to consider whether the Keezhmalai boy who replaced him was suitable.

Jogi's rapturous feelings when he left the temple, where he had been doing penance for many years, to set foot on the ground where he had played happily as a small child, were indescribable. Every house in the hatti had changed. His own house—its newness undimmed when he had left—now looked dilapidated with the limewash peeling off. Only two buffaloes were left in the cowshed. The edumane of the house was where his father lay all the time. The mortar and pestle to grind medicinal paste was at his bedside. The chest which once overflowed with grain now stood empty. The madi clothes that his father used to wear in the hagottu still hung there, but were now filthy. The stove, normally spotlessly clean, had not been mopped for many days. The castor oil pot, coated with grease and dust, lay among a lot of unwanted things.

His heart bled. In twelve years, the once prosperous household had become impoverished.

Jogi came and stood by the sallow anaemic form of his father. The father looked up at his son, eyes glistening with tears.

He had thought, 'I will depute my son to serve Hiriya Udayar. My debts will be cleared. My house will prosper.'

Was his house prosperous? No. The illness had pushed the toiler into bed. But now, his son was home. Jogi was home. He heaved a sigh of relief. His heart swelled and he became short of breath.

Jogi, his son, stood before him. Though lean, he was sinewy. His once white body had now acquired the redness of the earth. When the father cried, 'Jogi!' and clasped his son's hands, tears flowed unrestrained from his eyes.

'I've been reduced to depending on charity for food, my son. Unable to toil and sow, I have to ask others for food, Jogi.' The son's hands were soaked with the father's tears. With those hands, he wiped the tears away. 'I am home, Appa. The skies have not fallen. I have my hands. I am your son. I am here to till the fields. I will grow enough to feed a thousand men, Appa. I am your son, your son.'

Shedding tears of joy, the father got up from his bed and enfolded his son in his arms. 'You have served Ayyan. You will have no worries,' he blessed.

Madhi went near him and said, 'Bless him that he may lift the round stone like a ball of kali and bring Paru home. When I went the other day to gather firewood, I went to Manikkalhatti. I went to demand boldly. 'Has the promise that Paru will marry my son been forgotten at the sight of silver coins?' By the grace of Devar, my father spoke of a trial of strength. I said Jogi would also contest, that he would also be there to lift the round stone at the Hethappa temple. Give him your blessing.'

Lingayya knew about the contest. He also knew that Madhi had tried to postpone the day of the contest so that Jogi could participate in it. But Jogi did not know the whole story.

Lingayya did not reply. Rangan, the Rangan whom he had brought up like his own son, who had strayed from the path of honesty—how could anything good happen to him? Though born in a community that considered milking as a sacred duty and milk as sacrosanct, was he working honestly as a maistry in the dairy farm? Didn't his eyes betray that he stole milk and sold it on the sly to make money? If he had been leading a blameless life, would he not have approached his uncle and made peace? Lingayya would have been at peace if Rangan had stayed away. Yet, once he had seen Rangan, his loving heart had begun contemplating means by which he could make him change his ways. His face brightened at the thought.

Lingayya thought, 'Jogi is like gold. Whomsoever he marries, he would turn into gold. But Rangan! He needs a fine girl as a life companion to transform him into unalloyed gold. At birth he lost his mother who would have loved him and supported him. He has now come of his own accord to marry Paru. Let him not be disappointed this time also. Let her come home as Rangan's wife. Let him shed his crooked ways.' However, he kept his own counsel and concealed his inner turmoil.

'Why are you silent? You never opened your mouth even once to wish our family well. Don't you want to give your whole-hearted blessings to your son? Do you know how I agonised all these years when I thought of my son sleeping on just a piece of jute? You have sacrificed this family's prosperity for the sake of your brother's all these years. This time I will not give in.'

The outpouring of her tormented heart shook Lingayya. After entering his house, she had never demanded anything for herself all these years. Was it not his duty to give his blessings to Jogi? To utter one word to gladden a mother's heart?

His hand shook as he placed it on his son's head and blessed, 'May Paru come to our home. May the stone be light to your touch.'

It was much later that Jogi came to know the details of the contest.

Madhi had cooked a feast rich in ghee and milk. Till then, they had never partaken of a feast without inviting the people from the opposite house. That day they did not do so. Madhi longed to see father and son eat from the same vattil.

Lingayya came and sat in the ogamane to please Madhi. In the centre of the shining vattil, there was golden-coloured sweet pongal cooked in milk, kuzhambu with beans and potatoes and chutney made of greens.

Lingayya had no taste for food. Jogi was shocked to find that his father did not swallow even one handful of what he had taken from the vattil, but kept staring at him while he ate the indescribably delicious food cooked lovingly by Madhi.

'Appa, you haven't eaten a single morsel.'

'A whole kurinji-span has gone by since he ate properly. If he relishes his food, he will become alright. They say it is all because of a spell cast by the wicked Kurumbas. I've repeatedly complained to the village elders. I wonder whom they were planning to harm, but the curse has fallen on us,' said Madhi.

The food in Jogi's palm did not reach his mouth. Constant fever had sucked the vitality out of his father's blood. Was it the Kurumbas' doing? Why should they do it to his father, who had never meant any harm to anybody? Had he robbed their honeycomb? Had he taken their harvest without paying for it?

'Amma, has our Kurumba priest stopped coming?' he asked.

'A fortnight ago he brought honey. I took some honey for medicine from him and paid him with samai and potatoes grown by you in the temple land. He then said that he would perform *poosai* to the Gods and chant mantras. I am a woman, what more can I do?' she said.

Jogi made up his mind. Marriage was not his priority. Asking the Kurumbas to exorcise the spell they had cast on his father was his first duty.

Around three that afternoon, the sun peeped out from behind the clouds and smiled gently. He changed his clothes to go out. He took a silver coin from his mother.

To reach the Kurumba settlement he had to take the path that descended from Manikkalhatti and entered the forest. Most Kurumba settlements were inside the forest. Though they lived in low-lying areas where water stagnated, they never seemed to fall victim to the fever. He wondered why.

Many years had passed since his last visit to the Kurumba settlement. Even the previous time, he had gone in search of a cure for his father's illness.

The jungle path had not changed. The once fallow lands were newly covered with rows of potato plants, making Mother Mountain look as though she were wrapped in a skirt. Here and there the landscape was dotted with tea bushes. Potatoes were food. But tea? It was money. What was more important? Food? Or money?

Walking rapidly, he reached the bend in the Kumari River below Manikkalhatti. The path on the other side of the hill led to Kothai. One could spend the whole day gazing at the beauty of the Kumari River as it splashed and gurgled, twisting and turning between the two hills. The slopes were covered with thorn bushes and the scattered keno and cassia trees were in full bloom. The blue kurinji was everywhere as if to say, 'There is no place without me'.

Entering the forest, Jogi followed the single track beside the river. He hoped that Paru would be there, gathering twigs with the girls from Manikkalhatti. The path suddenly turned away from the river. At that point, the river curved and cascaded over a rock. Below that was the whirlpool that had brought Krishnan and Paru together.

Jogi climbed higher as he wished to view the waterfall from above. Suddenly he stopped in consternation. He felt as if a bee had stung him. Beneath a keno tree in full bloom... what did he see! It was not a dream!

Jogi wiped his eyes. He looked again and again without blinking.

The scene that met his eyes hardly ten feet away could not have been an illusion! *As* he watched, the evening sun bathed them in light.

Averting his eyes from them, he turned his gaze on the tree. Minigey vine twined itself around the tree in a close embrace.

There was no doubt about it. It was Krishnan in a yellow woollen shirt with a collar. A white cloth was wrapped like a turban around his head. Jogi could see only Krishnan's face. He was smiling. There was a touch of femininity in his face. Undoubtedly handsome, he was a good match for Paru, who stood looking up at him.

To lift the round stone was no problem for Jogi. For years, the young men of the hatti had been trying to lift the stone in sport to toughen up and test their strength. There was a knack to it. The oval-shaped stone had to be turned over with hands crossed like a chain in order to dislodge it. On innumerable occasions, Jogi had rolled the stone and lifted it two feet above the ground. Till his mother had mentioned it, he had not realised that it would be child's play for him to win the contest.

However, what he saw now disturbed him. Would it do any good to win Paru, when it meant separating two people in love?

Suddenly, a shadow crossed Krishnan's face. Their throats seemed clogged by sorrow as they stood there, oblivious to the passage of time. Jogi was also in the same frame of mind.

'Paru?' said Krishnan.

'Don't you have faith in me, Paru? Don't you believe I'll win?'

Jogi thought that Paru made no reply.

'Our true love will not fail. Just you see, Rangan will not be able to lift the stone.'

'How do you know?'

'He's not the type to do hard physical work.'

'How could he have saved money if he has not worked?'

'His eyes reveal that he is an out-and-out cheat. He has used coolies to work the land. God alone knows what tricks he has practised to pay them.'

'My fear is that he'll try some tricks now. What if he resorts to black magic to lift the stone?'

Krishnan laughed aloud. It was not genuine mirth. He laughed so as to dispel Paru's fears, but it was like trying to disperse clouds by blowing hard on them.

'Do you believe in all this hocus-pocus, Paru? It's all just an eye-wash. Whoever comes between us will go away defeated. Tomorrow I'll go to Maragathamalai. I'll spend the night on the temple thinnai and practise lifting the stone,' he said.

It would not be true to say that a spark of jealousy had not scorched Jogi. It had, but only for a moment. He conquered it by changing his line of thought. 'Paru is like my younger sister who died a long time ago,' he told himself firmly, and touched his eyelids with his fingertip in silent prayer.

His mother wished to see Paru light the lamp in their house and take over its responsibilities. So she had ensured that he would compete. It had also been his wish. But the moment he had seen and heard them, he had become a new man. The desire to possess her was supplanted by another wish.

He could withdraw from the contest. But Rangan? How could he be eliminated? Would he resort to tricks as Paru feared? When Krishnan practised lifting the stone at night, should he, Jogi, show him how?

What irony! What kind of contest was this in which one competitor helped the other to win?

Jogi left as silently as he had come, crossed the river and reached the other bank.

Eight

Jogi met the Kurumba priest on the path, even before he reached the settlement.

'Appada! Isn't it only today that you left the Ayyan temple? Come! Come!' he welcomed Jogi.

'I was on my way to meet you,' Jogi said and sat beneath a tree.

'If you had sent word, wouldn't I have come? What's the matter?'

'Why don't you also sit down? I have come for a cure for Ayyan's fever. It has lasted almost one kurinji-span,' said Jogi.

'That's the recurring fever.'

'Yes, his entire body has turned yellow. He hardly eats. Ammai has tried all sorts of medicines. Whom has Ayyan hurt? He never harboured hard feelings even against those who harmed him. How can he survive if he cannot eat anything? Look here, I beseech you. Whether it is black magic or a spell, I'll give you five measures of tinai and samai. Relieve him of his illness. How much longer can he remain so weak?' pleaded Jogi.

'Aiyo! Don't talk like that. I swear by our deity, *Jadasami*, none of us has cast a spell on him. We're not mad to do such a thing. Don't ever think like that.'

'Then, can you cure him of this debilitating fever?'

'As soon as your mother spoke about it, we performed a special poosai for his recovery. It's the recurring fever. It'll be like that.'

'Whatever it is, I believe you know how to brew medicine to cure it. At least tell me what to do?'

The priest smiled ingratiatingly. Guessing correctly, Jogi gave him a silver coin.

'Wait here, I'll be back,' said the Kurumban, and disappeared into the forest. The generation that would be sceptical of black magic was yet to be born.

Many thoughts crossed Jogi's mind. For generations, his people had believed that the forest-dwelling Kurumbas' magic spells could grant them their wishes. At the time of sowing and harvesting, they were the first to be honoured with gifts of grain. Would their ancestors have done it without a reason? Were they such fools? The Kurumbas must surely possess some special powers. Why not test it?

He made up his mind in a flash. The priest returned with something hidden in the folds of his clothes. They were roots, freshly dug up and tied in small bundles. Would he disclose what they were?

'What root is it?'

'Please don't ask me. I have recited incantations to make it effective. Make a brew and give it to your father every day. In time his fever will go.'

Jogi carefully hid the roots in his clothes. Tentatively he began, 'I wonder if it has reached your ears? Ten days from now there is going to be a trial of strength. The contest involves lifting the round stone in front of the Maragathamalai Hethappa temple.' He paused.

Before he could elaborate on this, the priest said, 'Yes. I heard about it this morning. It is a contest for the hand of the girl from Manikkalhatti and you're also… carry on.'

'I've come to you for another favour,' said Jogi.

What would a contestant wish for? Obviously to win and claim the girl's hand in marriage.

'Don't worry, I'll give you a root over which I have cast a spell. Tie it around your wrist. The round stone will be as light as a puff of wind in your hands. Jadasami will be with you,' said the Kurumban.

Jogi was in a dilemma. What would the Kurumban think if Jogi told him that it was not for him? Should he ask him to pray for Krishnan's victory?

'You… what I'm saying is that whomsoever she wishes…'

The Kurumba interrupted him. 'Don't worry about that. The girl will seek you out. Like a bee drawn to a flower, her heart will turn to you.'

'That's not what I wish for. All I ask is this; do something to ensure that the one whom Paru loves wholeheartedly will lift the stone. It will be a tragedy if she loves one and another wins,' said Jogi.

The Kurumba was amazed. Did such men really exist?

'Why are you silent?' Jogi asked.

'If you wish, I'll give you a root made potent by my spell. If she keeps it in her hand, she'll get the man she desires.'

'Will you give it to me now? If you come to the hatti tomorrow, I'll give you a silver rupee for it.'

'Now? Impossible!'

'I'll come back tomorrow. Keep this matter to yourself.' Jogi took leave of him.

As he made his way home, the waxing moon was moving majestically across the sky. Changing into madi clothes, he milked the buffaloes and said his prayers. He then made the brew with his own hands and took it to his father.

'Did you see our land, Jogi? The soil to the right has turned red and become infertile,' said Lingayya.

'We'll soon make it black, Appa. My only aim right now is to see that you recover,' said the son

The next day, when Jogi tied a measure of grain from the temple land in a small bundle and set out, Madhi enquired, 'Are you going to Manikkalhatti, my son?'

'No, Amma. I'm going to the Kurumba settlement. Could you spare me another quarter of a rupee?'

He met the Kurumba priest in the same place and gave him the grain and the money. The priest gave him a root that was two inches long.

Thanking him, Jogi tucked it safely in the folds of his clothes and took the path to Manikkalhatti. Near the waterfall, in fact, in the very same spot as on the previous day, stood Paru. He felt his heart lurch. Paru! He had not been able to get a glimpse of her face the previous day. Krishnan was away in Maragathamalai, so what was Paru doing there alone? For whom was she waiting? This was the meeting that should have made his dreams come true; the long-awaited meeting that should have lifted the veil between them, giving their yearning hearts a chance to rejoice. But now, it was a meeting where he would have to steel his turbulent heart.

Under the pretext of gathering firewood, was she waiting for Krishnan? Why was she there, all alone, without her friends?

Had she seen him from a distance? Realising that he was approaching her, she pretended to be very busy tying the bundle of twigs. Jogi stood where he was. Many, many years had gone by since she had last seen this man who could claim her as his bride. He was now her lover's rival. What did she want to tell him? Why did the surprise in her eyes turn to tenderness?

Just for an instant. Then her large black eyes did not dare to meet his.

'Paru!'

Speaking in a gruff voice, he took out the precious object that had been safely wrapped in a minigey leaf.

'Wear this around your neck or waist. You will get the husband you desire, Paru.'

When his words, uttered in a faltering voice, fell on her ears, she looked up startled. He did not have the sheen of prosperity like Krishnan. His cheeks were not rounded. But the glow on his face was something she had never seen on anyone else's. It confounded her. Why had he appeared suddenly? What was he saying?

She was in a daze. Jogi spoke in a tranquil voice, 'I got this specially from the Kurumban. Paru, you are my younger sister. I am competing for the sake of my mother, but I will not exert myself. I know to whom you have lost your heart. Take this. Your beloved will win the contest.'

Her dark eyes were damp as she stretched both her hands to receive the root. She rested it reverentially on her closed eyelids. The load on her mind seemed to have evaporated. Light in spirit and heart as never before, Jogi made his way towards Maragathamalai.

Nine

The festive air in tiny Maragathamalaihatti that day was similar to the atmosphere in the capital of Panchala, when princes from all over had come together, hoping to hit the fish-shaped target and claim Princess Panchali as a bride. Three young bulls were to take part in a trial of strength to win a maiden's hand. Gathered in the sacred precincts of the temple to watch the fun were not only the elderly panchayat members but also friends from neighbouring hattis and acquaintances who had heard about it. It was a unique opportunity for Kariamallar to sing the praises of his grandson who had done so brilliantly in his studies. He had gladly volunteered to feed all those present.

Paru's grandfather was in high spirits, as though he had regained his youth. Whenever he saw young maidens, he teased them mischievously, 'Hey girls, bring fifty young men if you can. I'll take them on, lift the stone and carry you away.' Excited by the feast and crowds, Rangan's father sang paeans of praise about all three suitors, Krishnan, Rangan and Jogi. To make the onlookers feel that all three of them were equally deserving, the elders who had arranged the contest were impartial in their praise of them.

Before the day of the contest, Rangan had paid two or three visits to the hatti. The contest was on a Monday. He arrived by Sunday bearing numerous gifts for the bride. He had faith in his own strength. During the days preceding the contest, he had been on a nourishing diet of eggs, fish and meat and had practised lifting weights. He believed that Krishnan, who ate samai and rice, would not be strong because he lived on vegetarian food. Jogi was beneath his notice. Emaciated fellow, who had become desiccated by eating just once a day! Rangan had no doubt about his impending victory. He wore a Glasgow mull dhoti, a shirt and a cap. He had expensive liquor at hand to boost his spirits before he lifted the stone. Krishnan was as confused as Rangan was cocksure.

On one hand, Krishnan was sure of Paru's love for him. On the other, he was confused by what Paru had told him about Jogi and the root he had given her. Were Jogi's intentions truly altruistic? Or was it a ploy? Contrary to his belief that it was Rangan who would resort to black magic, it had turned out to be Jogi. The question was not whether or not the spell would work, but whether his intentions were honourable. Though Krishnan was mature and rational thanks to his education, his inner turmoil caused lines to appear and disappear on his broad forehead. How could he look cheerful when he was so perturbed? How could he be full of enthusiasm?

Paru was naive. Placing her full faith in the Kurumban's root, she walked around proudly, confident that no one could equal Krishnan. Almost everyone from her village had gathered in Maragathamalai that morning to watch the fun. The sun, accompanied by a light drizzle and a gentle breeze, slowly swept across the sky to see the spectacle. The only ones absent were the young women who were forbidden by custom to step into that sacred place.

In deference to his mother's wishes, Jogi had fasted the night before. In the morning he had bathed, smeared sandalwood paste on his forehead and stepped into the maidan like a streak of light. His father, not wanting to miss the event, was seated in the first row.

At the appointed time, Paru's grandfather stood up and said, 'Friends, only in stories have we heard of *swayamvarams*, where a princess could choose a husband from among many suitors. I feel proud that you have come in large numbers today to witness this unusual spectacle, where three men are going to compete for the hand of one young maiden. It was in jest that I had said, 'The one who lifts the stone wins the girl!' But a grand competition is really taking place. I'll tell you what the rules of the contest are. The contestant has to roll the stone, lift it with his hands, straighten up and take two steps forward. It has to be witnessed by the members of the panchayat. He who rests the stone on the ground or drags it, loses the contest. If no one is able to achieve this, the one who lifts the stone the highest will be declared the winner. I think all three contestants will accept the conditions.'

The crowd noisily voiced its assent. When the uproar had subsided, Jogi was the first to be invited to the trial of strength. All eyes turned towards him as he stood next to his sick and frail father.

Jogi came forward, removed his turban and paid obeisance to God, the spectators and the members of the panchayat. He masked his true intentions with a defiant and aggressive stance. Posing as though he were keen on winning the maiden's hand, he walked towards the stone embedded in a corner of the field.

The excitement among the young girls, who were forbidden entry into the temple yard, was at fever pitch. Some watched from a distance, others stood on tiptoe. Some came running to Paru who was sitting in the edumane of her uncle's house. They teased her and giggled, pretending that they had come with news. Concealing her impatience, Paru sat blushing while the girls teased her. She was unshaken in her belief that her lover would be victorious.

Sounds of clapping, deafening shouts and laughter drifted from the temple yard, making Paru's heart beat faster.

'Who's it? Who's it?' In alarm, she peeped out. A girl taunted laughingly, 'Jogi was the first to try. He has lifted…'

'Ah!'

Words stuck in her throat. Her face darkened; her eyes wore a glazed look. Another girl rushed in with fresh news. 'Jogianna could not lift it. It's now Krishnan Anna's turn,' she whispered and sped back.

Appa! One load off her mind. Jogianna would not have lifted the stone. He had served in the temple. Would he lie?

Touching the root, which she had tied to the bead necklace tucked away in the mundu covering her chest, she prayed fervently. She visualised the stone that she had seen as a child, and imagined it being rolled and lifted by Krishnan. His face, which already had a touch of femininity, would redden, the veins on his forehead would stand out. Had he lifted the stone?

She seemed to hear a great uproar and applause. No, she was mistaken, there was no sound of clapping, only a great uproar. Would none of her friends come to her with the news? Losing patience, she brushed aside all inhibitions and peeped out of the front door.

Had Krishnan been able to lift the stone?

No, the stone was testing his strength to the utmost. How could those soft hands, which were only accustomed to turning pages, gain strength in the ten days he had been handling the stone? How could they suddenly become powerful? Jogi's defeat was proof of his good intentions. Now it was Paru's love that spurred him on. Face scarlet, struggling to breathe, beads of perspiration dotting his forehead, he managed to get a grip on the stone.

An inch, a hand-span. 'Bale! bale! Krishna!' Vociferous cries of encouragement and shouts split his eardrums. He bent and raised the stone above the ground, but he could not straighten up. The weight was crushing his legs, besides which his bent elbows constricted his breathing.

What was he doing? Was this love? A contest? A plot? A trial that would squeeze his life out? Was Krishnan, well-educated and refined, going to lose his life? Aiyo, what foolishness! Was a maiden's love worth all that much?

'It is. I will win her,' he resolved silently. But he could not straighten up while holding on to the stone. He staggered and fell and the stone slipped out of his hands.

'Aiyo!' Kariamallar ran towards him, alarmed. The stone which had slipped out, fell into the pit and became embedded there.

Kariamallar gathered Krishnan in his arms. An agitated crowd surrounded them. There was chaos, with some of them sprinkling water on him and others making anxious enquiries.

Krishnan stood up abruptly. 'Go away all of you. I'm all right, Thatha.' As a shame-faced Krishnan walked away, his pride injured, he could hear Rangan cackling. His contemptuous look seemed to say, 'He fell down like a girl. He is fit for nothing.' Even Jogi found Rangan's reaction distasteful.

Paru's grandfather quietened the crowd and invited Rangan to step forward.

Ignorant of the happenings in the temple yard, Paru's heart flickered like the flame of a lamp. There was no one with her. Everyone had heartlessly left her alone. Had her beloved won? Or had he not? Victory or defeat, she should have known by now. Why hadn't she said firmly, 'I don't want a contest! I don't want a trial of strength! He's the one I love. Ask the others to go away.' No one had any valid reason to dislike or oppose her choice. Words spoken in jest had made her a prize in a contest.

Yet, she would win her heart's desire. The Kurumban's root was infallible. If she were fated not to get her heart's desire, why should Jogi have taken the trouble to give her this talisman? Everything would happen according to Devar's will!

Aha! What uproar! What thunderous applause! Her heart leaped. Her friends came rushing in.

'The one to lift the stone was that annan.'

'Didn't I say so?'

'I knew it all along.'

'Why don't they understand my agony and come out with the name of the winner?' thought Paru.

'Paru is going to be a rich woman,' said one.

'Not only a rich woman! A grand lady who will be going to Othai,' said another.

Jogi and his mother came back with grim faces. There was not a vestige of joy in Jogi's face. So who wore the garland of victory?

'Who is it?' asked Paru, her heart in her mouth.

'Come on. Let his name resound in her ears!' The loud burst of laughter increased her annoyance.

In the middle of this tumult, Rangan, wearing a blue and yellow garland, his eyes glinting with triumphant and mocking laughter, strode towards her house, accompanied by Rangammai, his father and others.

She felt the Kurumban's root burn her breast. That deceiving sinner Jogi! Had he plotted for the sake of Rangan? Betrayer! She wanted desperately to flee immediately to Manikkalhatti, but her legs gave way. She could only sit wearily on the floor.

Ten

The Kurumban's root had apparently cured his father's fever. Jogi had found that the fever was abating and loosening its grip on his father's ailing body. So he had been confident that the contest would bring Paru and her lover together. It had not happened.

Rangan had won though he could not take the two mandatory steps with the stone towards the panchayat members. When Krishnan had tried to stand up, the stone had slipped from his grasp and he had staggered backwards and fallen. Moaning and groaning, Rangan had lifted it off the ground and stood upright. That was all! It was decided that he was the victor.

The wretched Kurumban had duped Jogi. The stone which had fallen had flattened the garden of love. How could he face Krishnan? How could he look Paru in the eye? His mind had been whirling with unhappy thoughts, but at last the truth was clear to him.

The Kurumban had given him a bitter medicinal root for the fever. It had entered the bloodstream and cured the illness. How stupid of him to have ascribed magical powers to a mere root! Why had wisdom not dawned on him earlier? He should have gone ahead boldly and stopped the contest for Paru's sake.

Not having the heart to participate in the festivities around him, he made his way alone to the cowshed. Once her son had been defeated, Madhi had not wished to see anyone else win. She had gone to the fields.

In the house opposite, Rangammai, with the help of those who had accompanied Paru from Manikkalhatti, busied herself in preparing a feast.

Leaning on his stick, Lingayya went looking for Jogi. Finding only Paru and a few others in the edumane, he went to the cowshed.

As he had expected, he found a sad-faced Jogi there. Should Jogi feel shattered because of a mere girl? He gently raised his son's chin, 'Jogi!'

In a listless tone Jogi replied, 'What, Appa?'

'Are you unhappy, Jogi?'

'Why should I be unhappy?'

'Your face gives you away. But doesn't Rangan have the first claim to Paru?' his father said with a gentle smile.

'Mm! Even if he has the right, it is unfair and we should stop the marriage,' said Jogi, lips trembling.

Lingayya was shocked. 'What happened was by Devar's grace. I always wished for a good daughter-in-law for my brother's house. I prayed that his son should take on the responsibility of the family and show an interest in the land. I was anxious that the family should not decline and become useless like infertile red soil. Thanks to Hiriya Udayar, a good girl like Paru has come into their family. Should you give room to jealousy in your heart, Jogi?' His fingers ruffled Jogi's hair soothingly.

'You don't know the truth, Appa. I'm not jealous. Thanks to the blessings of Hiriya Udayar, I constantly try to keep my mind pure, like soil which has been prepared by clearing it of thorns and stones. But you have separated two united hearts. You have separated Krishnan and Paru. The usual saying is, 'the man garlanded by the elephant is the one fit to rule; the man chosen by a girl is the right husband for her.' Changing it to 'the one who lifts the stone wins the bride' has done immeasurable damage. Haven't we already suffered a separation in our family because of incompatibility? Now you're getting the same Periappa's son married to a girl who does not love him!' The son's penetrating gaze sent a shiver down the father's spine.

Yes, it was the truth. But… but…

He had known Paru ever since she had been a little girl. He did not think she was mean or selfish. She was as beautiful as Rangan's mother had been. Like Jogi's mother, she possessed the rare qualities of equanimity and modesty.

He expected her to help her husband, be a companion to him, nurture the soil, beget children and be a stable factor in the family. For these reasons, he was in favour of her becoming Rangan's wife, rather than Jogi's. Poor soil needed good seeds. Lingayya felt that Paru had the capacity to anchor Rangan to the soil and wean him away from his crooked ways.

'Appa, Krishnan and Paru love each other. It will be wrong to keep them apart,' Jogi said heatedly.

'Maybe, Jogi. But I feel that Rangan should marry a good girl who can sacrifice her love and her desires and face life steadfastly.'

'What cruelty, Appa!' Jogi shouted.

'Listen patiently, my son. What is the object of marriage? The land where we have lived together should be made fertile and it should be cultivated. Many children should play in our courtyards. Cows and buffaloes should grow in numbers. This is why man and woman should share a life together.'

Jogi was speechless. Lingayya continued, 'Krishnan is educated. He belongs to a well-knit wealthy family. If his wife expects him to fulfil all her desires, he has the means to do so and thus ensure that she remains in his family. A girl with expectations who comes as a bride to my brother's house will be disappointed and might seek a separation. Paru will bring a sense of contentment to the family. A girl like her is needed to make Rangan prosper. Are you listening, Jogi? Periappan has no attachment to his family. He never worries about anything. He grabs the pleasures that come his way and loses himself in music. I've never come across anyone like him. Rangan is different from him. I'm afraid that he has moved away from the simple life linked to the soil. That's why I blessed him and wished him success in the contest, Jogi.'

Till then, Jogi's young mind had felt that the dreams and desires that revolved around a woman were the most important things in life. Only now did he understand that beyond the longings of youth lay a greater truth and that life was founded on that truth. Life was not meant for the pursuit of happiness alone.

What is achieved without effort gives happiness. Does one consciously derive pleasure from tilling the soil, sowing seeds, seeing plants grow and bear fruit, bathing in the waterfall or seeing milk frothing from the udders while milking? No. These are routine activities, done for the common good. Yet, they make one happy. In the same way, bringing a girl into the family and working selflessly with her for the sake of the family, the hatti and the world, would bring happiness.

How beautifully his father had put it! What had his mother got out of the family? Had she not come into their house as the personification of love and sacrifice? In spite of all their difficulties, why did she not leave the family?

'I spoke childishly, Appa. The sorrow I felt on seeing Paru's face made me speak hastily,' he said.

'Such emotions are only natural at your age. Conquer them, my son,' said his father.

Both returned homewards.

Paru was alone in the edumane. As soon as she saw them, she turned her face away. Tears of anger gushed forth from her eyes.

'Paru, look at me, my child,' Lingayya raised her chin with love and concern in his voice.

Her feelings were like a tidal wave caused by a massive landslide. However, she controlled them and held back her tears. She looked up at Lingayya.

'Are you terribly upset, Paru?'

She lowered her face. The tears spilled over.

'Silly child, why are you upset? A woman, like a fire, is a powerful force in shaping the family. This fire should burn brightly without smoking. You are entering this house with the strength to make sacrifices for the family, prepared to give up even milk if necessary. Your coming is auspicious, a sign of good fortune, and it will fill the empty coffers of this impoverished family. Do not allow petty feelings to get the better of you. A great responsibility has been thrust on you. You are coming to give succour to a soul bereft of love and to bring light into this family, my child.'

'Mama,' moved by his words, she fell at his feet.

An auspicious day in the month of *Avani* was fixed for the ceremony. On that day, Paru would enter Rangan's home, bringing joy to it. Jogi, Lingayya and Madhan accompanied Rangan when he went to Manikkalhatti attired in new clothes, carrying gifts and two hundred silver coins. Rangan then brought his bride home to the sound of Kothar music.

When the bride arrived at the entrance of the house, which had been smeared with red earth, Madhi, as the senior woman and mother-in-law, intoned, 'May you take responsibility for the growth of this family, which has continued from generation to generation like water flowing from a pot.' She poured water three times on the hands of the bride. It spilled over onto her feet. Taking a bead necklace strung with a gold wire, she placed it around Paru's neck and welcomed her to the house.

Rangammai led her elder brother's bride into the edumane, seated her on a blanket and placed a brand new vattil in front of her. Madhi served her cooked samai with fresh milk. Paru did not feel like eating it.

The hatti girls gathered around her to tease her. One of them brought Rangan in and said, 'Feed her, Ranganna.'

When Paru, red in the face, had tasted the milk and samai, Rangammal poured water over her hands.

Kothars played their music. The new water pot, engraved with designs and smeared with turmeric and sandalwood, shone like gold.

Rangi offered it to her brother's wife. Surrounded by girls and *sumangalis*, the bride made her way to the stream to fetch water. This ritual was symbolic of the fact that the bride had begun her household duties.

As she re-entered the house with the water pot to the sound of festive music, her uncle's words flashed across Paru's mind. 'This house is mine. The responsibility for this house is mine!' The strength of womanhood filled her mind and body and gave her a sense of pride. Mean and petty thoughts found no place in her mind at that time.

Part III

One

The gentle sun of the month of *Masi*, a dazzling jewel in the sky, had come with his youthful glorious smile to see the mountain damsel who had spread a blue silk mantle over herself. Her joy knew no bounds at the sight of her radiant lover. Perhaps she had spent the night beautifying and adorning herself with flowers and pearls!

Words are inadequate to describe the iridescent lustre of the pearl-like dew drops on the green grass, the new waterfalls sparkling like strands of diamonds on the slopes, the lively smiles of flowers of many hues. This was the auspicious day in Masi, when the mountain damsel greeted the sun after having triumphed over the vicissitudes of biting cold and cruel rain. The wild howling wind had abandoned its frenzied dance and it now rejoiced, enveloping the fir and eucalyptus trees in a friendly embrace.

Rows of white-clad hill folk, beloved sons and daughters of the mountain, descended the footpath leading to Keezhmalai, like a flock of white pigeons moving in an orderly formation across the sky. These honest, simple people made their way over the hillside, and converged on the vast, lush green expanse to celebrate their prosperity.

They had gathered to celebrate *Kenda Habba* or the fire-walking festival, when they worshipped Devar who had given them land, water and air, and ensured that they remained prosperous. On that great day, they sang the praises of Lord Siva, who bears the moon and Ganga in his hair; they prayed that they remain contented, that the seeds sown by them bear rich fruit, that their cattle increase in number, that samai and honey be abundant and that all their efforts be crowned with success. It was the sacred day when a fire was lit in the sanctum of the Madalingeshwara temple in Keezhmalai, while the chant of *'Harahara, Harahara'*, reverberated through the hills and valleys. People sang and danced in a frenzy of devotion at the sight of the fire-walkers coming down the hillside. The people who had been born in these hills and had taken their first steps, played and faced sufferings there, came with the sole purpose of being one with Devar. Descending in streams to join the sea of humanity in the Keezhmalai shola, they danced and sang devotional songs with fervour, blowing *kuzhals* and beating *maddalams.* Girls and boys in new dresses flitted about gaily like butterflies. Everywhere, one could hear the innocent chatter and trilling laughter of the hill women, in new mundus, their black curls peeping out beneath white pattus. The path to the temple through that huge shola encircled by green hills, was lined with shops piled high with poriurundai and fruit; children shrieked noisily as they whirled on merry-go-rounds. There were numerous attractions: shops selling pots and pans where women clustered, bundles of black sticks, cows with bells around their necks, calves and as offerings to Devar, huge pots overflowing with milk from the cows which had just calved.

Like a *mantapam* surrounded by water, a little hut stood in the midst of that beautiful valley, away from the noise and merry-making. In this tiny hut, like the bright light shed by a little oil lamp, shone the presence of Ayyan, the living force behind every blade of grass, the Ayyan of these children of nature who were content with simple living. To the right of the temple, in a pit seven feet long and three feet wide, logs of eucalyptus and aquila burnt fiercely, exuding a fragrance like that of sandalwood and incense. Streams of people descended into the hollow; each family in turn entered the little temple with offerings of coconut, fruit and milk. The crowding inside caused a suffocating atmosphere in the sanctum.

Five or six priests of the Odiyar sect stood in front of the *Nandi* outside the sanctum. They received the offerings of the throng, broke the coconuts, offered prayers to Devar and sprinkled coconut water on the men, women and children who bowed and touched their feet, and also blessed them.

Beyond the fire pit, on what looked like a natural stage, groups of young men from every hatti danced and sang with bells around their ankles and sticks in their hands. The dancing and singing went on and on; when one group left, another took its place.

Paeans in praise of the celestial dancer, Lord Siva, and his consort Hethaiamma mingled with the breeze and wafted over the hills. On one side stood men of the older generation like Kariamallar, Paru's grandfather and Rangan's father, Madhan, wearing huge turbans and *virva* leaf-shaped earrings with double loops. They were young at heart despite the lines on their faces. Hands linked to form a circle, legs moving in rhythm, they danced while the others chanted, '*Yea! Hou! Hou! Hou!*'

As the sun approached its zenith, the devotional fervour of the crowd reached fever pitch. In the midst of the crowd, innumerable miniature chariots made of coloured paper bobbed on the shoulders of the men dancing frenetically. To prevent these frenzied devotees from falling into the firepit, two men holding green branches in their hands, pushed them away with warning cries. The huge logs had burned leaving behind ruby embers.

People from Maragathamalai and Manikkalhatti formed a part of this huge throng. Paru, who had experienced one kurunji-span of married life, went in search of Girijai, dragging along her little daughter who was wearing a coloured *pavadai*. If Girijai stood any longer watching Jogi, who was part of the *bhajan* singers who were singing devotional songs, she would miss the fire-walking.

Madhi was not to be seen either.

Paru tried to push through the crowd and climb up the slope.

Appappa! What a crowd!

Aha, there was Krishnan's wife, the Thenmalai woman, fashionably dressed in a sari and blouse, her hair in a knot with flowers around it; kumkumam in the middle of the green tattoo marks on her forehead; dazzling diamond nose-ring; pomegranate-red rubies glowing in her ears instead of the traditional gold earrings; a necklace with a pendant; gold bangles on her wrists. She was the mother of two lovely children, a boy and a girl, and the wife of the man who had once been the hero of Paru's dreams! Krishnan, who had studied law, had a flourishing practice in Othai. He owned a house there and had recently bought a car. The progress of Maragathamalai was dear to his heart.

Once in a month or so, their black car would come up the new red mud road that snaked around the mountains. This would signal their arrival to the hatti folk. The boy in trousers and a shirt and the girl in a pavadai would play outside their house. The young and old of the hatti would gape open-mouthed at the children and their car. Paru would sometimes run into the Thenmalai woman while returning from the field.

'Are you well, Akka?' she would enquire with a smile.

Paru could never bring herself to smile back. But she would ask, 'Are you well, Akka? Have you just arrived?'

'Yes, the school was closed. We have to return tomorrow,' would be the reply. The happiness in her voice would bring forth a sigh of yearning from Paru's heart.

On that day, as well, the Thenmalai woman stopped Paru with, 'Are you well, Akka?'

Paru looked at her fixedly for a moment and mumbled, 'Are you well?' as a matter of form, then turned her eyes towards the crowd above her.

Rangan was escorting the English couple from the estate. He was chattering in English as he led the Englishwoman by the hand through the crowds. In what way was he inferior to Krishnan in looks or in reputation? In woollen trousers and coat, wearing a big turban and a watch, he looked every inch an important man. He had become a man of means, leasing acres of land near Othai and growing potatoes there.

Yet…

The sight of the Thenmalai woman caused a tumult within Paru. She tried to quell it by diverting her thoughts.

Rangan's father had left the old people to take charge of the young bhajan group. Even at the age of sixty, how rich and resonant his voice sounded! How supple his body was as he swung and swayed, stick in hand.

Krishnan's father enjoyed being a generous host. Mixing *panchamrutham* in big vessels, he was serving large helpings of it on leaves to the bhajan singers, who relished the mixture of fruit and honey.

'My son Gopalan and your daughter are playing, hand in hand. Just look at them!' laughed the Thenmalai woman.

Paru's older daughter was just seven, the younger, five. She had dressed them up herself. She had oiled their hair well, combed it, plaited it and tied it with a piece of pink wool. The older girl had a dusky complexion and her father's large eyes, while the younger was a replica of Paru. It was her hand that Krishnan's son swung back and forth joyfully. The other two girls were leaning against a tree, talking.

In spite of their finery, both Krishnan's children were the spitting image of their mother, with their oddly shaped heads, narrow temples and slightly sloping foreheads.

Only two of Paru's children had survived after four or five miscarriages. As for Krishnan, he had left for Madras to study law after losing in love. The very next year, he had married his Thenmalai aunt's daughter. Two years later, when he had started practising in Othai, the Thenmalai woman had joined him with their eight-month-old child.

As Paru watched, burning with jealousy, Krishnan came up to her. Paru's heart beat rapidly. She somehow composed herself.

'Are you well?' After so many years, he was addressing her, with a sheepish smile.

Paru could not answer.

'I was cheated. The traitors cheated me, talking of contests, this and that... Look at this Rukmini, ugly and thick-waisted after two children. I should have been in her place,' wept her heart.

'Where's Rangan? I don't see him,' Krishnan asked with the same sheepish smile.

'How should I know? Must be somewhere in the crowd,' she replied.

'I hear the crop was struck by disease this year,' he continued.

'So they say.'

'Isn't Mama going to walk on the kenda this year?'

'He is.'

'Why don't you come to Othai one of these days with Jogi and Girijai?'

Burning with resentment, Paru summoned a wry smile. 'Has Rukmini Akka ever invited me? After all, her car comes here; has she asked me to go with her?' she demanded.

'It's my fault, Akka. I'm inviting you straightaway. Come with us now,' said Rukmini, smiling to reveal teeth stained by chewing betel leaves.

By then, drumbeats and shouts announced the arrival of the fire-walkers.

Seven men, their shaven heads smeared with sandal paste and their necks adorned with garlands of *kadamba* flowers, came singing and dancing. The sounds of the Kothar's musical instruments—the kuzhal, the *kombu*, the *thaarai* and the *thappattai*—seemed to rend the air. Bearing *kavadi*-shaped cane bows on their shoulders, the men had to jump into the firepit and walk across it seven times, while the chant of '*Harahara Harahara*' resounded all over the hills. The first man belonged to Thenmalai; the second to Kothai; the third was Lingayya. How could a body, enfeebled by pain and fever and wizened with age, glow like that? For several weeks, he had slept on a sack and purified himself by fasting and other rituals. Virtue and piety were his riches.

While the onlookers showered them with flowers, they circled the pit three times and walked across it. When they stepped out of the embers with even the little hairs on their big toe unsinged,[1] Madhan danced like one possessed, crying out, *'Jayajaya Mahadeva, Harahara Shambo.'*

As Paru stood, lost in the music, Girija and Madhi came looking for her.

'Akka! We've been searching for you everywhere.'

Girijai held out a leaf containing panchamrutham to Paru.

' Liar! I was right here, looking for you. You were too busy gazing at Jogianna dancing to look for me!'

'Go on, Akka, teasing me as if I were married yesterday.' Girijai turned her face away shyly.

'You both give that impression. Isn't that so Athai? You tell me. Does she ever leave Anna's side?' asked Paru smiling.

A pall of gloom descended on Madhi's countenance. Seven fire-walking festivals had passed since Jogi's marriage. Did he deserve this after serving Devar? Even if the house wasn't filled with the patter of many tiny feet and childish prattle, couldn't Devar have granted her family at least one child?

Madhi had never hungered for gold or jewels; she yearned for a child, but Devar had denied her even that

How could she separate a couple, who like a pair of lovebirds, could not bear to be apart? How could she ask Jogi to agree to take a second wife?

As she stood there, her face creased with sorrow, there was a commotion in the crowd.

In a blind panic, Madhi demanded, 'What is it? What is it?'

'Lingayya… Jogi's father.'

A medley of voices; Madhi broke through the crowd and ran towards him.

With his sandal-smeared body, the old man who had walked across the fire without even the hair of his big toe being singed, lay like a golden tree that had been felled.

---

[1]The celebrants, before going through the ordeal, count the hairs on their toes. If any are singed, it is a sign of approaching ill-fortune or even death (Thurston).

Girijai and all their friends and acquaintances followed Madhi. Only Paru stood still as if in a swirling mist, brooding over the Thenmalai woman's good fortune. The Thenmalai woman's smile seemed to mock her.

The whole crowd rushed towards the tree near the temple. So far, there had been no untoward incidents at the fire-walking festival. That day was no exception.

'My father is feeling weak. He is old, after all. Move a little, give him some air,' said Jogi.

'It was only after he had circled the fire three times and sprinkled milk that he fell unconscious,' Rangamma's husband added.

Madhi wrung her hands in utter despair and prayed to all the Devars. Girijai stood by crying. Meanwhile someone brought hot tea. Krishnan, who knew that a medical student from Kothai was around, went and fetched him.

The young man, Arjunan, pushed his way through the crowd. As he felt Lingayya's pulse, everyone watched him with awe and respect.

He said smiling, 'There's nothing to worry about.'

Jogi tried to pour some of the sweet tea down his father's throat.

Turning towards the west, Madhan prayed, '*Basaveswara! Nanjundeswara!*'. I will come to your temple. Save my brother,' and began to sing fervently.

Perhaps that floodtide of music encompassing the names of Devar struck Lingayya's ear and awakened his benumbed senses. He slowly opened his eyes. Severe fasting, penance and age had shrivelled his face, and his eyes were sunken. Yet, they were shining.

'Appa, have some tea,' urged Jogi. He moistened his father's parched lips and tongue with tea. Lingayya looked around at everyone. 'Where am I?' he asked weakly.

The faltering voice did not seem to belong to him.

'You've just walked on kenda under the temple tree,' said his brother.

'Madhamma,' he called, in the same faltering voice.

Madhamma went up to him with tears in her eyes.

'Where is Girijai? Where is the child?'

'Mama!' Still crying, Girijai went and stood at his feet.

'Don't cry, my daughter. Before the next kenda festival you'll hold a fine boy in your arms,' he said.

There was pin-drop silence. Lingayya again looked around him. 'Why are you all standing here? We have walked on fire in the presence of Lord Madalingeshwara and have been blessed. Continue singing bhajans. I'm exhausted and I would like to sleep,' he said.

Almost immediately his brother resumed his singing. The bhajan singers beat time to music.

'What's all this? He's ill. If there is a car, he should be taken to the hospital in Othai,' said a voice in the crowd.

Arjunan said, 'Yes, that's right.' Several voices called out for Rangan.

After all, the Englishman at Johnson Estate was his friend; he could get hold of a car. But no one was aware that Rangan had left soon after the fire-walking to join the English couple in a picnic.

It was Krishnan who brought his car. While Lingayya was being lifted and placed in it, he again lost consciousness.

Madhan was terrified; Madhi wrung her hands. Why should he be taken to the hospital? So far no one in the hatti had been taken there. What would they do to him in the hospital? Kari's father, who had gone there from Manikkalhatti, with a sore on his back, had been cut up and killed by the English doctor.

In the car, Madhi started sobbing. To the alarm of Krishnan who was driving, she implored him not to take Lingayya to the hospital.

'Go back home, Krishna, go to the hatti,' said Madhan restraining Krishnan with his hand.

What could Krishnan do? He turned the car in the direction of Maragathamalai.

Due to his efforts, there was a good road to Maragathamalai. There were also other changes that had taken place in the last twelve years. In the dense sholas, the crackling sounds of great eucalyptus trees being felled could be heard constantly. Sunbeams entered and played in that hitherto impenetrable shola. And the hills to the west of Maragathamalai, which looked like herds of elephants and had been completely covered with a blue mantle of kurunji flowers, were now dotted with clumps of healthy tea bushes.

Near the rocky outcrop of Maragathamalai, a small school had made its appearance. Little shops and labourer's huts, which had so far been found only near the Johnson estate, had now sprung up on the path to Maragathamalai. The hatti dwellers, till then, had cultivated samai, ragi and potatoes for their own use and had not known that they could make money by selling them. They now worked on the land, planting tea, with the sole purpose of becoming rich.

Kariamallar and the members of his family had taken up the cultivation of tea, and they intensified their efforts each year. They did not toil on their own soil. They hired a few labourers from Pollachi to work on their lands. The money from tea had transformed Kariamallar's lime-and-mortar corner house into a much taller and wider double-storeyed one with all conveniences.

When Krishnan's car did not stop in front of his house but halted at the other end of the street, those who had not attended the fire-walking festival rushed to their doorsteps to watch what was happening.

Madhi, calm and composed, swiftly made up a bed for Lingayya on the bench in the edumane.

Though most of the families were now fairly well-off, the difficult situation in Jogi's house remained unchanged. Girijai and he worked hard to grow ragi and samai. They were not in debt at the moment. The two buffaloes in the shed had become four. Yet they were not flush with money.

Though Rangan had leased land near Othai to grow potatoes and dealt in thousands of rupees, he was not a source of support to the family. When he sold his crop, he would make a trip to Mysore and Bangalore. Or he would squander his money in Othai.

Paru discovered that her husband did not wish to be imprisoned in the cage of family life and disappointment with life had taken bitter root in her heart. Whenever she saw Jogi or his father, that bitterness boiled over and turned to hatred. She believed that they had ruined her life. Rangammai's husband was the only one who did a man's work in their house. Rangammai, ill and exhausted after enduring a life-threatening pregnancy every two years, struggled to rear her children, and seldom left the house.

Paru toiled on the land, working out her frustrations on Mother Earth. Jogi, like his father before him, assumed responsibility for Madhan's family, giving help whenever needed.

By the time Madhi made the bed, Girijai, Jogi and the others had reached home by the short cut. Quickly lighting the fire, Girijai made coffee. Madhi covered the feet which had walked on fire with a blanket and sat near her husband, her mind in a whirl.

'What was the use of marrying Girijai to Jogi? They had no children, while Rangammai had five, three of them boys.'

Bringing the coffee in a big vessel, Girijai poured some into a tumbler and offered it to Krishnan who was talking to Jogi in front of the house.

'Krishnanna, have some coffee,' she said.

'Oh! What is the need for all this?' said Krishnan, taking the tumbler.

At that moment Madhan went up to Lingayya, a bottle of liquor hidden in the folds of his dhoti. He had not forgotten that his brother had repeatedly told him that getting drunk was a sin.

He had urged Lingayya many times to drink in order to regain his strength.

'Not that, Anna. It destroys one's morals and fills the mind with dirt. It degrades a man,' Lingayya had refused firmly. In spite of Lingayya's exhortations, Madhan's fondness for liquor and his faith in its powers had not diminished.

Madhan's plan to give a drop of the liquor he had brought to his unconscious brother as medicine did not succeed. The minute he opened the bottle, the smell alerted his brother's senses.

Lingayya's eyes opened sharply. They looked steadily at his brother and at the bottle in his hand and Madhan's courage ebbed away. Fearing that his brother would knock the bottle from his hand, he placed it on a high shelf.

Lingayya's parched lips parted. 'My brother knows that this is one principle I cherish. Does he want me to give it up?' he said, looking towards his wife.

Without a word, Madhi poured some coffee into his mouth. When he had drunk it, she wiped his face.

Hearing voices, Krishnan, Jogi and Rangammai came in. Lingayya smiled at them. 'Where is Rangan?' he asked.

After a moment's hesitation, Jogi replied, 'He has gone to get medicine from the hospital.'

Lingayya smiled again. 'Nothing is wrong with me. Why are you all here? Go on, go to the temple and sing, dance and eat. Madhamma, have you eaten?'

Madhi nodded.

'Go then. Go, Krishna, I am all right. Let Ammai remain here, the rest of you can leave,' he commanded.

Every year, on the night of the festival, there would be continuous singing of bhajans, dancing and narration of epics in front of the Madalingeshwara temple in the light of flaming torches. Petromax lamps made their first appearance that year. The stage was decorated with garlands of leaves and flowers. A troupe had come specially from Mysore to present a *koothu,* a performance in folk art, of *Harichandra*. Except for Madhi, Jogi and Girijai, everyone had gone back to Keezhmalai.

Jogi bowed before the lamp, put on madi clothes and went to the cattle shed. Madhi sat by her husband's side, her eyes fixed on him. He told her that an arm and a leg had become so heavy that he could not move them.

'Aiyo!' Shaken to the core, Madhi raised his legs and hands and stroked them, weeping all the while. 'Is this also fate?' she cried, and her husband tried to console her.

'It is all for the best, Madhi. In a way it makes me happy. Devar's mercy…'

'Aiyo, are you in your senses? Why do all misfortunes come to us when Devar's name is constantly on our lips?'

Again and again, she touched his limbs and tried to raise them. All sorts of fears assailed her as she ground some garlic into a paste and applied it on his limbs.

'Don't worry, Madhi. The same thing happened to my father. He couldn't even speak at the time of his death.'

'Why do you talk like this? What will happen to me after you are gone?'

'Will I go away, Madhamma? We have something precious that no one else has,' he laughed. 'How can I have the heart to leave this house, Jogi and you? I will come back to this land. I'll come to play in your lap. Hasn't my son served Hiriya Udayar Ayyan? Have I knowingly harmed anyone? Why should Ayyan be cruel only to me? I am happy today. Ayyan has not blessed this house with a child. I will soon leave this form and come back as a child. Madhi, my son will always be happy. Girijai will always be a joyous young girl in this house. I will return. Isn't this what I prayed for today when I walked on fire? You should be happy about it; why are you crying, Madhamma?'

Madhamma had no answer. Her body heaved with sobs.

Two

Monstrous, black, monsoon clouds, ready to devour the mountain damsel, wandered at will that night over street and house and hill, egged on by the fury of the triumphant wind. Overcome by sorrow, the mountain damsel shed tears onto the earth. Unable to bear this piteous sight, the waxing moon vanished. The streets of Othai, deserted even during the day, bore no signs of life that night. It was a month since the sun had opened his eyes. The days and nights seemed endless. In the rainy season, Rangan's house in Vandushola served as a gambling den for him and others of his kind. That week, fearing that the potatoes would rot in the soggy earth, Rangan had already dug up three-fourths of his crop and sold it. He was flush with money and coins jingled in the house. Little wonder then, that he and his friends were possessed by a mania for gambling and drink.

The pear bush planted by Rangan long ago had grown wild and seemed to shelter the house beneath its branches. In the dark, the tree shielded the house as if to say, 'I know what's going on inside; but he planted me and reared me. I will not be ungrateful.' Inside, the game, which had commenced at seven that evening, was still in full swing well past midnight. The cigarette smoke that filled the room created the impression that the dark clouds outside had drifted in. Like the moon struggling among the clouds, a candle in a corner battled with the smoke and tried to shed light. The stench of liquor and the greed for money, which dominated the players, had destroyed their good sense.

Benjamin was shuffling the cards. He was a polisher in a carpentry workshop. Although skilled in making wooden articles and floors gleam like marble, it had never occurred to him to make his mind pure like marble. Ross, the other player, was an Anglo-Indian. He played the trumpet in the local band. Once he had money in his pockets, his sole aim was to gamble. Having finished off half the bottle, he puffed away at a fat cheroot. He had been enormously successful that day, winning all of Rangan's potato money.

Taking the last hundred rupee note from his pocket, Rangan flung it on the table. 'No luck today. What dreadful rain, pouring non-stop for three months,' he grumbled, looking at his cards.

When he announced, 'This is the last game,' Benjamin glared at him.

With a smile on his smoke-stained lips, Ross threw down his cards. Luck had not favoured Rangan the whole day. His hope of recovering his losses by placing all he had in the last game went up in smoke.

When the church clock struck two, the others went home, leaving Rangan alone. Swallowing the remaining liquor, he fell on the cot and cursed the rain!

The potato money had disappeared as though it had never existed. The debts that had to be repaid seemed like monsters waiting to devour him.

Chut! It was all that wretched Paru's fault. Ever since she had come into his life, money had slipped through his fingers. He earned well, but his earnings disappeared as fast as they came in.

As he lay, furious and confused, he saw Paru in his mind's eye, goading him to anger and jealousy. How many dreams he had woven around her!

He had dreamt that his marriage would destroy Krishnan's arrogance, but there he was, in his double-storeyed house, gloating over them! The whole hatti bowed to him as if he were a god. He deceived the villagers by pretending to be working for their welfare, while actually promoting his own interests.

Was Paru any better? Hadn't she moved closely with Krishnan before her marriage? Even on the day of the fire-walking festival, they had been seen conversing with each other. Dishonourable fellow! If that were not bad enough, he had sent his car to take her to Othai. Did his education give him the right to do anything he pleased?

Only the previous day, Rangan had heard of Paru's visit to Othai from a Toreyan's son who was a coolie in the potato *mandi*, where the vegetable was stored. The day before that, the deceitful, lying woman had insinuated that Rangan was a good-for-nothing. It was not impossible to get rid of the wretched woman and bring home the willing Gowri who had captured his heart five months ago. She also belonged to Manikkalhatti. She had wanted to marry him even before her first marriage. But she had been married off to someone in Kothai. Right from the start, the husband and wife had not got on. To make matters worse, her husband had cast her aside and became a Christian.

When Gowri had returned to her parental home, Rangan had made her his woman before anyone else could do so.

In his inebriated state, he spoke aloud, revealing emotions that were buried deep within him. There was no one to hear him except the smoke-covered walls that knew all his secrets.

When he awoke at last with a clear head, it was almost noon. The sun was playing hide-and-seek with the clouds. Only then did he fully realise that he had lost all his money.

An acre of potatoes was still untouched. It had been planted later. The leaves had not dried and curled up. He had decided it was too early to dig them up. But what had happened to them in the endless rain? Perhaps he could recover at least half of them.

He had to meet Gowri's brother, pay at least fifty rupees and bring Gowri home. But as for summoning the panchayat to rid himself of that cheat Paru, would Lingayya, who had been bedridden for the past five months, allow it?

Deep in thought, he got up and washed his face. As he was coming out of the 'military' hotel in the bazaar after a meal, he saw the Johnson estate car going back from the bazaar. Only the Englishwoman was in the car. Seizing the opportunity, Rangan saluted her with an ingratiating smile and jumped in.

He got off near the estate and walked straight on. As he approached Maragathamalai, he was gripped by a sudden urge to see Gowri. Without warning, the sky became overcast and there was a violent clap of thunder. As he hurried on, he saw Krishnan standing under a silver oak tree in the middle of young tea bushes.

'O Ranga, how are you? How is your chithappa? I came just a while ago,' said Krishnan, walking towards Rangan.

He was the husband of the woman Krishnan had once loved. Krishnan was very upset with his wild ways. Of late, he felt a desire to reform Rangan for Paru's sake. Whispers of Rangan's association with Gowri had reached him in Othai, as well as, in Manikkalhatti and in Maragathamalai.

At the sight of Krishnan amidst his thriving tea bushes on the slopes, Rangan's resentment flared up.

'What would I know about my family matters that the big shot lawyer doesn't know?' he replied gruffly, going off at a tangent.

'No... no. Since you are going towards Manikkalhatti, I enquired about your uncle's health.' To check whether Paru was still with Rangan, Krishnan asked, 'I hope everyone is in the hatti?'

'That is what I asked you. Hey, you think I know nothing? I'm going to file a case against you and tear your reputation to shreds in the panchayat.'

Krishnan was alarmed at Rangan's sudden anger and provocative comments. He could not understand why Rangan was angry.

'What is wrong, Ranga? What are you saying?' he asked.

'You ask me what I am saying? Watch your words!'

'What has happened? I don't understand. Are you serious?' repeated Krishnan, not losing his composure.

'Why is a big shot like you meddling in our affairs? Who sent a car to fetch another man's wife? Who? Tell me, you blackguard!'

Krishnan had not expected the matter to turn so sordid and ugly.

'Oh, are you referring to Paru's visit to Othai? It was Rukmini who invited her and sent the car. I had gone to Mettupalayam. Ranga, is it you, talking like this? I can't believe it.'

'Oho! Big shot lawyer, isn't he? He knows how to twist words.'

Perhaps even Devar couldn't bear the way he deliberately baited Krishnan; strong winds and heavy rain lashed the hillside.

Finding Rangan's company repugnant, Krishnan walked away in the rain towards Manikkalhatti. He was on a visit to his aunt and uncle there. Krishnan was a busy man; success in his profession and contentment in family life had effaced his old feelings for Paru and made the past seem like a distant dream. However, the sight of Paru, reduced to a shadow of her old self, pained his heart. Fate had cheated the poor girl. Time and again, it lacerated Paru's wound, not letting it heal. The memory, which had almost faded from his mind, was still fresh in hers.

It was true that he had reminded Rukmini to send the car to fetch Paru and her children to Othai. Rukmini derived great pleasure in showing off to the villagers her husband's wealth and position and her educated, modern friends. Apart from that, there was no trace of jealousy or spite in her. He was fortunate in that.

Paru had come, but sensing at once that Rukmini's boasting only intensified the pain in Paru's heart, he had been unable to join in their conversation and had left the house.

He had returned home the day after she had gone back to the village. Rukmini had brought up the topic of Paru when he sat down to have his night meal.

'Paru Akka is unhappy, poor thing. Neither she nor her sister has a male child. As for Rangan… do you know something?' she had asked mysteriously.

'So he wants to get married again, does he?' asked Krishnan, not touching the food on his plate.

'It is because the old man is against the practice that he has not sought a second wife even for his own son. He has been bedridden for months unable to move his limbs. He keeps saying, 'I'll die. I'll return as my son's child.' Not that Paru admits it, but she is unhappy. She only spoke of land and cultivation.'

Then, as an afterthought, she added, 'I wonder whether she feels it would be better to make a clean break than suffer in a place where she is unwanted. While talking of someone else, she said, "Some people are fated to be unlucky. They should not test their luck again and again."'

Instead of cherishing and valuing what belongs to them, some people abuse it and also flout the norms of decent society. Why did Rangan have to be one such person? When would such demeaning practices disappear from society? How would Paru ever find solace?

Not only did that base fellow Rangan pluck a flower only to toss it aside and reach for another, but he also justified it. How could a man with a wife like Paru and two lovely daughters desire another woman? For Krishnan, that rainy night stretched on endlessly; he could neither sleep nor enjoy the companionship of his loving relatives.

Three

With a roaring sound, rain lashed down in silvery sheets and the water flooded the already wet earth. Children dipped their feet in rainwater and then dashed back into the house, adding to the damp mess on the floor. In every corner lay soiled, wet clothes and piles of rubbish. It was only fifteen days since Rangammai had given birth to a child. The baby girl, wriggling on pieces of cloth, wet them ever so often, adding to the growing unwashed pile in the corner. Since there was no outlet for the smoke from the wet firewood, it filled the house. Paru was finding the housework more and more irksome, but now it seemed she had no way out of it. She could not work outdoors in the rainy season. She had never seen such unrelenting rain! Had the skies burst?

The rain that had started on the tenth of *Aani* had not let up till the end of *Purattasi*.

Dark clouds often settled on the hills. To show their gratitude for the resting place, they would delight the mountain damsel by showering rain on her and covering her with a green silk mantle. But this year, how it poured! Had the sun run away and hidden himself: Was he too terrified of the wild winds to show himself?

How would her young plants survive this unceasing rain? It was a month since she had gone to the fields. Rangammai's pregnancy, the housework, Lingayya's illness and the rain—all these had conspired to keep her housebound. She had been returning home in the drizzle after weeding her potato patch when Rangammai's daughter had come to call her, saying that her mother was unwell.

She had never felt so restless, even in the days when Rangan had totally forgotten her existence and not come home for a month. Apart from her children, nothing in life gave her as much joy as the land. The land gives life; it gives strength; it gives food. It receives the same lives into its bosom one day. There had been a time when she had never thought of the land, when her mind had flitted like a butterfly, weaving a web of dreams in the first flush of womanhood and the thrill of new love. After the stone in the temple maidan had destroyed that web, her mind had turned to the land.

Would her beloved plants, carefully nurtured as if they were her own children, be bruised and flattened by the merciless rain? Every day, Rangammai's husband, protecting his head with a sack, would make a trip to inspect the fields. And every day Paru would ask him, 'How are the plants, Anna?'

'They are fine, Anni. Rangan's potatoes which fetched him thousands can't compare with yours,' he would laugh.

When Jogi stood outside his house or came in carrying Rangammai's son, she would ask him the same question. Even Lingayya's health seemed less important to her.

'This is Anni's perpetual worry,' teased Rangammai's husband one day.

'Jogi's plants are his children. It is the same with this Anni,' Rangammai laughingly joined in.

Though her words pained Jogi a little, he did not show it. 'So what? There's nothing wrong in treating plants as your children. The earth is the mother; the plants are children,' he said.

Then, in reply to Paru's query, he added in a worried tone, 'The water channel has eroded and the water has stagnated. I dug up some earth to fill it. There's been too much rain, too much water. I don't know what's going to happen.'

Paru was never affected by her husband's gains and losses. Jogi was hard-working. His wish was that everyone should prosper and be content. So his worry caused her pain.

'Jogianna, why not plant tea in your three acres? However much it rains, it'll give you money,' suggested Rangammai.

'It costs money to plant tea. Then what do we do for three or four years till it starts yielding? Tea and coffee can only bring us money, Rangammai. But ragi, wheat and potatoes fill our hungry stomachs,' answered Jogi.

'Can one do without money nowadays? It was only because of tea that Krishnanna's house could be extended,' said Rangammai. Jogi did not relish her argument.

'I'm going, Anni,' he said, and left.

Jogi reached home. He could not believe his eyes! Was that really Rangan, seated by Lingayya, sobbing as though his heart would break? His coat and dhoti were dripping wet. What could have brought him here in the driving rain?

'I've been punished for all my sins, Chithappa. I ignored your words of advice and I have been punished. Aiyo, Chithappa, how frail you have become. You put me above your own son and did so much for me, yet I ran away. Can you bring yourself to forgive me, Chithappa?'

Jogi was absolutely stunned. Behind him, Girijai and his mother also stood like statues.

Tears trickled down Lingayya's cheeks.

'Two thousand rupees gone forever! Like my mind, which became blemished, the potatoes became spoilt and diseased. Just as my crooked thinking wiped out your advice from my mind, rats and pigs dug up my crop and destroyed it. Devar has tested me. He is saying, You have lived a wasteful life. Now pay for it.'

Were Rangan's tears and remorse genuine?

Jogi couldn't imagine Rangan crying like that. Had the wily Rangan really been humbled? Had Rangan, who dressed and behaved as though tens of thousands of rupees passed through his hands, fallen so low?

From Lingayya's emotion-choked throat, came a broken cry, 'Ranga!' At once, Rangan laid his head on his uncle's chest and sobbed.

'You were father and mother to me, Chithappa. One day when I lay hungry on the watch-platform, you took me home, fed me and gave me advice. What can I say, Chithappa? I have come to you burdened by debts. Will you forgive me?'

'It doesn't matter, Thambi, forget about the past. Let your ills go the way of the potatoes. Honestly, I'm not sorry about the potatoes. I'm happy, Ranga, really happy.'

'Chithappa, you are Devar. Aiyo, why didn't I realise your worth all this time?'

'That day you stood before me flaunting your wealth. My blood boiled. The look in your eyes told me you were not honest and straightforward. My heart cried, 'Is this the boy I raised, carrying him in my arms?' I hit you. Today, though you have come as a poor man, I am happy and content. Devar wants us to earn an honest livelihood with our hands, Ranga. Life means living in harmony with your wife, without hurting her.'

His speech was impassioned and he gasped for breath.

'That wretched fellow has also served a notice on me. I came to my senses when I was hauled to court and found my reputation in shreds. Who would give me three hundred rupees to repay him? Whom have I got in this world? Besides you, who is there to share my woes, Chithappa?' Rangan's weeping had the power to touch anybody's heart.

'Don't cry, Ranga, don't cry. Though bedridden, I've been holding on to life these past six months just waiting for you to have a change of heart and return to me. Even if I had swallowed the *veeraraya panam,* I would have survived. Now I can go to the land of the Devars in peace. Wealth and money are not important. Life has meaning only when you work hard on the land with your hands, share your food and live in amity with everyone.'

Lingayya then called out, 'Jogi!'

'Ayya,' said Jogi stepping forward.

'Anna has come home. We have no more worries. Fetch my bag from the hagottu,' he said.

Jogi's face darkened.

Madhi was thunderstruck. 'Is this right?' she asked.

It was hard-earned money, set aside for an emergency. About two hundred and fifty rupees. Had he come to snatch away even that? Madhi could not reconcile herself to it.

'Don't interfere, Madhi. When good times come, some expenses may crop up. After all, don't we give the Kurumbas their dues because we fear their spells? Don't you want your husband to die with peace of mind?' asked Lingayya.

'You leave me with nothing to say,' mumbled Madhi tearfully, moving towards the ogamane. Turning round, she said sharply, 'Why doesn't he sell or mortgage his land?'

Lingayya gave her a steady look. He was deeply disturbed and he looked very frail.

'What sort of talk is this? Can we snatch away the land that feeds Rangi and her children? Can we take away an inch of the land which is as dear to Paru as a mother, as a child? How could you think like this?'

Jogi brought the bag.

Lingayya counted each coin. Keeping the bag by his pillow, he said, 'Ranga, stay here tonight. You can go tomorrow.' At night he said to Madhi, 'Take out my vattil. Today I am going to sit and eat with my sons.'

With a strange sense of foreboding, Madhi asked, 'Must you?'

He sent Girijai to fetch Paru. 'Come here, daughter. My son has come home. Now you have no worries,' he blessed her.

Paru was shaken by the extraordinary light in his eyes. That night, he was the chief actor on the stage.

In the morning, Rangan took the money after counting it. 'I'll fling the money at him and come back Chithappa. You are Devar who saved me from going to court' were his parting words.

Lingayya's eyes shone; his heart was full; he blessed his nephew.

The overcast sky cast a pall on the day.

Madhi, Girijai and Jogi stood outside, watching Rangan go. As his figure receded, becoming smaller and smaller till only a white speck could be seen descending the slope, a mist came in from the north and enveloped him totally.

With the feeling that a *kalipurushan*, a man who portends strife and discord, had collected his wages and left, they went inside.

Seeing his father sleeping, Jogi covered his head with a sack and went out to the fields, sighing. Girijai and Madhi were at the back of the house.

Soon afterwards, Madhi seemed to hear a feeble cry 'Madhi!' Before she could put down her washing and run to him, his life had ebbed away.

Four

Madhi did not realise that he had called out to bid her farewell. How could she?

Lingayya's face was like a flower freshly plucked from its stalk. The eyelids were closed as if in deep slumber. A smile lingered on the lips as if an inner joy had bubbled forth. The countenance was serene and tranquil as never before. The body lay there, a shell that had released the breath of life imprisoned within it.

'Did you call me? Are you feeling sleepy so soon? What is it?' she asked, lifting his right hand. Gently, she shook his face and then sprang back as if scorched by fire. The face drooped like a flower broken from its stem. Frantic with fear, she touched his chest; held her hand in front of his nose; then pressed his hands and legs.

From the pit of her stomach came a cry of anguish, 'Jogi! Giri! Aiyo!'

Putting down the samai she was cleaning, Girija rushed in. 'Athai, what is it?'

Frantically rubbing the soles of his feet, Madhi said, 'Giri, go and call Jogi, Periappa and everyone else.'

Her voice faltered, thick with tears, over-burdened with grief. Did the piece of thread she had placed near his nose flutter with his breath? Or was it with her agitated breath? Nothing made any sense to her.

The news spread like a forest fire, bringing crowds of people to his bedside.

'Ammai, bring the veeraraya panam quickly,' said Madhan, fetching milk from the hagottu. It was Rangammai who ran to bring the gold piece, the size of a four anna coin, dipped in ghee. Madhan's eyes brimmed with tears.

'Am I still alive only to do this for you Thambi?' Choked with emotion, he placed the gold piece in his brother's mouth and poured some milk over it.

At the sight of the gold piece slowly sliding down the tongue with the milk, Madhi covered her face and wailed, 'Aiyo!'

Just then Jogi came running, wet and mud-splattered, after hearing the news from Kakai.

He had come tearing home on being told that something was wrong. When he saw the milk being poured over the veeraraya panam, he rushed forward crying, 'Appa!'

'Don't cry, Jogi,' his uncle calmed him down, tears spilling down his own face.

Kariamalla embraced him lovingly. 'Don't cry, Jogi. Your father has gone to a fitting place, to the holy feet of Isan,' he said, trying to control his own grief.

Men, women and children streamed in through the narrow doorway, stood tearfully at his feet and paid their respects, exclaiming, 'What a great man he was! How serene he looks! How radiant! He was a god!'

It had become an open secret in the village that Rangan had borrowed money from Lingayya that morning.

'He doted on him more than on his own son. It would seem he held on to life only to meet him one last time and eat with him,' people whispered.

Paru stood silently in a corner watching all that was going on. The news that Lingayya had given money to Rangan, who had always postured as a rich man, evoked in her a searing anger against the dead man.

Wasn't he the embodiment of evil; had he not schemed to spoil her happiness and succeeded in doing so? Had he ever shown her any compassion? What spell had he cast, more potent than the Kurumba's root, which had enabled his nephew to lift the stone? The milk-smeared lips, which were closed, seemed to wear a triumphant smile. She wanted to shout, 'Are you happy that you turned an innocent girl's joy into sorrow? Even on the day of the contest, I would have refused to enter this house. Like offering bitter medicine coated with jaggery, you enticed me with honeyed words and convinced me to do so! What a fool you made of me!'

Her white-hot rage found release in tears. It was in the same room that he had given her advice. 'If he marries the girl of his choice, he will walk on the straight path of virtue. Don't disappoint him, my girl, I beg of you,' he had said. He had deceived her. He had softened her heart and stamped his own image of Rangan on it. Had it lasted though? The fine image that he had created had melted in the heat of marital discord. All her love was now lavished on her two daughters. Her only aim in life was to work hard for their well-being.

Who was responsible for all this? Who?

What was so great about Rangammai? She couldn't even hold a pitchfork. Yet her husband cherished her.

Girijai was skinny, small and dark-complexioned. Though she was barren, her husband loved her.

Why, Chithappa? Didn't you yourself wish to bask in the love of your dear Madhamma till your dying day? Yet you broke a young girl's heart.

The sight of his calm countenance unlocked the sluice gates of her heart and unleashed a flood of bitter memories.

The rain stopped completely and darkness descended; the smell of wet earth and the dank breeze were in tune with the grief-laden atmosphere in the hatti.

After lighting the lamps, Madhan stood in front of the house giving a Toreyan instructions on who was to be informed. The next day was Tuesday, inauspicious for performing the cremation. So it was decided to postpone it to Wednesday. The Muttukothars were informed accordingly. Rangammai's husband got ready to convey the news to Rangan in Othai the following day.

The huge crowds, which had gathered for the funeral, had to be fed. Elaborate preparations were made. With the head of the house gone, his son and wife were numb with grief. Who would arrange for the necessary grains and foodstuffs? Rangammai opened the palapetti and dipped into the savings. Heaps of potatoes and quantities of grain poured in from all over. From Kariamallar's house came a hissing petromax lantern.

Women worked in groups, chattering. With so much activity, it did not seem like a house visited by death.

Returning to Othai with the money borrowed from his uncle, Rangan repaid his petty debts. When he went in search of men to dig up the remaining potatoes, his eyes alighted on the poster of a new film at the cinema hall. It was Tuesday, the day of the shandy. He decided to dig up the potatoes the next day, hoping the sun would shine. He spent the evening at the shandy and the cinema, returning to his Vandushola house only after nine at night.

Before he could open the front door and go in, he saw a squat figure, shrouded from head to foot, standing under the pear tree. It could have been a demon or a ghost in the dark.

Rangan feared neither demon nor ghost. 'Who is there?' he demanded.

'It is I, Ranganna; Rangammai's husband.' Without turning the key in the lock, Rangan asked irritably, 'What brings you here?'

'Jogi's father, Chithappa has passed away. There is no money for the funeral expenses. Chinnammai is banking on you and has asked me to fetch you,' explained Rangammai's husband.

Five

Can anything compare with the joy of being free after a lifetime in prison? Are there any bounds to the rapture of the earth when it beholds the sun, which rents the sombre shroud of night to each day to free it from its dark prison? How can one describe the delight of the fledgling that sprouts wings and flies out of the prison of its nest? Can one imagine the fragrance immured in buds mingling with the dawn breeze when it is released by the unfurling of petals?

When the soul imprisoned in the cage of the body is born on this earth, is bound by various shackles that are a part of life, struggles against odds and finally attains its freedom, can it be an ordinary event? Jogi's father had followed the path of truth all his life and wished no one any harm. The village folk believed that the soul of such a person, when freed, would seek to become one with the infinite Supreme Being. Is it any wonder then that they traditionally celebrated the death of virtuous honourable elders as a happy event?

How does man, forgetting himself, show his intense joy? Without his being aware of it, music is born; unconsciously he moves his hands and legs to express his happiness. Music and dance are an integral part of the heritage of the hill folk who are so close to nature. Death is the most important event of their lives. From time immemorial, music and dance have been an essential accompaniment to the last journey of the liberated soul as it traverses the darkness of hell and merges with the Supreme Being.

Each of the various tribes that regarded the blue mountain as their mother claimed kinship with the land and had put down roots in it. Though they were disparate entities, it was a mark of their greatness that they lived in harmony, helping each other in times of need. With their skilful hands, the men of the Kothar tribe fashioned pots, implements and other items necessary for everyday living and sold them to the others for grain. They were also well-versed in music and played the kuzhal, thaarai, maddalam, thappattai and parai. Their auspicious music was considered an essential part of the Badaga rites in life and in death.

That is why Thorayamallan's son Bettan conveyed the news to the Kothamalai Kothars who belonged to that region.

On the same Tuesday night, sticks, twigs and stalks had been collected to construct a seven-tiered funeral car[2] to carry the great man's body.

All the people agreed that the old man should be given a funeral befitting his stature. It was Machan who sent for Rangan. He had never delved deeply into his son's character. The father believed that his son was an all-powerful man who had borrowed money from Lingayya only because of financial constraints.

Rangammai's husband had gone to fetch Rangan on Monday. Why had he not come back yet?

Madhan became restless. An accomplished dancer, he had participated in many ceremonies. Now his younger brother, who had been entranced by his music like a snake by the snake charmer's magudi, had shed his mortal coils. Overriding his grief was the urge to fulfil the dictates of tradition by having a grand funeral. For the first time, he was spiritedly participating in a family function even though his brother was not there.

Why had not Rangan come? The cloth and silk necessary for the seven-tiered funeral car had to be bought.

Rangan's absence at that time, especially when Lingayya had given him all his savings, provided an opportunity for tongues to wag. The barbs hurt Paru.

Had her husband ever helped the family? Why expect him to do so now? When she had a hundred and fifty rupees with her, was it right on her part to have kept quiet when her father-in-law had had to borrow money for the funeral from Kariamalla against a promissory note? Paru had saved the money after years of toil. Why had she saved this money? Was it to buy gold and silver? No, certainly not.

It was her dream to buy an acre of flat, rich, black land where the stream curved into the valley. Every time she passed it on her way to Manikkalhatti, she would yearningly pick up

---

[2] It is made up of five to eleven tiers, decorated with cloth and streamers, and one tier is covered with black chintz and resembles a mantapam. Thurston refers to it as a funeral car.

some earth in her hand. The black soil would give bountifully like a loving mother. Every potato grown in the moist soil would be the size of a coconut. There was an orange tree there. When she had come to Maragathamalai as a bride, it had been a small bush. Now it was laden with fruit. And what delicious fruit! She had tasted it. It was as sweet as honey! Perhaps the soil and river water had combined to create such sweetness in the fruit and fragrance in the flower!

The land belonged to Krishnan. Neither he nor his wife or children would till that soil and put down roots in it. They would not lose by selling it to her. But was her husband the kind to buy her anything she desired? Didn't she know that he might bring another wife home any time? She had saved the money for the land. Paru had dreamt of asking Krishnan directly and his wife's invitation to visit Othai had come as a golden opportunity. It had been the main purpose of her visit to Othai.

But Krishnan had not even made casual conversation with her. She had had time only to listen to Rukmini's endless boasting, so there had been no chance to bring up the subject of the land. Unused to asking for anything, she had not been able to bring herself to talk to Rukmini about the land.

Having thought it over, Paru went to her house and returned with the currency notes she had kept hidden under her pillow. Calling her father-in-law aside, she offered him the money.

Madhan looked at her in astonishment. 'Where did you get this, Paru?' His voice broke.

Paru disappeared indoors without answering him.

On Wednesday, before the sun reached its zenith, men clad in white had gathered like a group of white cranes on the green fields atop Maragathamalai. Rangan and Rangammai's husband arrived only at noon. Rangan was secretly relieved that the family had begun the rites without waiting for him. However, he approached his uncle's body and shed tears.

'You were father and mother to me, Chithappa. Only the day before yesterday, you spoke to me, sat beside me and ate with me. How could you leave us so suddenly? What plans I had made! When I saw the Nandanar bioscope yesterday, I wanted to take you to see it. You would have watched it enthralled with tears in your eyes. I had plans to take my Chinnappa to Perur, Chidambaram and Bhavani.' His torrent of words and tears moved all those present.

Soon afterwards, Lingayya's body was brought outside the house on his cot and the rituals began. Shedding tears, Rangammai bathed her uncle's golden body. Madhan dressed his younger brother in a new dhoti, shirt, coat and turban and fixed two shining silver rupees on his broad forehead. Then Lingayya was laid on the decorated funeral car.

The Muttukothan, who had supplied him with pitchfork, scythe and spade in his lifetime, brought him implements for the last time, tearfully recollecting his generosity. Madhi's sister-in-law and the Mookkumalai relatives brought sweetmeats in baskets. Madhan and others had collected every single thing necessary for the last journey: jaggery and tinai flour, samai and rice, chickpeas, puffed rice and tobacco.

Womenfolk, both relatives and acquaintances, paid their last respects to the body of that virtuous man by standing with folded hands around the funeral car. Some of them expressed their reverence by ringing a bell.

Streams of people came to pay homage to Lingayya, who was departing to adorn the holy feet of the Almighty; they saluted him by touching the head; the youngsters touched his feet in reverence and placed pieces of white cloth with yellow and red stripes inside his kupatti as their last offering. Elders like Kariamalla stood respectfully near the head of the car with tearful eyes. The Toreyas who were like children to him and had served him all his life, bowed and touched his feet and shed tears.

Madhan, along with a group of men clad in shiny satin and silk skirts and turbans, danced around the funeral car to honour the body.

The Kothar music boomed. The dancers linked hands around the funeral car, six tiers of which were decorated with multi-coloured cloth while the seventh was covered in black.

The minute they started dancing in tune to the beat, Jogi, who, all this while had been dazed and numb, lost in a world of grief, suddenly rushed forward like a torrent unleashed by dislodged boulders. No one could figure out whether he was aware of what was happening or knew what he was doing.

His beloved father, who had brought him up in that house was gone. The light, which had created him and given him life, had gone out. The precious gem that had lived in that house had vanished. The mango tree that had adorned the courtyard had fallen.

At such a time, he thought, should they be singing and dancing to the sound of kuzhal and muzhavu, wearing gaudy clothes?

Jolted out of his lonely world of grief, he was infuriated by the noise and colours. A burning rage consumed his respect for tradition and custom. 'Stop!' he shouted like a maniac and savagely broke apart the linked hands.

His uncle was aghast, so were the crowds of women; the Kothars were stunned and their music was stilled.

'How long have you been wishing for my ayyan's death? Go! Go! Go away!' he shouted. In a frenzy he screamed at the startled Kothars, 'Who asked you to come? Go away. If I hear one more beat of the parai, I'll snatch it and fling it away.'

At that moment, Krishnan took a step forward. He had paid his homage to the deceased and was standing to one side. As an educated person who commanded respect in that gathering, he was in a position to say, 'It's true. It is better to give up these unsuitable customs. In a house visited by sorrow, wouldn't music, dance and feasting only add to the grief of those affected?'

Still reeling from the shock, Madhan caught Jogi's hand and asked him, 'Jogi? What's all this?'

Jogi could hardly bear the sight of his uncle clad in his gaudy silk dancing costume. He was caught in a vortex of violent grief and fiery emotions and the sequence of past events unrolled in his mind: the miserable poverty in his house because of his uncle, the inexhaustible patience with which his father had borne that burden and his continued support to the opposite house.

'What do you mean? Were you waiting for this? You destroyed my father little by little. Now you come beating the kottu, wearing silks and skirts; and you rejoice. Go away, all of you; leave me and my father and mother alone.'

Girijai's father tried to pacify him, 'Calm down, Jogi. Who is there to comfort your mother, if you succumb to grief and react so violently? Don't the ceremonies have to go on?'

'Don't you know how much my father had to suffer for the sake of his brother's family? Just yesterday, before his death, he gave the weeping Rangan money without even counting it. Today they have forgotten everything. When my father lies dead, how dare Periappa dance after drinking from the bottle his son sneaked in? My heart burns,' Jogi said furiously.

'Yes, we should stop singing and dancing on such occasions.' This was the voice of Arjunan, the young doctor who had taken Lingayya's pulse on the day of the festival.

'Yes. Our forefathers had adopted some practices which appear out of place today. Do we have to follow them?'

'Are we savages? Why sing on a sad occasion?'

'I agree.'

Several young men came out in support of Arjunan's opinion.

Krishnan played the role of mediator. 'Yes, it is a matter for reflection by the elders. So many of us abhor the funeral customs of the Todas and their habit of drinking. We should also alter some of our traditions and customs with changing times. Without studying these customs and deliberating why they have been instituted, it is not right to adhere blindly to them because they are part of our tradition. The elders should think about it without getting angry or upset.'

Krishnan's words and the respect with which he was heard sparked off Rangan's jealousy.

'How dare you poke your nose into other people's affairs? Who the hell are you?' he asked, taking a step forward.

Madhan lost his patience. Was there to be no dancing for his beloved brother? No Kothar music?

He was normally indifferent to what went on around him. The only things that were part of his bloodstream were drink, music and dance.

He had led the dancers in many funerals. When he was around, how could his dear younger brother have a funeral without any ceremony? Madhan was an inarticulate person who could not express his innermost feelings. 'Is my brother to be cremated like an orphan? Is this proper, Krishna?' he asked in despair.

'When the world has gone dark for Amma and me, is it right for you to dance? If you are truly grateful to your brother and his family, leave my father in peace. Show me the way to lessen my burden of grief or go away,' Jogi pleaded tearfully.

Meanwhile some young men, who had gone to school and had been exposed to other cultures, sympathised with Jogi and urged Krishnan to make another plea.

Every one of the elders said, 'How can it be right? Should the traditional rituals be suspended? Doesn't Lingayya have to be sent on the right path?'

Jogi approached the Kothars and said, 'Don't think that you will be deprived of your share of grain. Please go away.'

'Don't be childish, Jogi,' said the uncle from Mookkumalai.

'Yes, after a while he may say, "My father is not dead. Are you waiting to cremate his beautiful body? Go away," and then push us away,' Rangan said sarcastically.

'Ungrateful fellow! We didn't ask your opinion,' shouted Jogi, spewing hatred.

Krishnan was worried that Jogi's outburst would fan the small spark into a roaring fire. Ignoring Rangan's earlier unjust accusations, he said, ' Is this the time for both of you to lose your temper? Ranga, it is not proper.'

'The great lawyer has come to talk of right and wrong. Who are you to butt into the family disputes of others?' asked Rangan. Kariamalla, unable to bear his insolent words to Krishnan, said, 'Mind your tongue, Ranga.'

'Save your advice for those who are arrogant because of money, position and education. This is our personal affair,' Rangan retorted hotly.

An old woman interrupted, saying, 'Jogi, go in. Let the rites continue. Would your father have approved of your behaviour?'

'That's just what I'm wondering. There's no need for celebrations and dancing. Whatever has to be done for my father, I'll do it with sincerity and feeling. Those of you who have nothing to do with this can leave.'

Agreeing with Jogi, Krishnan told the Kothars, 'Let's not have all this. Please go.'

With long pent-up fury, Rangan sprang on Krishnan and sent him reeling.

'Starting a quarrel, are you?' he roared.

The crowd, which had already been divided, split into two camps when the verbal battle escalated into a fist-fight. Arguments and counter arguments were bandied. The Kothars waited for a long time and then left, worried.

Dusk fell.

Those in the crowd, who were envious of Krishnan's wealth and his education said, 'What role does he have to play here? His education has made him so arrogant that he thinks he has the right to speak like this.'

Kariamalla could not bear the way Rangan had needlessly taunted Krishnan. He was now determined to prevent the singing and dancing at all costs.

'I'll call the police. We will perform the ceremony come what may,' said Rangan.

Matters reached a head. Night fell without any ceremony being performed.

The next day, the disagreement created a schism among the hill folk, dividing them into two separate factions. A huge crowd gathered at Maragathamalai.

Rangan brought the police in. Jogi was horrified at the way the whole affair had assumed monstrous proportions.

Did his father die to bring about a rift in the people? Would his soul find peace in the midst of strife? On the last day, hadn't he shared his food with Rangan for the sake of unity in the family? He, Jogi, had shattered the ideals for which his father had striven till his last breath, the minute he had died. Hadn't he been the one to start the quarrel?

He berated himself; blamed himself; cursed himself for having lost his temper.

After the police came in, the two groups retreated, threatening violence. Since it started raining, dancing was out of question. In the house, the wife became a widow and, in the village, enmity triumphed. Jogi was consumed with grief and rage.

Six

Rivalry and jealousy may add spice to life, but too much of it can prove poisonous. Traditions and customs never meant much to Rangan. When Jogi alone had come forward to stop the Kothar song and dance, he had not seriously opposed him; but the minute Krishnan opened his mouth, he had struck like a snake emerging from its pit. The fire, which had been smouldering within him all along, now erupted like a volcano.

Merely showing his anger at Krishnan was not enough. He had to equal Kariamalla's wealth and influence in the village in order to oppose him. Rangan harboured no enmity towards Jogi for he did not consider him an equal. But he was determined to go all out to become Krishnan's peer. He had not, so far, engaged in tea cultivation. He would plunge into that activity now and work single-mindedly to achieve success. Yes, he would work hard, equal Krishnan in status, and see to it that his importance in the village was destroyed.

While Rangan was full of such grandiose plans, Jogi was torturing himself with feelings of guilt about his angry outpouring. The day following the milk ceremony at the funeral, he went to talk to Rangan and Madhan. He feared that his uncle might have borrowed from Kariamalla for funeral expenses. But Jogi knew that if he took Kariamalla's side, he was likely to antagonise Rangan. If he quarrelled with Rangan, his father's soul would not rest in peace. Hadn't he already dishonoured his father's words by calling Rangan ungrateful? Even while participating in the milk ceremony, Rangan had not exchanged a word with Jogi.

It was drizzling. Rangan stood outside his house with a cheroot in his mouth.

Jogi approached him and said gruffly, 'Anna.'

His eyes full of contempt, Rangan looked at him disdainfully.

'I was devastated with sorrow and spoke angrily to you. Ayyan would never have permitted this, Anna,' said Jogi.

'Whatever it was, you acted rashly, siding with that new-rich fellow. You have both joined forces against me since the day I married the girl you both coveted. Weren't you party to the conspiracy to send Paru to Othai in my absence, without my knowledge?'

Jogi was horrified at the nasty and unexpected turn in the conversation.

'Sivasiva! I didn't even know about Anni's trip to Othai. I had gone with Girijai to Manikkalhatti that day. Don't hurt me with such words, Anna.'

'Whom are you trying to fool? I know everything.'

Sparks of anger flew from Jogi's eyes. 'If I'm so vile, may the Goddess *Mariamman* put out my eyes!' he shouted.

Hearing raised voices, Paru emerged from the house. 'Aren't you ashamed of yourself? Nobody is preventing you from bringing another bride. So there's no need to accuse anyone else falsely. I've never stood in your way; nor will I ever do so. I am not the kind of person you think I am. This marriage has been such an ordeal that I don't wish to go through another,' she said. Without waiting for a reply, she went off to her fields, heedless of the drizzle.

For a moment Rangan was taken aback by her unexpected interruption. Jogi wanted to put an end to the matter. 'I didn't come here about that. Ayyan should have gone peacefully, but we had all that fuss with the police. My conscience is pricking me; I have been at fault. I had made a promise to Ayyan. He wanted these two households to live unitedly as one family. If one household goes hungry, the other should not eat. I am determined to fulfil his wishes,' he said.

'I am all for it. It was you who joined hands with that fellow and turned against your brother and uncle. They divided us. They think they are great because of their four patches of land and money! I'll show them that I can do better,' said Rangan, calling out to Rangammai and her husband. The quiet, peace-loving couple, who were playing with the new baby, came at once.

'Look here, if you as much as exchange a word with those who started the quarrel the other day, you and your children will have to find somewhere else to live. Remember who has given you this house and land to grow your food. Do you understand?'

'Don't I know that, Anna? If anyone meddles with us, I'll finish him off then and there,' said Rangammai's husband.

The matter was closed for the moment.

It was like a conspiracy; no one in the village turned up for the final rites on the tenth day.

Kariamalla was a man to be reckoned with and no one dared to cross him. The news that Jogi had joined hands with Rangan kept even next-door Belli away from the rites.

Jogi was pained. The rift should not have occurred. Kariamalla had so often lent them a helping hand when they had been in difficulties. Rangan would return to Othai the next day. How would he, Jogi, live there after having antagonised the whole hatti? But who could convince Rangan?

As soon as the final rites were over, Rangan returned to Othai to seek financial backing for his new venture. The house seemed empty. In ten days, Jogi's mother had aged considerably. Hadn't she lost her other half who had been her strength and support? Divested of the *elemukkuthi*, hands bare of the bangles which she had placed at her husband's feet, she reminded Jogi of a tree with yellowed leaves that might fall any day.

One evening, soon after sunset, a shaken Girijai came looking for her husband who was about to enter the hagottu.

Two buffaloes were missing; they were not in the shed nor in the pasture.

In earlier times, when Jogi had been a child, a whole hill had been set aside for grazing cattle. Now, except for one slope, coffee and tea bushes covered the entire hillside.

'Are you joking? Where could the grazing cattle disappear? Ask Rangi's son, Raman,' said Jogi.

Fear crept into her eyes. 'I went to search for them. Bellianna says that a cow from the big house came into our patch yesterday and ate up all the cabbage plants. So Raman's father beat the cow and broke its leg. Now their servants have caught our buffaloes and shut them up in the big house.'

Devare! As far as he remembered, such mean acts were unknown in the hatti. The villagers, who normally just drove away other cattle from their fields, had now become alienated from each other and went about fuelling the feud.

When Jogi went to fetch the buffaloes back from the big house, one of the gardeners was watering Kariamalla's cattle.

'Can a dumb creature distinguish between your land and mine? What is this new custom of shutting them up?' demanded Jogi.

'Who is introducing new customs? Your brother-in-law beat up our calf and broke its leg. We have merely tied up your cattle and fed them. Pay one rupee and take them away!' said Krishnan's younger brother Ajjan from within.

Jogi was stunned.

He went home with moist eyes, brought the money and collected his buffaloes.

Ever since more people had come to work in Kariamalla's tea estates, law and order had begun to deteriorate in the area. The system of each one taking a turn at the night-watch had almost disappeared. The coolies who worked under Kariamalla guarded his estates. A handful of others living in the hatti maintained the old traditions and customs; they cultivated the land jointly and guarded it in turns. Yet the feeling of togetherness which had been there earlier, had gone. This had not been so apparent for a long time. With the incidents on the day of Lingayya's death and in the ten days that followed, the lack of unity among the people and their fallout came out in the open.

All those who belonged to the hatti had lived graciously and in unity like a single family! They had worked hard, enjoyed the fruit of their labour, shared each other's joys and sorrows and eaten together. When anyone had fallen ill at sowing or harvesting time, others had stepped in to do their work and give them their share of the produce. When Jogi had been in the temple, his father had been ill and bedridden for months, even years together Could he now forget the help rendered by Kariamalla's family and others? His mother had related many touching incidents that highlighted their generosity and warmth.

Jogi spent that whole night reminiscing with nostalgia…

One incident came to his mind.

Normally, one would eat the new grain only after offering it to God at the harvest festival, which was celebrated on a day decided upon by all the villagers in that area. Once, the stock of grain in Jogi's house had been used up ten days before the festival. It was not wrong to cut the new crop and eat it before the festival, but it was held that those who did so could not participate in the sacred rites in the village nor go to the homes of their relatives and join the festivities. That particular year, in Kariamalla's daughter's house in Manikkalhatti, the Linga-offering ceremony for the Saivalinga Badaga boys was to be celebrated.

Jogi's father had been miserable the whole night. After much thought, Madhi had left for the fields to cut the tinai before daybreak. Kariamalla, on his way to invite Lingayya for the ceremony, had met her.

He had asked her, 'Where are you going so early in the morning?' Jogi's mother had stood sheepishly, full of sorrow, shrinking with shame.

He had immediately understood her predicament and had hurried back to his house. In a short while, a Toreyan had come bearing a basket of samai and potatoes on his head and left it at their doorstep… Jogi's father had narrated this incident to him; so had his mother. How could such a man become an enemy?

Jogi felt a burning sensation at the bottom of his heart, similar to the pangs of extreme hunger; his eyes filled with tears and he could not close them.

By his side, Girijai slept. Though he could not see her in the dark, her childlike face, reflecting her innocent nature, came into his thoughts. Fear stabbed him.

They had no children. After him there would be nothing, nothing at all.

Had he spawned only enmity? A trivial disagreement had become a full-blown one. Where would it end? Would he see it end?

In the morning, the spark lit by him had become a raging fire.

'Jogi! Jogi! Hey!'

Startled by Madhan's voice, he got up, adjusting his dupatti.

'What an atrocity! That damned labourer, Govindan, has broken my son-in-law's leg,' he shouted.

Jogi was thunderstruck; he ran out.

Rangammai's husband, his body splattered with mud, sat shivering and crying, while blood flowed down his leg. Rangammai was cursing the corner house in a voice that evoked memories of her mother.

Rangammai's husband had gone for the night-watch. The rainwater had stagnated in Paru's field and would have spoilt the potatoes. While he was making a breach to let the water flow out, he had been caught by the neck and pushed down. When he had turned his head, he had recognised Govindan, Kariamalla's gardener.

'Hey, how dare you let the water into our field and damage the crops? I'll kill you,' he had threatened. In the resulting fight, he had broken the leg of Rangammai's husband. He, in turn, had grabbed Govindan's dupatti and had raised a hue and cry.

Though the hatti had been startled into wakefulness, nobody had come forward to intervene in the fight.

Jogi asked, 'Whatever it is, wasn't it wrong of you to direct the water towards their fields?'

'Do they have the right to impound our buffalo and ask for payment?' retorted Rangi's husband.

'Will Ranganna take this lying down? How dare a labourer beat up my husband like this? Should we be cowed down by their wealth?' wailed Rangi.

'Let it be,' Jogi sighed wearily as he washed and bandaged the broken leg.

But the incident did not fade away so easily.

Rangan came to the hatti the next morning.

A mixture of pride, joy and arrogance together with aggression suffused his face with colour. The previous day, Dame Fortune had been on his side in the point-to-point race and had given him a prize of a thousand five hundred rupees.

As soon as he had heard what had happened, he had raced home. He took Rangammai's husband on horseback to the government hospital next to the Johnson estate and returned bearing a certificate.

He rested only after he had filed a case accusing Kariamalla's man of trying to shift the boundary stone of the field and alleged that the man had tried to murder Rangammai's husband when he had caught him in the act. He even found some witnesses to swear to this. Jogi, having lost all that was dear to him, was submerged in a sea of sorrow.

Seven

The black cloud, which had been playing hide-and-seek with the hilltops, had bidden farewell to Mother Mountain and disappeared. Wild winds and rain had followed in the wake of the clouds. Before Mother Mountain could recover, the biting frost had arrived flexing his icy fingers as if to say, 'Did you think it was over?'

How merciless he was! Overnight he would blacken the earth, destroying the verdure. The minute the tender shoots peeped out of the moistened earth, he would char them. Because of his cruelty, the trees would shrivel, shed their leaves and stand looking pathetic. It was unbearable to see the animals tugging at the dry grass, only to sigh, weary with disappointment.

While Mother Mountain with her soaring peaks awaited the touch of her lover, the sun, the tears she had shed all night at the cruelty of the frost, froze. She could have gazed forever at the beauty of the red orb as he appeared. Perhaps the long wait, when she had yearned for him, seemed to make him more attractive when he came. On his arrival, the frost could only vanish, tail between his legs. After all, he would be reduced to water by the first golden rays.

Saying, 'I'll destroy your arrogance,' the sun would transform him into vapour with his rays and then smile soothingly at Mother Mountain.

Madhi hurried, seeking the spot where the sun's golden-red rays fell. The slopes, hollows and roofs were covered with what looked like crushed sugar crystals. Though Madhi wore sturdy slippers, the frost had found the spaces between her toes and they hurt as though stung by acid. Rubbing her toil-worn, gnarled hands, she tucked them inside her shawl. The first rays of the sun warmed her.

As the days went by she found that she could not withstand the cold. In the year and a half since her husband's death, she looked nine years older, wrinkled and shrunk. Like Madhi, the tree near the temple had withered and was shorn of all leaves. When Jogi had tended the fire, green, cultivated land and flowering shrubs had surrounded the temple. Either before Jogi or after him, nobody had involved himself so completely in the task of tending to the temple.

Jogi was in the cattle shed, untying the buffaloes as he said his prayers to the sun and Girjai was carrying dung to the manure pit. The wood fire she had lit in the kitchen crackled, emitting blue smoke. Otherwise the house was silent; nothing stirred.

The frost had melted. Madhi squatted in the patch of sunlight. Her half blind mother-in-law used to sit in the same spot unable to bear the cold while she and her husband had been similarly busy with the morning chores. How many years had sped by! The sun's rays fell on the same spot, in the same season at the same time. Nothing had changed; the older generation rested while the younger ones worked.

Yet there was one difference; Madhi sighed, thinking of it. Had her husband's mother basked in the sun all by herself?

In her lap, a chubby Jogi had squirmed and kicked his legs. Ever so often she had scolded him and held him firmly, her dim eyes staring into space as she had enjoyed the warmth of the sun.

The wrinkles on her face had seemed to proclaim that she had been a woman who had lived a full and satisfying life. In her lap had lain the living symbol of her hope for the future, a child who had warmed her comfortingly.

As she had revelled in the flailing of his arms and legs, her scolding had been really an expression of love.

When would Madhamma experience such joy? She had faith in her husband's words. She believed that he had possessed the power to foresee what was coming, either in his dreams or by some extraordinary intuition.

Even when he had been ailing, her mind had secretly nurtured and kept alive her husband's words foretelling that he would be reborn in her house. More than a year had gone by, but there were no signs of a new life.

Would there perhaps have been a son in the family if Paru had been Jogi's wife?

'Athai!' called Girijai, coming to stand by her. She was slender as a creeper, and her soft ear lobes reddened when she was emotional. Her delicate lips had been chapped by the cold and sun.

She was still young and there was no need to lose hope totally.

Aware of her mother-in-law's scrutiny, Girijai smiled shyly like a new bride.

'I've kept hot water for you to clean your teeth. Coffee is ready too,' she said.

Paru was already leaving her house, basket and pitchfork in hand.

'How are you, Athai? It's really cold today! The frost will kill the plants,' she remarked, smiling.

Madhi nodded. Foolish girl! She showered her love on the land and plants, and deluded herself that she was content.

By the time she had cleaned her teeth with a piece of charcoal and rinsed her mouth with hot water, Girijai was waiting with a brass kinnam containing coffee prepared by mixing coffee powder and jaggery in hot water. Jogi joined them.

Madhi slowly savoured the coffee that warmed her.

'Ranganna did not come home last night. The forest beyond the stream is being burnt down,' said Jogi.

His mother looked at him wide-eyed.

'To plant tea?'

'Yes, he has taken a big step. He is determined to convert the forest into a tea estate, and mint money.'

'Rangan has changed for the better since Ayyan's death. Ayyan was like Devar, his blessings will always be with Rangan. Even when he gets embroiled in cases, he wins. Even when he goes to the races, he returns with plenty of money,' Madhi said enviously.

'No, Amma, no. Rangan hasn't really become a good man, as you seem to believe. He has not won the case, nor has the other side lost. It has been postponed. When it is enmity that drives him to compete with Krishnan, how does that make him a good man? I am the one who started it all. It was my bad luck which prompted me to speak like that.'

'You're only talking about your part in it. Why can't the elders bring about a reconciliation?' demanded Girijai who had come back for the empty coffee kinnam.

She had never spoken like that before.

'Why would they want a reconciliation? Three-quarters of the village is on their side; moreover, they are also influential in other places,' said Jogi.

The sound of a car attracted their attention.

Was it Krishnan in his car, so early in the morning? Was something the matter? When Madhi, Jogi and Girijai peeped out, they were torn with fear. Four days earlier, fourth house Bojan's wife had taken ill with fever. Perhaps because the fever had become very high, she had been taken carefully on horseback to the hospital near the estate. They had seen her leave the hatti.

In earlier times, however trivial the matter, the villagers had acted as one family, sharing their joys and sorrows. It was no longer the case. They only knew that Bojan and his mother had left for the hospital three days earlier.

What could have happened?

Only Bojan and the old woman got out of Krishnan's car weeping, followed by the hatti people. Everyone in the hatti had come running out of their houses

In a short while, Rangammai's son came and said that Bojan's wife had died.

Fear and worry were writ large on every face. Krishnan left immediately. He had never gone back in such haste from the hatti.

How could a mother of four die just like that?

A couple of years earlier, the villagers had severed connections with the Kurumbas, as well as, with the Kothars. The practice of giving the Kurumbas their due had been discontinued.

How could she have died after three days of fever?

Madhan brought more news.

'The body was cremated there. It was plague.'

'Aiyo!'

The involuntary cry rose from Rangammai. Her husband had told her how his entire family had perished in an earlier outbreak of plague.

'We must do poosai to the Gods. We have neglected the poosai to Mariamma. When one becomes rich, God is forgotten,' said Madhamma.

'Why wait for Kariamalla? I'll do what Kariamalla, the elder of the village failed to do,' Rangan swore to himself. As though waiting for an opportunity to show his superiority, he decided to buy a cock on Tuesday, sacrifice it to Mariamman under the rock and invite the Kurumbas to offer worship. Meanwhile, Rangammai secretly threw the two writhing rats she had found in her kitchen into the manure pit. Though Madhi informed the neighbours about the poosai on Tuesday, except for a couple of villagers, everyone stayed away because they felt it was an act of defiance against Kariamalla.

The families of the two brothers went off to the temple early in the morning, taking all that was required for the poosai. Only Madhi sat in the space between the two houses. Krishnan, accompanied by health authorities and doctors, came to the hatti to inoculate the hatti folk against plague. They went from house to house to ensure that everyone was protected.

Madhamma kept sitting between the two houses. Krishnan, who was checking to see if everyone had been inoculated, walked up and down, casting uneasy glances at Madhi. He thought, 'Paru and Rangammai have children. Shouldn't they be inoculated? What have the children to do with the elders' quarrel? Were they aware of my plan and have deliberately gone away?'

When Krishnan walked past her without a word, Madhi felt deeply hurt.

He had gone from house to house to call out to the people asking those inside to come out and get inoculated. Didn't he have a word for an old woman sitting in the sun? Was she also an enemy? Instead of paying what was due to the Gods, what was the use of injections? Why should this disgraceful state of affairs have come about as a consequence of the death of her husband, who had never wavered from his faith in God and had led a virtuous life?

Madhi's wrinkled cheeks were wet with tears.

That week, two Toreyas in the hatti succumbed to the plague. On Thursday evening, Rangi's baby was feverish. By Sunday, the plague had rapidly devoured three of her children and then attacked Paru's daughters.

The people of the hatti were in the grip of terror. Some left; some others burnt their belongings.

Kariamalla's family shifted to Othai. The *Mahamari*, the pestilence, invaded the nearby hattis one-by-one. In the house of the uncle at Mookkumalai, with the exception of himself and his son, the entire family fell prey to plague. The boy who guarded the fire in the temple was the next victim. The fire was extinguished and the temple shut.

When Paru saw the flushed faces of her precious children, her insides burned. 'I chose the names Lakshmi and Jaya with such love. My beloved children, I thought I would build a life around you,' she agonised.

Rangammai, who had lost three children in a row, lay in a stupor, unwilling even to light the fire.

'Amma, Amma!' moaned Paru's children.

What could Paru do? Was the poosai to God of no use? Why should the dreaded disease seize the tender young bodies? What was left for her? The frost had charred even the green shoots at the top of the trees.

Rangan was aware of her silent misery and with tears in his eyes, he fetched the doctor from the hospital near the estate.

'It is more dangerous than a tiger or leopard, it should have been prevented. Let us see,' said the doctor, prescribing some medicine.

'Why do you spare me when you want to take away my children? Oh, Mariamma, take me also!' prayed Paru, holding her children in her arms all night.

But once Mariamma had taken away those tender creatures, she left Paru's house, deciding that there was nothing left for her to do there.

Reeling from the shock of the worst blow that fate had dealt her, Paru wept uncontrollably.

Madhi could not find words to console her. Would the children have survived if they had been inoculated? While she spent sleepless nights yearning for a child, why did God pluck these two blossoms? Were both the houses destined to become barren?

She hated the sun, which though it exuded gentle warmth, seemed merciless to her. Addressing the blue sky, her embittered heart cursed, 'So you are gloating over your son, are you? O Sky, your child, the sun, will go away and you too will suffer!' Shutting the door, Madhi embraced Paru and wept. Rangammai and her husband left for Kothai with their remaining children, to escape death.

The hatti was deserted, the houses barred and bolted. In that desolate village, there was only one person who continued to do her duty. She consoled her sister and mother-in-law, cooked food for the menfolk of both houses and flitted from one house to the other trying to infuse some life into them. That person was Girijai

Eight

Just as a person debilitated by a long illness slowly regains his sense of taste and his body gets suffused with fresh blood, Mother Nature began to turn green after the severe frost.

After the fire-walking festival, everyone was engaged in tilling the soil. The people who had left the village returned and applied a fresh coat of limewash to renovate their houses. There was a new priest at the Ayyan temple. This time it was the son of Rami, a local.

Who can heal wounds better than time? Madhi recovered from the tragedy. Even Rangammai got over the loss of her children. Only Paru was inconsolable. It was as though the severe blow dealt by death had sent her into a state of shock. Unaware of whether it was night or day, she sat sighing, her hair unkempt, going without food or water.

Once he began to cultivate tea, Rangan did not go to Othai to lease land to grow potatoes. He took contracts for felling trees. He also bought artificial fertiliser and helped Jogi to plant potatoes, cabbages and wheat. However, when he returned home, there was no one to welcome him with a warm smile.

Madhan slept all the time and was a spent force. Where was the music of the earlier days? The dancing? The rituals? The traditions? How society had changed in two years! In most places, it was considered uncultured to invite Kothars to perform and their music was no longer welcome.

So Rangan's father had become a spent force.

What of Paru, his wife? Did she spare him a glance? The joy in her face had disappeared. Her golden glow had faded. Dark circles around her eyes, protruding cheek bones, parched cracked lips, was this the Paru of his dreams, the girl he had married? Was this the same Paru who had once made the young men's hearts flutter?

He had given up drinking and gambling. Obsessed with his rivalry, his sole aim in life was to mint money by growing tea. But even he was moved to compassion at the sight of Paru.

He had separated a young maiden from the man she loved and had married her. In reality, how many days had she lived with him as a loving wife?

Didn't he see Girijai with a spring in her step, looking like a new bride even today, the liveliness of childhood and the glow of youth undimmed, shyly lowering her eyes when she met Jogi's glance. How happy Jogi was with her! When they worked together in the field, laughing and exchanging loving glances, one could see that the bloom in their marriage had not worn off.

It was only after he started moving with them closely that he had been assailed by new feelings. Resentment against his wife flared up for the first time.

Even in the first flush of marriage when he had lived in intimacy with Paru, he had not experienced even a fraction of the joy that was evident in Jogi's marriage. She had never glanced at him with unfathomable mysteries in her eyes, nor had she thrilled him with enticing smiles. Now God had snatched away the precious children born as a result of their marriage even before they were fully grown. But even a tree blighted by frost blossomed again with the advent of spring.

'Paru, can't you serve me food if Rangammai is not here? Can't you bathe and be clean?' he asked.

His voice was gentle.

Her eyes staring into space, she served him his food.

Rangammai's son, Raman, came in and sat down. He was the oldest of the children and was about fifteen. A simple fellow, he helped his uncle in the fields and learnt the work. He also wanted to learn how to drive a car. The cheerful warmth of a close-knit family was dear to him.

Paru had served only one helping of rice in the vattil.

'Come, Rama. Sit down, what are you waiting for?' asked Rangan.

'Mami has forgotten me. Now that Jaya and Lakshmi have gone, she no longer bothers about me. Mami, if you have a daughter even now, I'll marry her. Don't forget me,' he teased.

He had a special affection for his aunt. He spoke to her every day and tried to bring a smile to her melancholy countenance. But she seemed beyond reach. It was as if she preferred to remain in her self-imposed isolation, allowing no one to trespass on her privacy.

'Why, Mami, why so silent? I haven't let Mama even set foot on your land. It doesn't matter that you forgot to serve me now, but how could you forget your land? It is overgrown with thorn bushes. Are you feeling sorry for them and giving them a chance to grow after so many years?' the boy persisted.

The hand that was serving the food suddenly trembled at the mention of the land

Yes, she had forgotten her precious land in her grief. For the past three months, she had forgotten the land that was as much a part of her life as air and water. Hadn't that land generously yielded nine-fold at the last harvest?

Shaken out of her stupor, she suddenly became agitated. She had a strong urge to drop the vessel immediately and rush to the land.

'See, Mama? At the mention of the land, Mami becomes restless. Don't worry, Mami, I've cut the thorn shrubs and turned the earth with the pitchfork. Mami, why don't you plant an orange tree there with your hands?' asked her nephew.

At once, Paru remembered the black soil. She said, 'We must get a good sapling. I've really wanted to plant an orange tree for years.'

Immediately, Rangan responded. 'Why just one, we can plant ten or fifteen. I'll bring a graft which gives fruit as sweet as sugar.'

'Just one will do,' said Paru.

'Your daughter will peel that fruit for me; isn't that so, Mami?' Smiling, Raman went to wash his hands.

Rangan beamed, but Paru did not smile. 'Not my daughter, but your mama's,' she said.

After finishing his meal, Rangan smoked a cigarette and went out for a while. When he returned, he went into the edumane.

Rangammai, her husband and children were all fast asleep in the ogamane. Raman was sprawled in the middle like a log. He was snoring. Raman was an innocent boy and he teased his aunt without a trace of shyness!

She had said, 'Your mama's daughter.' What could it mean? Did she intend on being a wife to him or not? Rangammai who had lost three children had gotten over it and was now happily sharing a loving intimacy with her husband. Girijai, who had not borne a child as yet, did not grumble.

What was in Paru's mind, wondered Rangan.

Addicted as he had been to many pleasures, he was provoked to violent anger by Paru's indifference.

He got up, walked past the sleeping forms and went to the rear of the house. A gunny bag was spread out near the woodstove, a thick blanket by its side.

Paru was not lying down. She was sitting up.

He could not see her face in the dark. Was he looking at a lonely figure disappointed with life? Or was it a woman who was a picture of grief?

His violent anger suddenly ebbed away, leaving him chilled.

For the first time, he wondered whether he had wronged her. For the first time, the thought occurred to him that he might have crushed the delicate blossom with his brutality.

When this thought came to him, several truths struck him. In that very house, hadn't his step-mother left his father? Hadn't Gowri, with whom he had become close, left her husband?

Why did Paru not behave that way? She never showed the least desire to leave his house. Girijai at least often went to her parental home in Manikkahatti with Jogi. Why did she never go anywhere?

Paru was not like the girls he normally encountered. Unlike her husband, who had sought another woman because he had not found fulfilment in marriage, Paru had never looked at another man.

Had he not hurled obscene accusations at Krishnan that were false, in spite of knowing in his innermost heart that Paru was chaste.

Whatever he felt about Paru, he did not dare to think ill of her. There were ways to get out of a marriage, but she was steadfast.

Pushing aside these thoughts, Rangan slowly approached her and sat down beside her. She was startled. Did she fear a nocturnal intruder with evil intentions?

She was not wearing a pattu on her head. She was clad in an araimundu and a shawl. He whispered in her ear, 'Look at me, Paru, why are you still harbouring sad thoughts?' and gently held her hand.

'No,' she said. From the way her hand trembled in his, he could sense her body shaking violently.

'What do you mean, no? That's all we were fated to have. But hasn't Rangammai, who has lost three children, overcome her grief?' he asked, his voice faltering.

She did not give him a direct answer. Gazing elsewhere, she said, 'Marry Gowri.'

'Paru!'

'Yes. Bring her home by next month.'

'What are you saying, Paru?'

'Isn't it true that you're having an affair with Gowri?'

He hesitated; faltered; then admitted it.

'Paru? Is that why you're angry? Do you not wish to stay in this house, Paru?'

'Did I say so?'

'Then, I don't understand.

'All I need in life is my patch of land.'

'If you want me to give up Gowri, I'll do so. Why do you talk like this? Today, in your presence, I realise that I am guilty.'

'No, I'm the guilty one. Our elders have said that it is wrong to be envious if other people's buffaloes yield milk in plenty or if their land is green and fertile. I was envious of others' lives. I envied them their children. My children were snatched away by Mariamma. If I crave for a child now, it might make me envious. Whenever my desires go beyond limits, God strikes a blow. I want nothing any more. Marry Gowri.'

'Paru!'

His voice sounded strange to his own ears.

'I… have unheedingly crushed your feelings. I was a brute who didn't realise that you were so sensitive. Do you hate me, Paru? Do you hate me for ruining your life, Paru?'

It was not true to say that he was entirely lacking in gentleness. Her eyes lit up when she realised that even he could occasionally rise above the base emotions that dominated him.

'Why would I hate you? You were entitled to marry me. You won me in an open competition and made me yours.'

'The competition was held only because of me.'

'Why harp on the past? There is such a thing as fate.' He took both her hands in his. He was agitated; whether it was due to anger or pity, he did not know.

'Paru, did you never want me? Were you ever happy with me?' It was the cry of a desperate heart unable to accept failure. Had he deluded himself all along that he had vanquished Krishnan? Wasn't it true that she had never loved him? Was Krishnan crowing triumphantly because he was aware of this?

How could a mind ruled by jealousy see straight?

'Why ask me all this now? It is not as if we were married only yesterday,' said Paru.

'Answer my question. Do you want to leave me because you have had enough of me? Though you came to me as my wife, you cheated me. You have no love for me. You are living here out of duty. Isn't that so?'

His voice rose in anger.

Tearfully, Paru asked him, 'Why are you harassing me and hurting me deliberately?'

'Traitor!' He flung off her hands and got up, then went and lay down in the edumane, still seething.

What a hard-hearted woman she was! Though he had begged and pleaded, she had not lied or spoken soothingly to assuage his jealous heart.

His heart pounded as he lit a match, went to the grain bin and pulled out the bottle of liquor buried in it. As he drank, trying to forget his failure he resolved to make arrangements to fetch Gowri the very next day.

The following day Paru did not welcome the dawn from within the house. With her body thrilling to the touch of the cool earth under her feet, she saw the sun as it rose in the east.

A new hope; a new light; a new life!

Lost in thought, she stood in her field and scooped up the earth with both hands.

This is the essence of my existence; the joy of my life; the soil, my mother, my child. This is everything. This will not betray me. Fire and disease cannot separate me from it; they cannot snatch it away. My land!

Nine

Time knows no fatigue as it makes its eventful way forward, creating and destroying. As it rolls along with the changing cycle of the seasons, it never glances back at the path it has traversed.

Madhi's hair was now silver, her hands and legs were like dry-twigs and her skin was criss-crossed with innumerable wrinkles. In the house opposite, Rangammai's son Raman had become a strapping youth. Rangan had begun to see the green tea leaves yield money. He had bought a lorry for six thousand rupees to carry the produce. He had rebuilt his house, making it larger and more comfortable. After she had entered the house,

Gowri had given birth to two fine boys. There had been many changes in the last few years.

Madhi had believed that God had cheated her! Was his father also cheating innocent Jogi! Was he reborn as a son to Rangan? Whom did Lingayya consider his son? Rangan or Jogi?

Her spirit was broken by age and disappointment. Would she wither and die disappointed? After living for five kurunji-spans, would she never hear childish prattle in her house, never see the family's hope for the future?

It was time for the Sakalathi festival.[3] The hatti houses were thoroughly cleaned and swabbed. In the evening the womenfolk decorated the floor of the entire house with beautiful *kolams.*

As a young bride, Madhi had used only white ash to make kolams. But Gowri and some other girls did not behave like women of her generation. Many hatti girls had become fashionable and wore saris. They went off in groups to Othai to enjoy the races and other diversions.

Every Tuesday, without fail, Gowri would go with Raman when he drove the lorry to Othai. Could she be blamed? What was there in Madhi's house? The same samai, the same wheat, the never-ending toil. But Jogi and Girijai never seemed weary of this life.

On the day of the Sakalathi festival, wheat flour *dosais* were prepared and stacked in a pile. A little rice and butter were placed on the pile. Three wicks dipped in castor oil were placed on the mixture and lit. The dosais were waved round the heads of all the children of the house to ward off the evil eye, then taken to their field and thrown in it with the words, 'Sakalathi has come!' Prayers were then chanted.

Madhi felt there was no fun in celebrating festivals in a childless house. But Jogi kept up all the traditions. In the

---

[3]The Sakalathi festival is celebrated in the month of *Aippasi* or Karthigai. Prayers are offered to God so that the family and the crop flourish and wheat flour dosais are offered as *bali* or sacrifice to ward off evil spirits.

evening, after throwing the dosais in his field, he sat beneath the lamp and began to say his prayers.

Madhi lay in the edumane with her eyes closed. The melodious chant fell sweetly on her ears. It soothed her worn nerves, like the comforting warmth of a mother's lap, like a lullaby. Had she slowly drifted into sleep? It could not be called sleep.

Groups of people are going somewhere. Is it an army? Or a battalion of women? They do not wear the pattu and mundu. They are wearing brightly-coloured clothes, bracelets on their wrists and auspicious *pottus* on their foreheads. They are running swiftly, led by a woman like Durga, the goddess of war. Behind them, in hot pursuit, come sword-wielding soldiers on horseback.[4]

The woman, the first to cross the river, looks at a distant temple gopuram with folded palms, tear-filled eyes and an anguished heart.

'Oh, Siva, swallower of poison! Oh, Ammai, save us! Oh, Nanjundanayakane, Nayakiye, prevent them from crossing the river! Oh, God of the dark neck, are you going to help those villains?' she prays tearfully, desperately.

Ah! A miracle! A torrent gushes forth from the riverbed like the Ganga from the matted locks of Siva. Is the roaring, swirling, frothy water a flash flood? Or has it been caused by the grace of the mighty God? The horses speeding like the wind come to a frightened stop before the turbulent waters.

Eyes shining with gratitude, the women sing in praise of Basavesa. There is a tinkle of bells, a fragrance of incense.

---

[4] In the 18th century, during the reign of Tipu Sultan, the Badagas came from Mysore to the Nilgiris through the Bandipur forest. It is believed that Tipu was smitten by a girl who lived with her seven brothers in a village called Badagahalli. He wanted to marry her. To avoid it, the family fled to the Nilgiris. With Tipu's men giving chase, they crossed the dry bed of a river and prayed to Nanjundeswara to protect them. Floods rose in the river bed, forcing Tipu's men to retreat. This is part of the Badaga oral tradition.

Madhi woke up suddenly at this juncture. The sound of bells, the sound of prayers! She realised it was Jogi, seated beneath the lamp, praying to Siva.

She quickly sat up, filled with an inexpressible joy.

'O Nanjundeswara! Great is your mercy! Was this dream your doing? Was it to reassure me, saying, "Why are you worried? I'm here. Have you forgotten me?" You have reminded this ignorant forgetful woman that you are the Lord of our clan. How can I thank you?' she wondered. With tears in her eyes, she ran and prostrated herself before the lamp.

'Jogi, Iswaran has blessed us. Take a vow to visit the Nanjundeswara temple and tie some silver coins in a cloth. Girijai, prostrate yourself before our Lord,' she commanded.

Jogi looked at his mother, amazed. 'Amma!'

'Yes, son. I saw a scene in my dream. I saw the riverbed filling with water as soon as the woman crossed it and the soldiers and horses falling back. Forgetting the Lord who swallowed poison, we are complaining that we don't have a son. He has reminded us of His existence.'

Jogi and Girijai bowed in the direction of the Nanjundeswara temple and tied some silver coins in a cloth.

Those who have faith are not disappointed. After several years of marriage, Girijai showed signs of carrying a new life within her. There was no limit to Madhamma's joy. Jogi's happiness knew no bounds. The face of Girijai, who flitted around with childlike exuberance, acquired a new radiance. It wore an expression of indescribable shyness and contentment. Paru was delighted by this change in Girijai. Surprisingly, even the women who had become aloof because of the feud surrounded Girijai as if she were a new bride and teased her.

An overjoyed Madhi invited the women to a feast of rice and *payasam*.

It was the custom in those days to perform the *kanni kattum* or tying of the *mangalasutram* only when a girl became pregnant for the first time; but Lingayya had changed the custom when his son had been married. The day Girijai had entered their house as a new bride, bringing the sacred water, Jogi had tied the mangalasutram around her neck. Hence the *kalippu*, the pregnancy, was just celebrated with a feast.

Kariamalla's family, which had always been the first to attend any ceremony in their house, was not in the hatti that day.

Ten months went by.

Girijai's labour pains began on a wet day at the start of the rainy season. Her mother arrived in haste from Manikkalhatti. Eager groups of old women and young girls clustered in front of the house.

The sky was overcast. Night passed into day, day into night. To the poor girl, lying like a broken reed, experiencing the excruciating agony of a first labour, there was no end in sight. Jogi's heart oscillated between agony and eager anticipation.

Four days crept by. Rangan went to the estate in search of a doctor. There he met an old, white Catholic woman called Miss Wood. The old woman had come thousands of miles to serve the people in the name of religion. Taking a few essential items, she got into the car with Rangan.

The old woman was feared as one who was out to convert all of them to her religion. Everyone, Madhi included, was against her coming into the hatti. Rangan cowed them down with a shout. Miss Wood realised that even the most experienced doctors would find Girija's case a difficult one.

When Miss Wood, with the idea of saving the mother if not the child, suggested to Rangan that Girijai should be taken to the Othai hospital, Jogi was panic-stricken. While Rangan made the necessary arrangements, Jogi looked to the west and prayed, 'God, this has come about because of your grace, don't cheat me.'

As Madhi waited, waves of fear pounded her heart. Bojan's wife had died in hospital while…

Krishnan had brought doctors to the hatti to give injections to the people. God had taken away Paru's children, who had not been given the shot.

Girijai was taken to hospital in an unconscious state.

For those who had been waiting with anxious hearts for four hours outside the closed door, the cry of a baby above the roar of the rain was like sweet honey.

Suddenly the door opened. Even before the white-clad nurse could step out, Madhi eagerly tried to barge into the room.

'It's a boy,' said the nurse, banging the door shut.

Jogi stood by, eagerly expectant.

Why was the child still screaming? Lost in the intoxicating bliss of the baby's voice, Madhi forgot the plant that had yielded the fruit. She was desperate to see the child. She craved to feast her dim gaze on the flower-like face. Her hands ached to lift up the child against her wrinkled cheek.

Why did this white-gowned woman allow this long-awaited child to cry for so long? Oh God, were they heartless? When Madhi, losing patience, knocked at the door, the nurse peeped out and scolded her. 'Go away, old woman.' Without opening the door fully, she pushed Madhi away and asked, 'Who is the husband of the girl?'

Jogi, terrified, rushed in. The door was shut again.

'Wretched woman!' said Madhi.

Jogi entered the room and looked at his wife. She lay like a flower on the hill slope, which though flattened by the rain, still looked fresh. There was a rubber tube tied around her arm. Something had been placed in her nostril. The white lady doctor was holding Girijai's hand and checking something.

'Girijai!' he shouted.

She looked at him with a smile on her face. When she moved her lips, only he could understand what she said.

'Please show us the baby,' Jogi said desperately.

The nurse brought the crying baby in her arms and showed it to them.

Girijai gazed at it. Her eyes brightened. A smile played on her lips.

'A boy, Girijai, by Isan's grace!'

Girijai continued to smile. Her eyes remained bright.

Shrugging helplessly, the doctor left the room.

The white-robed nurse's dark eyes widened and her red lips drooped. Her cry of 'Oh God! She's gone!' was followed by Jogi's anguished shout of 'Girijai!' which shook the entire building.

The child cried itself hoarse.

The rain poured relentlessly on.

Part IV

One

A shiny black car wound its way along the paved road below the hillocks. The school bell shrilled. The children were jubilant since it heralded freedom from lessons. Hordes of children emerged from the building like birds released from cages. Were there so many children in Maragathamalaihatti? Paru recollected the old days: a boy here and there, lazing on the hillsides, grazing cows. The forestlands had now become cultivated fields and the hillslopes were covered with lush green tea bushes.

Once, entire hills had been completely blue with kurinji flowers. But there was not one single kurinji to be seen now! It had last flowered the year Lingayya had walked on fire for the last time. So much had happened since then. One whole kurinji-span had gone by since Girijai had given birth to Nanjan.

It could not be said that all the schoolchildren were from the hatti. Many tea estate labourers had come from faraway Malabar and Kongai. New houses had sprung up on the hills and in the valleys. Tea factories spewing smoke had now found a place on the hillside. Gone were the days when at least one girl and one boy from each house of Maragathamalaihatti tilled the soil and toiled to support the family. Now some of the men were too lazy to work for their household. There were better options! A man could wear shirt and trousers and think of taking a bus from Keezhmalai into Coonoor town; of course, he could always go to Othai!

There were so many distractions to while away the time in Othai: horse racing, cafes, cinema halls. Could palates tickled by *bajji*, *bonda* and masala dosai relish the taste of korali and samai anymore?

There was not a single person in Maragathamalaihatti who was not consumed by a desire for riches and education was a prime requisite for earning money. Frustrated by the fact that they were not educated, all the parents sent their children to school. Women hankered after a variety of materials and saris; they yearned for things beyond their reach. Was this unique to Maragathamalaihatti? No, there was a revolution in the lives of all the hill folk.

'Hoi! Hoi!' A band of children shrieked as they ran behind Krishnan's car which was coming up the road. It was a brand-new, shiny car with the figure of a bird, with outspread wings, perched on the bonnet.

When she was returning from the fields, Paru saw Thenmalai Rukmini getting out of the car with her grandchildren.

Wearing a sandalwood-coloured sari, she was leading her granddaughter by the hand; diamond eardrops dangled from the child's ears. There were glistening chains around her neck and gold bangles jangled around her wrists. What if her daughter was short and had an oddlyshaped head? Krishnan's son-in-law was none other than the young doctor Arjunan, who had checked Lingayya's pulse on the day of the fire-walking festival. The wedding had taken place in Othai and he ran a clinic in Krishnan's house. A beautiful baby girl was born to them soon after the marriage. The baby was neither like her mother nor her grandmother. She was fair like her father.

Heedless of the light drizzle, Paru stared at the shiny, black car as she walked past, pitchfork in her hand. She remembered the day of the fire-walking festival at the Madalingeswara temple, when the Thenmalai woman had remarked pointedly, 'Your daughter and my son have become friends.' Her daughter was no longer alive. With the families consumed by hatred as a result of their rivalry, Paru had not been invited to the marriage of Krishnan's daughter. Rukmini's kindly enquiry, 'How are you, Akka?' was a thing of the past. For over two generations, there had been no occasion for the two families to come together.

'Amma, I'm getting a prize at school!' said Nanjan, running up to put his arms around Paru's neck. He was fair-complexioned with curly hair and clear light eyes like his mother. He had his father's features.

It was habitual for him to smile and blush ever so often like a girl.

Paru looked lovingly at her son and enquired, 'Re! What prize?'

'How can you understand all that? Do you know in which class I am? In the eighth, third form.'

Paru laughed 'Aye! How wonderful!' she exclaimed.

'Do you know who won the prize for getting the first rank?'

'Who?'

'Guess who?'

'The greedy Nanjan who can drink several tumblers of payasam sweetened with sugar.'

'Oh Amma!' Nanjan grumbled and ran inside with his books.

Paru gazed fondly at him, forgetting to go in to wash her hands and feet. Leaving his books inside, he rushed out again. He walked and ran like Girijai. None of Gowri's three sons or her daughter had taken to Paru. On her own, she had assumed the position of Nanjan's mother and moved into Jogi's house immediately after Madhi's death. When Rangammai's eldest son Raman married and took up the duties of a householder, he also moved in with them, in keeping with Jogi's wishes. In both houses several changes had taken place. However, nothing had changed for Paru till the birth of Nanjan. Twelve years ago, into her arid life had come a little boy, like a spring of water. By the grace of Nanjunda, this son was borne by Girijai especially for her. He was a favourite of Rangammai, Raman and his wife.

Just one kurinji-span in age, he was so intelligent! So smart! When he read his English lessons aloud or recited Tamil verses which he had set to music, Paru stood entranced and was filled with pride. In her plot of land, she planted potatoes and sold them. She gave the money to Jogianna to buy clothes and eats for Nanjan.

Rangan and Gowri were a little envious of Nanjan. None of their sons studied well. The eldest had failed in the sixth class.

All he had learnt was to fritter money and time on cigarettes and films in Othai. The second, who was older than Nanjan, did not complete class three. Rangan beat his next two children, a boy and a girl, and packed them off to school.

The tea gardens were giving them an income. Rangan concentrated on competing with Krishnan in diverse ways. When Krishnan set out to build a school, Rangan ran buses. If he planted coffee and cardamom, Rangan did the same. Though he tried his utmost to prove that he was in no way inferior to Krishnan, he was not successful.

Krishnan's fame had spread all over the district, beyond Maragathamalaihatti and Othai. Acting as the leader, he had spearheaded the independence movement in his district and gained fame as a hero. A band of twenty or thirty young men had, under his leadership, agitated in the vicinity of the Johnson estate, shouting, 'White man, quit India.' When they had destroyed the bridge connecting the bungalow and gardens to the world outside, the white man's government had arrested Krishnan and his companions.

Rangan, who was well acquainted with many white people, had been momentarily overjoyed when Krishnan had been arrested. However, Krishnan's fame had spread when he had been released from prison. At the time of independence, when he had been honoured and acclaimed by the people, it was like oil being poured on the flame of Rangan's jealousy.

Though he tacitly encouraged his elder brother's deeds which were instigated by jealousy, Jogi remained unchanged. Once the baby was left in Paru's care after his wife's death, he confined himself to tilling his patch of land. He controlled his desires and spent his time doing his duty like a *karmayogi*.

In the last three kurinji-spans, life had totally changed. Boys were no longer initiated into the ritual of milking at the age of nine nor were they entrusted with household duties. Rangammai's family eked out a living on Jogi's land. Raman drove Rangan Maman's lorry and earned a salary of forty rupees.

Nanjan, who had run out to play, came running back, remembering that he had a message for Paru.

'Our headmaster is coming to meet you, Amma.'

'Who is the *headmashtru*?'

To meet her? Why would he come looking for an old, white-haired, wrinkled hatti woman?

'Yes, Amma, he wants to meet you. He asked me to tell you this morning. It's you he wants to meet.'

Che, he did not even belong to their caste! He was an outsider who spoke Tamil.

As she hurriedly went to the entrance, Rangammai, who was clearing the courtyard of twigs, said, 'I believe the people from the *skol* and *headmashter* are coming. Jogianna wants coffee to be prepared.'

'Why?'

Though Rangammai knew why he was coming, she said, 'I don't know,' and went on to sweep the edumane. They herded the children to one side, warned them to be quiet, spread a gunny bag over the bench and placed a plate of betel leaves and betelnuts on it. A pot of water for the coffee was on the boil.

Jogi ushered in the headmaster who came surrounded by all the hatti children. He had to bend low to enter the narrow doorway to their house.

'Please come in,' Jogi welcomed him warmly and bade him sit down.

'As an elder you should sit first,' said the headmaster, waiting for Jogi to sit down. Nanjan brought them coffee in tumblers.

'Why this coffee?'

'What else could we offer you? You teach our children,' said Jogi. Turning around, he called out, 'Rangammai, bring some good buttermilk for Ayya.'

'When I come to your homes, you ply me with hot and cold drinks. I've come to you for a big favour and you probably know about it. I've already sent word through Nanjan,' the headmaster paused.

'Yes, I heard,' said Jogi. His face was downcast.

'Krishna Gowder has already donated five acres of land on the other side for the school building. You know that we have to build rooms for classes nine and ten next year. It will become a high school. The present building is not enough.'

'Yes, of course.'

'If your patch of land could be added to it, it would be of help.'

Paru could not follow every word of the conversation as it was in Tamil, but the meaning was clear to her. Her heart leaped in alarm. Had they come to snatch her possession?

'I've heard from the higher-ups. I know that you will raise no objection whatsoever since it is meant for a school building for children,' said the headmaster.

Paru came and stood at the doorway. Jogi did not reply.

'In the high school, we need individual classrooms for Science and Engineering. As it is we have more than two hundred children and the numbers can only go up and not down. More and more children want to study,' said the headmaster.

Jogi glanced at Paru's face as he spoke, 'We have no objection to donating it. But this parcel of land is as dear as a son to Anni. She is the one bringing up Nanjan.'

'The district board will give you a handsome compensation,' the headmaster said trying to tempt her.

Overcoming her inhibitions about talking to a stranger, Paru blurted out, 'Can you equate money to my land?'

Unfamiliar with the language, the teacher asked, 'What is Amma saying?'

'Her world is her land. You cannot equate this land with Krishna Gowder's. He pays coolies money to cultivate his land. For one who owns hundreds of acres, five acres is nothing. We've had this land for generations. My Ayyan cultivated it. It is Anni's only possession. She cannot bear to part with it.'

The headmaster looked troubled.

'Do I want it for my own use? If you think it over carefully, Gowdare, you will realise that it is for your children's education and for your people's progress. What you do for education is far, far greater than any good deed you perform. I did not think you would deny the children education.'

'How can you understand our anguish, Ayya? Is this mere soil? Isn't this the essence of our being?' Paru asked with tears in her eyes.

Finally, after drinking the cool buttermilk the headmaster spoke gently, 'This is a good opportunity for your children to study, for your children to progress. Think it over,' he said and took leave of them.

When Rangan heard of the headmaster's visit on his return from Coonoor, he rushed to see Paru.

'Paru, Paru!'

Paru, sitting in the ogamane like one demented, did not get up. Rangammai was the one who came out of the house.

'Did you consent to give up the land?' he asked Paru.

Paru silently shook her head in denial.

'You are right. Come what may, we will not agree to it. It is them versus us. Let's see who wins,' and vowing vengeance, he left. Paru knew only too well that his stance was not out of sympathy for her, but out of enmity towards Krishnan.

Two

Paru did not sleep the whole night. The headmaster's words kept ringing in her ears.

'For your children's education, for your children's progress.'

Wasn't school essential if Nanjan wanted to study further and further? Krishnan was in Chennai. His children had studied there. Personally, Krishnan stood to gain nothing if the Maragathamalai School expanded. Yet he had donated land and helped in other ways. Even if Krishnan's children did not go to this school, his younger brother Ajjan's children would do so. So would many other children, including Nanjan. Was it right that she stall all these efforts?

What would she do if she gave up her patch of land? In the old days, there was vacant land here and there. Now, whichever way one turned, there were estates, huts, houses. The winding path, where previously only one or two shops had stood, was now lined with them. Where was the land for her?

As her thoughts unfolded, a wisp of desire, which had lain hidden in the farthest corner of her heart, slowly surfaced. The same rich black land with its orange tree was still there. Coffee and cardamom were cultivated there. Could she get that land in return for hers? Would Krishna Gowder be willing to give it to her? Once, long ago, her desire had impelled her to go to Othai to ask Krishnan for the land, but now. . . ?

Was the relationship between the families still the same? Disputes and lawsuits had put a strain on it.

In his time, Kariamalla had spared no expense to take care of his tea estates. After that, Krishnan's younger brother Ajjan had returned to look after the land. He saw to it that the workers had benefits like thatched huts that did not leak and that they had time off when they fell ill. These efforts had yielded good results.

However, three-quarters of the land cultivated by Rangan had been leased by him. The few tea gardens he owned had withered due to lack of manure and now looked barren.

The coolies who came to work for him for six annas a day did not have proper huts to sleep in. It was a piteous sight to see the ill-clad workers wriggling like worms in slush during the monsoon, when their shoddily thatched huts leaked.

The women who plucked the tea leaves would suddenly gang up and stay away from work and the men would refuse to weed the land. Rangan would abuse them, accusing them of being in the enemy's pay. He would get Krishnan's men beaten up and the feud would escalate till matters ended up in the law courts. This happened frequently.

How could she approach Krishnan when the situation was like this? Would her husband's people allow her to enter the house of the man who had become their bitter enemy?

She could not see an end to her inner turmoil. But by the time dawn broke, she had made up her mind.

Before leaving for school the next day, Nanjan asked her, 'Amma, will the school take our land?'

When he uttered the words 'our land', Paru, overcome with emotion, hugged him. 'Yes my son. Will you study and become greater than Krishna Gowder and buy large tea estates and a car?'

'Amma, do you know what I want to study?'

'Tell me, my son!'

'I'm going to join the Engineering section in the fourth form. I'll go to college at Coimbatore, Amma.'

'Is that what Krishna Gowder did?' asked the poor woman.

'No, Amma. I want to build a school, bridges and all kinds of things…' said Nanjan. Shedding tears of joy, she clutched him, her face against his.

Shouldn't her brilliant intelligent son, who had been born by the grace of Nanjundan, have a good education?

'Will you ask the headmashtru to come, my child?' said Paru, as her son left for school.

Around seven that evening, hearing of the headmaster's visit to the opposite house, and of Paru's decision to give up her land, Rangan stormed in.

'Paru, Paru!'

'Yes?' she said, calmly.

Nanjan was inside having his meal.

'What did you tell the skol headmaster?'

Paru stood quietly without replying to him, and Jogi, who did not wish to remain there any longer, went outside.

'What did you tell him? Who gave you permission to give it up?'

'Why? This land was given to me by Maman. It belongs to me. Is it any concern of yours what I do with it?'

'Since when have you become so bold?'

Paru laughed mockingly. 'Does it matter to you what I do? The relationship between us was over long ago. Do I come in your way?'

'Impertinent woman. Did Chithappan tell you to do what you like with the land?'

'Why are you shouting? What is the point of being jealous?

Our children will go to the school. My son will study there.' She moved away, putting an end to their conversation.

'Jogi!' called Rangan, turning around. Jogi was nowhere to be seen.

Rangan could not find a victim on whom he could vent his anger. He could find no outlet for his feelings of jealousy and his fiercely competitive spirit. For years he had suffered, stretching his resources to the limit. He had tried all means to become wealthier and more popular than Krishnan! But he had met only with failure!

Krishnan was a member of the district board; he was invited to attend receptions at the Government House. Whichever way he turned, Krishna Gowder's fame haunted him.

He would be an honoured guest at the opening of the Maragathamalai High School. He would be praised to the skies for his donations and his help; there would be clapping and cheering as he got out of the car; he would be greeted with rose garlands.

What did Rangan have? In truth, his debt was equal to his capital.

He charged into the house. His son and daughter were fighting beneath the lamp. Puffing a cigarette, his eldest son was playing cards with a couple of his friends. In his anger, Rangan rained blows on the children who had been squabbling and separated them. Just then, Gowri entered the room. She had put on weight and had become ugly.

'Why are you beating the children?' she asked.

'Is there nothing but trouble when a man comes home?'

'Do you expect children to be quiet?' she asked, and then added, 'Would you like some coffee?'

'I don't want anything,' he replied, climbing up the stairs.

Gowri realised that the time was not right to broach the subject of the 'gold swastik' chain to Rangan.

Her ears were sharply tuned to village gossip, particularly to news of the latest jewellery acquired by Krishnan's wife. Instead of asking Rangan directly for jewellery, it was enough to say, 'I believe Krishnan's wife has bought…' And Rangan would get it for her, even if it meant going to Kovai.

She was content with Rangan because of the generous streak in him. For the very same reason, she prided herself on her lot, which she felt was better than anyone else's. Land or water meant nothing to her.

The scene created by her husband did not affect Paru. She was more worried about getting another piece of land before she parted with her precious patch.

Why should she not visit Krishnan once again? He would never think of hurting her. She was aware that it was Rangan, not Krishnan, who was the cause of the enmity between them. For that matter, was Thenmalai Rukmini her enemy? 'I hope all is well, Akka?' she would ask Paru with sincerity. Would she perhaps treat her differently now as the wife of the enemy? To be honest, did she have any relationship with Rangan? If she could own the patch of rich black soil which she desired, she could return to Manikkalhatti, where she had been born. The enmity and alienation which now prevailed, would not affect her.

What about Nanjan? Could he not go to school every day from Manikkalhatti? She would give him dosais and coffee in the morning; pack his lunch in a nice new tiffin carrier; she would take his food in the carrier when she went to work on the patch of land; he could come at mid-day to have lunch under the orange tree…

Her daydreams were endless.

The next morning, as soon as she woke up, she decided to go to Krishnan's house without anyone knowing about it. When Nanjan left for school, she changed into a fresh white mundu and a blouse that she had hardly worn and draped a shawl over her thundu.

She walked down briskly towards Keezhmalai. Rangammai had gone to collect firewood and Raman's wife was busy in the kitchen. She did not come across anyone as she slipped out of the house.

She knew that the Coonoor bus went from Keezhmalai. She could either go to Othai from there or take the shortcut to Othai on foot.

She walked on without deciding which way to go. The bus stop was in a clearing and there were remnants of the forest beyond the path, with clusters of shrubs and trees here and there. The bungalow beneath the bridge, which had once belonged to the Englishman, had been shut up. A couple of tea shops had cropped up near the bus stop. The gramophone in Nair's tea stall was croaking. At a distance, beyond the path, two men were sawing a large log.

Speaking in her own tongue, she asked Nair, 'When is the bus due?'

Nair, who understood her, replied, '12 o'clock.'

While she was trying to decide whether she should wait or walk on, she saw a shiny, black car in the distance. Her heart almost missed a beat when she recognised the car.

Was it Krishnan who was coming to the hatti? Or was it his wife and daughter?

She was still standing there when the car turned the corner and went past her. She saw Krishnan in the front seat and briskly followed the car.

Three

Krishnan Gowder was also taken aback when he unexpectedly caught sight of Paru. He wondered what had brought her there.

Many years earlier, she had entered his heart and made his thoughts tingle; she had filled all his dreams. But now there was only a dried-up scar in the place she had once occupied in his heart. But the scar had not allowed him to let his memories fade.

At first, he had not been aware that her patch of land had been included in the school's plan. Whenever he had seen Paru tilling her land, she had seemed to him a picture of disappointment, a symbol of defeat in life. He did not know whether it was true or whether he was imagining it.

When he had come riding on horseback, one day, many years ago to the hatti, he had come with so many dreams, some of which he had realised. In two kurinji-spans, his people, who had been in darkness, had received the light of learning, and had been awakened. Earlier, the number of literates among the hill folk could be counted on the fingers of one hand. Now many of them had come up in life and returned to educate their people and bring pride to their land!

As far as he was concerned, though some of his dreams had come true, had they made his life brighter?

His dreams were like the sun which rose even during the monsoon and climbed to the zenith, but whose brilliance was obscured by the dark rain clouds.

Did the lives of the hill folk steeped in their hoary heritage shine in the glow of this new education? No, not really. Hattis with two or three hundred people stood split into two. Like a contagious, deadly fever, the spirit of disunity had spread from hatti to hatti. Factions, enmity, jealousy, rivalries, disputes and lawsuits affected one and all.

Krishnan yearned to make peace with Rangan and had made many efforts to do so.

Grandfather Kariamalla had been like a pillar in the hatti. His family and Lingayya's had been very close. At the time of Kariamalla's death, Jogi had disappeared, blatantly proclaiming his ingratitude. The thought of it brought to the surface Krishnan's resentment towards Lingayya's family.

Even so, his conscience would not permit him to be petty-minded towards Rangan. Whenever he visited the hatti, he had a sneaking desire to find a way to end the animosity. He even hoped that Paru's land would provide him an opening to arrive at an understanding with Rangan.

On seeing Paru, Rukmini, who was also in the car exclaimed, 'Isn't that Paru Akka?'

'Hm,' replied Krishnan, sighing softly.

'Where is she going?' she asked.

Krishnan did not reply.

Whenever he visited the hatti, the villagers paid him a visit on some pretext or other. Wheat, rice and castor seeds were drying in front of his house, which was no longer what it used to be. The interior of the house was now like a mansion. It had expanded to accommodate wide halls, storerooms and storage space for potatoes, high doorways, benches, chairs and almirahs.

The sight of the car would draw men and women of the neighbourhood to his house the minute he entered it and sat down. He had to sort out single-handedly all their problems.

Kari's grandson refused to work in the fields. He had failed twice in the eighth class. It was Krishna Gowder who had to find a way out.

Third house Rami's elder sister's daughter-in-law wanted Krishna Gowder's opinion about giving her daughter Lingamma in marriage to an educated boy.

Opposite house Uchan came seeking money and a letter of recommendation to take his polio-affected son to Coimbatore for treatment.

Why did all these people have to come on that particular day and make Krishnan's head ache? Why was he so irritated by the old men who considered talking to him a privilege?

He waited till dusk had fallen, then took his walking stick and went for a stroll towards the estate. As soon as he reached the cultivated land, a small boy playing with a top came running towards him.

Who could it be? Whose son was he? His face bore a strong resemblance to someone he knew. His gait reminded him of an acquaintance. Two girls picking tea leaves looked up as they met.

The boy stood looking at him hesitantly for a while.

'Who are you, my child?'

'I am… I am… can you come with me please?'

The boy pointed to the banks of the rivulet. Who was this boy who was asking the great Krishna Gowder to follow him?

All of a sudden recognition dawned on him.

'What is your name?'

'Nanjan; Jogi Gowder's son,' he replied

'Oh! Aren't you studying?'

'Yes, in the third form.'

'All right. You can go. I'll follow you.'

Top and string in hand, the boy sped away while Krishnan stood gazing at the disappearing figure. After a few seconds had passed, he took a deep breath as though he were coming out of a dream.

Who was calling him? Where were they asking him to go? Why had he agreed without questioning the boy further?

He was assailed by doubts. Was this perhaps an invitation to end the long-standing enmity? Had a boy really come to him? Did Jogi really want to prolong the feud? Would Jogi, who was the epitome of goodness, harbour enmity in his heart?

Never. Jogi was a straightforward and honourable man who loathed fighting. He disliked Rangan. It was fear of Rangan that had made him run away from the hatti and hide when grandfather Kariamalla had died. Jogi had been forced to nurture the feud with Karimalla's family to honour his father's last wishes and preserve the unity between the brothers. So it must be Jogi who had wanted to meet him, he thought.

The rain was unpredictable towards the end of *Vaigasi*. Because he did not have an umbrella, Krishnan quickly climbed down the slope. There were tea gardens dotted with silver oak everywhere. Care and good manure had made each plant thrust through the soil, spread, sprout and thrive.

Paru's small patch of land in the flat earth near the school seemed like a poor girl overshadowed by affluent people, or like a small hut hidden behind a big mansion. A solitary orange tree stood on it, heavy with flowers. The scent of the blooms evoked many memories as he went near it.

Had the fragrance of the unfulfilled desires of her barren heart been released to emanate from the flowers? Orange trees in bloom were a common sight. Were any of them as sweet-scented as this one? Planted and tended by Paru herself, it would soon be felled when the school building came up. Was this tree as precious to her as an only son to his mother?

Krishnan looked around. Memories of holidays spent on that hillside, swapping stories with Jogi while the cattle grazed, rushed to his mind. They had plucked and eaten the coral-red berries from thorny bushes. White buttercup-like flowers had bloomed on the slopes in the evenings.

He turned and walked towards the banks of the rivulet. There were vegetable patches beyond the tea bushes; farther away stretched uncultivated lands like an uneducated mind; on the banks of the rivulet there was still a profusion of bushes in some places. As a child, he had walked along the river bank to Manikkalhatti. The Kumari River cascaded down to a whirlpool where it met the rivulet. One day, twenty-five years ago, young Krishnan had sat on a rock in the middle of the water. Just watching the whirlpool had given him a thrill as though he were touching a virgin.

As he walked along the stream, his attention was drawn to the yellow flowers of a keno tree in bloom. Wasn't the sacred tree considered dear to Lord Muruga? The stolen hours with Paru under the keno tree were now a mere memory, which was best forgotten.

He stopped suddenly. He could not believe his eyes and he was taken aback. It was the dream he had had twenty-five years earlier.

It was Paru! Clad in a white mundu, draped in a shawl, it was undoubtedly Paru. Yes, Paru. She had followed him; she had sought him out!

Though the light was fading, how could he fail to recognise Paru!

'Paru!' She looked at him with trepidation.

'I sent word through the child. I have run a long way.'

'Was it you who sent word to me, Paru?' His normally firm voice faltered.

'They are taking away my land! What shall I do?' her tremulous voice was barely audible.

'I am also upset about it, Paru. It was the first thing that struck me when I saw your land. I thought you would not have parted with it.'

She was deeply touched by his words. In spite of his busy eventful life, did he still have time to think of her with concern?

'Nanjan goes to skol! My son. Did you see him?'

'Your son?'

'Yes. Girijai gave birth to him and left him in my care. Isn't my son a fine boy? He comes first in skol. He is clever like you.'

'Bless him. If you're happy, I am content, Paru. I am sure he will study well.'

'I'm giving away my land to the skol. Instead of which… I…'

'What do you want, Paru? If it's land that you want, tell me where it is,' he said anxiously.

'Where you have planted coffee. It is the patch of land with dark soil above the bend in the rivulet. I had come to Othai even earlier to ask you for it.'

Hardly had she finished speaking, when Krishnan sensed someone emerging from behind the bushes. The next minute, both of them felt heavy blows raining on their back.

Before Krishnan could react, Paru had crumpled to the ground in shock.

Four

'Stop it, you cowards! Who are you?'

Swinging his cane in all four directions, Krishnan sprang up like a twenty-year-old.

Men rushed away through the bushes, their footsteps thudding.

'Paru, are you hurt? Hooligans! Hitting a woman! Why should Maragathamalai hatti come to this sorry state? Paru!'

Before he could bend down and gently lift her up, a figure approached, shining a torch. When the figure aimed the beam at him and laughed, Krishnan was shaken.

'Oho! Is it the big shot, Krishna Gowder?' The mocking laughter grated harshly on Paru's ears. It was Rangan's eldest son, Lingan.

'One should not look closely into the lives of big shots. However, to waylay a woman returning from gathering firewood and frighten her…'

Paru reacted sharply 'Linga! What's all this?'

'Are you asking me, Periamma? Haven't you been insulted? What a shame! People call him a great man! He has hired men to beat up a woman and tried to grab her land. How could all of us, Appan, Pattan, Chithappan, sons, keep quiet? When I saw him, I was suspicious and hid myself. I dread to imagine what would have happened to you if I hadn't been here. Come along now. How can we watch this injustice and remain silent?'

Lingan dragged Paru by the hand. Her hands, which were drained of youthful freshness, were caught in his rough ones.

'No, Linga! We don't know who came and beat us up.'

'Who else could it have been? Drunk with power, he is trying to bully us. Is there not enough space in this vast mountain for a school? How craftily he has lured you here and sent his henchmen to beat you up!'

Shaken to the core, Paru felt as though she were losing her mind. She knew that in Maragathamalai, where there were no venomous snakes, her husband was like one. Wasn't Lingan the son of a snake? Where was the comparison between Krishnan and this callow youth? To stay on would only cause an unsavoury incident.

A stream of foul accusations and defamations against Krishnan, his kith and kin, poured forth from Lingan's mouth.

Paru wept inwardly. Oh God, only you know the truth! Hadn't Krishnan come with good intentions? A skol for her son. Rich black soil promising a good harvest for her. After all, she had severed the relationship with her husband long ago.

Even before she entered the hatti, dragged by Lingan, his loud curses brought everyone to their doorstep. Paru cowered and shrank, humiliated beyond bearing.

'What? From the big house? Did he beat her? Paru Akka?' voices whispered. The hatti people were no longer averse to expressing their feelings in words.

Rangan rushed in, 'Arre, Linga!

Paru's heart fluttered like a flickering flame. Was there no limit to injustice? Nanjan ran to her and hugged her.

Driven by his son's anger, Rangan behaved like one possessed.

'Can we remain silent in the face of such an atrocity! He talks of school and donations while committing evil!'

'Can we ignore this, Appa?' asked his son.

'Why should we? I'll get a doctor's certificate to testify to the wounds, take him to court and make sure that his name is mud,' vowed Rangan.

'May the accursed court go up in flames,' said Paru.

'You're a traitor to your husband's family!' hissed Rangan.

'Appa, Periamma talks without understanding Krishnan's treachery,' said Lingan.

'Shame on you! You are staying in my house and betraying me; why don't you get out?' screamed Rangan and called out, 'Jogi, Jogi.'

But Jogi was not there.

After remaining silent for a moment, Paru tearfully cried out, 'I'll go. I'll leave with my son, I'll have nothing to do with this soil.'

Her husband laughed harshly. 'Son? Whose son is he? Will a son of this house go with the woman who wants to leave the family?'

As though impaled by a spear, Paru stood stunned.

Nanjan was a son of his father's family. Was he her son? If a woman left home, even her own children would no longer belong to her. Nanjan was Girijai's son, not hers. He belonged to Jogi's house. Only if she thought of this house as hers would Nanjan be hers. If she wanted to consider this as her home, she would have to accept that she was the wife of the man who stood in front of her.

'Why are you dumbstruck? If you want to stay here, you'll have to obey me. If you want to be an accomplice to the enemy, go away.'

What could Paru reply? What could she say?

'Today he sent his men to beat up one of our women, tomorrow he'll abduct our son.'

Her blood ran cold at these words. A snake mistrusts another snake. A wrongdoer will always suspect his enemy of doing wrong.

Krishnan's men would never have beaten her up. That was indisputable. But…? Her husband could have sent his men to do it. He would get men to bear false witness. If she dared disobey him, he could harm her beloved child.

Did the boy belong to her husband? Rangan was even jealous of Jogi. He might also keep that in mind and seek revenge on her.

She was terrified. Unconsciously, she tightened her hold on Nanjan.

'Why are you keeping quiet? Do you want to leave this house?'

Pale with fright, she slumped wearily in a corner. Rangan had not finished with her.

'Swear by Mariamman as witness that you will not be Krishnan's accomplice.'

Her tears flowed freely. She gazed at Nanjan's innocent face. Terrified that he, who was dearer to her than life, would come to harm, she said, 'I swear by Mariamman, I am not Krishnan's accomplice.'

'Then, the truth is that he sent his men to trick you into meeting him, threatened you and forced you to give up your land; he beat you up.'

Iswara! If she did not agree to be a false witness, did it mean she was an accomplice?

Paru fell at his feet, 'I beg of you. Once, a long, long time ago, it's true that I had thought of marrying him. That thought has since turned to ash. Even that ash has been dissolved in the tears flowing from my eyes. Leave me alone. There's no connection between him and me. I have no connection with anyone in this world but this child. Don't drag me through the courts.'

Jogi stood near the doorway, his heart choking as he witnessed the scene.

He had gone to Nair's tea shop on the upper road, where he had been listening to chit-chat. Nair had extolled the efficacy of a new medicine that healed all wounds. Uchan had claimed that all the white men's achievements could be ascribed to their eating meat. The news of the commotion caused by Lingan dragging Paru home had not yet reached their ears. He was horrified at the scene that met his eyes as he entered his house.

Had the quality of life been inferior before progress made inroads into the hatti? Had there been a difference between those who were higher and those who were lower? Had they fought over land? Had one starved while another grew fat? When one household had had its ups and downs had the other been a mere spectator? What had destroyed his magnanimity? Hadn't it been destroyed when they had no longer been content with samai, tinai, korali and milk? Hadn't the money from tea and potato destroyed it? Hadn't the fashion of wearing shirt and trousers destroyed it? Hadn't hunger for gold and silk destroyed it?

Who was the cause of all these changes in Maragathamalaihatti? It was Krishnan. Was it Krishnan alone? Wasn't Rangan also responsible for this? Both of them together had become poisonous insects sucking the hatti of its vitality.

The future was bleak. Educated boys would make piles of money. The arrogance of money and the power that went with it would make them go to court and fuel enmity.

Paru, his elder brother's wife, the epitome of love, grace and humility, had prostrated herself at the feet of Rangan, the jealous monster. How could one conquer jealousy?

Jogi watched the scene with tear-filled eyes.

Rangan did not know how to deal with Paru, who was trying to win him over with tears.

'Why are you sobbing away like this?' he demanded.

'I don't want anything to do with the courts. Leave me alone.'

'You wretched woman.'

Rangan kicked her and left without noticing Jogi. Paru remained inside, holding on to her son, trying to control her sobs.

Rangammai and her daughter-in-law and children paid no heed to this commotion. They had gone to sleep. The lamp had not been lit in the niche. Raman was away, driving his lorry. Did the brothers join together only against the common enemy?

A long time passed before Jogi went in looking for a blanket. Paru seemed like a statue in the darkness. She was not asleep.

Fate was adept at interfering and playing with people's lives; separating and uniting, giving and taking away!

'Anni.'

Though inured through the years to joy and sorrow alike, the concern in his voice broke down her defences.

'Jogianna.'

Sobs broke out and the tears could not be dammed.

'Nothing will happen to Nanjan, isn't it, Jogianna?'

'Don't lose heart. This mountain soil was sweet to me when our life was honey and milk. Now, when our life has turned sour, the soil has turned salty and bitter.'

As he spoke, she continued to sob.

Five

The next morning, dense clouds like a woman heavy with child, descended painfully on the hillsides. From somewhere, a healing wind also blew hard.

Jogi forgot his land and water that day. He did not milk the buffaloes when he got up in the morning. He did not stand outside and pay obeisance to the Sun God. After thinking things over at night, he had come to a decision. He extracted from a small box kept in the grain bin, the three hundred and odd rupees, which he had kept tied in a cloth and earmarked for an emergency. In the days gone by, it would have been equal to three thousand rupees. Since everyone had grown greedy and started hankering after money, it had become worthless.

Jogi took all the money with him and draped a woollen blanket around himself. As he was about to leave the house, Lingammai asked him, Haven't you milked the buffaloes? Can I get you coffee?' He decided to milk them before leaving. Immediately he washed his feet and hands. He went into the hagottu, changed into madi clothes, washed the honai and went into the cattle shed. After milking, he recited the morning prayers and drank the coffee prepared by Rangammai's daughter-in-law. He left the house while Paru was busy getting Nanjan ready for school.

Jogi hurried towards Keezhmalai, leaving behind the accursed soil that bred hatred. The wind blew hard and the rain fell like sharp needles. The rain was welcome for it would make the land lush green!

He avoided Keezhmalai and walked towards Mookkumalai. In the distance, he saw the men who cultivated potatoes, vegetables and wheat, hoeing the land. He saw the owners of the plots, with gunny bags or blankets draped around their shoulders, turning the soil, impervious to the wind and rain. Those who planted tea and coffee and employed others to look after the crops had no respect for the land. They made money to enjoy themselves in Othai and Coimbatore. Here and there, he saw goats and cattle searching for patches of grass. Gone were the days when vast pastures on the slopes had been set aside for cattle to graze. Now, there was nothing but tea everywhere!

Was that all? The alien culture of the outside world had taught them other things as well. How degrading that the very elders who had considered those eating meat as belonging to a lower caste, now took pride in the fact that their children ate it!

Smoke spiralled from the chimney of a tea factory on the slopes of Mookkumalai. At every turn there were factories that dried the fragrant green tea. He had heard that Krishnan was going to put up a factory with the latest machinery at Maragathamalai! What new disputes would it stir up, he wondered.

In Mookkumalaihatti, the sun played hide and seek, shining one minute as though it were smiling and hiding itself the next minute behind a veil of passing clouds. Overjoyed that it had rained, people were tilling the land. Tea and coffee plants were a rarity on that hillside. Probably the greed for money had not yet touched these people.

Potatoes flourished in some areas. How powerful the chemical fertilisers were! They had the power to bring out all the vitality of the soil in one go! An old man chewing betel leaves and tobacco sat in the midst of the men and women who were working on the land. He seemed drained of vigour as he feebly turned the soil and then rested from time to time. His body had been toughened by exposure to cold and frost over the years. Gold earrings with double hoops dangled from his earlobes. His turban wobbled. He must have seen at least seven kurinji-spans.

Jogi ran up to him calling, 'Mama. Mama!' The old man's eyes strained to recognise him.

'It's Jogi. Isn't it?'

'Yes, Mama.'

The very sight of his uncle made Jogi's heart melt. A feeble old man, pitchfork in hand, turning the soil!

Did he not have a son? There was one left, but he was of no help to him in his old age.

'Are you well? How is everyone?'

'M… Mama… why are you turning the soil yourself?'

'My educated son has flown away to earn a livelihood. And this old man has his land to look after. Is everyone in the other group well?'

For one who had fled to forget the enmity that had pervaded his hatti, the word 'group' was like a spear entering the heart.

The old man squatted on the ground and lit a fat cheroot.

'Mama, how long is it since Siddan came here?'

'Hm… What can he do in the village? His education and career have weaned him away from the village. My other children were wiped out by the plague and now there is no one left at home even to quarrel with. I have my land, my self-respect and my hut. I huddle in a corner of it. What has brought you here?

Have you finished turning the soil and sowing the seeds in your field? I believe there was some trouble even yesterday?'

The pain in Jogi's heart was unbearable.

'You must forgive me, Mama. I've come to forget about groups, quarrels and animosity. Don't talk about it. Ayyan used to say that in order not to ruin the life God has given us, all of us should live together in harmony. As soon as he died, the fight started. The thought that I may also have been responsible for this makes me feel guilty. In your feeble state of health, for whom are you turning the soil and sowing seeds?'

'There's still some strength left in this body given by God. On whom can I rely? Even if there are no sons to share the work, there is a son to feed.'

The old man laughed bitterly.

Taking the pitchfork from him, Jogi said, 'I'll turn the soil.'

'You?'

'Yes. Don't feel sorry that Siddan had no attachment to the land and has left it. Look upon me as Siddan. Don't talk to me of groups and differences. If you let me work on your land, I'll accept it as a boon.'

'Jogi,' cried the old man, his eyes moist. 'After all, how can I forget that you have spent eight years in the Hiriya Udayar temple? Yes, there is land but no one to work on it. Only an old man remains. An old man!'

'Mama, I consider you as my father. Give me the pitchfork. The soil at Maragathamalai has turned bitter. This Mookkumalai soil is mine.'

The old man looked up at the sky in gratitude.

'My son and daughter-in-law have deserted me in my old age. Only this morning I shed tears thinking "what's the use of having a son?" In the olden days, if one became disabled, there was always someone who would help. Jogi, it's because there are still some good people like you, that the wind blows, the rain falls and the frost appears at the right time.'

'The only reason why Annan wants us to stay together is because he wants me to support him in the quarrel. I've come to take refuge with you. I have three hundred rupees with me. You could either accept it as rent for the land or as money to cover my expenses. I've come to stay.'

'You are the son who has come to carry the burden of my old age.' The old man hugged Jogi. In the warmth of the embrace, they were oblivious to the chill of the drizzle as it started to rain.

Jogi returned home in the heavy downpour, full of joy at having found refuge beyond the pale of enmity and anger. Paru was mending a torn blanket. Peering at the rain, she looked up worriedly and said, 'Nanjan has gone out without an umbrella.'

Without a word, Jogi went in and looked around the house. When he had left home with the money, he had had no intention of returning to Maragathamalaihatti. He was leaving the house where he was born, where he had grown up, the house that was a part and parcel of him. The thought that he was leaving his home where each nook, each little object, each door and each wall seemed to speak aloud, evoking memories, made him realise that he had left without bidding farewell. Then there was Paru Anni! The mother who was bringing up Nanjan! Should he not take leave of her?

'Anni, I've something to tell you,' he said. The gravity of his voice made her aware that it was no ordinary matter.

'What is it?'

'Where is Rangammai?'

Rangammai, who was grinding grain into flour, came out.

'I have decided to go away to Mockkumalai.'

The needle slipped from Paru's hand. Rangammai stood in stunned silence.

'In this hate-filled atmosphere, I feel suffocated. You and the children till the soil. I'm leaving.'

'And after you leave? Jogianna, this hill has turned sour. What will be the fate of my children?' asked Rangammai.

'Don't worry, Rangammai. Ayyan will be pleased that your family is tilling his land. I feel as though I were treading on thorns or walking on the edge of a saw. My conscience and my relationship with my brother make it impossible for me to carry on here. I'm leaving. I want to take the boy with me,' said Jogi.

'So you are taking the boy! Are you also cheating me? Are you taking Nanjan away from me?'

'Is it necessary for him to grow up in this climate of anger and ill-feeling? With the enmity continuing generation after generation, his heart will also be filled with it.'

'You are separating me from my son! Is it fair?' Paru asked tearfully.

Looking down at her, Jogi said, 'I am not proposing anything unfair, Anni. If you wish, you can also come with us for Nanjan's sake. Mookkumalai Maman will give shelter to all three of us.'

Paru got ready to leave the very same day.

Six

The gentle Purattasi sun was soothing to the old man's body. Feeling secure that a man and a woman had come to work in his desolate home, the old man seemed to have become ten years younger.

On one side, the green of samai and wheat cooled the eye. On the other, the potatoes bursting from the soil ready for harvesting brought contentment to the mind. The buffalo brought by Jogi was heavy with calf. What luck in his old age! Two treasured children of the soil. Had they not proved that they had a golden touch?

Jogi had left early to inspect the field.

Paru had to feed Nanjan and also pack food for school. She could make her way to the field only by midday, when she had finished her housework. Nanjan was through with the school at Maragathamalai and was now going to Othai. To satisfy his hunger for knowledge, he did not mind trudging eight miles over hills and valleys and through forestland every day. Her son, though not born to her! Some days Paru's eyes were full of pain when she saw Nanjan setting off for school, wearing shoes and a coat to protect him from the cold and rain, carrying his schoolbag and a tiffin carrier. She would stand at the doorway till he climbed down the lower slope.

She had big dreams of Nanjan growing up and achieving great heights. As though he could read her mind, the old man asked her with a smile one day, 'Has the boy left for skol?'

'Of course, he'll never stay behind even for a single day. See how far he has to walk!'

'What's he going to do after studying like this?'

'What a question, Mama? He'll be the most educated person in the hills.'

'What use is it to you if he becomes a big man, you foolish girl?'

'What use is it to me? I'll be proud when the son I have brought up becomes great!'

The old man laughed at her naiveté. 'Why should you be proud? I don't understand.'

'How can I make you understand? He'll read many books and do many good deeds. He'll travel in a car. I'll be indescribably happy.'

'Foolish girl! If he becomes such a great man, is he going to be bothered about you? When education, youth and modernity combine, he'll be ashamed to admit that you are a relative.'

'Mama!' Paru's face reddened with anger, 'Don't think all other children will be like your son.'

'Why are you getting angry when I speak the truth?' the old man laughed again.

He continued, 'What would a well-educated boy do in a hatti? Have you thought about it?'

'He'll work in Othai. He'll travel by car.' How could she envisage anything other than Krishnan's popularity and the esteem in which he was held.

'You'll toil in the soil till you die. He'll say he is not earning enough and ask you for more. He'll forget this soil and will not show respect to his parents. He'll seek a girl worthy of his youth and education. He'll listen to her words.'

'Why are you so keen that my son remains uneducated?' shouted Paru.

'You should not be let down like me in your old age. You've faced many setbacks when you were young. I'm talking to you as though you were my daughter.'

Paru did not reply. Would Nanjan really let her down? Never, never.

The son who lived in Coimbatore would write to the old man every month. When Nanjan read the letter to the old man, Paru's heart would swell with joy. 'No, my son will never reject me,' the poor woman would console herself.

Changes swept the country and the world. But were enmities forgotten?

The dispute about the school, the cause for the enmity, which spread its hood like a cobra between the two families, remained unresolved due to a lack of concerted effort. Paru's appeal for land lay like a thorn deeply embedded in Krishnan. He knew that Jogi had shifted to Mookkumalai and that Nanjan walked eight miles to attend school at Othai. Hadn't his son Gopal completed his teacher's training and starting working in the same school that year! What if Jogi had uprooted himself and moved away only to forget the feud? Should he, Krishnan, not lend him his support? Was it a good thing to allow the rift and hostility to spread from generation to generation? What was the reason for it? How could he bring about a change of heart? These questions had crept into Krishnan's thoughts and made him lose his peace of mind.

Rukmini was unhappy about Krishnan taking the car to the hatti after five in the evening. Naturally, deep down she was afraid, as feuding factions were on the rise.

What did it matter whether the hatti had a school or not? What if someone stopped the car and harmed him? While Rukmini was worrying about this, Krishnan had already stopped the car near Keezhmalai and was walking to Mookkumalai in the falling darkness. As it had rained the day before, the bridle path was slippery.

At that moment, Jogi was climbing up the slope carrying the salt, matchbox and a bottle of groundnut oil that he had bought from the shop in the adjoining estate. In days gone by, the *kalayams* overflowed with castor oil. The lamp in the niche would cast a pearl-like brilliance. When Nanjan returned from school at seven o'clock, a lighted lamp would be there so that he could study. But castor oil was no longer available! That was the reason for the groundnut oil in the bottle.

Thanks to Krishnan, the path to Maragathamalaihatti had been made smooth. It was no strain to go up the path or climb down. But since no one in Mookkumalai had done well, the path remained uneven. However, there was neither rivalry nor jealousy in Mookkumalai.

For some days after Jogi had left, he was afraid that Rangan might pick a quarrel with him, demanding, 'Why did you leave?' As days passed by, this fear left him. There was no one to bring news of the town or the country to Mookkumalai. He was content with this life! There were no great desires; no great losses.

He found it a strain to carry four measures of salt, the jaggery and provisions on his head, and panted as he walked uphill. Ahead of him, he suddenly saw a tall figure, walking stick in hand, wearing trousers, coat, shoes and turban. In a simple hatti like Mookkumalai, there was no one who dressed like that.

Jogi did not know why, but he felt angry. He bit his tongue and walked faster to catch up with the figure ahead of him. Unaware that he was being followed, the figure ahead of him kept walking fast.

Jogi recognised the figure. He did not have relatives in Mookkumalai. None he could consider his equal in status, none as educated as he was. What brought him there? Why had he come to this peaceful spot to raise the flag of enmity? Jogi sighed angrily.

Turning his back on relatives and enemies alike, he had come away. If Rangan learnt that the man from Othai had come to renew contact with him, would he remain silent? Would he not rush up the very next day, demanding, 'Why did you invite the enemy and make friends with him?'

Let the two of them thrash each other. Let them threaten each other. Why drag him into it?

However fast he walked, he was able to overtake Krishnan only when they had almost reached his house.

Paru was in the kitchen and the old man was praying near the lamp. Nanjan, who had returned just then, was telling his mother all about his day at school.

Jogi put down his bundle as soon as he entered the house. He then took the lamp from the niche and rushed out again. The old man thought to himself, 'Perhaps there's a fox on the prowl.'

'Stop! Stop right there.' The words blazed with the emotions that had been suppressed for a long time. The vessel of tea in Paru's hand slipped from her grasp. She ran outside.

Jogi stood there with the lamp in his hand; his body was shaking, his lips were quivering. She saw... Was it a dream? Was he real?

'I have fled from quarrels and dissensions. Have you come to destroy our peace even here! Go! Get out!'

Was it Jogiannan screaming?

'Jogi, should this enmity not end? I have come to put an end to it. I have come to lighten my burden of grief,' Krishnan's words were hardly audible.

'If you come now with words of friendship, will the enmity and hatred end? Why didn't you think of it earlier? You looked upon us as enemies and opposed us. Didn't your workers, your family and the whole hatti persist in being antagonistic towards us? You got everyone except those who belonged to our family inoculated against the plague. Even when we were in danger, you continued to be hostile. Ammai lamented all her life, all her life. We don't need your money or position or respect. Go away. Don't come to ruin our peace and happiness. If I renew contact with you, the enmity between the two of you will flare up! Go away! Go away!'

Even if thousands of sharp stones had been flung at him, they would not have pierced and torn Krishnan's heart as Jogi's words did.

Every 'Go away' from Jogi's lips attacked him like thousands of spears. Unable to bear it, the lonely figure of Krishnan melted away in the darkness while Paru looked on.

His fury having abated, Jogi replaced the lamp in its niche and sat down, breathing hard.

No one spoke.

Seven

It was not Gopalan's turn to take class that day. But the social studies master was absent and so he had come to Nanjan's class to teach them during his free hour. When he substituted for another teacher, he would pass the time mingling freely with the students and chatting informally with them, thus keeping them in high spirits.

All the boys chit-chatted with each other; they laughed; they even began to sing.

'Sh!' Gopalan rapped the table and asked, 'What's all the noise about?'

'We live in freedom, *Saar*. Aren't we all kings of this country?' said one student, reminding the others that Republic Day was just around the corner.

'Is that so? I'm going to ask you a question,' laughed Gopalan. 'Who was the first one to proclaim, "We are kings of this country"?'

For a while there was silence.

'Mmm… Bheeman, why don't you answer?'

Bheeman stood up.

'You don't know? Let the next one answer. You… you…' One by one they all stood up. One cheeky youngster stood up stiffly and said, 'Premkumar, the cinema star, Saar.'

Those who knew the answer, and those who did not, joined in the teacher's laughter.

'So you think it was Premkumar who proclaimed it? How many times did you see his film *Vaazhkai Thirai?*'

'Five times,' answered the lad.

The loud laughter, which burst out for the second time, could be heard in the next classroom.

It was then that Gopalan's glance fell on Nanjan, who sat with his head on the desk. He had not joined in the loud talk and noisy laughter.

Gopalan rapped the table and said, 'Forget it. Here's someone who is confident that we are all kings of this country and feels that he has the freedom to sleep blissfully. Let's ask him. He'll certainly know the answer.'

As all eyes turned to Nanjan, the laughter was loud enough to make the thatched roof fly off.

Startled, Nanjan looked up.

'Adada! How can he help it? Soothing sunlight is streaming in through the window. He has come in after his morning meal. Doesn't he have the right to fall asleep in the classroom?' When he realised that the teacher was poking fun at him, Nanjan looked around. Again there was laughter.

'Why are you all laughing? Keep quiet. Let's see whether he has understood the question,' said Gopalan.

'I've a splitting headache, Saar,' said Nanjan.

Never before had he been inattentive in class, nor had he been the object of laughter and ridicule. An impoverished student, a solitary figure who trudged all the way from Mookkumalaihatti, he kept to himself in class. He was usually first in class. From the very first day that he had started coming to Othai, the feeling that everyone looked down on him had been building up within him. He had neither an educated father nor uncle he could boast about. Even his uncle, Rangan, was unlettered. No one close to him was well educated. He came to study with the sole purpose of doing well and being a credit to his family. When he looked at Gopalan, the animosity and acrimony that existed between the two families pervaded his mind like a dark cloud.

'Should you sleep in class just because you have a headache?'

'Then I'll leave the class, Saar.'

Nanjan collected his books and walked out without another word.

No one had expected him to walk out so boldly, so insolently. Nanjan was not the sort to behave like that. Why had he behaved in such a manner? It was because of hunger. He hadn't eaten anything since morning.

The land given to them by the old man had not yielded well that year. There was little left, after giving the old man's son money whenever he demanded, feeding four mouths and paying for Nanjan's education. Paru, who was not used to asking for anything, skipped one meal a day. She brewed coffee only for her son and the old man, and hid their want from her son. Even Jogi often went hungry.

That morning, she had made just two ragi *adais*, one for the old man and the other for Nanjan. Nanjan looked into the kitchen and asked her, 'What about Appa? And you?'

Paru, who had been smearing the adais with butter, replied, 'There's more, eat up.'

'Where is it? Show me!'

Paru had removed the twigs from the wood stove and put the fire out.

At his age, the old man had a craving for tasty food. He was in the habit of giving Nanjan a few coins to buy him bajjis, bondas or sweet laddus at Othal on his way back from school. The old man had initially supported Jogi and treated him as a son. But now he behaved as though by giving them the land, he had earned the right to order them around as if he were their master. Nanjan's blood boiled at the thought. The old man's son and daughter-in-law came to the hills, but never to Mookkumalaihatti. The son would go only to his wife's house. All they wanted was money from the land. They were not interested in the house or the land. Even if he came only for a couple of hours, the son behaved as though the old man had given away his possessions to them as charity.

Nanjan was old enough to understand all this. In the morning, the old man had given Nanjan four annas, asking him to buy sweetmeats and savouries. Had he ever given four annas to Nanjan as a treat? Nanjan, after having trudged eight miles on an empty stomach, would hand over the eats to the old man before going to the kitchen for his cup of tea, which was lovingly and caringly prepared by his Ammai.

That morning, discovering the truth that they often kept no food for themselves, he had lost his temper.

'Am I the Bakasura, the glutton, in this house? There's nothing for you and Ayyan. I'll not touch the adai or coffee.'

'Don't hurt us in this manner, Nanja,' Paru implored tearfully. 'There's wheat. I'm going to grind it and make kali. You have to walk eight miles to school and eight miles back. At your age, is this nourishment enough? Listen to me.'

'No. I'll not take more than a third of it,' he shouted, 'You're doing this day after day to make a sinner out of me, can't you see?'

Jogi, who had walked in after letting out the cows to graze, understood why Nanjan was so angry. They had not experienced such poverty since Paru had come to their house. As a young man at Maragathamalaihatti, he had certainly seen poverty. But the all-important sense of togetherness had not been lost; the poor and the wealthy had stood side-by-side. Hunger had been unknown.

Now, though the earth was green, the heart was devoid of compassion. Was this the punishment for forsaking one's own land? Jogi's spirit was broken.

Swallowing his grief and gulping down a mouthful of buttermilk, he went out. The old man, totally unconcerned with what had happened, continued to smoke serenely.

Nanjan was seething with wrath. At whom was his anger and frustration directed? He did not know. Taking it out on his mother, he picked up his books and set out for school.

Even as the first bell rang, his stomach began to rumble as usual. Bidding it to shut up, he concentrated on the simple interest problems set by the teacher.

By the time the second bell rang, his stomach had lost patience. 'Have you forgotten me?' it called out repeatedly. Hunger gnawed at his insides. He immersed himself in grammar.

When the bell rang, all the boys trooped out for lunch. Nanjan came out. Down the slope there were shops, cinema theatres, tea and tiffin stalls from which the aroma of mouth-watering spicy food wafted.

The demon in his stomach ran amok. Gritting his teeth, Nanjan turned away and climbed upwards instead. He gulped down water from the tap. Unwilling to see anyone, he sat on the grass and opened his English text. 'Where there is love, there is God.' Tolstoy's short story that had been taught in class. When he read about the old woman and the boy who stole the apple, his mouth watered and his cheeks ached. He closed the book and lay down on the grass.

When he heard the school bell clang, he staggered into the classroom. That was all he knew till he walked out.

On his way home, the feeling of enmity that had always been at the back of his mind, flared up at Gopalan's laughter, like his hunger. The radio at the hotel blared out the song, 'Amma… I'm hungry…'

At the close of the monsoon during the last half of the month of Karthigai, Othai appeared like a garden in the sunshine. As he walked mindlessly along the garden road, he suddenly remembered the four anna coin the old man had given him that morning. He walked into Ooty Bhavan and ate two dosais and drank a cup of tea. For the remaining anna, he bought some savoury that he put away in his bag.

The dosai and tea made no difference to his headache. He wiped his face and went into the botanical garden. The expanse of green grass and the flowers calmed him.

Girls from the English convent were rolling down and playing on the grassy slopes. All in the same blue uniform; hair in two plaits; pink cheeks, which were a sign of affluence; coral-coloured lips. Sounds of happiness mingled like a melody with the gentle breeze. A white teacher sat on the bench, knitting. That little girl playing with a blue ribbon…

Nanjan looked intently at her. That girl, studying in an English convent with other affluent girls and the daughters of white men, was the daughter of Dr Arjunan. Krishna Gowder's granddaughter. He had seen her several times in her uniform when she visited Maragathamalaihatti.

Even the girls from that family were well educated. While he… he…? He stood there with thousands of thoughts jostling in his brain.

A little later, the teacher left surrounded by the girls. Only then did Nanjan become aware that it was getting late. As he left, clutching his books, something got entangled in his chappals.

It was a blue ribbon, the one she had been playing with. He picked it up, rolled it and put it away in his school bag. He walked on, vowing that whatever ills befell him, he would endeavour to pursue higher studies, earn a name for himself and become their equal.

Eight

The adai and butter that Nanjan had refused to touch remained on the plate. The twigs in the stove had cooled and turned to ashes. Paru's tears had dried on her cheeks.

The disheartened boy had left home on an empty stomach! Wretch that she was, she had let him go hungry! Even though she had not borne him, was he not dear to her! Knowing that he had not eaten even a morsel of food, she had allowed him to leave! Why had she not thought of running after him and bringing him back? The boy had to walk eight miles on an empty stomach, without even a sip of tea! She had made him angry.

As she sat in a daze near the woodstove, the old man came along and asked her, 'What's the matter? Why haven't you gone to fetch water?'

The hawk-eyed old man had sat quietly and watched the boy leave on an empty stomach and was now questioning her!

'Nanjan left for skol without eating anything, Mama!' said Paru, her eyes spilling tears again.

The old man smiled. His smile, revealing his smoke-stained teeth, made her furious. 'He's growing up. Is he going to be bothered with you or me?'

'You speak without pity, Mama.'

'I am saying this only because I feel sorry for you. What is this education for which you are sacrificing your life? How is it going to help you? You foolish girl, learn to survive.'

What could Paru say? After thinking it over, she came to a decision and wiped her eyes. Had she been separated from her husband? Had she gained freedom with the help of the panchayat? No! Was the land that had been cultivated by Jogianna a gift to Rangammai's family? Why should they not give them at least a small share of the harvest? They would need a lot of money when Nanjan finished school at Othai and went to college at Coimbatore.

Many were the days when the younger brother had helped out the elder brother's family. Shouldn't Rangan, out of gratitude, help out by paying for the education of his younger brother's son?

Had she revealed to Jogi that she was going to Maragathamalai to seek help, she doubted whether he would have agreed to it. In any case, she would have to stop shedding tears and find an answer to the problem before Nanjan returned home in the evening, hungry and tired.

She completed what had to be done at home and left for Maragathamalai, as though she were on her way to work in the fields.

After she had slipped out of Maragathamalai in the dark and crossed the Kumari River, she had not gone back to the hatti again. She crossed the river now, paying no attention to the changes that had taken place beyond it. She walked with the sole purpose of completing her mission and returning to the hatti before nightfall.

Work on the Maragathamalai school building, which had been held up due to disputes, had just begun again. Rangan seemed to have got the contract. In a blue serge coat and turban, he stood in the midst of carpenters, masons and helpers, issuing orders.

Avoiding the climb, Paru went around the hill and reached the house. A lorry was parked on one side; perhaps Raman had come home for his noon meal. He came out to wash his hands after he had eaten and was the first to spot her.

'How are you, Mami? Not a day passes by when I don't think of you. They cut down the orange tree yesterday. While I was eating, I kept thinking I should come to see you. After you left us, you never came back.'

'Did I leave you for good? Are you all well?' Paru asked about everyone's welfare and distributed an anna's worth of chickpeas to the children.

Lingan appeared, sporting a budding moustache, wearing a gold chain and clad in a *lungi*.

'What brings you here, Periamma?' he asked.

Rangammai and Gowri made the customary enquiries. Paru had gone away and not kept in touch with them. So when they surrounded her and talked to her, making her feel part of the family, she felt greatly comforted and happy.

Rangammai's hospitality overwhelmed her. Raman climbed the loft and brought down the oranges that he had secretly put away for her. When Paru saw the oranges, tears trickled down her cheeks. She had nurtured the tree as if it had been her child.

She had a strange feeling that the fruits in the basket were saying, 'Mother, we have lost our real ammai.'

She gave an orange each to the children around her.

'Anni, they've had enough. Rama! Put the rest away in a corner. She should take them for Jogianna and Nanjan,' said Rangammai and she enquired, 'How is Nanjan?'

In a voice tinged with pride and sorrow, she related how he was doing well in school and bringing home prizes, and how he had to walk sixteen miles over a stony path.

'I see him in Othai when I take the lorry to the shandy. Mami, let me peel an orange for you. Please have it. Rami, why are you standing around? Get her something to eat,' he hustled his wife. By then, Rangammai had appeared with a vattil heaped with rice, keerai kuzhambu and cabbage

'Come, amme, come and sit down,' Paru invited everyone around her to partake of the feast. Gowri who had been standing beyond the door also came in and helped herself to a handful of food.

Many days had gone by since she had eaten with her relatives.

'When will Lingan's father come home?' Paru asked Gowri.

'He'll come to have his tea,' replied Gowri, wiping her wet bangles with the end of her sari; gold bangles; a sari of the same colour.

When her husband could afford to spend so much, would he not give fifteen rupees a month for Nanjan's schooling? She did not have to worry about going to his house, as Rangan himself came to his younger brother's house.

'Are you alright? Is Nanjan doing well at school?' A discreet enquiry.

'Yes… I… I…' words failed her. Even when they had been living as husband and wife in the same house, she had never asked him for anything.

'And Paru, is Mama keeping well?'

'I… I need some money. That's why I came.' Paru spoke without lifting her head.

Without a murmur, he took out a ten rupee note from his coat pocket and gave it to her. Overcome with gratitude, Paru said, 'Maman is sending money to Siddan. What we grow is enough for food but Nanjan is now in high school. We need more money to buy school books and clothes. If you could give me a similar amount every month…' Paru stopped.

'I'll not remember. Come and ask for it or send Nanjan. Rangamma, has Anni eaten? Have you given her coffee?' Rangan asked solicitously.

Paru nodded her head and put away the money carefully.

'Are you leaving now?'

'Yes. I've come away without telling Jogianna.'

'Rama, give her a lift up to Keezhmalai in the lorry,' Rangan ordered him and left.

Raman stacked gunny bags containing two measures of wheat, potatoes and oranges in the lorry. He made her sit beside him and started the lorry. As it bumped along the uneven surface, Paru was inexpressibly happy.

Her husband was a good man. Gowri, Rangammai and Lingan were also good people. How affectionate Raman was towards her! Her land, her people. In this happy frame of mind, words poured from her mouth.

'Is Devaki also going to skool, Rama?'

Raman replied, 'Ch! You cheated me by not having a daughter to give me in marriage. Will I forget that? When Nanjan comes home with all his degrees, can my daughter afford to be uneducated?'

Overjoyed, she closed her eyes.

'The next seven years should rush by with the speed of the lorry. Then…' She could not contain her joy.

She pictured Devaki bedecked in gold ear studs and dangling eardrops, wearing a dazzling silk sari just like the daughter of the Thenmalai woman, standing beside her Nanjan. May that day come fast, she prayed.

The lorry came to a halt.

Paru lifted the bag containing the wheat and rested it on her head. One of the coolies who had come with them in the lorry, carried the sack of potatoes for her.

'I'll take leave, Rama.'

'I'm in a hurry. Please tell Maman that I'll come again,' said Raman.

With the load on her head, she walked briskly to keep pace with the coolie and climbed up Mookkumalai. The path was not as even as the one to Maragathamalai. Her only thought was whether Nanjan had returned home hungry. She had not wanted to put even a morsel of Rangammai's food into her mouth as her thoughts had been on Nanjan.

While climbing up, she noticed five or six men in white uniforms, wearing hats like white men, going towards the hatti. She also saw that Jogi was with them.

Who could they be? With the advent of coffee and tea, such officers had become a common sight.

The thought that Nanjan would be wearing such clothes one day burgeoned in her mind.

Reaching home, she boiled the potatoes and pounded the wheat and ground it coarsely.

Before it became dark, she fetched water and made tea for the old man. She cooked the wheat and made kuzhambu and then lit the lamp in the niche.

In every home, the men who had gone out to work had returned. The cattle had come back to their sheds. Women had lit their woodstoves and the twigs crackled. Paru kept going to the door and looking out.

The boy who had left early in the morning hadn't returned yet! Normally, he would have been back by this time. But he had not left in the normal way that morning! Had he perhaps fainted on the forest path? Why hadn't he come back yet?

Even Jogiannan had not returned! Had the men she had seen, the brown sahibs, come for hunting? Jogiannan hunting? Impossible!

As time passed, she grew more and more fidgety.

Mother Mountain was ready to fall asleep, covered in mist.

Jogi came in shouting, 'Anni,' in an unusually buoyant tone.

As soon as she saw him, she blurted out, 'Nanjan has not yet come home.'

'It isn't time yet for his return,' Jogi said. 'Listen, Anni. Do you remember, when we were children, Annan, Krishnan and I used to lie down on the slopes, while the cattle grazed? Do you remember that you lost a bangle? At that time…'

'Why talk about those times now?' Paru panicked. 'He didn't eat anything this morning, Anna.'

'Don't worry Anni, is he a small child? He would have eaten something,' he said and again began to talk with his old enthusiasm, Just listen to this; one day I, Annan and Belli—yes even Belli—argued about what we should do to cover the entire hillside with huge lights. It was then that Krishnan said, 'We'll cast spells and turn the river water into oil. We'll request the Muttukothars to make a big pot.' The time is not far when we will actually use the water of the Kumari River to light the hills, Anni.'

Jogi, who avoided uttering Krishnan's name because of the feud, forgot himself in his excitement, and kept talking of how darkness was going to be banished and how there were going to be lights everywhere.

Paru did not enjoy this conversation one bit.

'The officers roamed all afternoon. They surveyed the hills and forests and calculated the amount of water in the river and the amount of rainfall. I also went with them up to the sandal shola where they are camping. They have brought all kinds of equipment. It is amazing.'

Before she could understand what Jogi was saying, her heart recognised the familiar footsteps she had been waiting for. She went forward eagerly and met Nanjan as he reached the doorstep. He did not look famished and weary. She perceived a hitherto unknown confidence in his walk and manner.

'Nanja.'

Nanjan did not utter a single word. Hearing his footsteps, the old man got up from the bench in the edumane.

Before the old man could open his mouth, Nanjan announced, 'I lost your four annas, Thatha,' and then walked in. After washing his feet and face, he came to the stove and sat on the floor.

The fire was blazing. A pot with potato kuzhambu was on it. He opened another pot; broken wheat kali.

Paru, standing beside him, gave him an orange and said, 'Why don't you share it with Appan, Nanja.'

'Where did you get the orange? And the wheat?'

'The orange is from our tree. When Periappan cut down the tree, Raman kept some fruits for us. Can you guess how I felt when you left this morning, my child? I couldn't bear to see you go hungry.'

Nanjan's heart was touched by the caring voice. He wiped the tears streaming from her eyes.

'Amma! Amma! You should never cry. It was stupid of me to have lost my temper,' he consoled her. He quickly took out of his pocket the savoury he had bought for an anna.

'Open your mouth, Amma.'

Jogi came in just then and he seized the packet from his hand.

'It is better to die of hunger than to stoop so low.'

Paru stood aghast.

'He starves us every day, Appa, and lives off our toil,' said Nanjan.

'You can tell the old man that you want money, but you should never stoop to this, Nanja. Never… never… How could you lie that you lost the money? Truth is more important than life! How much did he give you? Is this what you've learnt in school?'

'Four annas.'

Paru was relieved that he had not gone hungry. 'Jogianna, he was hungry,' she said, 'He will not do it again. I'll give Maman the money, so please drop the subject.'

But Jogi did not listen to her. He handed the packet to the old man.

Nanjan felt as though his heart had been torn apart when he saw the stricken look on his father's face.

Nine

'Gopala!'

'Yes, Sir.'

'Where are you going?'

'To cast my vote.'

'Which box?'

'The rose box.'

'In the hair of the princess?'

'Is the rose.'

'The most beautiful?'

'Is the rose.'

'The most fragrant?'

'Is the rose'

'People like most?

'The rose'

'What blooms in the evening, is the most fragrant and is coveted by the people?'

'The rose.'

'Look at the beautiful rose in bloom in a plant with thorns and leaves. Does the rose have education or glamour, pride or vanity, arrogance or a storeyed house—is it selfish or wayward?'

'No.'

'Then what does it have?'

'Beauty to enhance knowledge, a loving heart, magnanimity in its simplicity, eagerness to enlighten lives. That which remains fresh and steadfast, that which blooms and sheds radiance, while others thump their chests and brag that they can do this and that. That is the rose.'

'Vote for?'

'The rose box.'

'Which box?'

'The rose box.'

Could the clamour of the elections spare the hill folk? Rangan's symbol, the rose, was strewn everywhere, in nooks and corners, heights and hollows. Baskets of rose petals were trampled underfoot every day at the election meeting. Yellow roses, wild roses, white roses, common roses, roses of all kinds were plucked and heaped everywhere and the praises of Rangan were sung.

Rangan's men, wearing coats with roses pinned on them, extolled the greatness of the rose. Trucks and vans carrying pictures of Rangan, garlanded with roses and placed on pedestals adorned with roses, circulated on the hilly roads. Certain that victory would be his, Rangan spent money heedlessly for the sake of status.

If Krishnan had stood for the election, Rangan would not have been so sure of winning. Initially, Krishnan had planned to stand for the election as a candidate of the people's party. When he had learnt that Rangan was contesting, he had given up the idea.

Rangan least expected this. The other candidate was a well-known personality belonging to Kothai. The one chosen as the people's party candidate did not belong to the hill people.

If Rangan had known that Krishnan would withdraw, he would not have jumped into the fray. At this late hour, he could not step down.

The old enmity and the rift between the two families did have a part to play in the election. It could have been said that it was the main issue in the campaign.

Those who had raised their voices against Rangan, in particular on the day of Lingayya's funeral, and had said, 'We will progress, we will stamp out uncivilised traditions and look to the future,' had now joined the opposition.

Gowri walked on air! Was it an ordinary event? Her husband was going to hold high offices. Wherever she looked there were pictures of Rangan. Wherever she turned, roses and praises of Ranga Gowder. Were the praises confined to Rangan? Was anyone equal to Lingan in oratory? In every hatti, from every platform, he stood garlanded with roses, making flowery speeches. The son of the woman from Thenmalai might be a graduate but could he make such speeches? Even elderly Madhan, emerging from his dream world, took part in the glorious election campaign of his son. To attract crowds, he wore rose garlands and sang songs which he had not sung for a long time. He danced. He met all his old friends and chatted with them. He visited Toda settlements and enthusiastically assured them that if they cast their vote in the secret ballot in favour of his son, the intoxicating drugs that the government had banned would be made available to them. Needless to say, this election promise was the one aspect of his son's campaign which sparked the old man's interest and enthusiasm.

Jogi was totally unaffected by the excitement of his brother's electioneering. The commotion and the strife in the outside world did not affect him, nor did they affect Paru and Nanjan.

However, when Nanjan had to stand before his uncle and beg every month for a paltry ten rupees, he found himself shrinking with shame. If he went to the potato mandis at Othai, he would sometimes have to hang around for hours waiting for Rangan.

Rangan, feigning ignorance, would ask him, 'What is it?'

Nanjan would shamefacedly say, 'You said you would give me money if I came here.'

'Oh! So you think that this education is going to take you places! Does an educated chap weed the garden?' He would begin to lecture heatedly to the Gowder in the mandi.

Nanjan was sorely tempted to retort, 'Are your uneducated sons weeding the garden?' but would control himself with difficulty.

'Alright! Here, take this five rupees now. Come and see me at home later.'

Nanjan would have to walk ten times between the mandi at Othai and Rangan's home for the ten rupees.

He never breathed a word of these humiliations to his mother. It would have pained her and he did not want to see her unhappy.

He was becoming more mature day-by-day.

Nanjan had to pay the examination fees at the time when the electioneering was at its most intense. Even normally, it was difficult to meet Rangan. He was not at the mandi, he never went home and to meet him in the tea estate was impossible. Gowri knew that Nanjan would come for the money. Let him come and ask her! Why was he so proud?

Nanjan, expecting her to give the money on her own, shied away from asking. One day, he was dispiritedly returning to Maragathamalai after failing to meet his uncle. When he lacked fifteen rupees what was the use of thinking about Coimbatore or college? He would have to start looking for a job on completing school.

His mother did not know that he had to pay the examination fees. Did his father ever have a thought for this world? A deep sigh rose from within him. He felt that his heart would break.

The Karthigai sun was blazing. There had been no rains that year. The earth was scorched, the grass had withered, here and there cows tugged at the dried-up roots and looked up in disappointment. Had the earth ever been so parched in the month of Karthigai?

Nanjan, coming along the Keezhmalai path saw a rose painted on the Mookkumalai rock. Limewash had dripped down the rock making it look like a demon's face.

The Kumari River had become a thin trickle over a bed of pebbles. The lorry driven by Raman was parked in front of Nair's shop. The sides of the lorry had hoardings of Rangan with folded hands, flanked by two huge painted roses. A crowd had gathered to gape at it.

Nanjan waited to see whether his uncle was inside the lorry. While he was standing there, Raman came out of Nair's shop. He was wearing khaki pants and shirt and a woollen muffler. Seeing Nanjan, his eyes widened and he came towards him.

'Nanja! Are you returning from the hatti? Come, let's have a cup of tea.'

He gripped Nanjan's shoulder and led him into the tea shop.

Nanjan smiled, 'Busy with the elections?'

It was a long time since Raman had spoken to Nanjan. At sixteen, Nanjan had left childhood behind and was growing taller day-by-day. His voice had broken, indicating that he was growing up.

'Are you having holidays?'

'Yes, revision holidays for the selection exam,' replied Nanjan.

'Next year, you'll be going away to Coimbatore?' Raman smiled as he passed him two bondas on a leaf.

'What about you?'

'I've just eaten. What brings you to the hatti? To see Periappa?'

Nanjan's face clouded immediately.

'Nanja, what's the matter?'

'Nothing, Athan. How can I go to Coimbatore for higher studies? I don't have money even for the selection exam.'

Raman was taken aback for a moment.

'Are you upset because of that? Silly boy! How much money do you need?'

'Fifteen rupees.'

A lot of election money was passing through Raman's hands at the time. In truth he was the one worrying about the election expenses.

He feared that the tea estates and leased lands would be sacrificed at the election gala.

Raman depended on Rangan for his livelihood and was paid forty or fifty rupees by him. Rangan, his mother's brother, thought nothing of earning money or squandering it. But what about him?

He quickly extracted two ten rupee notes from his pocket and gave it to Nanjan.

'Why are you getting upset over this? Thousands of rupees are being swallowed up by riff-raff. When you need money, ask me. Is Mami all right? And Maman?'

Beaming gratefully, Nanjan folded the currency notes and put them away.

'I'll never forget this. I didn't know how to tell Ammai that I hadn't managed to get the money, so I never mentioned it.'

'You did the right thing. We live in Jogi Mama's house and live off the produce of his land. My wish is that you should study well and earn a good name. Whenever you need money, ask me, Nanja.' Raman spoke with feeling and bid him goodbye.

Nanjan studied night and day. Night and day, petromax lights burnt. Electioneering, fist fights and wordy duels shook the peaceful hill region.

The day Nanjan had learnt that he had been 'selected' and had gone to pay the fees, the excitement of the crowds about the results of the election had reached fever pitch.

As soon as the men in Ranga Gowder's party heard that he was leading, they raised slogans from the rose bedecked lorries which had been kept in readiness for the victory procession.

Liquor bottles for a grand celebration were kept hidden under mounds of roses.

The party which did not belong to the hill people, polled few votes.

Only the count of the votes cast for the big shot from Kothai with the elephant symbol was still to be known.

When Nanjan came out after paying his fees, joyous cries of victory pierced and rent the air. The jubilant cries of lorry-loads of excited people singing and parading in the streets; many-hued shawls on all the mountains; turban-clad crowds.

Who had won?

As Nanjan walked briskly down the slope, a police lorry went by, laden with people who had caused confusion and trouble. An inebriated young man who was swaying, raised his hand and babbled, 'Victory to the rose: rose, king, queen.'

A group of people travelling in a lorry and showering pamphlets, laughed at him.

One such pamphlet flew down and fell on Nanjan.

'Victory! Victory! Heartfelt thanks to all those who have overwhelmingly supported the might of the elephant.'

Did that mean that the rose had lost? Had his uncle been defeated?

Nanjan derived a vicious pleasure at his uncle's defeat. Eager to convey this in person to his mother, he walked home swiftly.

Ten

Spring came as usual to visit the Mountain Beauty as he did every year. Why had the beauty, who used to welcome him with a profusion of flowers, a smile playing on her lips, her complexion fresh, changed beyond recognition?

Where was her youthfulness and freshness? Where were the gurgling streams? Why had the tender branches that swayed in the gentle breeze become withered? Would the blazing sun never disappear?

Once the forests had vanished, rows of potato plants covered the bare hilltops stretching to the horizon and delighting the eye!

That year there was no moisture in the earth. People planted potatoes and stood imploring the skies. Mother Earth, seeing the people's plight, fumed helplessly.

Jogi had planted the entire field with only potatoes that year. The old man agonised, gazing at the blue expanse of the sky where not a speck of cloud could be seen.

'The boy has to go to Coimbatore to study. We planted potatoes on leased land. Lord of the sky, do you have no mercy?' Paru grieved.

'Our future hinges on the potato seedlings in the ground; our mother, ammai, earth and sky, don't cheat us,' Jogi was not the only one to implore the skies and weep.

The wealthy, who had planted lakhs of potato seeds, as well as the progressive people who had forsaken belief in God, were all praying for rain. Men of many beliefs, each according to his faith, invited the rain clouds by performing poosais and rituals, by dancing and singing. Those who had come to spend money like water on gambling, horse racing and other pleasures, were surprised to find Ooty parched and dry.

Meetings were held, people made speeches, the press published photographs on the plight of the drought-stricken people and wrote reams about it.

The skies did not relent.

Twenty days had passed since the potato seeds had been planted. Within thirteen days of the planting, the skies should have darkened and the rains should have come. Where had the dusky beauties, who normally came and stayed on the mountain tops, gone? Was it because of man's ingratitude?

Rangan had striven hard to acquire status by squandering lakhs of rupees. He had lived like a millionaire, but had now lost his estates, cattle and influence in one sweep and become a pauper. Karuppiah, who had looked to him for support, became the owner of his potato mandis, and Chinnapillai inherited the tea estates. All that remained was his ancestral land. There were no men to work on it and no money to cultivate it. Raman began to drive the lorry in Karuppiah's mandi. To forget his family, which consisted of a wife who raved and ranted because of the loss of her jewels, good-for-nothing sons and an old father who resorted to begging, and to obliterate the memory of his defeat and disgrace, Rangan sought the solace of drugs. He even directed his attention to the production of intoxicants. His animosity towards Krishnan had increased since he felt that Krishnan's support to the opposition was the reason for his downfall.

None of this affected Jogi. From the day he was born and throughout the years when he had been growing up, he had seen many men change, but the skies had never cheated him like this. What could he do if the very skies cheated him? On the twenty-second day, when there was still no sign of rain, Jogi felt his heart break and sink to the pit of his stomach.

He lacked the will to pull out a plant by the root to see whether there was any moisture left. Not a single drop of rain had fallen!

Though the summer holidays had begun, Nanjan continued to go up to Ooty. His thoughts were not on the earth or the sky. When his uncle, Rangan, himself, was broke and there was no one who could help him, what was the point of dreaming about going to college? He belonged to a backward class, he was entitled to preferential treatment in the matter of admission into college but who was there to bear the other expenses? Would his father borrow to see him through college? What could he offer as collateral?

Loath to see his mother's face and the desperation in his father's, Nanjan spent the better part of the day away from home.

What could Paru, whose dreams had been woven around the soil, do? She had coped when many of her sweet dreams had been shattered. All that remained now was the dream that

Nanjan should go to college. Her dream depended on the soil. If that dream was also shattered, how could she bear it?

She did not dare to look at Jogi's face. She hid herself, fearing that she would forget her resolve if she saw the tears in the old man's eyes as he gazed at the sky, forgetting even his tea and tobacco.

Even on the morning of the twenty-fifth day, clouds did not gather in the sky. Paru furtively pulled out a seedling from a corner of the field.

Iswara! Is this your wish? There was not a drop of life-giving moisture in the soil. The seeds she had planted had shrivelled and withered. They had become blighted empty shells.

Her heart broke.

She crumpled on the hot earth and sobbed. How was she going to overcome this? How could she console herself? Her beloved crop! Was it a mere day or two days old?

The pitiless cold of the evening fell on the hot dusty soil. Even then the heat of the agony in her heart did not subside.

'Mami, Mami! What's the matter?' A frightened Raman shook her out of her stupor.

'Mami?'

Dazed, as though her house had fallen on her head and crumbled, she slowly opened her eyes.

'It's getting dark. Are you feeling faint, Mami?'

'Faint?' The dam burst and tears were unleashed. She could not utter a single word.

'Why grieve like this, Mami? It's Iswaran's will. You coped even when the great disaster struck Periamaman.'

'Rama, all the Gods are angry with us. Your Maman's greed and jealousy have brought disaster to the well-being of the family. Both Mamans fanned the hatred. Jogi Maman drove out Krishnan Annan who had come home seeking his friendship. Rama, how can I face Nanjan? He has done well in the exam. What will he do here if he cannot go to Coimbatore? This potato plant, like my life, has become a blighted empty shell. Just as fate plotted against me, the skies have also plotted against me,' she ranted like one demented.

Raman consoled her, 'Perhaps this one potato is like this. Get up, Mami. Don't worry about Nanjan's education. I'm here. Get up.'

Had she heard right? Was she imagining things?

'You!'

'Yes, Mami. Can I, Raman, forget that I am living off Maman's soil? Shouldn't your heart always be loving and caring? Get up. Nanjan will certainly go for higher studies. I'll do everything I can to fill this one bright lamp in our family with oil and keep it burning. Get up.'

'Rama, can I believe you, Rama?'

'Shall I swear by this soil, Mami?'

'Thambi, Rama, how can you undertake this big responsibility?

'Don't you have faith in my words, Mami? Will we perish just because this one harvest has failed? Are you the only ones to have suffered a loss? There are others who have borrowed lakhs to plant potatoes.' His tone was kind and caring. She leaned gratefully on the support he offered.

He was short like his father and he smiled and spoke innocently; Rangammai's son, who wished everyone well.

'Isa, you have tried us sorely. At least spare these good people!' A mother's heart blessed him.

A month later, when almost all the seeds had turned to dust, there was thunder and lightning, which struck young trees, splitting the trunks into two. This was followed by heavy rain.

Jogi did not recover even one tenth of what he had sown. But Paru's hopes were rekindled when she saw the wet earth and she hastened to turn the soil.

Yes, her Nanjan would certainly study more than Krishnan and would be greatly respected. Raman had undertaken the responsibility. He was a good boy. He would keep his word. Isan's grace and power were eternal. A few problems might appear now and then, but should one buckle under them?

Part V

One

Even as the Nilgiri Express was steaming to a halt at Mettupalayam station, the passengers who alighted ran to find a seat on the first-class bus to Ooty. Ignoring the cries of 'Porter! Porter!' Nanjan ran at full speed, carrying his box. Had he not done so, he would not have been lucky enough to find a place in the bus parked at the railhead. He was returning from an interview at Madras, prior to joining duty.

As Nanjan ran, he saw a young girl with her hair in two plaits, dressed in a crepe *davani* and wearing velvet slippers, jumping out from the first-class compartment that was in front of his. As she hurried along, a man carrying her small leather suitcase ran ahead.

The bus, which was little better than a covered bullock cart, was referred to reverentially as 'a first-class bus'. However, even those who travelled in the first-class compartment in the train had to compete with the rest, to find a place in the bus that reached the top of the hills ahead of the slow mountain train. During the season, owners of bungalows in Ooty also competed for seats in the bus. The conductor of the bus had the privilege of waving his hand and cheerily saying 'Full up!' even to rich men flashing *navaratnam* rings on all ten fingers, race-going millionaires and merchants with leather bags bulging with invaluable papers, and driving away. It was no surprise that Nanjan ran for a seat, pitted as he was against these heavyweights.

As he had expected, the queue for tickets for a place in the twenty-seater bus wound its way right from the railhead to the bus-stop. However, Nanjan elbowed his way through the crowd, deaf to the conductor's shout of, 'Saar, please stand in the queue.'

'Coonoor, one.' Nanjan managed to get a ticket by holding out a two-rupee note above the raised hands of all the others.

He scrambled into the bus, reserved a seat by placing his handkerchief and newspaper on it and then got down to have a cup of coffee. He was extremely happy. His nerves tingled with the joy of being free.

His dream had become reality and his mother's fervent wish had been fulfilled. Raman had kept his promise to his aunt, Paru, and had given money for Nanjan's studies, in fifties and hundreds, over the past six years.

Nanjan was now a graduate in Civil Engineering. Many other educated young men of his community were also, like him, coming forward to build a wonderful future for their country. Nanjan was one of the group of young experts, all of whom were part of a mammoth project in the Nilgiris, at Maragathamalaihatti, the very place where he had been born and brought up.

What greater happiness could he have expected in life? A good degree, a good job and earnings in hundreds, which he would give his mother and make her happy. He finished the idlis and coffee and made his way with a light step to the bus that was about to leave.

The driver, seated behind the wheel, honked. As he boarded the bus, he had a rude shock.

The crepe-clad beauty was sitting in the seat that he had reserved with his handkerchief. She was nonchalantly turning the pages of an illustrated magazine and chewing her fingernails.

Nanjan was shy by nature when it came to facing girls and talking to them. But when he saw that there was no place to sit in the bus, which was packed to capacity, he realised that he had no option but to make her vacate his seat.

How cheeky of her to remove his handkerchief and newspaper and take his seat!

'Excuse me, this seat is mine,' said Nanjan, confused and flustered.

She did not appear to notice that he was standing next to her and did not look up.

Left with no other option, Nanjan raised his voice and called out, 'Conductor! This is my seat!'

The conductor, who was counting the money, was about to tell the driver to start the bus. He heard Nanjan and looked up. 'Get down, the bus is full,' he said indifferently.

Holding out his ticket, Nanjan said heatedly, 'I bought a ticket and reserved this place earlier by leaving my things which have now been swept aside.'

'Ade,' finding that he had inadvertently got caught in a quarrel, the conductor pleaded, 'What's to be done, Saar? Why did you leave the bus? Get down, there's another just behind this one!'

Nanjan grew red in the face.

'How unfair! I reserved this place before I got down.' He glared angrily at the girl. He was startled when he recognised her.

'What if you had reserved the seat? You should give in because she is a "lady". Catch the next bus. After all, you're going to Coonoor, aren't you?' the conductor pleaded once more.

Nanjan could not be appeased. With the aggression natural to youth, he said, 'Being a woman does not mean she can behave unfairly. The next bus is due an hour later. Ask her to vacate my place.'

Getting up abruptly, the girl moved to one side. She said in English, 'Here's your seat, you can take it.'

No one in the bus expected her to do this.

Slightly taken aback, Nanjan's face darkened. He sat down angrily, opened the newspaper and held it in front of his face. Inexplicably, his heart beat faster.

The conductor was in a fix.

There was a murmur of voices in the bus.

The conductor grumbled, 'What is this, Saar?' A woman passenger and her two children had occupied three seats. 'Can you keep one child on your lap, please?' he requested her.

The woman did not wish to do so.

Meanwhile someone from the rear of the bus got up. He offered his seat to the girl and got down, bag in hand, to catch the next bus.

She took his seat.

Nanjan felt as though someone had slapped him.

As the bus began to move, he felt as if everyone was looking at him. He felt guilty for having behaved boorishly towards a woman and for having made a scene. He felt sorry that his conscience troubled him at a time when he should have been enjoying the journey.

Not wanting to meet anyone's eye, he looked out till the bus reached Coonoor.

The bus came to a halt at the noisy and crowded Coonoor bus stop.

As he was getting off the bus, he turned when he heard a voice asking, 'How are you, Vijaya amma? Did you fare well in the exams?'

Though he was loath to linger, he had to wait till his small box had been unloaded from the roof of the bus.

When Krishnan Gowder, stick in hand and a turban on his head, came near the bus, the crepe-clad girl jumped down, laughing excitedly. Pushing back a lock of hair that had fallen on her forehead, she replied, 'I've done well, Thatha! I was afraid that you might not come.'

'Not come? I'd sent word to the driver yesterday that I'd be coming to the bus stop. But even if I hadn't, surely a girl who has travelled alone so far will be brave enough to get to Ooty. Did you get a good seat?'

Her eyes fell on Nanjan, who stood aside, pretending to look up at his box. Her grandfather looked back and did not fail to spot Nanjan.

'Oh! Was Nanjan in the same bus? Don't you know Nanjan, amma?' as he spoke, he turned to Nanjan.

A little smile played on her lips. Was she smiling thinking of him as an ill-mannered peasant? Why should Krishnan, an enemy of the family, talk to him? Nanjan did not turn to face him.

'Are you returning from the interview, Nanja?'

'Yes,' he replied, feeling discomfited.

'Have you not been assigned to the Kumari River project?'

'Yes.'

'Vijaya, this is the son of our Jogi Gowder. You've done our hatti proud, Nanja.' Krishnan Gowder looked from one to the other.

She giggled, covering her coral-red lips with a silk handkerchief.

Nanjan could not bring himself to smile. He felt uncomfortable.

His box was unloaded. 'I'll take my leave,' he murmured and turned away.

Raman was employed as a jeep driver in the project. When Nanjan had left for the interview, he had said he would try to meet him at Coonoor. But he was not to be found in the crowd. As he waited for the bus going to the Kumari River dam site, he saw Krishnan Gowder and Vijaya driving away in a big blue car.

Nanjan could not get over the shock of Krishnan Gowder coming up to him and starting a conversation, that too when his granddaughter, who was studying in a college in Coimbatore, was with him.

What would she be telling her grandfather about him? Would she be laughing at him? He had last seen her in a blue convent-school uniform. She had grown so tall! Why had Krishnan Gowder introduced him to her?

The minibus bound for the Kumari River project site groaned to a halt. There was such a crowd scrambling to get in. Were there so many people in Maragathamalaihatti, his birthplace? People from all over India had come to this out-of-the-way place to build the dam.

Nanjan leapt in and found a corner seat.

'Where to?' Conductor Chinnayya, his classmate from Maragathamalaihatti, asked him teasingly. Nanjan replied with a smile, 'Keezhmalai.'

As the bus bounced along the badly paved new road, he felt happy and cheerful as he got to know the newcomers to the Blue Mountains, and struck up a conversation with them.

'Tea, Saar. Tea bushes all over. Did you see that, Meenu? Those look like coffee bushes.' The middle-aged head of the family, wearing a shirt, a coat and a woollen muffler against the cold, was jumping up and down excitedly.

'Meenu, Meenu,' he called to his wife from time to time.

Wrapping her Conjeevaram silk sari around herself tightly, she complained, 'I can't bear the cold. What sort of a place is this?'

Their bright-eyed son eagerly piped in, 'Won't there be tigers and cheetahs on the road?'

'Don't open the door at night. It is then that they come out,' the father replied.

Nanjan controlled his laughter with difficulty. The gentleman turned to Nanjan. 'Saar, are you also going to the project site?'

It was Nanjan's first opportunity to tell someone that he had become an engineer.

'I finished college only this year. I'm coming back from the interview,' he replied jauntily.

'So you are also new to these hills? It's already so cold. I believe tap water will freeze in December! How will we cope?'

Nanjan was amused, but answered him with a straight face, 'That's not true. I know because I belong to this place.'

The man's eyes widened. 'Is that so, Saar? Really, Saar? Are you settled in Ooty?' he asked.

'No, I was born and brought up in Maragathamalaihatti. I belong to these hills. My parents live in Keezhmalai,' Nanjan said with a smile.

'Really? I'm so glad to meet you and talk to you. My name is Panjamritham and I'm an accountant attached to the project. I was nervous about coming here, Saar. My wife can't stand the cold even in the plains,' he began, and then went on to stump Nanjan by quizzing him on matters about which Nanjan knew nothing.

'Saar, I believe that the kurinji will bloom this year. Has it flowered? Can you show it to me?'

'I myself don't know the flower, Sir. I don't remember ever seeing the kurinji.'

'Ade! I believe your people measure time in terms of the flowering of the kurinji?'

'Yes. You will have to talk to the elders about it. It is referred to as *kattegida* in our language.'

By the time the bus reached Keezhmalai, they had become good friends. Nanjan got down at the bus stop and took leave of them.

The place where the bus halted was a far cry from the jungle path of yesteryear. All along the route, boulders had been dug up and broken into huge slabs. Many feminine hands had laboured on this job. The thrill that he experienced when he heard the din created by thousands of hands at work in the sholas, was new to him.

As soon as he got down, a beaming Raman came towards him from a nearby teashop. Making kind enquiries, he took the box from him. Where was his father, wondered Nanjan. He had always been at the bus stop to receive Nanjan when he returned home from college.

Before he could look for his father, he saw his mother standing on the path to Mookkumalaihatti. He took long strides towards her.

Paru could not speak. Misty-eyed, she saw her Nanjan, her son, her life, now grown up, his eyes sparkling with intelligence. Her dream had come true.

Two

Having fulfilled his long-cherished dream, Nanjan had returned home. Why had his father not come to receive him? Was he unwell, perhaps?

'Is Ayyan well, Amma?' he asked.

'He is well. He said he would come. He went to Maragathamalaihatti yesterday. There he is!'

Nanjan watched his father approach. Why had his face lost its usual brightness? Why was his father, who had been boasting to one and all that Nanjan would come home as an engineer in six months' time, looking so gloomy and unhappy?

'Is it the heat, Appa? Are you ill?' he asked in a worried tone.

'Is your father such a great man that he is unused to sun or rain?' asked Jogi. The bitterness in his voice alarmed Nanjan. He had never heard his father speak like that. Was it the weariness of doling out money in fifties and hundreds?

Could Raman, on his own, have borne the entire cost of his education? Could Rangan have helped? He had lost not only his money in the elections; he had lost all hope for the future and had turned to drugs. His son, Lingan, had got a contract to supply milk to the ever-growing populace in the dam colony. The second son, Dharman, was employed in the dam project and the third son was trained to project pictures in the new touring cinema at Maragathamalai.

Nanjan was fully aware of the financial situation in Rangan's family. No help could have come from that quarter. As for his father, he was still sending money to Siddan even after his uncle's death.

Could his father have incurred a lot of debts? Had he mortgaged his land? In his eagerness to study, Nanjan had never given a thought to it.

Nanjan suddenly realised that the footpath had become a proper road that curved along Mookkumalai.

'Jeeps can go on it. They say there'll be a tunnel under our hill to carry water!' said Raman.

'Amma, I think they'll put me in the tunnel-digging section. We can have electricity even in our house. You press a button and there'll be light! The water from the dam will pass through the tunnel in big pipes, which will turn huge machines and produce current. The cinema in Maragathamalai will come to Mookkumalai also. Now the current is coming from elsewhere.

We will dam the water from the river and the waterfall and generate our own electricity. We will use the electricity for factories, for manufacturing machinery and for cooking and heating. There will be work for lots of people. They will have food to eat and clothes to wear.'

Carried away by enthusiasm, Nanjan went on with his explanations. He had never failed to come and tell his mother about the modern advances he had seen or heard about.

But did Paru appreciate all that he said? Was she truly happy about the revolution that had come about in the hills?

Her happiness was bound up with Nanjan. His coming had brought about a revolution in her life. If tomorrow, the progress he envisaged spread over the hills, as far as she was concerned, he would be the architect of it all. In the blissful glow of hearing his voice, her heart was full. Whatever he said was all right with her.

But Jogi launched into a tirade, 'So you say many people will get food to eat and clothes to wear? People living here will go without food. To give jobs to educated fellows like you, they are drilling land, ravaging Mother Earth. Men are mad after money. Can money and land ever be equated?'

Nanjan was stupefied.

Was this the same man who used to say enthusiastically, 'This mountain will be covered with lights. I dreamt of it when I was young.' What was the reason for this change?

Dismayed, he said, 'Appa!'

Paru paid no heed to the conversation. She was not in control of her senses; she could neither listen nor analyse.

Jogi took hold of himself and said, 'Forget it. It was not right on my part to have spoken to you like this as soon as you arrived.'

The whole of Mookkumalaihatti had gathered to welcome Nanjan.

Paru recalled the day when Krishnan had come to Manikkalhatti on horseback and the entire village had collected to see him. The girls had worn white mundus then. Today they were wearing coloured saris and *davanis*. There were affectionate enquiries of 'How are you, Nanja? Aren't you going to work here?'

As Nanjan stepped into his house, he saw a girl in a coloured davani darting into the kitchen. He knew at once who it was.

'Amma, you never told me? Re, Devaki! Why are you running from me?' he laughed, putting down his box.

Devaki came and stood before him, her head bent, a shy smile on her lips. She was short and well-built like her father. Dark-complexioned, she had big eyes and thick black hair. She wore a flowered pavadai and voile davani, a blue choli with elbow length sleeves and a black bead *mala* around her neck.

'Re, Devaki, how did your maths exam go? Why have you stopped talking all of a sudden?' teased Nanjan.

When she ran inside, seized with shyness, he was reminded of the morning's incident. Would she have ridiculed him when talking to her grandfather?

Paru laughed when she saw him still standing there.

'Wait, Rama. Nanja, let's have coffee,' she said. She went into the kitchen and brought coffee for everyone.

'Has Devaki come alone? What about Athai and the others?' asked Nanjan.

'I asked only Devaki to come. She has written her tenth standard exam,' said Paru, brimming with pride.

'That's why I asked about the maths exam.' Addressing Raman, Nanjan spoke enthusiastically. 'Athan, we'll now have to find a groom with an M.A. for Devaki.'

While Raman smiled without saying anything, Paru dashed out from the kitchen.

'What a thing to say, Nanja! Devaki studied only for your sake. To marry an educated cousin, she can't be an uneducated fool.'

Nanjan gave his mother a stern look. A chill ran though his body. Was this why Raman had taken such an interest in him and paid for his studies?

'Have you taken a decision on your own, Amma? Will an educated girl marry a man who's been like a brother to her?'

Nanjan spoke laughingly, but Paru did not relish the remark.

'As her mama's son, you are the right husband for her. Raman has always thought of you as a son-in-law. Isn't that so, Rama?'

Nanjan did not wish to prolong the conversation. He said, 'Alright,' and closed the topic.

Soon after the meal, Jogi and Raman left the house.

Nanjan lay down for awhile. But he grew restless. He suddenly thought of something, went to the edumane and rummaged through the box containing his books and clothes.

Group photos of his class taken every year in college, the prize book won at the Tamil Manram Bharathiyar poetry competition, a pen gifted by an outstation friend. Engrossed in the memories that each one evoked, he spread them all on the floor. Finally he reached for the yellowing paper lining the box and shook it out. Underneath lay a folded blue satin ribbon, intact.

How long had that ribbon remained there! Picking it up, he recalled the vow he had made one day in the garden at Othai.

He had fulfilled his vow. The owner of that ribbon had become a willowy and beautiful woman! And what a boor he had been to have insisted that the seat was his. How foolish he had been! It showed that he had grown up in a hatti and did not know about the niceties of behaviour! He was trained only to tackle rough jobs. On the other hand, having been steeped in European culture, which had become part of her nature, she talked and behaved politely. It must have been the conductor who had pushed his handkerchief to the floor and given her the seat.

How stupid he had been! It was this stupidity that had made him behave so boorishly. When he had rudely insisted that the seat was his, she had given it up.

'Che!' Nanjan felt that unless he apologised to her that very instant for his behaviour and showed her that he was a cultured well-mannered chap, he would know no peace.

Why had their archenemy, Krishna Gowder, who had never spoken to him, greeted him at the bus stop with the familiarity of an old friend? Why had he introduced Nanjan to her as Jogi

Gowder's son? Why had Nanjan, who regarded Krishnan as an enemy and had always been slightly jealous of him, not been angry?

What if his father, who was already perturbed, got to know of it?

He could not fathom what was bothering his father. Perhaps he had taken loans of two or three thousand rupees? What if he had? Nanjan could repay them now in monthly installments. Even as he thought of discreetly finding out about the debts from his mother, she walked in, bringing *urundais* made of roasted peanuts and jaggery. She saw the satin ribbon in his hand.

'Re, Nanja, have you bought the ribbon for Devaki? So were you joking when you talked of being her brother?' she asked, eyes shining.

Nanjan collected his wits about him and asked her, as if in jest, 'Does the ribbon seem new? It is a very old one. Look, Amma, guess who it belongs to?' He felt as though he had managed to surface after almost drowning.

With a beating heart, Nanjan was just about to reveal the secret. Paru, who had no inkling of what he intended to say, laughed. 'Whose is it? Is it your sister's? Did you pick it up at your Periappa's house?'

'No, Ammai, no.'

'Then? Oh! Had Devaki plaited her hair with it?' There was a mischievous teasing glint in her eyes.

'Far from it, Amma. If you guess correctly, I'll give you whatever you ask for.'

Paru laughed aloud.

'You are my biggest prize! What more do I need?'

'Don't you want anything else?'

'Nanjan should marry Devaki. Ammai's lap…'

Suddenly a shadow covered the light in his eyes.

'Why should I marry now, Amma? How much has Ayyan borrowed to educate me? From whom has he borrowed?'

'Borrow? He hasn't borrowed, Nanjan. Raman offered to educate you. He did it for the sake of your ammai. You will marry his daughter. I know that this ribbon is Devaki's. Isn't it?'

Nanjan didn't have the courage to dash her hopes to the ground. At last, he had discovered the motive behind Raman's desire to help him.

He sighed deeply. Shaking his head, he turned his attention to the groundnut urundais.

Three

The gentle breeze heralding summer was soothing to Nanjan when he came out after spending the whole day standing in the tunnel. It was two weeks since he had started working. From the outside, he looked into the horseshoe-shaped tunnel dug into the hillside. The workers engaged in this great endeavour, their skin coated with mud and stone dust, were busy carrying slabs of stone and dumping them outside. They belonged to the night shift. Those in the day shift had already left by five in the evening. Inside the tunnel, which was a few hundred feet in length at the time, the racket of the noisy machines boring into the hillside, compounded with the sound of those pulverising the rock, was nerve-shattering. Spending eight hours a day in that din had gotten on Nanjan's nerves for a couple of days after he started work.

He felt ill at ease when he saw the mask-covered faces of the workers. His endurance was tested when he was assaulted by the ear-splitting noise that made conversation inaudible. However, he got used to it soon. As he stood outside the tunnel and glanced down at the hills all around, he saw houses, scattered lights that had multiplied to hundreds of thousands and a black shiny, meandering rivulet in the far distance. Some hillocks were still covered with tea bushes, a few conical silver oaks and tea factories with smoking chimneys. He became aware that a brand-new world lay spread out before him.

The growing number of people had to struggle hard to earn a living. Man had mastered power and knowledge. Man had progressed by breaking down hills, levelling valleys, damming rivers and capturing nature's energy.

Nanjan shook his chilled body. The young man in charge of the night shift had arrived. Cordite sticks and explosives would be inserted in the holes bored into the rocks during the day to blast them at night. After removing the pieces of rock, they would start drilling again.

As soon as his replacement arrived, the jeep carrying Nanjan and his boss left the Maragathamalai slopes and brought them to the project office located in the sprawling housing colony of the dam.

Nanjan was going to the canteen for a cup of tea, when…

Wasn't that his father? Why was he standing in front of the project office? Was it to see him? Nanjan, knitting his eyebrows together, went to him and touched his shoulder from behind. 'Appa, what brings you here?'

Jogi turned around. Nanjan tried to contain the sorrow that arose in him when he saw his father.

Why did his father look so sad? Did he feel that his educated son was indifferent to him? His father was standing at the office of the Deputy Collector of the project, clutching a long, brown paper envelope in his hand. Like a flash of lightning, he realised why.

'Why have you come here, Appa? Whom do you want to meet?'

'You can go, I've come to see the Collector,' his voice betrayed the immeasurable anguish that lay within him.

'Won't you let me see him and explain? What do you wish to tell him? Why don't you tell me what the matter is, Appa?'

A *dawali*, peon, came up to Jogi, 'Old man, how many times do I have to tell you that the Collector will not be seeing anyone today. Come back tomorrow.'

Nanjan saw his father's eyes fill with tears. He did not speak. He started walking towards Mookkumalai. Nanjan, who did not want to discuss the matter on the road, followed him, his mind beset with many thoughts.

At home, Paru was grinding batter. Knowing that Nanjan, having lived outside the hatti, was used to variety in food, she had learnt to make idlis for the morning meal. The joy and enthusiasm in her heart brimmed over as the dhal being ground foamed up. Nanjan knew that his mother was unaware of the sorrow that troubled his father.

Removing his shoes and changing his clothes, he washed his face, hands and feet before going upto his father, who sat in a corner, broken in spirit.

'Appa, will your land be submerged when the dam is built?' he asked.

Jogi looked up and thought, 'How unemotionally he says, "Your land".'

'Traitor to the soil, you have lost your heart to money! You speak totally without feeling. Do you realise that it's this soil which has fed us for generations?'

These words burst from his incensed heart. As though he was ramming a bolt on his feelings, he closed the conversation by flinging the brown paper envelope at Nanjan.

Nanjan opened the letter. As he was reading it, Paru brought tea and fruits. She looked from one to the other enquiringly, her brows knitted.

The dam would not submerge the land belonging to the uncle from Mookkumalai which Jogi was cultivating. However, a wide road encircling the dam would pass that way. There would be godowns to house important material for the project. To store it, the government would be acquiring land, which would include Jogi's uncle's land. The letter had come a few days earlier.

Why should his father be so upset about it?

'What if we lose the land? The government will not just take it away. They will pay us a good sum of money for it,' said Nanjan.

Paru understood at last. Thunderstruck, she exclaimed, 'Our land?'

'They are going to snatch the food out of our mouths and pay us money in return. Who wants this money?' Jogi spluttered.

'They grabbed the land at Maragathamalai to build the colony and now Rangammai's family is suffering. Like a predatory snake they are coming here to snatch the food from our mouths. How can we tolerate it? Who wants the dam and the electric lights? They are snatching away our food and giving it to strangers. These Governors and Collectors!'

It was a cry of anguish from the heart of an old man who knew no other life.

'Nanja, you tell the Collector durai. What will we do without land? How can we give up the soil which is yielding well?' said his innocent mother.

For a couple of minutes, Nanjan's mind was a blank. The rock could be blasted to bore tunnels but people could not be separated from the soil that was a part of their being. He stood helplessly as he realised it.

'That blackguard Krishnan. He has had a hand in this conspiracy too. He has not lost even four full acres of his land. I ran away from a faraway place and came here, crossing mountains. Why are they snatching away my land?'

Had his father, who had all along appeared as a personification of peace, become mad? Was he so angry that he had lost his senses?

'Appa!' cried Nanjan, in alarm.

'You have always believed that your brother should prosper, that men should prosper and that the whole world should prosper, and wished everyone well. Is it you speaking like this? Aren't you receiving money to give up your land so that our people and our country can reap the benefits? Crores of rupees are being spent on this magnificent project that will harness the skills of men. Don't talk in ignorance, Appa.'

'Ignorance? You, who were born yesterday, how dare you talk with contempt, calling me ignorant? Is this what education has taught you? The soil has fed and clothed us. The blood that courses through our veins comes from the soil! The land is your mother! How would you know the worth of the mother who has given birth to you? Scoundrel! My heart burns! It is like a volcano erupting! As soon as you have finished your education, you are talking of giving away the land for money! Can paper currency be equated to a mother? Can one put a price on a mother?'

Jogi's body shook and his lips trembled. His passion for the land was palpable. Nanjan stood paralysed with fear. Could bundles of currency notes be used to sever a relationship that had lasted for centuries?

'How would you know the worth of the mother who has given birth to you?'

The words pierced Paru's heart like a lance. With that one sentence which implied that she was not Nanjan's mother, he had wounded her heart with a red-hot spear. Without saying it in so many words, he had said that he had given his son on loan to her!

Paru was devastated. 'Why are you talking like this to Nanjan? Have I not been his ammai?' she cried.

The loss of his land had plunged Jogi into a sea of unbearable sorrow. So thoughts which were alien to his nature occurred to him. He had no control over himself.

'If you had really been his mother, you would not have given him the education which has made him a traitor to Mother Earth who gave birth to him. You slaved, you earned money from the land and when that was not enough, you begged for money from all and sundry! I was always certain that if he was educated, he would grow away from us. Which educated chap has been up to any good? You have not been a true mother to him. No mother would bring up her son to be a stranger to his father. Has this chap ever discussed school or college with me? Has he shown me any respect?' Nanjan interrupted him, losing patience with this vituperative tirade, 'How can you talk in such a childish vein, Appa?'

Tears fell from Paru's eyes. 'Your talk is crueller than the loss of my land. Nanja, I am your ammai. Don't deny it. Distraught by the loss of his beloved soil, Annan is talking senselessly. Go to the Collector or Governor and save our land. We have already given land for the school. We don't own any land in Maragathamalai. If we lose this, what will we do for a living?' she asked.

Nanjan tried to reason with them. 'Neither the Collector nor Governor can help you. Aren't you and Ayyan getting on in years? How long can you continue to toil on the land? Think about it. As an engineer, I'll progress in my career. You will have no worries in your old age. You can live in comfort in a big house. Aren't you always talking of how great Krishna Gowder's family is?' The mention of that name triggered a fresh torrent of words.

Don't mention that traitor's name. He is the cheat who ruined my life long ago. Though he has hundreds of acres, he did not have to part with even four. He is a crook. With the arrogance of education, he caused disharmony in the village. He created factions and dissension. He dragged my elder brother and me through the courts. He was the cause of our family's downfall. Rangan, who stood as majestically as an elephant, was reduced to nothing. To earn a good name, Krishnan cunningly persuaded the chap from Kotagiri to stand for elections and took revenge on us. Now he has instigated everyone and plotted to snatch away my livelihood. Come what may, this Jogi will never give up this golden earth. He is prepared to die, if necessary.'

What could Nanjan say?

The land would go. He feared greatly for Ayyan's sanity. Sleep eluded him that night. His mind was in turmoil.

He dragged his feet unwillingly when he set out for work in the morning. Raman, seated in the jeep in front of the office, ran towards him.

'Nanja, I have to discuss certain matters with you at leisure. Can you meet me alone this evening?' he asked.

Nanjan stood with his hands in his pockets. Many thoughts flitted across his brain and he kept staring at Raman. He asked, 'What is it about?'

'I have to tell you something. I am worried that I might have made a big mistake. Come with time to spare.'

Raman could not linger there with him. His boss was already in the vehicle. Nanjan stood gazing at the jeep that meandered along the winding roads to disappear in the distance.

Four

Hillview Mansion in the Anandagiri area of Ooty wore a festive air that day. Gleaming cars stood at the entrance. In the front garden, girls in bright silk saris and children in beautiful woollen clothes and shoes bore testimony to the gaiety within.

Gopalan's wife, Krishnan Gowder's daughter-in-law, had become the mother of a baby boy and had just returned from the hospital. She was the daughter of Bette Gowder, owner of the Pasumshola tea estates and factories. All the members of her family had come with her.

Krishnan Gowder's daughter, Vijaya's mother, who had been as slender as a creeper ten years ago, was now plump after successive pregnancies. She had become lethargic and moved around less. As mistress of the house, she sat in one part of it ordering everyone around. Not a day passed when the ground floor of the mansion did not resound with the noisy mischief of children, chatter of relatives and laughter of friends. Did a wealthy and influential person ever lack friends or relatives?

To the right of the mansion stood the imposing Ananda Nursing Home. Dr Arjunan, who had returned from abroad after specialisation, was now training two young doctors. Krishnan Gowder was especially proud and relieved that domestic problems or other dissensions never distracted his son-in-law's attention from work.

The feast over, Gopalan's wife, Jaya, and her mother relaxed and spent the afternoon sitting and talking with Vijaya's mother and grandmother. It was obvious that Jaya's mother was captivated by Vijaya. Her fair complexion seemed as though it had been distilled from moonlight and her two plaits moved on her shoulders like serpents. All morning, she had run hither and thither looking after the comfort of the guests and talking animatedly with them.

Gopalan's in-laws were very keen that their son should marry Vijaya. Jaya's mother broached the subject, 'Won't Vijaya be getting married this year?'

Grandmother Rukmini looked at Vijaya with a smile and said, 'Her father wants her to study medicine.'

'Oho! So he wants the daughter to remain with him and is looking for a doctor as a son-in-law too, perhaps?'

'Yes. But her grandfather wants her to get married. Two or three people have approached us,' said the grandmother.

'What does Vijaya want?' asked Jaya's mother, laughing. On hearing this remark, Vijaya, who had been flipping the pages of a magazine, pretending to be indifferent to the conversation, turned red.

'What will Vijaya say? At the moment she agrees with her father and talks about going to medical college,' said her mother.

'So you have not given a reply to those who have approached you?'

'One of them would not have suited her—he was short. The other's birth-star was not compatible with Vijaya's. There are plenty of educated boys these days. We can wait,' said the grandmother.

'Why don't you get Vijaya married to our Natarajan? The marriage has to be conducted before he leaves for America. His father says that he could then take his wife along with him. As you mentioned, there is no dearth of educated boys. But there are not many educated girls to suit them,' laughed Jaya's mother. She turned to Vijaya and asked, 'What do you say, Vijaya? Why don't you become our daughter-in-law?' As though she had just remembered, Jaya's mother added in a voice tinged with pride, 'He said he would come here after the tennis match in the evening.'

Vijaya had seen Natarajan five or six times in Hillview. He had completed his B.Sc in Textiles. He was fat and tall and looked middle-aged. Vijaya, who had been sitting with her head bent, got up abruptly and went out of the room.

The offer for Vijaya's hand made grandmother Rukmini truly happy. Natarajan owned estates that yielded an income of lakhs of rupees. He was educated and just the right age for her granddaughter. She had really been waiting for them to come up with the offer.

'Why has Vijaya left the room?' asked Jaya's mother.

'When there's talk of marriage, which girl won't be shy?' asked the grandmother.

When Natarajan came in the evening to Hillview Mansion after the tennis match, Vijaya was not at home. She had gone to the pictures with one of her college friends who had turned up for the season. Her grandmother was a little put out.

After all the guests had left, Rukmini went upstairs where her husband was relaxing with a cigarette. Now that she had become old, she found it difficult to climb the stairs. While she was going up, she could hear someone talking. Since there was another staircase in front, the women of the house were not usually aware of who went upstairs. After all, there were many who came to consult the lawyer or the doctor.

However, the voice seemed vaguely familiar. It was a rustic speaking in their mother tongue. She was undecided whether she should enter when she reached the upstairs hall. The grey walls and the matching sofas and carpet, all looked brand-new. An electric heater in the corner made the room comfortably warm.

Krishnan was seated on a sofa. Raman was perched on the edge of the sofa opposite. He looked ill at ease as though he was aware that he did not have the status to sit with Krishnan as his equal, but was doing so under duress.

Who was he? Had he come from the hatti? Rukmini remembered having seen him somewhere, sometime. Seeing her, Raman stopped talking and hastily stood up.

He folded his palms together in greeting and enquired, 'Athai, are you well?'

'Who are you, Thambi? I can't place you. We hardly come to the hatti these days. When we do, I'm totally occupied with the children. Are you from Maragathamalai?'

'Yes, Athai. I'm Rangamma's son. You know Jogi Mama? In Mookkumalaihatti?' Raman elaborated.

Rukmini was totally stunned for a minute. Did he belong to the family of the sworn enemy? Why had he come here in secret? What was brewing?

'Rangamma's son?' she asked in a dazed voice.

'Yes, Athai, we live in Jogi Mama's house.'

Swallowing her anxiety, which had formed a lump in her throat, she asked, 'Is Rangamma well? Where is your wife from? Do you have children?'

'My wife is from Manjakombai. I've two sons and two daughters. The eldest daughter has studied up to the tenth in Maragathamalai School and has just finished her final exam.'

'Oh! Such progress!' thought Rukmini. Aloud, she said, 'Is that so? Very good! When your mamans are hostile even without setting eyes on us, you've been very kind to come. It makes me happy. Have some coffee.'

'Don't bother, Athai. I've had my meal.'

'That's no excuse. I did not know earlier that you were here. Not a day passes when I don't pray to Devar that the feud should end. The two families were so united in your grandfather's time. I am glad you've come discreetly to help end the feud. Are you working in the estates?'

'Only on Maman's land. The Kumari River Project has acquired even that. I am a jeep driver there.'

'That's good. Wait, I'll bring some coffee,' said Rukmini, going downstairs.

'Sit down, Rama. Why do you keep standing?' asked Krishnan. Raman sat down again, feeling ill at ease.

'I want this marriage to take place so that the enmity ends with this generation, Rama. What hurts me most is that Jogi judges me wrongly. In the olden days, marriages between great kings helped them to stay friends. Explain this to Jogi Mama. If Rangan's sons were educated and suitable, I would have chosen one of them for Vijaya. Tell Jogi I look forward to the day when he will come to my house to ask for my granddaughter's hand. Tell Paru also. It doesn't matter if you think I offered to pay for Nanjan's studies with selfish motives. The two families must come together; there must be an end to the rift.'

Raman was a simple, inarticulate soul. He felt hurt and letdown, as if something which had been within his grasp had slipped through his fingers. With what hopes and desires he had educated his daughter, Devaki, so that she would be worthy of Nanjan! These people would give a lot as *streedhanam*. Several estate owners would ask for Vijaya's hand in marriage. But what about Devaki? Probably only the loud-voiced Lingan, Rangan's son, would come forward to marry her. The brute!

'Why, Rama, don't you agree?'

'Of course, I'm happy. I'll tell my mama. But… but, I also have a daughter. We brought her up believing that Nanjan would marry her. All of us were happy about it.'

Krishnan sat upright, frowning. 'Is that so? Is that so?'

Old memories unfolded in his mind, one after another. Would his efforts cause harm by separating two hearts that beat as one? After Nanjan and Vijaya had arrived on the same train, Vijaya had blushed shyly whenever Nanjan's name was mentioned. He had felt confident that his wish would be fulfilled.

While Krishnan and Raman tried to come to terms with the situation, each in his own way, Rukmini came in with coffee, laddus and vadais.

Though Raman normally had a good appetite, he could not bring himself to eat anything. He drank just the coffee and got up to leave.

Raman's family had survived because of his uncle, Jogi. Vijaya, the doctor's daughter was worthy of Nanjan. Let good things happen in Jogi uncle's family. What could a poor man like Raman do for Nanjan? Consoling himself, he said aloud, 'I'll tell Jogi Mama.'

As though relieved of a burden, Krishnan also stood up and said, 'Is that so? But will it make Nanjan unhappy?'

Raman remembered Nanjan's question, 'Will an educated girl want to marry a man who has been like a brother to her?' Wasn't that Nanjan's view?

'It was the elders' idea. I don't know how Nanjan feels,' he replied.

Yes, Nanjan should marry a girl from an influential family. He, Raman, would not stand in his way.

'Rama, if that's the case, my brother Ajjan has sons who would suit your daughter. I'll get her married to a good boy. Tell Jogi Maman. We must come together. We must put an end to the enmity. The rift must be mended.'

Raman was moved. How magnanimous of Krishna Gowder! What a large house he lived in! He had a heart to match!

'I'll take leave.'

He bowed and went down the stairs. Krishnan stood watching him till he had crossed the front verandah and disappeared from sight.

Her Kashmiri shawl rustling, Rukmini came in and stood by him.

'After all these days, just as I thought it was all behind us, why has he come? Is there trouble brewing?'

'Not trouble. The time has come when the feud will end.'

'You said the same thing earlier. You went to their house and came back humiliated. Forget it now. I've some good news for you.'

'What news?'

'Vijaya has studied enough. We don't have to educate her further just because it is her father's wish.'

'Is this the good news?'

'No, no. Jaya's mother has asked for Vijaya as a bride for Natarajan. Their tea factory alone is wealth enough. They've bought new machinery and rollers for five lakh rupees. The boy is young, he is going to America.'

She spoke without a pause. Krishnan remained silent.

'Why don't you say something?'

'Even though I hadn't expressed it, I didn't want Vijaya to study further. I had found a husband for her eight years ago. Did you know that?'

Rukmini looked at him as though she were in a trance.

'I undertook to pay for the boy's education without anybody's knowledge. He is the right husband for our Vijaya. She has met him. He is an engineer in the Kumari River dam.'

Startled, Rukmini asked, 'Are you talking about Jogi's son?'

'Yes. It is the only way to end the feud. By God's grace, the marriage should take place. I asked Raman to come to discuss it,' Krishnan said in a firm voice.

Five

At 5.30 in the evening, Nanjan stood waiting for Raman at the canteen door.

He thought, 'What is he going to tell me? Will he talk about the money he has borrowed to educate me? Will he talk of my marrying his daughter at such an awkward moment? I know about the loan. Why does he want to talk to me alone at leisure? Does he sense that I am not showing any eagerness or desire to marry Devaki?'

There was a cool breeze. Raman ran down the steps.

'Have you had coffee?'

'No, Athan.'

They went in for a cup of coffee.

Nanjan asked, 'Shall we go home?'

'No, I have the jeep. I'm expected at the dam site. Let's talk on the way,' said Raman.

They got into the jeep.

Raman started the conversation. 'How is Maman?'

'Land, land. That's all he can talk about. I am worried he will lose his mind. If I could somehow get him an acre of land elsewhere, the road-building work could start on his plot.'

'And Mami?'

'She is worse than him. Should she not try to understand the situation? Stones can be crushed, mountains melted, but it's impossible to change their minds. Let's forget it. Now tell me, I don't know why you wanted to talk to me at leisure.'

'We are forever beholden to Jogi Maman. Mami has a soft corner for me. I took a certain decision without consulting them, believing that it was for the best. Did you ever wonder how I was able to send you money on my income, in spite of the fact that I have a large family?'

'Am I not old enough to wonder how you managed, Athan? I was thinking about it just now. I will repay whatever you have borrowed to the person who lent you the money. Never doubt it.'

'I did not borrow the money, Nanja. Would a person with a chronic illness say no to one who offers him medicine? Do you remember the year the monsoons failed and the potatoes turned to dust? Mami was in despair, Mama was not in his right mind and you were loafing around in Cthai, never coming home.'

Nanjan listened silently.

'Jogi Maman helped us survive. I thought it was not right to see him suffer. I promised Mami I would help them. Rangan Maman had stood with his legs too far apart and toppled over. He had lost all his money. What could I do? I tried everywhere for a loan. I had banked on Gounder, the mandi owner. Then one… one day…' Raman's voice became gruff.

Nanjan was intent on watching Raman take the hairpin bend.

'Krishnan Gowder saw me one day in the mandi and drew me aside. What could I do, Nanja?'

The truth became clear to Nanjan.

'Has he been paying for my education all these years?'

'Yes, he told me that I should not tell anyone that he was helping out. He gave me two hundred rupees then and there. He is truly a great man, as lofty as a mountain. Jogi Maman forbade him from entering his house. The other maman hired men to beat him up. We were guilty of wrongdoing. What a great man to think of doing good to the wrongdoers!'

'Have you not told even Ammai, Athan?'

'They would have misconstrued Krishnan's motive and reacted with suspicion. Did I have a choice? Where would it have led? If Jogi Maman knew, would he not have pulled you out of college? I thought it best to keep it to myself.'

Nanjan recalled his encounter with Krishnan Gowder at the bus stop.

'I pray fervently that Devar always showers good fortune on you. Krishnan Gowder sent for me day before yesterday. He has a palatial home. I have never been inside it till today. I met Athai. He asked me for a favour in return for his help. It was not really a favour; on the contrary, he offered you something very dear to him. Custom dictates that Maman should approach him. This enmity should not be continued from generation to generation. Krishna Gowder has asked us to wipe it out. He offered you his daughter's daughter...'

Raman left the sentence in mid-air and concentrated on turning the vehicle.

Was it true? Had Raman showered him with a basketful of flowers? The mention of Devaki as his bride had left him cold. Now, he felt the first joyful stirrings of a hitherto unknown emotion.

Having had a hand in moulding him, had Krishnan also contrived to throw them together? Would a far-thinking man like him bring up the subject of marriage without consulting her? Then the beauty must have consented to be his wife. His wife!

Nanjan felt that he could not bear such happiness. Raman, sensing his reaction, felt sad.

Nanjan was educated. Nanjan had never worn dirty clothes and grazed cows or goats. While he had been at school, his mother had made sure that he had not got his hands dirty. It was obvious that Nanjan did not care for Devaki. But...

Krishnan Gowder was a great man, loftier than a mountain. Let his efforts bear fruit! A man of his word, he was bound to ask for Devaki's hand for his nephew.

Nanjan masked his feelings. 'I am confused. Ayyan is a broken man since he lost his land. The man who paid for my education is our sworn enemy. Still he has come forward to offer me his granddaughter's hand in marriage. How can I force my father to make a formal proposal?'

'Be patient. Are you for this marriage? Did I do wrong? At least it's off my chest. May you be happy and healthy, Nanja!'

'How can I express my thanks for your affection and for the courageous step you took?'

Pain mingled with happiness and sorrow mingled with joy came in waves. Nanjan was unable to speak further.

It was dark when he climbed up Mookkumalai and reached home. The thousands of lights on the slopes and valleys tried to outshine the stars in the sky. The house was not desolate and dismal, as he had expected. The agitated voice he heard as he climbed the steps was not his father's. In fact, it was the venom-filled voice of his elder uncle, Rangan.

Nanjan entered the house, removed his coat and asked calmly, 'Are you all right, Periappa? How is Thatha? You were away when I visited your house.'

'Yes, I was away at Manikkalhatti. I am not going to stomach it. Is it not treachery to do us out of what is rightfully ours and heap wealth on others? How can outsiders and intruders who have come to our hills deprive us of our land? What injustice is this! I forbid you to work on the project! Yes!'

Thoroughly shaken, Nanjan quietly went inside to change.

Jogi looked at his elder brother expectantly. With even greater reverence, Paru looked up at her husband.

'We can teach them a lesson if we unite and fight! I can induce all those who have lost their land to join in the agitation. When Rangan takes a step, he never fails! Jogi, how did we drive the white man out of our country? Satyagraha! We will do the same thing now. These hills are ours. We don't want these lights if it is going to deprive us of our land. We'll foil their conspiracy!'

'There is one more thing. Not one of those on the project who earns a fat salary belongs to our hattis. Intruders! It makes my blood boil! Did they compensate us in advance?'

Nanjan lashed out, 'Periappa, don't jump to conclusions. Our people are not yet qualified to earn such salaries. They are still being educated. They are learning new skills. They will soon become eligible for better jobs. Let's be reasonable in our demands. They will be met. What you are proposing is impractical. You are not going to be done out of your compensation. Periappa, are you aware of the extent to which natural resources are tapped in other countries? Why should we remain buried in the dirt? Should we not progress? Can you visualise the number of industries that will draw power generated by this project? And think of the benefit to succeeding generations. You need to have a change of heart. Villages will be no different from towns. We will enjoy all the amenities here, in our hatti. We have already taken great strides forward!'

'Think! Was there a pucca road from Maragathamalaihatti to town in your days? Were there good schools for our boys and girls? But for the contact with the world outside, would it have been possible to enrich our soil, grow tea and reap solid cash? Periappa, you have first-hand knowledge of all this. Compare the hatti of today to that which you left at the age of twelve for Othai. Why, even I had to walk to Othai to study. Could we cover the distance from Keezhmalai after sunset? Don't you enjoy the bright lights, the radios in every corner, the exhibitions? Nothing is gained by envying those who have done better than us. We should learn from them. We should be friends with them. You have to give up this obsession with the land for the good of the future generations.'

Having Krishnan Gowder in mind, he used all his persuasive powers to make them change their attitude. But did he meet with an iota of success?

Merely blowing hard can snuff out candlelight, but Rangan's jealousy was like a blazing fire. Jogi's passion in life was his land. Nanjan's speech only inflamed them more.

Rangan laughed harshly. 'He was born just yesterday, yet he presumes to advise us! Thambi, are we envious of those who have done better? Can you not guess from his treacherous words whose stooge he is? I was afraid that you might not take it well and that Paru would be upset, so I've kept quiet about what happened. Ask this chap whether or not he spoke to our sworn enemy at the bus stop at Coonoor?'

Periappa's eyes held a vengeful gleam.

Ah! Jogi could not believe his ears. He became as still as a statue.

The youthful blood in Nanjan's veins boiled. 'Courtesy demands that you speak when you are spoken to. What is there to hide? Krishna Gowder spoke to me. I also spoke to him. You may be enemies, why should I take sides?' asked Nanjan.

Rangan shouted, 'Take note, Thambi. You two-timing rascal! He hired men to beat those who brought you up. He destroyed your family!'

'If you wear tinted glasses, everything will appear dark to your eyes, Periappa!'

Rangan's eyes glittered malevolently, like those of a snake ready to strike. 'De! Say that again!' he hissed.

When Rangan leapt forward, Paru screamed, 'No, no, Nanja!'

'Sh! Why should the truth make you angry? You are the root cause of our family's downfall. You stoked the enmity.' Nanjan could not be restrained.

'Nanja! Don't be disrespectful to your Periappa!'

Jogi controlled his feelings. Nanjan had hit upon the truth, knowingly or unknowingly.

'Disrespect will breed disrespect. You can neither see straight nor think straight. For you, happiness is seeing your enemy begging for alms. Would you spend money in fifties and hundreds to educate your enemy's son? When your enemy is thirsting for your blood, would you offer your precious daughter in marriage to his son, especially when she has been brought up in the lap of luxury?'

For a minute, it seemed as if the whole universe had come to a standstill. The awful silence was broken by Rangan's insane laughter.

'Oh! The reason for the youthful outburst is clear, Thambi. Krishnan has this chap in his pocket,' he shouted angrily.

Nanjan had made a clean breast of everything. Given the grist to the mill, there was no holding Rangan down.

'The scheming devil! He plotted to strip us of all our wealth. Now he is trying to lure our son away. Does he think he is honouring us by getting his granddaughter married into our family?'

Again, Rangan laughed like a madman.

Every word drove the truth home to Paru like blows from a red-hot hammer.

Rangan continued 'She has studied in an English convent. Can she make a cup of coffee for you? Grind batter? Water the buffaloes? Do we have a car? How is she going to while away the time? Are there cinema theatres here? They will keep the son-in-law with them. He'll have a car to take him to work. Doesn't it stare you in the face? Maman's educated son, Siddan, is an example. Does Krishna Gowder's daughter live with her in-laws in Kotagiri? Wasn't it her husband, Dr Arjunan, who came to live with his wife? Girls from the Anandagiri bungalow will never stay in the hatti. On the contrary, the sons-in-law have to move in with their wives.'

'Stop! Stop!' Paru sobbed.

Her husband's words bombarded her dream mansion from all sides.

She remembered the words of the uncle from Mookkumalai. Would she also suffer the same fate? Would her Nanjan abandon her?

How vehemently Nanjan had rushed to Krishnan's defence! He would surely equally vehemently retort, 'Stop it. I am not that kind of person.

Every nerve and pulse in her body yearned for her Nanjan to say those words.

But he did not say anything. Nanjan did not utter a word. 'Nanja, have you been struck dumb? Deny it; think of Paru, the ammai, to whom you are everything.'

'If you want to get a glimpse of your son, you will have to wait for hours outside gates guarded by mastiffs. You will see your son get down from the car and saunter away, nose in the air. With your dirty mundu and *pattu*, you will not be welcome in their house. His wife will say, "Why does she have to come here so often? Did she give birth to you? If she needs money, why not give her ten or twenty rupees every month?" And his wife's words will be law,' goaded Rangan.

'Aiyo!' wailed the stricken Paru.

Nanjan could not fathom the strength of the maternal feelings that lay within her. How could he gauge them?

'Do you have anything to add? Come out with it.' Nanjan's voice was tinged with sarcasm.

'Does the truth hurt?'

'Hurt? Are you really our well-wisher? Your jealousy cannot bear to see me come up in life. I should throw away my job. I should not marry a girl from a good family. You used to make me walk ten times for ten rupees! You ridiculed our poverty publicly. You! You caused our ruin by wanting us on your side only when it was time to confront the enemy!'

Why did he not utter one single word that could give hope to her sinking heart?

'Nanja!' A flash of lightning. The voice of Jogi, who had till then been silent, as if turned to stone, jolted Nanjan.

'Are you siding with the enemy in this house? Is this why you went to college? Get out!'

Nanjan staggered out and sank to the floor in the edumane. His parents' ignorance was like the impenetrable darkness.

Not mere ignorance. Blind love coupled with blind ignorance that overrode the innate high ideals of his father. Even a thousand, ten thousand kilowatts of electricity could not pierce the blind ignorance. What further catastrophe was this going to cause? Stage a satyagraha for the land? The mere thought filled him with shame. His uncle Rangan's arrival had made sure that there would be no change in his father's attitude.

With the natural ebullience of youth, he could not see how marriage to Vijaya could affect his mother adversely. His uncle's words had no impact on him.

He would live with Vijaya in his own house in the colony. When he returned home tired after a day's strenuous work, looking forward to a pleasant evening, he would be joyfully welcomed by Vijaya. One look at her face and his weariness and fatigue would dissipate like the mist. He would walk with her at sunset down the winding paths! All his life he could enjoy the beauty of the Kumari River waterfall with Vijaya by his side!

Such beautiful daydreams were a balm to his troubled soul after the storm.

Mookkumalaihatti was electrified but their house did not have a connection. Enveloped in darkness, he was blind to everything but his thoughts. He did not care less whether the brothers had eaten, slept or gone out.

Much later, Paru came, lamp in one hand and a plate and kinnam in the other.

There was rice in the aluminium kinnam, sweet dosai on the plate. Sweet dosai was her son's favourite dish. Paru had prepared it in the evening, while waiting for her weary, dirt-covered son to return from his workplace.

'Nanja,' her loving voice seemed to come from another world. His eyes remained closed. Could such a tender voice belong to such an ignorant person? Could that ignorance be washed away or removed? Would they be adamant and refuse to allow it to be removed?

'You haven't eaten anything, Nanja. I have made your special sweet dosai.'

Her son did not open his eyes.

'I don't want anything, Amma!'

To one like Paru, who was beset by fears, anything dark seemed like a ghost! Had the beauty, who was yet to step into the house, already taught him to hate his mother? Was she already trying to pluck from Paru the son who was part of her being?

Controlling herself, she called to him in a voice that would have melted stone. 'Nanja!'

Nanjan did not reply.

The old uncle from Mookkumalai had once said, 'He'll seek a girl worthy of his youth and education. He'll listen to her words.'

His cruel cackle rang in her ears.

Nanjan was her only compensation for the cruel blows, defeats and setbacks she had suffered in life; she had pinned all her hopes on him. How could she let him slip away now?

'Nanja, won't you listen to me? Look at me, Nanja, I am your ammai.'

He only felt irritated by her tearful insistence.

'Do you have anything more to say? You need not have educated me. You need not have humiliated me. Is it fair to stand in the way of progress? What would you do to a rat that destroys the crops you have lovingly tended? Won't you kill it to save your crops? Periappa, who is filled with jealousy, is obstructing the construction and is like the rat. And you listen to him? You have put me to shame.

He had no idea of the cruel blow he was inflicting on his mother!

'Let us forget about the land, Nanja. But you must promise me then…'

'What?'

In a faltering voice, she pleaded, 'I have never looked upon you as Girijai's son or Jogianna's child. You are dearer to me than life. All I have hoped for is to see you grow up and lead a good life. Any mother would have wished for the same. You are my life. I am living just for you. You will never forsake me for anybody, will you?'

'You talk rot, Amma. Is it wrong to move with the times? Does it mean that I hate you?'

'Promise that you don't hate me.'

'Why should I hate you?'

'Your ammai wants you to make just one promise. She has hoped for only one thing in this life. Will you give your word?'

'What is it, Amma?'

'We don't need a bride from Krishnan Gowder's family. If you don't care for Devaki, I'll find you someone else to your liking.'

Nanjan could not breathe.

With bated breath, Paru asked, 'Will you promise me that?'

Nanjan's eyes did not waver. He remained silent.

'Say yes,' urged Paru.

'Why, Amma? Don't you want this feud to end? What harm did that poor innocent girl do to you?'

'I have nothing against her. Won't you listen to me?'

'If you have nothing against her, what is the need for this promise? Are you afraid I'll leave you for her, Amma? How can I? I have a job. Their doctor son-in-law needs a place to practise, so he stays in his wife's house. Do you think I'll do the same? How stupid of you, Amma?'

'No, Nanja. Dont talk of an alliance with that family. For two generations, nothing good has happened between the two families. There's been nothing but ill feeling between us. Stay away from them. We don't want their enmity nor do we need to have any connection with them.'

'You forget that I am beholden to them.'

'When we had not asked him, why did Krishnan Gowder support you secretly, with Raman acting as a go-between? Wasn't it wrong?'

'Iswara! You are seeing evil even in the best of actions. What can I do with you?'

'Let it be. We can expect compensation for our land. We'll repay Krishnan Gowder. Forget the girl.'

'Hm.' A deep sigh filled with irritation rose from within him.

'Say yes!'

'Yes, Amma.'

'Have a dosai, Nanja.'

'I don't feel like eating. Just leave me alone.'

'What happiness do you get from hurting me?'

'Have I ever hurt you? Haven't I said yes! Don't I have feelings too, Amma?'

She was startled. Something in his words suddenly struck her. 'Nanja, have you... you... seen her? Spoken to her?' she demanded.

'Amma, won't you leave me in peace? All right, I'll eat a piece of dosai. Will you go now?' said her son, taking a morsel of dosai and eating it with evident distaste, just to get rid of her.

Paru could do nothing. Her son had grown taller and more mature all of a sudden. He was a man. She, who had been a mother to him, had become a stranger to him.

How long had he known that girl? Hadn't he shown her a blue ribbon one day, long, long ago?

Her feelings battered her like unceasing sea waves.

The brothers returned home and fell asleep. Paru sat in the edumane, wide-awake. Nanjan did not sleep a wink either.

Six

Though deep down he loved Vijaya, he wished to avoid an encounter with her in deference to his mother's wishes. But it took place unexpectedly the very next day.

It was a Sunday. Not wanting to be in the house, Nanjan went to the dam. He stood at the dam site watching the preliminary work in progress. He noticed a sleek green car coming to a halt in the midst of the lorries carrying sand and stone. A tall girl alighted from it, the *pallu* of her green silk sari billowing in the breeze.

She… what a surprise! She walked towards the spot where he was standing.

It was… Vijaya!

His heart leapt uncontrollably.

'Thank goodness! We saw you right away. We came to see the work that was going on. My college professor and lecturer have come with me,' she said.

As she was talking to him, a fat woman and a thin dried-up one got down from the car and followed her.

'Meet Miss Uma Devi and Miss Chandra.' After introducing them, she continued, 'I was wondering who I'd find to show us around. This is Mr Nanjan from our village. He has just started working here.'

'We want to see the work that's going on here, Mr Nanjan. Could you take us around?' fat Uma Devi asked in a squeaky voice.

'I'll be happy to do it,' said Nanjan and began to explain all about the dam. He showed them where tunnels would be dug after the dam site was readied, and in which direction they would go. Then he took them to the slope along which the water pipes would be situated, and to the foundation of the hydro-electric project. While he was explaining everything to them, one part of his mind kept prodding him, 'I must apologise to Vijaya privately for my boorish behaviour the other day. I mustn't let this opportunity slip.'

When he had finished showing them around the project, Vijaya asked, 'Is that all there is to see?'

Nanjan said smiling, 'If you come next year, there'll be a lot more.'

'We're already tired. Considering my weight, even this walk was too much for me. Vijaya, your grandfather talked about a waterfall somewhere here. Let's not forget about it,' said Uma Devi.

'We'll have lunch there. Mr Nanjan, we'd be very happy if you could join us,' said Chandra.

'He'll come. How can we eat without him after dragging him all over the place? The Kumari waterfall is not very far from here. We can eat there, can't we?' said Vijaya.

Nanjan seemed taken aback. 'The path to the fall is not good and there is no convenient spot with a view of the waterfall where we can eat. We can sit above it, but there's no way you can get there. You can only admire the beauty of the waterfall from the road.'

'Why? Grandfather said we could climb down,' argued Vijaya.

'I only said that you couldn't manage it,' smiled Nanjan.

'What is meant by "you"?'

'He is referring to the women,' laughed Chandra.

Red in the face, Vijaya asked, 'Are women that helpless in your opinion?'

'You're trying to pick a quarrel with me! See for yourself. The slope is steep. From the road, the water falls between two hills to a depth of a hundred feet. On both sides, there are dense shrubs and coffee bushes,' explained Nanjan.

'We thought we could enjoy a meal seated on a rock while gazing at the waterfall!' sighed Uma Devi.

'Haven't you told us we can't do it? We'll roll down just to show you!' challenged Vijaya.

'Aiyo! Don't say such things. I'll get blamed if anything goes wrong!' Laughing, Nanjan got into the car.

Later, Chandra turned to Vijaya and asked her, 'You say this is your village. Haven't you ever been here?'

'We used to come to the hatti once in a while, but would return home immediately. Mr Nanjan would probably have come here more often.'

The car came to a halt. Getting out first, Nanjan pointed out the waterfall. Between steep slopes, the river cascaded down the hillside, narrowing and curving into the valley, to disappear finally like a snake slithering under a rock. The slope was completely covered with coffee bushes. Down below, the dense bushes on either side of the river were proof that people did not frequent the place. Seen from the road, it was a beautiful sight, but to the city-bred women, the thought of going down the slope on foot through the bushes was daunting.

Taking the food basket out of the car, Subbiah, the driver, asked her, 'Shall we go down, Amma?'

'Such a scenic spot where one can relax. Why can't it be developed properly? It's not too high. The water is trickling down in two thin dribbles perhaps because it's the cold season,' remarked Chandra.

'They've improved the place enormously by building roads. Why can't they cut the bushes and even out the rocks to make a proper path?' asked Vijaya.

'I'll convey the idea to those concerned. But for now, you are saying you don't want to climb down, isn't it?' asked Nanjan.

'Who said so?' Vijaya demanded. She entered the coffee estate and quickly climbed down.

'So Vijaya has taken up the challenge. I can't manage it,' said Uma Devi, sitting down on the two-foot-high stump of a cypress tree. Chandra had already stretched herself out on the grass beside the road. Only Vijaya, slender as a reed, was clambering down amidst the green coffee bushes.

Nanjan ran down another path to call the driver who was walking towards the river with the food basket.

Vijaya had climbed down nearly a furlong when she heard him call out to the driver. She turned back and joined him.

'Your teachers have not come down. Tell the driver to come back. Miss Vijaya, if I've said something wrong, I take back my words,' teased Nanjan.

'Hey, Subbiah! Come, come!' she called out waving her hand. How could he hear her above the roar of the water?

Thoroughly baffled, Subbiah turned back.

'If one crosses all these hazards and reaches the spot below, how beautiful it'll be! I can manage, but the other two can't.'

He was standing close to her. He could see the curls dancing on her forehead as she spoke.

'I have to ask for your forgiveness, Vijaya!' Opening his heart to her, he spoke softly, but she heard him.

'You are our sworn enemies,' she said, looking straight at him for an instant, her eyes brimming with mischief.

'Are you aware of how your grandfather wishes the feud of the sworn enemies to end?' he retorted.

'When you created a scene in the bus, I gave in. Luckily for you, I didn't know you were provoking a fight because we were sworn enemies. If I had known, I'd have dragged you to court!'

'Oho! Many thanks for being so magnanimous. Your grandfather has sent me a message. I want to know if it was sent with your consent.'

'What is the message?'

'Do you want to hear it from me, Vijaya?'

'There could be many things between sworn enemies. How would I know?'

Her lips spoke the words. But her eyes, shyly loving, looked down, announcing loud and clear that she knew what it was.

'You know. Vijaya, to tell the truth…'

Her face flushed and glowing, she turned and sped up the slope, ostensibly because Subbiah had already reached the top.

'Oh, Vijaya! Chandra was afraid that the three of you would get caught up in gossip and begin to empty the basket, forgetting all about us,' laughed Uma Devi. She then enquired, 'Mr Nanjan, do you and Vijaya just belong to the same village or are you also related?'

Nanjan responded laughingly, 'In my grandfather's days there were good relations between the two families. Then came the fight.'

'Adada! What a pity. And now?' asked Chandra.

'There is fighting and peace,' replied Nanjan, laughing again. With a rosy blush, Vijaya started opening the packets of food.

When Nanjan returned home that afternoon, his heart soaring like a lark in the sky, Paru was waiting for him with a worried face.

'So late, Nanja? It's late for your meal!'

'I don't want to eat, Amma.' As he had been away for a long time, all sorts of suspicions arose in her mind.

'Ah! Where did you eat?'

He wanted to relive the sweet memories of those few hours and savour them in silence. He was irritated when she questioned him sternly with a tearful face.

'Nanja, you are hiding something. You have come back after meeting her!' She burst into tears.

'What is this, Amma? You've become a nag. Can't you leave a man in peace?'

Yelling at her, he went out of the house again. Paru felt as if the world had come tumbling down on her head. Her son had already forsaken her.

He was her love, precious to her. How could she watch him go away from her? How could she bear it?

Of all the educated boys, why did Nanjan have to be ensnared by Krishnan? Weren't there enough sons from rich families? She could find no relief from the turmoil in her heart.

Jogi had neither land nor work. So, he went along with Rangan to meet the men of his generation and fan the flames of their anger by pouring out his grievances and plotting vengeance.

Offices sprang up and tin-roofed godowns came up in their fields. The sound of rocks being blasted to lay roads ricocheted from the hills. When he heard the sound, Jogi would clutch his heart. To Paru, it was the sound of Mother Earth shuddering in agony. It sent shock waves through her. Even when she sat in a stupor, staring into space, her body would tremble.

Nanjan gave Paru a part of his salary and spent most of his time away from the house. He distanced himself from the family and stopped going home from work at night. Then he began to visit them in the evenings once in three or four days. Gradually that also ceased. His house in the dam colony and his close friends held him back even at night. He got into the routine of coming home as a formality once in a way.

Seven

Nanjan was on the night shift.

It was eight o'clock when he entered the tunnel wearing knee-length boots and a muffler that covered his ears. Like the quiet after a thunderstorm, the clanging of the machines ceased, signalling the end of the previous shift. Water seeping from underneath had stagnated all over the floor of the tunnel. In the centre, a man furiously pushed a barrow-load of stone slabs along the rails. As Nanjan went farther into the tunnel, there was a strong smell of gunpowder and a cloud of stone dust filled the air.

Helmet-clad Dharman, who was finishing his shift, went past Nanjan. He was Rangan's second son.

Nanjan was aware that Dharman worked on the project, but did not expect to meet him in that section.

'Oh! Is it Engineer Saar?' Dharman's tone was mocking as he stood with a beedi between his teeth.

Startled, Nanjan looked him up and down and asked, 'Isn't it Dharman? When did you come here?'

'I've been asked to work here from today. I'm happy to work for the new engineer.' Dharman gave him a nasty look and walked away. Nanjan stood still till he disappeared from view at the mouth of the curving tunnel.

Sarcasm! Disrespect! Why was Dharman suddenly treating him like a stranger and behaving rudely? Dharman's elder brother was a loud-mouth who could spew venom. But he had always felt that Dharman, the younger, was quiet and restrained. If he shared his father's strong views, he should not be working here at all!

It was only when he emerged from the tunnel after the shift, in the early hours of the morning, that the truth dawned on Nanjan.

Notices plastered on rocks and on the huge pipes, which lay here and there, told him many things.

The workers had announced a massive strike.

'Our legitimate claims have been refused. To humble the high-handedness of the management, comrades, let us wage a moral war.'

Management versus workers! Soon after Nanjan had taken up the job, he realised that there was a deep divide between the management and the workers.

Did he not belong to the fledgling management cadre? Was that why Dharman's words were filled with hatred, sarcasm and disrespect?

The new divide broke up the unity between the haves and the have-nots. It created a new kind of caste by bringing together people who did not have a common background.

After keeping awake the whole night and walking up and down the airless tunnel, Nanjan was fatigued and weary. In addition to this, he was also troubled.

Back in his house in the colony, he washed his face, drank the coffee brought by the servant from the canteen and fell into bed. His eyelids closed the minute he lay down.

Outside, the winter sun was scorching. Three men shared the house with Nanjan. His colleagues from the day shift came in, laughing and chatting, with their boots clattering. They ate the food brought by the servant boys in a tiffin carrier and went back to work. After clearing away the meal and perfunctorily washing the vessels, the servants were soon engrossed in a noisy game of cards in the room outside.

Nanjan slept through all the activity.

The sun had set and it was teatime. The servants wrapped up the card game, freshened up and departed. With the front door wide open, the house seemed deserted.

Six months had gone by since Krishnan Gowder had sent word through Raman.

With no college to attend, Vijaya whiled away the time dawdling at home; she had lost her old cheerfulness and enthusiasm. Natarajan had not left for America. Because Vijaya was an educated, modern girl, Natarajan visited her twice or thrice a week at Hillview and made bold attempts to get close to her. Vijaya showed her dislike of him openly.

'If you reject all offers from good families, how can you be sure that your Jogi Gowder will approach you? I believe the boy never goes home,' Rukmini repeated hatti gossip to Krishnan and got him worried.

Krishnan Gowder left for Maragathamalaihatti on the pretext of inspecting his estates and took Vijaya along.

He left Vijaya at Maragathamalaihatti and as he turned the car around and went towards the colony, he spotted Raman and stopped the car.

'What, Rama? It's been a long time!'

'Yes. Is everyone well?'

'They are all well. Haven't you spoken to Maman?'

Raman's face darkened.

'Jogi Maman has become demented at the thought of losing his land. He and Periamaman are plotting all sorts of things. It's the talk of the hatti, haven't you heard?'

'Yes, I heard that he is going to join the workers' strike and stage a protest. Poor Jogi! I feel bad.'

'I don't know what went wrong in their house, but Nanjan doesn't seem to go home at all. What can I do?'

'Where does Nanjan live?'

'Over there. Come, let's go there. He was on night shift yesterday. I saw him return home in the morning,' Raman said, leading the way.

'Nanja.'

Nanjan was having a nightmare. Hemmed in by masked figures, he was struggling for breath, while all around him there was a tremendous din. He awoke with a start on hearing his name. For a moment he did not know whether it was a dream or reality.

'Were you on night duty? Are you unwell?' Krishnan Gowder pulled up a chair and sat down.

Rubbing his eyes, Nanjan sat up. His head had cleared.

'Athan, where are the servant boys? What's the time?' he asked agitatedly.

'The time is quarter past four. Have you had lunch? Can I get you some coffee?'

'Ade, have I been sleeping for so long! Why didn't someone wake me up?' he said, getting up. There was no sign of the servant boys.

'Do you have night duty at a stretch?'

'No, my turn comes once a week.'

'Can you not change to day duty?'

'That's what everyone wants,' smiled Nanjan. 'Please sit down. I'll be back in a few minutes. I've slept through lunch.' He went for a wash.

Raman brought a kettle of hot coffee, dosais and bondas.

'He has come here for the first time to end the feud. Should we not celebrate with a sweet, Athan?' asked Nanjan, solicitously offering the snacks to Krishnan Gowder.

'Don't bother, Nanja, you eat. Only if your Ayyan talks to me will the feud end. Raman would have told you everything.

'We don't deserve your magnanimity,' said Nanjan.

'Why do you talk like this, Nanja? Does Ammai not want it? Is Jogi against it? Or ... are you...' stopping mid-sentence, Krishnan looked keenly at Nanjan.

'They will not change their mind. They do not want the dam to be built. They say they don't want anything to change. Is that possible?'

'Then what do you suggest? asked Krishnan Gowder.

'What can I say? I've lost interest in everything. Even now, I fell asleep in sheer disgust. I didn't want to wake up.'

Krishnan Gowder was deep in thought.

As though it had suddenly occurred to him, Nanjan asked Raman, 'Athan, are you going to join the strike?'

Raman laughed.

'I plan to go away to Palani during that period. If I stay here and don't join the slogan-shouting procession, Lingan and Dharman will break my legs.'

'You've become friendly with the enemy, aren't you a traitor yourself?' Nanjan joined in the laughter as he addressed Krishnan Gowder.

Immediately he turned to Raman and said, 'If you are going to Palani, let me also come along, Athan. I think it will be better to get out of this environment for a couple of days.'

Krishnan Gowder smiled. 'I have an idea,' he said.

Nanjan looked at him enquiringly.

'I'll come with Vijaya and the other members of the family in the big car. Let the marriage be performed in the precincts of the Palaniandavar temple.'

Raman remarked as if in jest, 'A good idea. The strike is on Monday. Tuesday is out of the question. Find out whether Wednesday is auspicious. No. If Monday is auspicious, it's even better. We can leave on Sunday.'

This talk exhilarated Nanjan.

Krishnan Gowder spoke again. 'What a good idea! If we leave by evening, we can be in Palani by nightfall. Take four days off. The shock of the wedding will change the attitude of the elders.'

'You are hatching a plot.' Nanjan smiled shyly.

'You are willing, aren't you? Are you for it wholeheartedly? Believe me, I'm serious. Vijaya is not interested in the various other suitors who've come forward to marry her. Only when your name is suggested does she raise no objection.'

Nanjan's eyes were downcast.

'Shall I see Jogi today? Can I meet Ammai?' asked Krishnan Gowder.

Nanjan spoke hastily, 'No, please don't. You'll face unpleasantness.'

'That's not new to me.'

'It will be more unpleasant than the last time. Then you met only Ayyan. Now that his bitter disappointment has combined with Periappan's raging jealousy, we don't know what the outcome will be. No, please don't go.'

'Your ammai?'

'Ammai's world is very narrow. If you want to inform them and get their consent, forget about the marriage in this birth.'

'Then… I cannot force you to tell your parents. Nor can I force you to marry Vijaya for the sake of my selfish motive of ending the feud, especially if you have some other girl in mind. I've spoken to you only because I'm interested in your welfare and Vijaya's happiness. I have never wished anybody ill. Time and circumstances may have conspired against me. I am a coward.'

His voice was gruff as old memories surged up.

Nanjan thought, 'Can one compare this man's large-heartedness to the stifling love of Ammai, who is possessive just because she brought me up. I'll never come to harm by getting close to such a great man.'

'Nanja?'

'If Vijaya is willing, I am a lucky man,' he said, head bent.

Krishnan, seeing the light of a bright future, took leave of him.

The silent preparations for Nanjan's forthcoming marriage were as swift as those for the forthcoming massive strike. Krishnan sent word that the marriage would take place on Wednesday.

Nanjan could not get out of night duty that Sunday. He had to stand in for his colleague, who had been urgently summoned to Madras.

Having sent a message to Krishnan Gowder that he would be ready to leave early the next morning, he went to work on Sunday evening. As he returned home the next morning, he saw signs of hectic preparation for the workers' meeting. Expecting Raman to be in the house, he hurriedly opened the front door to find… Paru, his ammai, standing to one side.

Eight

It was Raman who had disclosed the plot to Paru. Raman had been unaware of the cause of the arguments between Paru and Nanjan and the reason for their subsequent estrangement. He had assumed that Nanjan would have told Paru about the marriage. It had not occurred to Raman that Nanjan would have contemplated marriage without the knowledge of the mother who adored him. He did not approve of Nanjan's decision nor did he want to discuss it with him.

Deciding that it was his duty to inform his aunt, he went to see Paru on Sunday afternoon. She was sitting in the sun in front of the house. Earlier, her eyes would have lit up and her face would have brightened at the sight of a visitor.

Now the sparkle and brightness were no longer there. Her face, already crisscrossed with wrinkles and even more shrivelled by the winter sun, looked shrunk and dried up, with the bones jutting out.

'Is it Raman?' she asked. With her life being so barren, she could not even manage a token greeting of, 'Are you well?'

'Are you well, Mami?'

Are you well! How could she be? A deep sigh seemed to burst out of her ribcage. She only nodded.

'Where is Mama?'

'I don't know where Mama goes, when he comes. Since he left, Mama doesn't even come home regularly.'

Raman felt miserable.

'When his son was here, Jogianna had some attachment to this place. He went away, Jogianna also goes away. Only I'm left in this house.'

'Does Nanjan never come here?'

'Once in a while. Why does he need his ammai now?' As she spoke, her eyes filled with tears.

'Mami… I've come to give you some news.'

'What is it?'

'Nanjan is getting married on Wednesday.'

'What?'

Did she hear a thunderbolt splitting the earth beneath her? She shuddered. Not noticing her reaction, Raman continued, 'It is Krishnan Gowder's granddaughter. Nanjan is lucky, so is the girl who marries him. The wedding will take place at the Velan temple on Palani hill.'

Spasms of pain seemed to squeeze her heart.

'He has plotted and planned this. It is his granddaughter after all. That scheming girl, she has devoured my son alive.'

Raman was taken aback. 'Mami, don't upset yourself.'

'Rama, won't you stop the marriage somehow? That wretch has got my son in his clutches. The house is barren without him, there's no life, there's just a void.'

'Don't cry, Mami. Isn't Nanjan's happiness yours as well? He has come up in life. You should rejoice, not be angry. Come with us. We'll go to Palanimalai. How nice it'll be if the marriage takes place amidst rejoicing.' His soothing words fell on deaf ears.

'It was you who deceived me and conspired against me. You promised to pay for my son's education and went and begged that wretch for favours. You pushed my son into the net cast by him.'

Raman was alarmed by her fury. 'Mami, why do you talk like this?'

'It would have been better had Nanjan never studied. He would have worked hard on the land. Then we wouldn't have lost our land. He needn't have fallen into their net. My son wouldn't have left me. Ayyo!

He couldn't bear to see her like that, her body shaken with sobs. He regretted going there.

After he left, Paru walked towards the dam colony like one possessed.

On reaching the colony, she saw a woman standing in the doorway of a house. 'Which is engineer Nanjan's house?' she hesitantly asked, in her own language.

'Oh, further up, the fourth house. There!' the woman pointed.

Two servant boys were playing with marbles in front of the house. She stood there, her heart palpitating.

'Who are you, Amma?' one of the boys asked her.

'Engineer Nanjan ...'

'Oho, he is on night shift. He's just left for work. It's half past five. Now he'll return only in the morning.'

The morning shift workers were returning in groups. Not quite comprehending what he meant, she lingered on, feeling awkward as she waited for Nanjan.

'He will come early in the morning, Amma. Go now,' the other boy told her very clearly.

Somehow she got through the night. Leaving Mookkumalai early in the morning, she reached the house in the colony. When she knocked at the closed door, Nanjan's colleague, a stranger to her, opened it.

Before she could open her mouth, he said, 'Come, are you looking for Nanjan? Come in, he should be here any minute.' Seating her in the front room, he went inside. The servant boy placed steaming hot coffee before her. This should have been the proudest moment of her life. Instead she stood there with her eyes glued to the front door. Each moment seemed an aeon.

At last, he was there. Hair tangled, clothes covered with black dust, bloodshot eyes. *As* he climbed up the steps, she was the first person he saw.

His mother!

An amalgam of obstinacy and foolishness, love and possessiveness. Should he be angry or pity her? Unsure, he just stood there.

'How come you're here, Amma?' he asked, concealing his shock.

'How could you do such a thing, Nanja? Without you, the house is so empty.'

She could not continue. Intense emotion strangled the words in her throat. She sobbed.

His two colleagues peeped in to see who was crying. He felt that she was humiliating him by creating a scene there.

'All right, I'll come home. You could have sent for me. Why did you have to come here?' he said.

'Will you come now?' she asked, wiping her tears.

'You are making my life hell,' he snarled.

'Don't talk like this, Nanja. Is it right to break your promise to me and get married? Will I suggest anything that'll harm you? Have I ever wished you ill? Do you know how I suffered when you had to trudge eight miles to school and back? One day when you went to school hungry, do you know that I actually went out to beg for food? Why are you deserting your ammai, Nanja?'

He was so weary that he did not have the patience to deal with the flood of tears.

'Why rake up those old stories now? I have finished studying. Appappa! You needn't have educated me at all,' he muttered, going inside with his head bent.

As he sat on his cot, head in his hands, he felt as if the whole world were spinning. Couldn't the past and the elders' differences be forgotten with the passage of time? Couldn't things be set right?

Who could have told her about the marriage? Had Krishnan Gowder paid her a visit?

His friends left for the morning shift. The servant brought him coffee and tiffin. After two hours had gone by, she peeped into his room. She had been waiting for him all this time.

He was to get married in two days' time. Krishnan's family would be waiting for him with Raman's car near Keezhmalai. What was he to do?

'Amma, if you really love me, come with me to my wedding. Don't be so stubborn. You can live happily with your daughter-in-law in a house like this.'

'They will take you away from me.'

'Amma, I promise you. I will never abandon you to become part of my wife's family. Come with me right now. Don't make yourself and me miserable. Do you really want me to get married in this furtive manner? How nice it would be if Ayyan is also happy!'

'Promise you won't abandon me as soon as you get married?'

'Promise, promise, promise! Trust me, I'm not so vile as to desert you.'

Her eyes never left his face. Could she depend on his promise and trust him?

'After my marriage we will live in this house with you and Ayyan. Ayyan is wrong to think that Krishnan Gowder is out to harm us. We shouldn't think that way. Nor would Ayyan, left to himself. He has been brain-washed by Periappa all along. Believe me, Amma!'

'I… I… shall I come with you?'

'I will be very happy! I'll just have a bath and change. The car will be waiting for us at Keezhmalai.'

Paru stood there torn by conflicting emotions.

A little later after informing the servant, he left, bag in hand, accompanied by his mother. He had not bought even a small gift for Vijaya.

As the two of them climbed up towards the road, they were deafened by shouts echoing all over the hillside.

From where had this huge crowd materialised? Men were waving red flags in front of the tin shed that housed the main office.

'Down, down! Down with the injustice of the management! Down with the management class which refuses us our rights!' Slogan after slogan was being shouted.

Paru was terrified. She did not know about the workers' strike. Were they the people who did not want to give up their land, she wondered?

She could not keep pace with Nanjan. Avoiding the ocean of humanity surging around the offices, Nanjan walked down by the short cut.

Appappa! What a crowd there was on the road, near Keezhmalai! There was no room for any vehicle except the jeeps and police cars. There were hundreds of policemen—special police in khaki uniform and ordinary police in blue.

Nanjan was inwardly seething. How would he find his way through the chaos and confusion to reach Raman? How could he pass through the crowds swarming all over the bazaar, and pouring out of every street and alley?

A premonition of impending disaster made him shiver. Holding his mother's hand, he again made an attempt to reach Keezhmalai quickly.

'Have all these people lost their land, Nanja?'

'No. These are people who have left their homes and come long distances to work here. They want more pay.'

'Have all these people left their native place and come here?'

'Yes, they have come from warm climates, braving the unaccustomed cold in order to make a living. There is no water in their native place, no jobs, no food. The dam provides food for all of them.'

There were sounds of gunfire!

Startled, Nanjan turned around. Paru, petrified, held Nanjan's hand tightly.

Where did the sound come from? Where?

He realised that the police, unable to control the situation, had resorted to firing.

His heart thumping, he stood to one side, unable to go forward or turn back.

The crowd in front of the office scattered like a swarm of bees that had been smoked out. Vehicles charged. The police penetrated the crowd, hemming it in.

Holding his mother's hand tightly, Nanjan took long strides down the short cut.

'Long live the revolution!' Fractured shouts from the scattered crowd.

At the Keezhmalai bus stop—where was Raman?

There was no sign of Krishnan Gowder's car or of Raman.

As his eyes searched among the milling crowds, they alighted on accountant Panjamritham. Before he could cross the path, an ambulance followed by four jeeps sped by.

Panjamritham hailed him. 'What, Sir, there seems to have been some shooting. Totally uncalled for,' he said.

'The whole thing baffles me,' replied Nanjan, eyes still searching for Raman in the crowd.

'I came to the office to ask for leave to go to Ooty. Fools! Those whose land had been acquired chose to join the workers' demonstration today. The man who was shot has been taken away in the ambulance. Did you see?'

'A man shot? Oh!'

Had his father, by any chance, been one of those 'fools'?

His blood ran cold at the very thought.

'Amma, Raman is not here. Let us get out of here and make our way to the hatti. There's too much confusion here,' he said.

Before he could take two steps forward, a car went swiftly past them. The sound of crying drifted across in the wind.

'Probably that is Range Gowder's wife. Poor thing! The bullet hit Range Gowder in the stomach and came out through the back!'

Nanjan felt as though someone had given him a hard blow on the head.

Range Gowder...

For a minute, everything went black before his eyes. His ears were blocked. Dragging his mother with him, he leapt into a bus that was about to start.

Nine

Paru did not understand what was going on, nor could she bring herself to ask Nanjan what was happening. Why was Nanjan not looking at her?

She wondered, 'Does Nanjan look as though he is about to be married? Is this the marriage procession?'

The bus was taking them somewhere at a maniacal speed. Where was it going? How could she find out?

Paru's insides churned. She felt uneasy. Nanjan made her lean against his shoulder. Even then he did not ask her, 'Ammai, what ails you?' Why did he not speak?

She was unaware of getting off the bus or of being put in a taxi by Nanjan. But at the entrance to the hospital, she opened her eyes.

She remembered the day when Nanjan's mother, Girijai, had been lifted from a vehicle at the hospital entrance and how, much later, everyone had got into the vehicle, wailing.

Who was dead? Who? Was it she, Paru? Was she moving around in the form of a spirit? Why did everyone crowd around her? Rangammai, her daughter-in-law, why were they all sobbing?

Jogiannan was weeping, 'I am a great sinner. I incited him.'

What had happened?

'I told him not to go, did he listen to me?' Gowri lamented.

The thudding footsteps of policemen went past them.

Krishnan… Krishnan… what brought him here? Had he also come for her funeral? Had she really died?

No. If she were dead, could she see so clearly? They had made her sit on a chair. Everyone around her was crying.

'Anni! Annan's raging jealousy combined with mine has scorched him. Anni, my annan Rangannan has gone!'

Ah! Had Annan gone? Annan, her husband, Rangan!

She was transfixed, as though something was weighing her down like a boulder placed on her chest.

'Jogi, be brave. What can we do? I came forward to give Rangan blood. I would have considered myself lucky if I could have saved him. But it was too late. Let our enmity end with the sacrifice of this life, Jogi.' Krishnan's voice was choked with emotion.

'I am a sinner. I sinned. I rekindled the flame of jealousy that was dormant. Krishnan, I was jealous. I was jealous because you did not lose your land.'

'Please don't say that, Jogi.'

Quivering hands were clasped in the presence of death and enmities forgotten.

Early on Wednesday morning, the golden rays of the sun pierced the clouds, embracing Maragathamalai.

The huge crowd that had gathered as one unit for the last journey of Range Gowder gave rise to a fear that Maragathamalai would be buried under its weight. Not since Lingayya's death, not since that death which had caused the birth of factions among the people, had such a crowd gathered for any funeral rite among the hill folk. So the people said.

During the funeral rites, there were no insincere tears, feasting or merrymaking. Each one paid his last respects, according to his custom, to the dead man.

His body shrunk and wrinkled like an overripe fruit, a grief-stricken Madhan, who had not stepped out of his house for many days, was brought by Krishnan.

For the past two years, the old man had been shut up in his room. His speech slurring, his mind wandering, had he lived only to see this happen!

Seated on a chair, he saw the crowds and his son's body on the funeral car. In a face shrivelled like an overripe fruit, the pupils of his eyes, which looked like withered seeds, floated in tears.

He touched Krishnan who was at his side; he held Jogi.

Sensing his wish, they raised him up. As tears streamed from the old man's eyes, it seemed as though an extraordinary light was pouring out of them.

Once on his unsteady feet, he looked up at the sky and chanted '*Hou! Hou!*' His words were slurred.

When the old man, holding on to Krishnan and Jogi, walked around the funeral car without missing a step, many others joined him.

It was not a dance.

Did he see his son's spirit soar in the sky, leaving behind the bodily form, the seat of worldly desires and passions? Were the movements of his body born out of the agitation of his mind? Or were they born out of happiness, that he would have, for one last time, the privilege of dancing at a funeral, a custom that had been discontinued since his brother's death? Or was it bliss, that he had waited for just this event and the time had come when he would find deliverance?

His feelings were indescribable.

The rites performed that day were not mere rituals. When everyone, including Rangan's wives, had paid their last respects, the most important part of the funeral rites of the Badagas, that of reciting a last prayer seeking forgiveness for all the sins that the dead person might have committed while in his bodily form, took place at the cremation ground. At Lingayya's death, as a result of the disputes and dissensions, it was done for the sake of form. It seemed as if the prayer for forgiveness had never been sung so movingly as it was by Jogi that day.

The sins of ancestors,
The sins of elders,
His sins,
The sins of clansmen,
Let all of them disappear!
The sin of displacing boundary stones,
The sin of telling countless lies,
The sin of not assuaging the grief of the poor,
The sin of tormenting the meek,
The sin of not being able to bear others' lands flourishing,
The sin of not being able to bear another's cow yielding milk,
The sin of not being able to bear another's prosperity,
The sin of having given room to jealousy,
The sin of having felled green trees,

The sin of having killed cows and cobras,

The sin of creating enmity by carrying tales,

The sin of having driven out those already shivering from the cold,

The sin of having polluted water,

The sin committed against kith and kin,

The sin of having denied drinking water,

The sin of having wronged his people.

Jogi asked forgiveness for the sins that numbered more than three hundred in all.

Were Rangan's the only sins that were cleansed by this prayer for the purification of the soul? All those gathered there washed away with their own tears the sins they had committed knowingly or unknowingly.

Jogi, as the one asking for forgiveness, begged forgiveness for each sin.

Soon, the flames of the pyre lit by Lingan were consuming Rangan's body.

After the crowds had left, two people remained till Rangan's body had turned to ashes and mingled with the earth. One was Paru, the other, Jogi.

Scenes from their lives, which had been intertwined with the life of Rangan, unfolded in their thoughts. Rangan, who was born in those hills, who had grown there, who had struggled in the battlefield of life, who had won and lost and who was now finally possessed by fire.

Rangan had become a memory.

Epilogue

Three years had sped by.

The day after the fire-walking festival in the month of Masi, Maragathamalai wore a festive look never seen before in the mountains. From every nook and cranny of the blue mountain, a sea of brightly clad people gathered at Maragathamalai, and their cries of jubilation filled the air.

Old man Jogi, who had seen five kurinji-spans, sat on the grassy slope enjoying the festivities. He had led a full life, and no one of his generation was alive in his family now. Once Rangan, who had been possessed by anger and hatred born out of disappointments in his youth, had become dust, Paru had not lived long. But she had not died without her desire unfulfilled. She had seen Nanjan and Vijaya live happily, bound to her by love. She had witnessed the happy event of Devaki, born poor, becoming the daughter-in-law of an affluent family when she had married Krishnan's nephew. Though Dharman and Lingan, after their father's death, had continued to go to court to stir up trouble, no major upheavals had ensued in their families. Krishnan had bound the two families irrevocably in the marriage pandal. Paru had seen all this in her lifetime.

Paru had peacefully breathed her last as she was weeding the potato patch on Krishnan's black earth. Mother Earth received her beloved daughter into her lap with great mercy, not allowing her to suffer in any way.

As far back as he could remember, Jogi had never seen such a festive crowd in the hills!

Was there such great rejoicing because there would be no more darkness? Was there great happiness because all their fears had been laid to rest? Were these the triumphant cries of a newly awakened young society striding forward on the path of progress? Were these the victory celebrations of a resurgent hill folk who had proved that there was no unawakened society in New India? Or was it a grand festival to felicitate those achievers who had ensured a marvellous future for those yet to be born in the lap of the hills?

Atop the pole of victory flew the brilliant tricolour flag. In the sacred hour when evening was drawing to an end, the Kumari River dam was opened to the acclaim of all those present.

The sluice gates were lifted to the ringing of bells; the heartening sound of the gushing water propelling machinery was sweet music to the ears; dazzling electric lights suddenly lit up the entire hillside.

There were tears of joy in Jogi's eyes. His heart sang in praise of the Almighty.

'Hara hara Siva Siva Paramesa!
Hara hara Siva Siva Basavesa!'

Glossary

annas: a unit of currency not used anymore

ayyan: sometimes refers to father, sometimes to God

devar: God

dharmadeva: God

dhoti: a sarong worn by men below the waist

dupatti: part of Badaga male attire

durai: refers to a white man, or to the boss

elamukkuthi: a nose ornament worn by Badaga women, which is removed at the time of her husband's death

hagottu: milk-house, that part of the *ogamane* in a Badaga house where milk is stored, and where no woman may enter

hatti: a Badaga village

Hethappa: deity of the Badagas

honai: a bamboo vessel used to draw milk from the udder

isan, iswara: God

kalam: vessel

karmayogi: one who believes that action is the best form of worship

kavadi: a bow-shaped structure carried by devotees of Lord Muruga as a sign of devotion

kinnam: a small bowl

labbai: a Muslim moneylender

lala: sweets vendor

lungi: a sarong worn by men

madi: freshly washed clothes worn by the Badaga before he enters the *hagottu* or milk-house

magudi: a snake charmer's instrument

mangalasutram: a golden disc on a string tied around the bride's neck at the time of marriage

maniakkarar: the official entrusted with the collection of revenue and the de facto headman

Mariamman: a local deity

mundu: a rectangular piece of fine cotton cloth worn shawl-like, over the shoulders and over a blouse by a Badaga woman

Nandi: sacred bull

ogamane: the inner room of a Badaga house

palapetti: a wooden box where the Badagas store the fruits of their labour

panchayat: a gathering of village elders where important issues are discussed and decisions are taken

panchmrutham: an offering to God made with five ingredients: jaggery, ripe bananas, crystal sugar, cardamom and raisins

pattu: a scarf-like piece of white cotton cloth, worn square across the forehead and tucked in at the back of the head

pavadai: a long skirt

pice: a unit of currency, a coin, not used anymore

sholas: groves

streedhanam: gifts from parents that a bride carries with her to her husband's home

sumangali: married women whose husbands are alive

thinnai: a platform adjoining a building

thundu: a dhoti-like rectangular piece of cloth, worn by Badaga women under the armpits and wrapped across the chest and reaching the knees

todamund: a Toda village

todas: a pastoral tribe indigenous to the Nilgiris

unkalam: vessel

vattathattu: a large round brass plate around which men from the same family sit and eat

veerarayapanam: when death is drawing near, a gold coin, called the veerarayapanam, dipped in butter or ghee is given to the dying man to swallow

velimanai: the outer room of a Badaga house

yama: God of death